Health Is Academic

A GUIDE TO COORDINATED SCHOOL HEALTH PROGRAMS

Health Is Academic

A GUIDE TO COORDINATED SCHOOL HEALTH PROGRAMS

Edited by Eva Marx and Susan Frelick Wooley
with Daphne Northrop

FOREWORD BY ERNEST L. BOYER

Teachers College
Columbia University
New York and London

Published by Teachers College Press, 1234 Amsterdam Avenue, New York, NY 10027

This publication was completed with fiscal and technical assistance provided by a cooperative agreement (number U87/CCU110236) with the U.S. Centers for Disease Control and Prevention, National Center for Chronic Disease Prevention and Health Promotion, Division of Adolescent and School Health, Atlanta, GA 30333. Its contents are solely the responsibility of the authors and do not necessarily represent the official views of the U.S. Centers for Disease Control and Prevention.

Education Development Center, Inc. (EDC) is an international nonprofit research and development organization that works with schools, universities, families, health care centers, businesses, and communities, addressing health and education across the lifespan. EDC provides a broad range of services, including training and technical assistance, curriculum and materials development, social marketing, policy development, and research and evaluation in areas that include coordinated school health programs. For more information, contact Education Development Center, Inc., 55 Chapel Street, Newton, MA 02158-1060.

Library of Congress Cataloging-in-Publication Data

Health is academic : a guide to coordinated school health programs / edited by
  Eva Marx and Susan Frelick Wooley with Daphne Northrop : foreword by
  Ernest L. Boyer.
      p.   cm.
  Includes bibliographical references and index.
  ISBN 0-8077-3714-3 (cloth). — ISBN 0-8077-3713-5 (pbk.)
    1. School health services—United States. 2. Health education—United
  States.   I. Marx, Eva.   II. Wooley, Susan.   III. Northrop, Daphne.
  LB3409.U5H417   1998
  371.7'1'0973—dc21   97-39385

ISBN 0-8077-3713-5 (paper)
ISBN 0-8077-3714-3 (cloth)

Printed on acid-free paper
Manufactured in the United States of America

05 04 03 02   8 7 6 5 4

To **Ernest L. Boyer,**

whose wisdom and commitment to the education
and welfare of young people served as a beacon to
educators and all others who share his vision that
children should be a nation's priority.

Contents

Foreword

Shortly before his death, Dr. Ernest L. Boyer, late president of the Carnegie Foundation for the Advancement of Teaching, began drafting for this book a Foreword that highlighted the urgent need for schools to address the health needs of their students. His untimely death interrupted its completion. Below are excerpts from Dr. Boyer's unfinished work.

Since the beginning of this century, when school nurses in Boston, New York, and other cities valiantly led the battle against infectious diseases and poor sanitation and when young girls, trained in school, became "health teachers" in their homes, it has been widely accepted that good health relates to learning. The educational and physical needs of children simply cannot be divided (Bremner, 1971). Health programs, consequently, have become an established part of the nation's schools.

Recently, however, school-based health programs have become casualties of budget cuts. For example, in New York City, 88 nurses were serving 1,000 school campuses, down from 200 nurses in one year as a result of budget cuts (Flax, 1991). What is especially disturbing is that these cutbacks are occurring at the very time the physical and mental health needs of children have increased. Consider, for example, that more than half the teachers we surveyed in a 1990 study said that undernourishment is a problem at their school and that 67% cited poor health as a problem (Carnegie Foundation, 1990). In addition, a survey of elementary teachers by the American Academy of Pediatrics and the National Parent Teacher Association found that one in eight young children has a health problem that impairs learning, and that most teachers believe the situation is getting worse (Hoff, 1992; Shea, 1992/1993). A third-grade teacher in a midsize city who was among the teachers surveyed observed: "Every year there seem to be more physical problems at our school that interfere with learning. I know that children who don't eat well or don't get rest can't do well in school. Yet that's exactly what I'm seeing more and more."

Mary Futrell, dean, Graduate School of Education and Human Development, George Washington University, observed that the relationship between a child's emotions and learning is a phenomenon every classroom teacher understands: "Just as a child who is hungry cannot learn, so too a child who is wracked with anxiety or mired in depression or burdened with self-hatred cannot learn" (Kramer, 1992). Clearly, schools are caught in a dilemma. On the one hand, they encounter children daily who have physical and emotional needs that cannot be ignored. On the other hand, schools are educational institutions. They cannot and should not become "social service centers," act as surrogate parents, or seek to solve every family problem.

We propose a middle ground.

While remaining committed, first, to the academic achievement of each student, the focus of the school still should be on the whole child. The school should provide basic health programs and services to meet the routine health and counseling needs of children, with the recognition that such support, which is so essential to the educational mission of the institution, will vary from one school to the next. In addition, the school should provide a referral service, building a partnership with other community service agencies to respond to family needs that are most acute. We believe that schools, while providing routine health care, should focus primarily on prevention. The health professionals in the schools should be considered teachers. The school nurse should meet regularly with classes to talk about wellness and good food, the value of exercise, and the damage that drugs, alcohol, and tobacco can do. The goal is to help young students learn to respect and care for their own bodies. It is imperative to interrupt the cycle of ignorance about good health that diminishes the quality of life for so many children, and also has such tragic consequences for the nation.

Helen Dugan, the school nurse at Center Elementary School in Kansas City, Missouri, is a gifted teacher who is enthusiastically welcomed into classrooms by colleagues. Offering a creative health curriculum, she invigorates classrooms, often using a puppet stage in the doorway, while the children inside call out questions and the puppets respond. Ms. Dugan says, "Teaching children about their own bodies and giving them skills to help their families is a big step toward prevention."

Perhaps the time has come to organize in every community not just a school board but also a children's board. The goal would be to integrate children's services and build a friendly, supportive environment for children.

Children can become a community priority.

In our hard-edged, competitive world, a community-wide commitment to help children may seem quixotic. Not only has the sense of neighborhood faded, but the very notion of community seems strikingly inapplicable to contemporary life. Absent larger loyalties, we are settling for little loyalties that diminish our national unity and widen the social separations. There is a growing pessimism in this country, a feeling that the social pathologies we confront may be just too deep to be remedied.

But good will runs deep in America. Throughout our history, citizens have shown their capacity to come together and organize energetically in times of crisis. We have dedicated ourselves to great causes, responding in times of need with vigor and an outpouring of concern. We are confident that with the right blend of commitment and imagination, communities in this nation can come together, once again, this time on behalf of children.

REFERENCES

Bremner, R. H. (Ed.). (1971). *Children and youth in America: A documentary history: Vol. 2. 1866–1932* (Pts. 7 and 8). Cambridge, MA: Harvard University Press.

The Carnegie Foundation for the Advancement of Teaching. (1990). *The condition of teaching: A state-by-state analysis.* Princeton, NJ: Author.

Flax, E. (1991, October 30). Budgets' ill health prompts cuts in school nurses. *Education Week,* 10.

Hoff, D. (1992, September 16). Students' poor health interferes with learning, teachers say. *Education Daily,* 1, 3.

Kramer, P. (1992, April). Fostering self-esteem can keep kids safe and sound. *PTA Today,* 10.

Shea, D. (1992, December/1993, January). Crisis in the classroom: How kids with poor health care lose in school. *PTA Today,* 6–8.

Preface

Coming together is a beginning; keeping together is progress; working together is success.

—Henry Ford

Concern about the health and educational achievement of young people and the recognition that education and health are inextricably intertwined have resulted in considerable interest in school health programs that engage the entire school system—instruction, services, community, and environment. This book presents for education decision makers and the larger community to which they belong an approach to integrating health into the academic fabric of their institutions to benefit the well-being and learning of their students.

A groundbreaking 1987 article by Allensworth and Kolbe in a special issue of the *Journal of School Health* on comprehensive school health programs proposed that a school health program might include eight components:

- health education
- physical education
- health services
- nutrition services
- counseling, psychological, and social services
- healthy school environment
- health promotion for staff
- parent/community involvement

Accompanying the Allensworth and Kolbe article were several articles by other authors that described each of the components.

In the ensuing years, the school health program concept has been widely discussed and applied, and many national, state, and local health and education organizations have begun to incorporate this approach. However, much work remains. Although school administrators and other decision makers generally understand that children must be healthy to learn, many still need to be convinced that school health programs must be a priority to ensure that children are healthy. Moreover, when convinced, school administrators need to know how to make a school health program a reality within their building. A reservoir of experience has accumulated that can help school communities implement, coordinate, and integrate the components to develop school health programs that work.

In the fall of 1994, the Division of Adolescent and School Health, Centers for Disease Control and Prevention, invited Education Development Center, Inc., to facilitate the development of 12 chapters that would further define comprehensive school health programs and their components (see the section "A Note on Terminology") and provide action steps for their implementation at the local, state, and national levels. The chapters would include:

- An overview discussing the concept of comprehensive school health programs; why they are needed from social, economic, health, and education perspectives; how they relate to education and health reform movements; and recommendations for their implementation.
- A chapter discussing implementation at the local level, action steps that school administrators can take to implement a comprehensive school health program, and the supporting role of district-level organizations.
- Eight chapters, each explaining the essential function of one of the components of a comprehensive school health program and action steps needed to implement it.
- A chapter discussing the role of state-level organizations and action steps they can take to support the implementation of comprehensive school health programs at the local level.
- A chapter addressing the role of national organizations and action steps they can take to promote the implementation of comprehensive school health programs at the local level.

A NATIONWIDE EFFORT

This publication is based on the knowledge and experience of those who best know the field—the many professionals who implement, teach, and conduct research about the various elements of school health programs and those who are responsible for administering them. In addition, more than 300 professionals, including school staff, principals, and administrators; members of local, state, and national organizations; and university faculty have reviewed the chapters.

The process began with an invitation to more than 70 national organizations whose constituencies implement one of the components of a school health program. The list of close to 60 organizations that participated appears in Figure 1.

In April 1995, representatives of these organizations met in Washington, D.C. to begin developing the content of a book about comprehensive school health programs. Participants met in eight working groups, one for each component, to address the following:

What are the essential functions of the component?
Who are the staff that implement these functions, what is their training, and what national professional organizations assist them?
How should staff who implement these functions work with staff in any of the other seven components?
What specific and feasible actions should the local school take to achieve the essential functions of the component and to enable staff in different components to work together?
What specific and feasible actions should the local school district, relevant state agencies, and relevant national organizations take to help the local school implement actions?
What ongoing measures do we have and do we need to monitor national, state, district, and local school actions?

At the same time, participants identified authors for each of the chapters. The national organizations met again in June 1995 to share their knowledge with the writers. The writers also met with focus groups of national- and state-level health and education professionals, school principals, school board members, health coordinators, and representatives of universities and voluntary organizations.

A NOTE ON TERMINOLOGY

The eight-component model has traditionally been referred to as a "comprehensive school health program." However, many meeting participants suggested substituting "coordinated" for "comprehensive" when referring to school health programs because some people confuse "comprehensive school health *education*," which relates to instruction, with "comprehensive school health *programs*." In addition, the term "comprehensive" might discourage an overburdened educational system from considering development of the model. The use of "coordinated" addresses the separation of compo-

Figure 1. Organizations Contributing to *Health Is Academic*

Advocates for Youth
American Academy of Child & Adolescent Psychiatry
American Academy of Pediatric Dentistry
American Academy of Pediatrics
American Association for Active Lifestyles & Fitness
American Association for Health Education
American Association of School Administrators
American Cancer Society
American College of Sports Medicine
American Dietetic Association
American Federation of Teachers
American Medical Association
American Nurses Association
American Psychological Association
American Public Health Association
American Public Welfare Association
American Red Cross
American School Counselor Association
American School Food Service Association
American School Health Association
Association for Supervision & Curriculum Development
Association of State and Territorial Health Officials
Association of State and Territorial Public Health Nutrition Directors
Communities In Schools, Inc.
The Council for Exceptional Children
Council of Chief State School Officers
Council of the Great City Schools
Employee Assistance Professionals Association
Food Research and Action Center
Girls, Incorporated
National Alliance of Pupil Services Organizations

National Assembly on School-Based Health Care
National Association for Sport and Physical Education
National Association of Community Health Centers
National Association of Elementary School Principals
National Association of Governor's Councils on Physical Fitness and Sports
National Association of Leadership for Student Assistance Programs
National Association of School Nurses
National Association of School Psychologists
National Association of Secondary School Principals
National Association of Social Workers
National Association of State Boards of Education
National Association of State NET Program Coordinators
National Coalition for Parent Involvement in Education
National Coalition of Chapter 1 and Title 1 Parents
National Conference of State Legislatures
National Council of Churches
National Council of LaRaza
National Education Association
National Environmental Health Association
National Federation of State High School Associations
National Health & Education Consortium
National Middle School Association
National Network for Youth
National Peer Helpers Association
The National PTA
National Safety Council

*Participation does not indicate endorsement of the entire contents of this book.

FIGURE 1. Continued

National School Boards Association	Society for Nutrition Education
National Urban League	Society for Public Health Education,
National Wellness Association	Inc.
President's Council for Physical Fitness	Society of State Directors of Health,
and Sports	Physical Education and Recreation
Public Education Network	State Directors of Child Nutrition
Public Risk Management Association	Wellness Councils of America
Society for Adolescent Medicine	

nents that "comprehensive" might imply and better communicates the integration that this book describes.

The more than 300 professionals who reviewed this book were polled on the question (Figure 2). Based on their opinions, this book uses the term "coordinated school health programs" rather than "comprehensive school health programs." This terminology emphasizes the interrelationships among components and the collaboration among staff, school administrators, and concerned community members while still connoting the inclusion and improvement of all components of the school health program. This is to say that coordinated school health programs should be comprehensive—an elaboration of the Allensworth and Kolbe model.

The focus is on taking concerted actions to achieve a common vision. Many schools and districts probably already have some or all of the components of a coordinated school health program in place. But it is likely that many components are not well developed and are operating independently of each other. This book will help decision makers and administrators examine ways to strengthen each component and bring them together to more effectively address the health needs of the nation's young people.

REFERENCE

Allensworth, D., & Kolbe, L. (1987). The comprehensive school health program: Exploring an expanded concept. *Journal of School Health, 57*(10), 409–412.

FIGURE 2. "Comprehensive" versus "Coordinated": The Pros and Cons

Typical reasons offered for retaining "comprehensive":

- The word "coordinated" does not encompass "comprehensive." The goal is to have a comprehensive, well-coordinated school health program. Omitting the word comprehensive may let administrators and policy makers "off the hook."
- The use of "coordinated" diminishes the aim of comprehensive school health programs by implying that coordination of existing programs is sufficient.
- Coordination is a low level of collaborative efforts.

Typical reasons offered for using "coordinated":

- School health programs need to be coordinated to avoid fragmentation and duplication, maintain accountability for all program components, increase effectiveness, and be cost-effective.
- The term "comprehensive" school health has been used in so many ways, particularly in health education, that it has become meaningless.
- "Coordinated" gives people credit for what's already in place and makes them more willing to participate.
- Seeing how the components relate as part of the whole will make communicating with school systems much easier.
- "Coordinated" seems to better reflect what we are trying to accomplish.
- "Coordinated" sounds broader and includes any agencies and individuals who work to improve the well-being of school-age children. It implies all school personnel working together to strengthen the health program and might help administrators understand the importance of a team effort in coordinating programs.

Acknowledgments

This book represents the collective wisdom of hundreds of people from around the nation who came together literally and figuratively to contribute to the well-being and achievement of young people. We are grateful to them for their intellectual contributions and their willingness to transcend professional boundaries to address their common concerns and hopes for youth. Their thoughtful comments and generous participation have set a standard for collaboration that we hope their colleagues will replicate at local, state, and national levels.

The authors of this book's chapters shared extraordinary dedication and enthusiasm. The energy and willingness to collaborate of these talented people did not flag during the long process of developing this publication. We greatly appreciate their contribution of time, energy, commitment, and patience.

We are most grateful to the Division of Adolescent and School Health (DASH), National Center for Chronic Disease Prevention and Health Promotion, Centers for Disease Control and Prevention, for the support that made this volume possible. We extend special thanks to Lloyd Kolbe, whose vision initiated this effort. Many others at DASH supported and advised us: Peter Cortese, Susan Giarratano, Pete Hunt, Wanda Jubb, Laura Kann, Mary Sue Lancaster, Elizabeth Majestic, Jim Martindale, John Santelli, Margaret Leavy Small, Marlene Tappe, and Howell Wechsler. We also thank Donna Brodsky of Cygnus Corporation for her meticulous and thoughtful editing that contributed to this publication's coherence, consistency, and clarity.

Donna Lewis, principal, Timberlane Elementary School, Falls Church, Virginia, merits special acknowledgment for suggesting the title *Health Is Academic.*

At Teachers College Press we are particularly grateful to Faye Zucker, whose dedication to and confidence in this project carried us smoothly through negotiations and production.

Many at Education Development Center, Inc., (EDC) contributed to this effort. Most notable are Cheryl Vince-Whitman, senior vice president, whose leadership based on years of commitment to school health issues guided us throughout the process; Tim Dunn, director of EDC's Center for School Health Programs; and Christine Blaber, an associate director of the center. No project of this magnitude succeeds without the painstaking, behind-the-scenes work of support staff. With conscientiousness and unceasing goodwill, Perryne O'Reilly, senior administrative assistant, kept us organized, transcribed interminably, and responded patiently to the varied needs of editors, authors, and reviewers.

Finally, we wish to express our gratitude to those who will use this book—the school administrators, their staff, and community members who are committed to taking the creative and challenging steps to help all young people become healthy, productive adults.

Floretta Dukes McKenzie, Ed.D.
Julius B. Richmond, M.D.

Linking Health and Learning: An Overview of Coordinated School Health Programs

1

Academic: of, relating to, or characteristic of school.
　　　　　　　　　　　　—American Heritage Dictionary (1993)

*Efforts to improve school performance that ignore health are ill-conceived,
as are health improvement efforts that ignore education.*
　　　　　　　　　—National Commission on the Role of the School
　　　　　and the Community in Improving Adolescent Health (1990, p. 9)

It is Monday morning physical education class and Terry is complaining again to her teacher that she has a stomachache. Last week, the teacher remembers, Terry sat out the class because her stomach was bothering her. The teacher asks herself whether she should send Terry to the school nurse this time. In second-period history class, Terry's teacher catches her dozing and, when the homework assignments have been collected, Terry's is not among them—again. Perhaps it's time for a parent–teacher conference, the teacher thinks. During lunch, Terry is quiet and withdrawn, poking at her food with a fork but not eating it. The teacher who is monitoring the cafeteria is concerned; Terry is usually an outgoing, good-humored person,

Health Is Academic: A Guide to Coordinated School Health Problems. Edited by Eva Marx and Susan Frelick Wooley, with Daphne Northrop. New York: Teachers College Press, 1998. ISBN 0-8077-3713-5 (pbk.), ISBN 0-8077-3714-3 (cloth). Prior to photocopying items for classroom use, please contact the Copyright Clearance Center, Customer Service, 222 Rosewood Dr., Danvers, MA 01923, USA, tel. (508) 750-8400. © 1998 Education Development Center, Inc. All rights reserved.

but she's been like this for the past several days. The monitor wonders if he should ask the school counselor to set up an appointment to talk with Terry.

Each teacher has seen a fragment of potentially worrisome behavior. Each has a nagging doubt about Terry's health or her academic performance. And if the problems appear to be serious enough to warrant intervention, that intervention is likely to be just as fragmented. A visit to the school nurse, a chat with Terry's parents, a referral to a counselor—these are the ways that schools have traditionally dealt with students' poor health or learning. But educators and school administrators across the nation are beginning to realize that such traditional piecemeal approaches fail to meet many students' fundamental needs as whole, complex people, nor do they use school and community resources coherently, effectively, and efficiently.

This book is about the growing understanding that piecemeal, competitive, or uncoordinated efforts to address the intertwined social, educational, psychological, and health needs of young people are counterproductive. They do not work for students, they do not work for teachers, and they do not work for educational institutions and their communities.

More important, this volume is about learnings of the past decade about better ways to approach the needs of children, educators, and schools. It is about the theory and practice of building coordinated school health programs designed to improve both the health and educational status of young people. It is about what has been done and what needs to be done (and how) to involve students, their families, and others in the community as full partners with school staff in helping students succeed both in their learning and in their journey to become healthy, productive adults.

Once it was common to define a school's mission in narrow terms focused on educational goals and methods alone. But as more and more teachers and school administrators have come to appreciate, there is an inextricable link between students' health and their ability to learn (World Health Organization, 1996). If schools do not deal with children's health by design, they deal with it by default.

Only when students are healthy will schools be able to fully meet their goals (Smith, 1996). According to Jean Schultz, National Middle Schools Association, many schools are working with their communities to "organize and optimize" their resources in ways that place students' overall well-being at the heart of the school program (Tanaka, 1996). These initiatives, called school health programs, are both comprehensive and coordinated (see Figure 1.1). They feature classroom activities, psychological and health services, and an improved school climate, and they build children's health so that they can succeed in school.

What is new about these programs is not their individual components—many schools already have most in place—but their quality, sophistication,

FIGURE 1.1. A Coordinated School Health Program

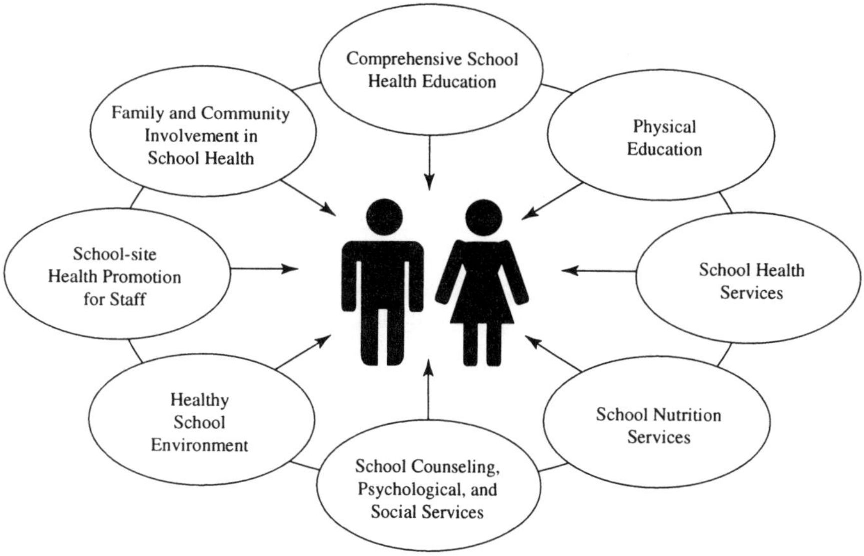

Adapted with permission from the Centers for Disease Control and Prevention

and coordination of effort. Figure 1.2 describes eight components that, when combined, offer a coordinated school health program. Representatives of the national organizations who participated in the development of this book (see the Preface) developed these definitions.

This volume discusses the eight components of a coordinated school health program and the organizations that support their development. It explains how a coordinated approach to students' health helps schools achieve their goals and enhance student well-being and achievement, clarifies the importance of the school's involvement, and describes ways to strengthen and coordinate a school and community's education and health resources for the benefit of children and their families.

BARRIERS TO STUDENTS' WELL-BEING AND LEARNING

Once the major health risks children faced were contagious diseases such as tuberculosis, diphtheria, measles, mumps, rubella, and whooping

FIGURE 1.2. Components of a Coordinated School Health Program

Health is not just the absence of disease—it is complete physical, mental, and social well-being. A school health program that effectively addresses students' health, and thus improves their ability to learn, consists of many components. Each component contributes in unique ways yet overlaps with other components in other ways.

Comprehensive school health education: Classroom instruction that addresses the physical, mental, emotional, and social dimensions of health; develops health knowledge, attitudes, and skills; and is tailored to each age level. Designed to motivate and assist students to maintain and improve their health, prevent disease, and reduce health-related risk behaviors.

Physical education: Planned, sequential instruction that promotes lifelong physical activity. Designed to develop basic movement skills, sports skills, and physical fitness as well as to enhance mental, social, and emotional abilities.

School health services: Preventive services, education, emergency care, referral, and management of acute and chronic health conditions. Designed to promote the health of students, identify and prevent health problems and injuries, and ensure care for students.

School nutrition services: Integration of nutritious, affordable, and appealing meals; nutrition education; and an environment that promotes healthy eating behaviors for all children. Designed to maximize each child's education and health potential for a lifetime.

School counseling, psychological, and social services: Activities that focus on cognitive, emotional, behavioral and social needs of individuals, groups, and families. Designed to prevent and address problems, facilitate positive learning and healthy behavior, and enhance healthy development.

Healthy school environment: The physical, emotional, and social climate of the school. Designed to provide a safe physical plant, as well as a healthy and supportive environment that fosters learning.

School-site health promotion for staff: Assessment, education, and fitness activities for school faculty and staff. Designed to maintain and improve the health and well-being of school staff, who serve as role models for students.

Family and community involvement in schools: Partnerships among schools, families, community groups, and individuals. Designed to share and maximize resources and expertise in addressing the healthy development of children, youth, and their families.

cough. Today, however, most risks have their roots in social or behavioral conditions (see Figure 1.3). Six preventable behaviors that are established in childhood account for most of the serious illnesses and premature deaths in the United States (Kolbe, 1990):

- tobacco use
- poor eating habits
- abuse of alcohol and other drugs
- behaviors that result in intentional or unintentional injury
- physical inactivity
- sexual behaviors that result in HIV infection, other sexually transmitted diseases, or unintended pregnancy

In some schools these problems are rampant. In others they simmer beneath the surface. When the problems emerge, they can disrupt individual students' lives, classrooms, and the overall school environment. When students are sick, distracted, or unable to attend school, schools become inefficient. When many students underachieve or drop out because they do poorly in school, both social progress and personal dreams suffer (Levinger, 1994).

Good health is necessary for effective learning. It is an asset for students facing intense competition, peer pressure, stress due to testing, and a full program of intellectual and physical activities. Besides a six- or seven-hour school day, many children participate in organized group activities before and after school; others entertain themselves and sometimes care for younger siblings until adults return from work. Many adolescents have part-time jobs. For school-aged youth, therefore, good health and healthy behaviors are important for them to keep up with their demanding schedules.

A TIME OF REFORM

The health concerns of children and youth are becoming acute at a time when schools, public education, and health care are undergoing intensive scrutiny. Education reform calls on schools to offer improved academic programs and to change the way they function. Schools are devising ways to develop active learners, use standards-based curricula, work with parents and the community, make more decisions at the school level, and increase accountability. Under school reform initiatives, educators are examining the causes of underachievement, frequently identifying poor health or psychological or social problems as factors (BellSouth Foundation & Education Development Center, 1994). A coordinated approach to addressing students' health can become one of the means to meet a shared outcome: productive

FIGURE 1.3. The Condition of Today's Students

One-third of children entering kindergarten are unprepared to learn—that is, they lack physical health, confidence, maturity, and general knowledge (Boyer, 1991).

One child in four—fully 10 million—is at risk of failure in school because of social, emotional, and health handicaps (Dryfoos, 1994).

During the 1980s, poverty among children in the United States worsened by 22% (U.S. Department of Education & U.S. Department of Health and Human Services, 1993).

Only about 70% of students finish high school in four years (Center for the Study of Social Policy, 1992).

More than 3,000 young persons, most of them children and teenagers, start smoking each day in the United States (Pierce, Fiore, Novotny, Hatziandreu, & Davis, 1989).

Between 12 and 22% of children experience mental, emotional, or behavioral disorders, yet few receive mental health services (Costello, 1989; Hoagwood, 1995).

Two-thirds of eighth graders have tried alcohol, and 28% have been drunk at least once (Johnson, O'Malley, & Bachman, 1994).

Twenty-two percent of ninth graders report carrying a weapon in the previous month (Kann, Warren et al., 1995).

Almost one-fourth of high school students report having seriously considered suicide in the previous year, and 8.6% made an attempt (Kann, Warren et al., 1995).

One-fourth of 10- to 16-year-olds report being assaulted or abused in the previous year (Finkelhor & Kziuba-Leatherman, 1994).

Over 40% of children living below the poverty level have deficient intakes of iron (Pollitt, 1994).

On any given night, more than 100,000 children are homeless (U.S. Department of Education & U.S. Department of Health and Human Services, 1993).

FIGURE 1.4. National Education Goals

By the year 2000 —

1. All children in the United States will start school ready to learn.

2. The high school graduation rate will increase to at least 90%.

3. All students will leave grades 4, 8, and 12 having demonstrated competency over challenging subject matter, including English, mathematics, science, foreign languages, civics and government, economics, the arts, history, and geography, and every school in America will ensure that all students learn to use their mind well so that they are prepared for responsible citizenship, further learning, and productive employment.

4. U.S. students will be first in the world in science and mathematics achievement.

5. Every adult American will be literate and will possess the knowledge and skills necessary to compete in a global economy and to exercise rights and responsibilities of citizenship.

6. Every school in the United States will be free of drugs, violence, and the unauthorized presence of firearms and alcohol and will offer a disciplined environment conducive to learning.

7. The nation's teaching force will have access to programs for the continued improvement of their professional skills and the opportunity to acquire the knowledge and skills needed to instruct and prepare all U.S. students for the next century.

8. Every school will promote partnerships that will increase parental involvement and participation in promoting the social, emotional, and academic growth of children.

—U.S. Department of Education (1991)

---

and capable students. Similarly, a primary objective of health care reform is cost savings; health education and prevention play central roles in accomplishing that goal.

Students' healthy development as a necessary companion to academic success is reflected in national initiatives such as *Healthy People 2000* (Public Health Service, 1991) and *Education Goals 2000*. Each of the *Education Goals 2000* (see Figure 1.4) has a direct or indirect link to the objectives of coordinated school health programs. Goal 1, that children "start school ready to learn," is the core of coordinated school health programs. If children have emotional problems, use drugs, have health problems, or do not have proper nutrition, they are not ready for optimum learning. Similarly, Goal 6, that all schools will be free of drugs, violence, and firearms, directly relates to a healthy, nondisruptive environment that allows all students to learn. Coordinated school health programs also contribute toward the goal of increasing the percentage of students who graduate by providing quality prevention programs (for example, substance use prevention and pregnancy prevention) that keep more young people in school. They prepare students to be critical thinkers and problem solvers; responsible, productive citizens; self-directed learners; and effective communicators (Boyett & Conn, 1991; Secretary's Commission on Achieving Necessary Skills, 1991).

Improving children's health is the ultimate commitment to the belief that *all* children can learn. When schools and communities ignore health problems that could reduce attendance and contribute to school failure, they deprive a child of equal access to an education.

MANDATE AND MOMENTUM

The concept of school health programs has evolved over the past several decades. In the beginning, discussions of school health focused on curricula. In 1987 the field took a quantum leap when Diane Allensworth and Lloyd Kolbe described an eight-component model of a comprehensive school health program (Allensworth & Kolbe, 1987). In the decade since, many schools and organizations that support children's health have prepared the groundwork for integrating the eight components into a whole (Kann, Collins, Pateman, Small, Ross, & Kolbe, 1995). Our improved understanding of risk and resiliency factors and the tendency of young people experiencing risk behaviors to exhibit more than one such behavior makes it necessary to develop programs that are comprehensive—that is, affecting the underlying and long-lasting knowledge, attitudes, and behaviors of students (Dryfoos, 1994).

Public support is strong for schools to take a coordinated approach to health-related services and education. For example, most parents, students, and school administrators believe that health education is at least as important as other subjects taught in school (Gallup Organization, 1994). Over 80% of respondents to another national survey favored providing health services in schools (Harris, 1992). "While schools alone cannot be expected to address the health and related social problems of youth, they can provide, through their climate and curriculum a focal point for efforts to reduce health risk behaviors and improve the health status of youth" (Kann, Collins et al., 1995).

The call for improved health comes from the corporate world as well as from the public at large. Business leaders express their concern about the employability of graduates and ask schools to contribute to building a healthy productive workforce (Secretary's Commission on Achieving Necessary Skills, 1992). The promise of preventing chronic medical problems and avoiding future medical costs has also prompted voluntary health organizations as well as insurance companies to support school-based health programs. "Most of those [health care] dollars are being spent on avoidable diseases caused by style of living (smoking, overeating, heavy drinking) and these expenditures often have very limited benefit to the patient," points out John Seffrin, executive vice president of the American Cancer Society. Such spending does little to change health status and "represents no investment in the next generation and our nation's future" (Seffrin, 1991, p. 135). Carefully coordinated investments can reap great financial *and* health rewards. Every dollar invested in effective tobacco education saves society an estimated $18.80 in health care and other costs caused by smoking. Each dollar invested in alcohol and other drug use prevention saves an estimated $5.69. And each education dollar to prevent too-early and unprotected sexual behaviors saves $5.10 (Centers for Disease Control and Prevention, 1997).

But even as coordinated school health programs gain more advocates, schools face a practical concern associated with widespread systemic reform: scant resources—money, time, space, qualified professionals, and public and political will. Many school practitioners realize that because they cannot work harder than they are already working, they must streamline their work. For some, streamlining means creating new strategies for coordinating, integrating, and redeploying resources to help students improve their health and school performance (Tharinger, 1995).

THE PROMISE OF A COORDINATED APPROACH

Students like Terry—and the millions of her peers—reveal health and learning problems in fragments; schools then often respond in a fragmented way. Efforts to prevent major health problems among young people must expand beyond "AIDS Day" or essay contests on the perils of drug abuse. We must "connect the dots" between health and learning. Limited resources and a shared commitment to children's well-being make a coordinated approach not only practical but preferable. Schools face myriad programs, guidelines, and requirements, and they must review, prioritize, and conceptually link the diverse programs and services available to students (David and Lucile Packard Foundation, 1995).

By addressing students' well-being and ability to learn in a less fragmented way, schools and communities can avoid gaps, collaborate on overlapping functions, and eliminate unnecessary duplication of efforts. As this book elaborates, a school health program is "comprehensive" and "coordinated" when it (Allensworth, 1995)

- focuses on the key risks to health and learning
- receives support from students, family, friends, and adults within the school and community
- draws on the thoughts and efforts of many disciplines, community groups, and agencies
- uses multiple programs or components
- provides staff development programs
- uses inclusive and broadly based program planning

The promise of a coordinated school health program thus far outshines its practice. But the experience of pioneers tells us that the model described and discussed in this volume "could become one of the most efficient means available for almost every nation in the world to significantly improve the well-being of their people" (Kolbe, Kickbusch, Draijer, Dick, Isaksson, O'Byrne, & Jones, 1994). Many school leaders report that their efforts at coordinating health initiatives result in improved attendance, less smoking among students and staff, lower rates of teenage pregnancy, increased participation in physical fitness activities, and greater interest in cholesterol levels and healthier diets. A better understanding of the relationship between health and learning increases use of school health and counseling services. In turn, use of such services decreases disciplinary problems and can delay onset of health risk behaviors such as sexual intercourse and use of alcohol and other drugs that jeopardize both students' health and academic achievement.

We know from research that schools offering individual components of a coordinated school health program can demonstrate both improved students' health and better academic performance. For example, evaluations of classroom curricula have revealed improved health knowledge, attitudes, and practices—notably the decreased use of drugs, alcohol, and cigarettes. Mental health and social service interventions have resulted in improved student functioning, increased attendance, and reduced teacher frustration. These interventions also reduce costs related to welfare, unemployment, and use of emergency services (see Chapters 3–10).

MAKING IT HAPPEN

Education reform initiatives will succeed only if they also address students' health and well-being. We and other contributors to this book do not call for a revolution in the schools. We do call for a new vision about the essential relationship between health and learning and we call on schools to enhance and reallocate existing school and community resources. This book does not offer a formula; instead, it discusses key elements of a change process that schools and districts can embark on to improve education for all. They include:

- *A customized plan.* Each school's or community's unique populations, needs, resources, problems, and financial capabilities will determine the make-up of a coordinated school health program. Needs, issues, and concerns differ among age groups and geographic location (see Chapter 2 for discussion of local planning).
- *Teamwork.* Teamwork is central at all levels: between local districts and state or national organizations; between the school and community players; among school administrators, staff, and students; and within classrooms, cafeterias, and clinics. A district's school health team should have representation from throughout the community to inform curriculum development, health policies, and service. All participants must share a commitment to four key practices: communication, cooperation, coordination, and collaboration.
- *Family and community involvement.* Effective school change involves students and their families. It requires mobilizing both school and community resources to make children's education and health a community priority.
- *A commitment to continuing improvement.* Systemic changes in schools require a long-term, steady commitment (Tanaka, 1996). Change requires professional development at the college and university level as well as ongoing training programs for administrators, teachers, and other staff. Research and evaluation efforts that monitor progress, demonstrate program quality and satisfaction, and inform program improvement will move schools closer to the goal of better-prepared students who can perform well.

A GUIDE TO THIS BOOK

The second chapter sets the stage for implementing coordinated school health programs by discussing what needs to happen in a school and how school districts can support these activities. The next eight chapters describe the individual components that comprise a coordinated school health program and how each component reinforces the other seven. Subsequent chapters discuss how state and national agencies and organizations can support coordinated school health programs. Each chapter includes action steps for moving toward the goal of a coordinated school health program. A summary chapter sets forth overall imperatives for action, guidelines for the future, and indicators for measuring success.

This book can be a catalyst for deep and positive change in schools. Its philosophy that healthy children learn more, its approach, and its tools reflect longstanding values of education. Only when schools and communities systematically tap and coordinate their resources will all children achieve well-being and success.

REFERENCES

Allensworth, D. (1995). *The comprehensive school health program: Essential elements.* Unpublished.

Allensworth D., & Kolbe, L. (1987). The comprehensive school health program: Exploring an expanded concept. *Journal of School Health, 57*(10), 409–412.

BellSouth Foundation & Education Development Center. (1994). *Education and health: Partners in school reform.* Atlanta, GA: BellSouth Foundation.

Boyer, E. L. (1991). *Ready to learn: A mandate for the nation.* Princeton, NJ: The Carnegie Foundation for the Advancement of Teaching.

Boyett, J. H., & Conn, H. P. (1991). *Workplace 2000: The revolution reshaping American business.* New York: Dutton.

Center for the Study of Social Policy. (1992). *The national education goals report: Building a nation of learners.* Washington, DC: U.S. Government Printing Office.

Centers for Disease Control and Prevention. (1997). *Is school health education cost-effective?: An exploratory analysis of selected exemplary components.* Unpublished manuscript, Division of Adolescent and School Health.

Costello, E. J. (1989). Developments in child psychiatric epidemiology. *Journal of American Academy of Child Adolescent Psychiatry, 28,* 114–120.

The David and Lucile Packard Foundation. (1995). *The future of children. Long-term outcomes of early childhood programs.* Los Altos, CA: Author.

Dryfoos, J. G. (1994). *Full-service schools. A revolution in health and social services for children, youth, and families.* San Francisco: Jossey-Bass.

Finkelhor, D., & Kziuba-Leatherman, J. (1994). Children as victims of violence: A national survey. *Pediatrics, 94,* 413–420.

The Gallup Organization. (1994). *Values and opinions of comprehensive school health education in U.S. public schools: Adolescents, parents, and school district administrators.* Atlanta, GA: American Cancer Society.

Harris, L. (1992). The public takes reform to heart. *Agenda (Winter),* 17.

Hoagwood, K. (1995). Issues in designing and implementing studies of non-mental health care sectors. *Journal of Clinical Child Psychology, 23,* 114–120.

Johnson, L. D., O'Malley, P. M., & Bachman, J. G. (1994). *National survey results on drug use from the Monitoring the Future study, 1975–1993: Vol. 1. Secondary school students.* Rockville, MD: National Institute on Drug Abuse.

Kann, L., Collins, J. L., Pateman, B. C., Small, M. L., Ross, J. G., & Kolbe, L. J. (1995). The School Health Policies and Programs Study (SHPPS): Rationale for a nationwide status report on school health programs. *Journal of School Health, 65*(8), 291.

Kann, L., Warren, C. W., Harris, W. A., Collins, J. L., Douglas, K. A., Collins, M. E., Williams, B. I., Ross, J. G., Kolbe, L. J., & State and Local YRBSS Coordinators. (1995). Youth Risk Behavior Surveillance—United States, 1993. *Morbidity and Mortality Weekly Report, 44* (SS-1), 1–56.

Kolbe, L. J. (1990). An epidemiological surveillance system to monitor the prevalence of youth behaviors that most affect health. *Health Education, 21*(3), 24–30.

Kolbe, L. J., Kickbusch, I., Draijer, J. G. H., Dick, B., Isaksson, A., O'Byrne, D., & Jones, J. (1994). *National and international strategies to improve school health programs.* Unpublished manuscript.

Levinger, B. (1994). *Nutrition, health and education for all.* Newton, MA: Education Development Center and United Nations Development Programme.

National Commission on the Role of the School and the Community in Improving Adolescent Health. (1990). *Code blue.* Alexandria, VA: National Association of State Boards of Education.

Pierce, J. P., Fiore, M. C., Novotny, T. E., Hatziandreu, E. J., & Davis, R. M. (1989). Trends in cigarette smoking in the United States: Projections to the Year 2000. *Journal of the American Medical Association, 261*(1), 61–65.

Pollitt, E. (1994). Poverty and child development: Relevance of research in developing countries to the United States. *Child Development, 65,* 283–295.

Public Health Service. (1991). *Healthy people 2000: National health promotion and disease prevention objectives—full report with commentary.* Washington, DC: U.S. Department of Health and Human Services, Public Health Service publication (PHS) 91–50212.

Secretary's Commission on Achieving Necessary Skills. (1991). *What work requires of schools: A SCANS report for America 2000.* Washington, DC: U.S. Department of Labor.

Secretary's Commission on Achieving Necessary Skills. (1992). *Learning a living: A blueprint for high performance.* Washington, DC: U.S. Department of Labor.

Seffrin, J. R. (1991). Comprehensive school health education: A responsible and responsive intervention to the HIV/AIDS epidemic and other health problems. In

Restructuring schools: Potential for students at risk (pp. 133–158). Washington, DC: Council of Chief State School Officers.

Smith, D. R. (1996). *Healthy children are prepared to learn. School health: Programs in action.* Austin: Texas Department of Health.

Tanaka, G. (1996). *What's health got to do with it? A case for health programs in middle level schools.* Columbus, OH: National Middle School Association.

Tharinger, D. (1995). Roles of psychologists in emerging models of school-related health and mental health services. *School Psychology Quarterly, 10,* 203–216.

U.S. Department of Education. (1991). *America 2000: An education strategy.* Washington, DC: U.S. Government Printing Office.

U.S. Department of Education and U.S. Department of Health and Human Services. (1993). *Together we can: A guide for crafting a profamily system of education and human services.* Washington, DC: U.S. Government Printing Office.

World Health Organization. (1996). *Promoting health through schools.* Geneva: World Health Organization.

Joyce V. Fetro, Ph.D., C.H.E.S.

2 Implementing Coordinated School Health Programs in Local Schools

School health programs offer the opportunity for us to provide the services and knowledge necessary to enable children to be productive learners and to develop the skills to make health decisions for the rest of their lives.
—National School Boards Association, et al. (1995)

I n recent discussions about preparing youth to take their places in society as successful and contributing adults, federal and state officials and leaders of national organizations have referred to the essential linkages between healthy development and educational performance and articulated their commitment to working independently and in partnership to address students' physical, emotional, and intellectual development (Figure 2.1). Many schools and districts also recognize the need to address students' health needs to maximize academic success. Yet within local schools, adoption, implementation, and coordination of the components of a coordinated school health program remain a challenge. To assist schools in this important undertaking, this chapter describes steps that site and district administrators can take to 1) establish and strengthen coordinated school health programs and 2) build district-level support for coordinated school health programs. Other chapters in this book discuss the nature and components of a coordi-

Health Is Academic: A Guide to Coordinated School Health Problems. Edited by Eva Marx and Susan Frelick Wooley, with Daphne Northrop. New York: Teachers College Press, 1998. ISBN 0-8077-3713-5 (pbk.), ISBN 0-8077-3714-3 (cloth). Prior to photocopying items for classroom use, please contact the Copyright Clearance Center, Customer Service, 222 Rosewood Dr., Danvers, MA 01923, USA, tel. (508) 750-8400. © 1998 Education Development Center, Inc. All rights reserved.

FIGURE 2.1. **Statements on the Linkages Between Health and Educational Performance**

To help children meet these [educational, health, and developmental] challenges, education and health must be linked in partnership. . . Health, education, and human service programs must be integrated, and schools must have the support of public and private health care providers, communities, and families. . . School health programs support the educational process, integrate services for disadvantaged and disabled children, and improve children's health prospects.

U.S. Department of Education & U.S. Department of Health and Human Services (1994)

Students who are hungry, sick, troubled, or depressed cannot function well in the classroom, no matter how good the school.

[Schools must] improve academic performance through fostering health and fitness of young adolescents, by providing a health coordinator in every middle school, access to health care and counseling services, and a health-promoting school environment.

Carnegie Council on Adolescent Development (1989, p. 9)

Programs should address universal requirements of adolescents in their communities, such as: health and physical well-being, personal and social competence, cognitive and educational competence, preparation for work, leadership, and citizenship.

For the first time in the history of this country, young people are less healthy and less prepared to take their places in society than were their parents.

National Commission on the Role of the School and the Community in Improving Adolescent Health (1990, Executive Summary)

No knowledge is more crucial than knowledge about health. Without it, no other life goal can be successfully achieved.

Boyer (1983, p. 304)

In the larger context, schools are society's vehicle for providing young people with the tools for successful adulthood. Perhaps no tool is more essential than good health.

Council of Chief State School Officers (1991, p. 4)

Figure 2.1. Continued

Poor health interferes with learning; good health facilitates it. *(p. 14)*

States and school districts should give teachers and principals the authority and resources to transform middle schools and junior high schools into health-promoting as well as learning environments. *(p. 13)*

Much of the current spending for adolescents could achieve better results if it were redirected toward fundamental, comprehensive approaches.
Carnegie Council on Adolescent Development (1995, p. 15)

nated school health program and the supports available at national and state levels.

COORDINATED SCHOOL HEALTH PROGRAMS: AN EDUCATIONAL INNOVATION

Although most schools have some elements of a coordinated school health program, few have a health program that includes all components at a fully functioning level, and fewer still effectively coordinate all. This book proposes an "innovation" for schools—to strengthen and coordinate all the components. Some educational innovations are simple and practical; others are more complex and theoretical. Some resemble programs already in place in schools; others are more novel. When educators introduce a new program, they might expect to implement the program exactly as described, with the unquestioning support of staff, students, families, and community members. However, a variety of barriers and challenges usually prevent full implementation (Rogers, 1983).

Successful implementation of an innovation depends on several factors, including characteristics of the innovation itself. According to a national focus group of school principals, board members, and district-level administrators convened to inform this chapter, the following characteristics contribute to successful implementation:

- Underlying purpose and potential outcomes
- Perceived value in addressing identified needs
- Clarity of purpose
- Adaptability

- Replicability
- Consistency with the school's mission and vision
- Ease of implementation (for example, requirements for additional training and resources)
- Credibility with school staff and the community
- Capacity for broadening the knowledge base of students or staff
- Potential to enhance, supplement, or support existing programs

The more of these characteristics inherent in an innovation, the more likely a school will adopt and successfully implement the innovation (Bosworth, Gingiss, Potthoff, & Roberts-Gray, 1995).

The focus group findings are consistent with characteristics that Rogers (1983) identified as critical to successful adoption or implementation:

- *Relative advantage:* Is the new idea, practice, or product better than what was in place before?
- *Compatibility:* Is it consistent with existing values, past experiences, and needs?
- *Complexity:* Is it perceived as difficult to understand and use?
- *Trialability:* Can it be tried on a limited basis?
- *Observability:* Are the results of implementing it visible?

By assessing coordinated school health programs using Rogers's five characteristics, schools can develop step-by-step strategies to promote such programs and support their adoption.

Relative advantage: If school communities perceive coordinated school health programs as more effective than existing fragmented programs, they are more likely to implement such programs. To determine the perception of relative advantage, a school community could ask the following critical questions: What are the perceived benefits and costs of implementing a coordinated school health program? Do the perceived benefits to the physical, mental, social, and emotional health of students, their families, and school staff outweigh those that currently exist? How will implementing a coordinated school health program affect teaching and learning at the school?

Compatibility: If schools and communities view coordinated school health programs as consistent with existing values; responsive to student, family, and staff needs; and supportive of school plans, they are more likely to support such programs. Questions that can help determine compatibility include: Are coordinated school health programs consistent with the philosophy and values of the school community? Does this model address identified needs, concerns, and interests of students, their families, school staff, and the community? Do coordinated school health programs support the mission, goals, objectives, and priorities of the school? How successful were past attempts to implement elements of a school health program? What facilitated and what impeded past efforts? How much change in existing programs and structures will this model require?

Complexity: If school administrators and staff believe that implementation of coordinated school health programs is easy, they are more likely to move forward with implementation plans. Some questions to answer about complexity are: Do staff understand coordinated school health programs and how such programs support educational achievement? Do key implementers understand the breadth and depth of each component of a coordinated school health program? How many school staff will be involved in implementation? How much professional development will staff need to implement a coordinated school health program? How much time, effort, and energy will implementation require? Are adequate human and fiscal resources available to support implementation?

Trialability: If a school can pilot some or all components of a coordinated school health program and in effect try out the concept, it is more likely to begin implementation. Questions about trialability might include: Can schools initially implement only one or a few components of a coordinated school health program? Can school communities implement the model in stages? How adaptable is the model?

Observability: If school administrators can document successful implementation of coordinated school health programs, they are more likely to facilitate their implementation. Questions that might help to verify the benefits of a coordinated school health program include: Are there examples of schools that have partially or fully implemented coordinated school health programs? Can the school community see some successes? Have staff, parents and other caregivers, and others confirmed the relative advantage of using this model?

SCHOOL AND DISTRICTS WORKING TOGETHER

Implementation of new programs can begin both at the school level or at the district level, each influencing the other. For maximum success, program efforts and support should occur concurrently at the two levels. School programs cannot survive for the long term without school board policy and support from district-level leaders. At the same time, successful implementation requires strong school-level leadership and strong local school support.

Most school districts have in leadership positions health education specialists, nurses, and other health professionals who are committed to meeting the health and safety needs of youth. Enlisting the support of other district-

level administrators, establishing an advisory committee, identifying supports and challenges in the broader community, and developing supportive
board policies can strengthen these people's leadership. At the school level,
principals or other committed staff can identify key players, establish Healthy
School Teams, and identify ongoing efforts and activities that contribute to
the school's health program.

Four key processes will help districts and schools strengthen support for
school health programs and plan and implement such programs—communication, cooperation, coordination, and collaboration:

- *Communication:* Sharing ideas among interested parties. Implementing
  strategies that facilitate communication within the school, between the
  school and the community, between the school and district offices, and
  between district offices and community agencies early in the process will
  strengthen ownership of programs.
- *Cooperation:* Informal relationships among individuals and organizations
  with related goals. If communication channels exist, individuals and organizations work together on an ad hoc basis even if they do not engage in
  common planning.
- *Coordination:* Regular meetings among individuals and organizations with
  related goals for sharing resources, plans, and needs. These meetings include discussions of potential sources of support, the health-related needs
  of students and their families, and gaps in meeting students' health needs.
- *Collaboration:* Formal relationships among individuals and organizations
  committed to a common vision, mission, and goals. The relationships
  could establish a new organizational structure with defined interrelated
  roles and responsibilities and involve shared leadership and consolidation
  of resources.

Ways to apply these processes in all phases of developing a coordinated
school health program appear throughout this chapter. Program development will draw on different processes at different times.

ACTION STEPS SCHOOLS CAN TAKE TO ESTABLISH OR STRENGTHEN A COORDINATED SCHOOL HEALTH PROGRAM

A coordinated school health program will look different in each school.
The needs, issues, and concerns of elementary students and their families (for
example, bicycle safety, fire safety, feeling good about oneself, using medicines wisely, good touch/bad touch) differ from those of older students and

FIGURE 2.2. Steps to Implement a Coordinated School Health Program

School Level	District Level
• Establish school-based leadership	• Secure district-level leadership
• Identify key players	• Establish a broad-based advisory committee
• Establish a Healthy School Team and select a coordinator	• Identify supports and challenges in the broader school community
• Get "buy-in" from other school-site staff	• Develop supportive board policies
• Establish a common language	• Train district and community advocates to sell the program
• Set up a safety net	
• Map existing school-based and community-based resources	
• Identify student, family, and staff needs	
• Identify programmatic needs	
• Develop an implementation and coordination plan	
• Identify existing and potential sources of funding	

their families (for example, depression, substance use, dealing with anger, HIV infection, pregnancy). In addition, the health-related issues in urban areas (gang involvement, for example) often differ from those in suburban and rural areas (access to health services, for example). Many health and safety issues (for example, flood, earthquake, tornado, or other natural-disaster preparedness; sickle cell anemia; lead screening) are determined by a school's geographic location.

Within a single school district, mandated elements of a school's health program (for example, health education and physical education curricula; vision, hearing, and scoliosis screening; tobacco-free school policies) are usually consistent across schools. Individual schools then tailor their programs to address the specific needs of students, families, and staff.

Regardless of which specific strategies a school deems appropriate and relevant, several steps can facilitate implementation of a coordinated school health program (Figure 2.2). Although the sequence will vary depending on a school and community's level of readiness, capacity, priorities, and available resources, most schools need to engage in all of the steps at some time.

Schools can take the following eleven steps to build or strengthen a coordinated school health program.

Establish School-Based Leadership

An essential key to success is a school principal or assistant principal who recognizes the importance and value of a coordinated school health program and how it can support teaching and learning within the school. The principal is an opinion leader who can support or undermine programs within a school through direct or indirect words and actions. A direct link between the school and the district office, the principal can often help to secure needed fiscal and human resources as well as administrative support.

Identify Key Players

Individuals with responsibilities for implementing the various components of a coordinated school health program also must participate. They include health educators, physical educators, school counselors, school nurses, school social workers, school psychologists, drug and alcohol prevention coordinators, food service staff, liaisons with parents and other caregivers, police liaisons, union representatives, clerical staff, bus drivers, and custodial staff. Because some of these key school staff wear several hats, one person might assume more than one role or responsibility. Other members of the school community also have important roles. Older students can provide valuable insights into students' needs and the appropriateness and effectiveness of interventions. Equally critical for effective implementation is the active participation of teachers and support staff who do not have primary responsibility for a given component; often, they act as the administrator's designee. School secretaries, for example, often facilitate or impede communications in a school. School volunteers and families and other caregivers are other key players whose support and participation are essential.

Key players can also include representatives of community organizations that serve the health-related needs of students and their families—the American Heart Association, American Lung Association, American Cancer Society, National Dairy Council, YMCA, and Boys and Girls Clubs, for example. Such players can be powerful allies and advocates for coordinated school health programs if they are included in discussions and planning from the outset.

Establish a Healthy School Team and Select a Coordinator

A Healthy School Team should include students, parents and other caregivers, community representatives, and key school staff identified above who have primary responsibility for implementing the various components of a coordinated school health program. The responsibilities of a Healthy School Team could include assessing student, family, and staff needs; mapping existing school and community resources that could contribute to a coordinated school health program; identifying gaps and duplications; developing action plans; and monitoring implementation.

An existing advisory or planning group—for example, a school council, student study team, student assistance team, safe school planning team, or crisis response team—might take on this role. If a school creates a separate Healthy School Team, that team should create linkages with other school teams, such as those considering school improvement plans, to ensure that the plan includes the various aspects of a coordinated school health program.

A coordinator at the school should lead the team and serve as the contact for coordinating and integrating community-based programs with school-based programs. The coordinator should have professional preparation and certification; be able to plan, implement, and evaluate a coordinated school health program; be familiar with existing community resources; and have connections to local, state, and national health and education organizations. Health educators and school nurses often have such abilities, training, knowledge, and connections.

The coordinator will need release time during the school day for coordination activities. A regularly scheduled meeting, held during the school day if at all possible, will facilitate the team's work. If meetings must be held after school, some type of compensation (for example, extended-hour pay) is warranted.

Get "Buy-In" from Other School Staff

The school culture, organizations, and social structure can either facilitate or impede adoption of any innovation. Key leaders can use their contacts to seek support from a school management council and opinion leaders in the school and in the community. Often, informing others about how a coordinated school health program addresses the "whole child" and contributes to a school's mission will garner desired support. If school staff believe that all children can learn and that each child should have opportunities, supports, and services that ensure academic success, they are likely to view a coordinated school health program as complementary rather than as competing for instructional time. If administrators see how this model will help maximize existing funding, time, and human resources, they are likely to view a coordinated school health program as good management rather than an added burden. Existing communication channels and networks, such as faculty meetings, daily announcements, bulletin board flyers, and informal discussions in the teacher's lounge or lunchroom, can help inform others.

In making the case for a coordinated school health program, the following points might help get staff "buy-in":

- A coordinated school health program can better address the health-related interests, needs, and concerns of students, their families, and staff, and improve students' academic performance.
- A coordinated school health program can help attain more than one-third of the 300 national health objectives (Allensworth, Symons, & Olds, 1994; Healthy People 2000, 1991).
- Improved health status improves school attendance and learning. National and state data from the Youth Risk Behavior Survey (Centers for Disease Control and Prevention, 1995) and data from a local health department can demonstrate the prevalence of health risk behaviors among youth.

Often, people are more receptive to a new concept if it appears doable. Thus, to get "buy-in," a school's health leadership might first determine needs and priorities and then begin finding ways to coordinate and strengthen existing activities without adding staff or space. As staff and students see how one component can support and enhance the others, they will become more receptive to the total concept—for example, strengthening an existing unit on tobacco use prevention in the health education curriculum by coordinating it with a program to monitor the blood pressure of current smokers (health services). Additional measures might include establishing and enforcing tobacco-free school policies (healthy school environment), offering smoking cessation programs to students (counseling, psychological, and social services), discussing the relationship between smoking, cardiovascular fitness, and athletic performance (physical education), offering awareness sessions for families on the effects of smoking and spit tobacco (family and community involvement), organizing stress management activities for staff (staff health promotion), and providing alternative healthy snacks (nutrition services).

Establish a Common Language

Common understanding of the components of a coordinated school health program among teachers, administrators, students, parents and other caregivers, community members, and other key players helps obtain "buy-in" and also facilitates implementation. If people define the same term differently, confusion often occurs. For example, some people believe that "health education" addresses only sex education; others think "health education" addresses only food groups; still others believe it addresses only disease prevention. Similarly, when some think of "health services," they visualize health aides weighing and measuring children and administering first aid; others see school nurses and other health professionals coordinating school-based services and serving as case managers for students with complex health problems. It is therefore important for the Healthy School Team to clearly define each component, to offer opportunities for discussion and clarification among all relevant groups, and to clarify misperceptions.

Set Up a Safety Net

At the start of the program, the Healthy School Team should identify factors that might impede implementation and develop a strategy to address each one. For example, if members of the team sense conflict because staff fear that a new initiative might replace an existing one, the team might call a meeting of all school staff who are affected by the decision to ask those who are uncomfortable with the team's proposal what they would support. Prior to such a meeting, the team could develop a plan for fielding questions by identifying possible questions and the individuals best able to answer them. The team could draw up a list of teachers and other school staff who are supportive of the concept of coordinated school health programs and who could talk with their peers who have reservations or concerns. Similarly, if the Healthy School Team sensed the resistance of certain community members, they could solicit the assistance of parents or other caregivers who might be effective advocates.

Healthy School Teams often find that it takes more time than expected to win people over to a new idea. An open, supportive, nurturing environment can go a long way to both allay fears and demonstrate the school's commitment to implementing a coordinated school health program. Involving staff and community advisory groups early in the process can help to meet challenges as concerns arise.

Map Existing School-Based and Community-Based Resources

Most schools have numerous elements of a coordinated school health program in place. Resource mapping is a technique that schools can use to depict what is currently in place in a school. Figure 2.3 shows a sample map listing both mandated and supplementary activities for a school district. The coordinated school health program model serves as a framework for thinking broadly and identifying duplications and gaps. As the figure illustrates, most health-related activities address more than one component of the coordi-

FIGURE 2.3. Sample Map of Health Activities, Services, and Policies

Activity, Service, or Policy	Coordinated School Health Program Component							
	HED	PE	HS	NS	HPS	CPSS	HSE	FCI
Skills-based health education curriculum (preK–12)	x	x					x	
Health advocates/liaisons	x		x		x	x	x	x
Speakers from community agencies	x		x					
Theatrical performances	x							x
Names memorial quilt	x		x					x
Red ribbon week/World AIDS day activities	x					x	x	x
Ropes courses, wilderness courses	x		x		x	x	x	x
Club live/Friday night live	x						x	x
Professional development in health education	x							x
District-wide health services/ screenings			x			x	x	x
Special education intake center			x			x	x	x
First aid manuals	x		x		x		x	
Awareness sessions on universal precautions	x				x			
School health center		x				x	x	x
Hepatitis B immunizations	x		x			x	x	
Computerized student health records			x					
Policy: use of tobacco, alcohol, and other drugs	x		x		x	x	x	x

HED = health education, PE = physical education, HS = health services, NS = nutrition services, HPS = health promotion for staff (staff wellness), CPSS = counseling, psychological, and social services, HSE = healthy school environment, FCI = family and community involvement.

FIGURE 2.3. Continued

Activity, Service, or Policy	Coordinated School Health Program Component							
	HED	PE	HS	NS	HPS	CPSS	HSE	FCI
Policy: anti-slurs	x						x	
Policy: sexual harassment	x				x	x	x	
Physical education curriculum (preK–12)		x					x	
Physical fitness testing		x						
CPR training	x	x						
Jump rope for heart	x	x						
Peer helper programs	x		x			x	x	x
Support services for gay/ lesbian youth	x		x			x	x	x
Student assistance programs			x			x	x	x
Crisis response teams			x		x	x	x	x
Family peer educators	x		x	x		x	x	x
Police resource officers	x						x	
Breakfast and lunch program	x			x				
Employee assistance program	x				x			

Source: San Francisco Unified School District.

nated school health program model. Figure 2.4 provides examples of activities, services, and policies that a school's map might depict.

Identify Student, Family, and Staff Needs

Much information on the needs of students, their families, and school staff is readily available. Databases, needs assessments, and reports from the school, the district, and the surrounding community are a good starting point for a Healthy School Team's needs assessment. Morbidity and mortality data

FIGURE 2.4. Examples of Health Activities, Services, and Policies

---

NOTE: These examples are not all-inclusive, but might prompt ideas for examining opportunities, supports, and services for students, their families, and school staff. Other chapters provide additional ideas.

- To support *planned, sequential health education*, a school might involve speakers from community-based agencies (e.g., American Heart Association, National Dairy Council, American Cancer Society, Department of Public Health) and participate in district-wide events (e.g., Great American Smokeout, Red Ribbon Week, World AIDS Day). Students might participate in health-related service learning opportunities (e.g., volunteering at community health agencies or youth-serving organizations, participating in SAFE KIDS coalitions). After-school health-related activities and clubs offer positive alternatives to substance use and gang involvement.

- To go beyond *physical education* classes that promote cardiovascular fitness through lifelong physical activity, schools sometimes provide opportunities before, during, or after school hours for fitness activities, intramural programs, and interscholastic sports programs. Students might participate in other activities that promote physical activity such as Jump Rope for Heart or walk-a-thons. Some schools develop partnerships with health clubs to expand the facilities available to students and staff.

- To support and enhance *school health services* that provide preventive services, education, emergency care, and management of health conditions, some schools host a health fair that offers cholesterol and diabetes screening, health risk appraisals, and health counseling. School or public health nurses provide immunizations and testing to students and staff (e.g., hepatitis B, tuberculosis, blood pressure, cholesterol). Links to community providers strengthen referrals and case management.

- To promote a *healthy school environment* that is conducive to learning; supports individual and family differences; and promotes personal growth, wellness, and healthy relationships, schools adopt supportive policies and procedures. For example, some school districts have policies that address comprehensive health education; use of tobacco, alcohol, and other drugs on campus; slurs based on gender, race, ethnicity, and sexual orientation; students and staff with HIV infection; preschool physical examinations; sexual harassment; and condom availability. In addition, schools might have disciplinary policies, safe school teams, crisis response teams, injury prevention programs, or universal precautions awareness sessions designed to maintain a safe and supportive environment for teaching and learning.

FIGURE 2.4. Continued

- To supplement the *counseling, psychological, and social services* that a school offers, schools identify, assess, and refer students who need assistance to outside resources. In addition, many schools offer peer helper programs and individual and group counseling sessions for students and families. All school staff could receive training on recognizing and reporting child abuse and identifying students at risk for suicide, substance use, and other health-risk behaviors. Depending on local needs, some schools offer students opportunities to discuss health-related issues (e.g., Alateen groups, facilitated support groups) or provide student assistance programs. Through formal agreements, community-based agencies often provide counseling services to students and their families.

- To offer a full range of *school-site health promotion for staff programs*, some schools provide awareness activities, health assessments, stress management and fitness activities, and health-related support services. Awareness activities might relate to good nutrition, fitness, or weight control. Some staff in every school might take training in first aid and CPR techniques. Some schools offer before- or after-school fitness, weight control, and aerobic programs for staff. Many districts offer employee assistance programs.

- In addition to providing nutritionally balanced breakfasts and lunches reflecting the U.S. Dietary Guidelines for Americans, *school nutrition services* can serve as learning laboratories that support classroom nutrition education. In some health education classes, students examine menus for salt, fat, sugar, and fiber content. Some children with special health needs require modified school meals. Many schools limit vending machine selections to healthy foods. As part of the school lunch, many schools offer salad bars and provide low-fat, low-salt, and low-cholesterol meals.

- To address the diverse needs of students and their families, maximize resources, and ensure that health-related messages are consistent in schools, at home, within the peer group, and in the community, schools *involve students' families and other members of the community.* Parents and other caregivers and community members participate in school-based advisory groups and coalitions and often volunteer in the schools. Some schools offer parents and other caregivers opportunities to participate in health-related fairs. Community-based agencies often provide additional health-related activities for students and their families (e.g., engaging alternative programs, such as ropes courses, wilderness trips, sailing trips; theatrical performances to enhance the educational program; facilitated support groups; linkages with clinics).

from the public health department offer a broad view of community health problems. The Centers for Disease Control and Prevention's biennial Youth Risk Behavior Survey (Kolbe, Kann, & Collins, 1993) provides information on the behaviors that youth engage in at various ages.

Information obtained directly from students, their families, staff, and community members will help the Healthy School Team to fine-tune the picture that the national and local data provide. The team can use both focus group interviews and informal surveys to gather in-depth information.

Identify Programmatic Needs

The coordinator and the Healthy School Team can use the resource map and the needs assessment to identify gaps in the school's health program and make decisions about how to strengthen or modify existing health-related efforts. They can prioritize the programmatic needs based on factors such as relative importance for academic achievement; resources required (professional development, funding, time requirements); number of students, family members, or staff that will benefit; and readiness of the school community.

Develop an Implementation and Coordination Plan

The Healthy School Team, in consultation with other school staff, can use the resource map and needs assessment to develop a multiyear plan for implementing a coordinated school health program that includes short- and long-term goals, measurable objectives, and specific program and evaluation activities. Both human and fiscal resources will limit how much a school can support and implement successfully in any school year. For example, a school that has a strong student assistance program might add prevention strategies and engaging social or recreation activities. Similarly, if both health education and physical education are in place, a school might add an assessment and referral system for students at high risk that utilizes family support groups. Chapter 13 suggests what a school might expect to accomplish in the early years of implementation.

Once a school has developed a plan, it must consider the support systems and mechanisms it will need to implement the plan:

- *Professional development for school staff:* The need for training will depend on the staff's professional preparation and experience with regard to specific health activities, services, and policies in the plan. For example, conducting a one-time school-wide event like a walk-a-thon might only require a staff meeting to discuss who will do what, when, and how. By contrast, implementing a student assistance program might require that a school team participate in several days' training in assessment, referral, and case management procedures and policies.

- *A plan for technical assistance and collegial support:* The more a new activity differs from past activities, the greater will be the need for technical assistance and support. In many instances, schools can tap district-level resources.

- *Ongoing communication among staff about what is and is not working:* Existing or new networks can facilitate communication between the site administrator and staff, between the Healthy School Team and staff implementing program components, and between all players.

- *A system for managing, monitoring, and evaluating the program:* Whenever possible, schools should use existing operations and systems. If effective communication channels are in place, for example, there is no need to change them or to create new ones. Similarly, an ongoing public relations campaign could communicate program successes to the community.

Questions that might guide the process of monitoring and evaluating the program include: Is implementation following the plan? How are students, staff, families, and others responding to the program? What, if anything, needs changing? How many youth and adults participate in the program? Is the program having an impact on educational achievement, health-risk behaviors, attendance rates, dropout rates, and other student indicators?

Identify Existing and Potential Sources of Funding

Finding and securing resources to support components of a coordinated school health program is a challenging task. Charting existing sources of funding as part of resource mapping for health activities, services, and policies can be a useful first step. Figure 2.5 provides a sample chart, showing federal, state, and local sources of funding.

In seeking new funding to implement additional activities, services, and policies, schools should determine whether (1) the district already receives funds that could support new or expanded initiatives; (2) the district is eligible for such funds; (3) the district makes allocations to schools; and (4) the school is free to pursue additional funding independently. Creative thinking, patience, and perseverance are critical. For example, schools might blend dollars from a variety of sources to implement particular health-related initiatives.

Procedures for applying for funding and eligibility requirements vary from state to state and district to district. To stay apprised of funding sources and opportunities, school health coordinators should establish a network of

FIGURE 2.5. Existing Funding for Coordinated School Health Programs

Funding Source	Coordinated School Health Program Component							
	HED	PE	HS	NS	HPS	CPSS	HSE	FCI
Federal Sources								
Centers for Disease Control and Prevention	x		x		x	x	x	x
Improving America's Schools Act, Title I			x			x	x	x
Improving America's Schools Act, Title II	x	x						
Improving America's Schools Act, Title IV	x	x	x			x	x	x
Improving America's Schools Act, Title XI	x	x	x	x	x	x	x	x
State Sources								
Tobacco Use Prevention	x					x	x	x
Tobacco Use Reduction/Cessation	x				x	x	x	x
Healthy Start	x		x			x	x	x
Medi-Cal Reimbursement	x		x			x	x	x
Child Health and Disability Program			x			x		x
Cardiovascular Health	x				x			
Gang Risk Intervention	x					x	x	x
Peer Leaders Manual	x					x	x	
Earthquake Preparation	x						x	
Local Sources								
San Francisco Unified School District General Funds	x	x	x	x	x	x	x	x
San Francisco Unified School District Buildings and Grounds							x	
San Francisco Department of Public Health	x					x	x	x

HED = health education, PE = physical education, HS = health services, NS = nutrition services, HPS = health promotion for staff (staff wellness), CPSS = counseling, psychological, and social services, HSE = healthy school environment, FCI = family and community involvement

FIGURE 2.5. Continued

| Funding Source | Coordinated School Health Program Component | | | | | | | |
	HED	PE	HS	NS	HPS	CPSS	HSE	FCI
San Francisco Children's Amendment, School Health Center			x			x		x
San Francisco Children's Amendment, Healthy Start	x		x			x	x	x
Other Sources								
California Wellness Foundation	x	x	x	x	x	x	x	x
University of California- San Francisco	x		x					
Merck Pharmaceutical Company			x					

Source: San Francisco Unified School District.

contacts in the community (at the local health department, for example), in the state (at the department of education and department of health services, for example), and at the federal level (a school district's lobbyists and the Federal Register, for example).

The brief summary of sources of federal, state, and local funding below can be a starting point for schools' fund-raising efforts.

Federal Funding. The federal government provides funding that supports systemic reform to school districts and local schools. The Improving America's Schools Act (previously the Elementary and Secondary Education Act) provides support for schools in low-income communities. Title I of the act (Services for Disadvantaged Children) makes available funding for schools to provide additional health and social services to selected students and their families; Title II (Professional Development) supports staff training that fosters school reform efforts; Title IV (Safe and Drug Free Schools and Communities) supports safe, violence-free, and drug-free environments for teaching and learning; and Title XI (Coordinated Services) allows school districts to use up to 5% of the funds received under the act to develop, implement, or expand a coordinated services project. After identifying student and family health and social service needs, local schools can partner with public and/or private agencies to increase access to coordinated services.

The Goals 2000: Educate America Act provides funding to schools or school districts (through their state education agency) for coordinated standards-based school improvement efforts. The Individuals with Disabilities Education Act of 1990 provides funds for special education programs for children aged 0–22 years with disabilities, including necessary health and social services. The Family Preservation and Support Program provides funds to departments of social services that schools could use to develop and expand a family preservation program (for families at risk or in crisis) or family support services (community-based prevention activities).

In addition, the U.S. Department of Education, National Institutes of Health, Centers for Disease Control and Prevention, and other federal agencies make available a variety of competitive sources of funding that schools and districts could tap to implement health activities and services. Schools can stay abreast of new and existing funding opportunities by subscribing to publications such as the *Federal Register* and *Commerce and Business Weekly* and by accessing on-line information through the Internet.

State Funding.   State funding for coordinated school health programs varies according to states' priorities. For example, Massachusetts makes a portion of the revenues from its tobacco tax available to schools for tobacco use prevention activities. Other states have funded statewide initiatives that address other categorical health issues or support child and family services. For example, California funds Gang Risk Intervention Programs and the Healthy Start Initiative. Finally, schools and school districts should explore options for reimbursement for services through Medicaid and Early and Periodic Screening, Diagnosis, and Treatment Programs (see Chapter 8).

Local Funding.   In addition to funding available from the school district, local funding sources might include the departments of public health and social services, and other city and county departments. Funds from these sources might support staff positions, health services based on referrals, or recreation programs at schools. Some cities have enacted city-wide initiatives for children's services, such as San Francisco's Children's Amendment (Proposition J).

Other Funding Sources.   Schools should not overlook sources of competitive funding, such as foundations. The Foundation Directory (available in many libraries) lists local, state, and national foundations and the issues and services they support. Often, schools can obtain funding and support from local civic organizations or businesses through adopt-a-school programs, for example, or by participating in research studies conducted by colleges and universities.

ACTION STEPS TO BUILD DISTRICT-LEVEL SUPPORT

To ensure the successful implementation and sustainability of an educational innovation such as a coordinated school health program, the external environment—the school district and the surrounding community—must support the program. The following steps can facilitate support for a coordinated school health program at the district level. Although some steps are similar to those at the school level, the key players and implementation strategies differ.

Secure District-Level Leadership

No matter how strong the principal (or assistant principal) and the Healthy School Team, how abundant the resources, or how supportive other staff, families, and community-based agencies, district-level leadership is critical for ongoing and consistent support of a coordinated school health program as part of school-level change. Ideally, the superintendent of schools and one or more members of the board of education—people who are committed to success for all children and who understand the importance of addressing the whole child—will spearhead the effort. If the superintendent and the board of education need convincing, people in the community or various district-level staff could provide the necessary access to them.

Also essential is a district-level staff person to coordinate health-related school and community activities that involve several schools. In larger school districts, this coordinator might be a health or education professional who is professionally prepared to advocate for and market coordinated school health programs; to conduct school and community needs assessments; to plan, implement, and evaluate coordinated school health programs; and to design professional development models. Professionals with these capabilities and skills are often active in local and state coalitions and also informed about state and federal funding. Such an individual also would have the ability to involve other district-level staff whose responsibilities include health-related goals and objectives, such as staff involved in curriculum improvement, health services, pupil services, bilingual education, special education, human resources, nutrition services, and physical education. In smaller school districts, a department head or curriculum specialist might support and lead this effort.

It is important for the school-level staff who are building a coordinated school health program to establish collegial relationships with one or more district-level administrators. By sharing information about what the school is doing and how the efforts support teaching and learning, school-level staff increase the chance that district-level administrators will advocate for a coordinated school health program and facilitate other essential support, including human and fiscal resources.

Establish a Broad-Based District Advisory Committee

This committee might assist the Healthy School Team by assessing the health status, issues, and concerns of children and their families districtwide; obtain input from the community about the overall direction of the program; develop a shared vision for the health of children and their families; make policy recommendations to the board of education; identify and help coordinate community resources; help secure district-level support for coordinated school health programs; and initiate planning for district-wide adoption.

Representation should include all levels of school administration (board members, district-level administrators, school-site administrators and teachers, and union representatives), community organizations (the local health department, organizations of parents and other caregivers, youth-serving organizations, voluntary health organizations), health care providers, representatives of the religious community, college and university faculty, law enforcement officers, elected officials, media representatives, and leaders of business and industry, as well as students. Issues the committee might address include: What are the district's mission and goals and the superintendent's priorities? How do district priorities relate to school initiatives? Is the coordinated school health program model consistent with district policy and direction?

Identify Supports and Challenges in the Broader School Community

Many supports and challenges for a coordinated school health program exist in any local community. Therefore, it is important to assess the community as well as the schools. Districts can use town hall meetings, neighborhood forums, focus groups, personal interviews, telephone surveys, informal discussions, and other forums and methods to identify:

- The community's and district's vision for youth and their families.
- Internal and external bureaucratic structures and processes.
- Community values and the political climate.
- Individuals who could positively or negatively influence program implementation.
- Events in the external environment, such as upcoming elections or a youth curfew proposal, that might influence program implementation.
- Individuals or organizations that might gain or lose as a result of implementation of coordinated school health programs.
- Other potential barriers or supports for effective and efficient implementation of programs.

At town meetings and community forums, organizers should seek an airing of opposing viewpoints. Charged issues—such as teaching about sexuality, making condoms available to students, or discussing sexual orientation— will vary from school to school and community to community. Hearing from parents and groups that have concerns about health-related issues can help clarify misperceptions and minimize conflict. The early involvement of people with a variety of viewpoints can minimize controversy later (Newman & Farrell, 1995).

Develop Supportive Board Policies

In most school districts, board policies already support various components of a coordinated school health program. School-level staff should identify relevant policies within the district and ensure that clear procedures exist for implementing the policies at the school site. They can also suggest new policies if gaps exist and eliminate unenforced and out-of-date policies. One way of ensuring that current policies are available to school staff, board members, students, and families is to develop and distribute a manual that consolidates school and district policies and procedures related to all aspects of a coordinated school health program.

Train District and Community Advocates to Sell the Program

Short summary statements about the strengths of linking education and health (see Figure 2.1), the health status of children and youth in the community, the incidence of health-risk behaviors among adolescents, and how each coordinated school health program component addresses the district's mission and goals can help sell a program. Opinion leaders who are respected in the district and community make good spokespersons to describe the coordinated school health program model and how it can support teaching and learning. These advocates could conduct awareness sessions about coordinated school health programs for board members, administrators, community members, family members, and others. Articles and stories broadcast in the local media, position statements, and program descriptions can help promote the program to the community and explain its potential impact on students and their learning (see Chapter 4).

ADDRESSING CONCERNS

No matter how promising a new program might be, some individuals or groups within the school and the community will have serious concerns about it. School and district staff must prepare thoughtful responses to likely concerns and take time to respond clearly and respectfully when the concerns arise. Some typical concerns, along with suggested responses that advocates can adapt for their needs, appear here. Many of the suggestions came from the focus group of school administrators from across the country who helped to inform this chapter.

- *Concern:* "We have no money, no training, and no facilities." *Response:* "Funding and other resources are limited. Let's look at what is already in place and what is new and different. Then we can decide how much additional money, professional development, and space we will need. For example, specific training might become part of regularly scheduled professional development days. By looking at what we have and coordinating our efforts, we might actually save money that we could use to implement additional programs and provide professional development."
- *Concern:* "There's not enough time. I can't do one more thing." *Response:* "In most cases, you will not have to do more than you do already. A truly integrated and coordinated school health program takes less time because it reduces duplication of effort."
- *Concern:* "We've always done it this way." *Response:* "Just because we have always done it this way does not mean it is the best way. As the needs and concerns of youth and their families change, schools must change to meet those needs. Change is difficult, but by not changing we are not supporting our students."
- *Concern:* "When I was in school, we didn't have a coordinated school program, and I still made it." *Response:* "The challenges young people face today are very different from those of the past. Working in isolation, today's teachers cannot meet the complex needs of students. In contrast to the 'old morbidities' (communicable diseases, for example), young people face 'new morbidities' (early, unprotected sex; eating disorders; substance use; violence; depression) that are highly correlated with school failure (Dryfoos, 1994) and reduced quality of life as adults. Without additional opportunities, supports, and services, many of today's youth will not acquire the knowledge and skills they need to become successful adults."
- *Concern:* "We're in the business of education, not in the business of health." *Response:* "That is true. But students who are hungry, sick, troubled, or depressed cannot function well in the classroom, no matter how good the school (Carnegie Council on Adolescent Development, 1989). Education and health are closely intertwined. By addressing the health needs of students and their families now, we should see increases in academic achievement and in the numbers of students who are capable of addressing future challenges."

- *Concern:* "If it ain't broke, don't fix it." *Response:* "It is 'broke.' Students are not performing to their maximum potential. Not all students succeed. Schools must provide additional opportunities, supports, and services that promote positive development of youth and their families to increase students' academic success."
- *Concern:* "What's in it for me?" *Response:* "Your job will be easier. When students' health-related needs are met, more students will arrive at school ready to learn. Their successes will make them more willing to participate and less likely to become disruptive. That—in the long run—will increase your success with more students."

SYSTEM REFORM EFFORTS: SUPPORTS FOR CHANGING THE WAY SCHOOLS DO BUSINESS

As part of "selling" a coordinated school health program—in a local school, at the district level, or to the community at large—advocates could describe how coordinated school health programs are consistent with current and future trends, including systemic education reform and Education Goals 2000, resiliency and youth development, community planning, and consolidating funding streams.

Education Reform and Education Goals 2000

Schools are changing the way they do business. Some reforms involve developing active learners, using standards-based curriculum, making more decisions at the school site, and addressing accountability and assessment. Health-related program components and activities link well to education reform, including standards-based units of study, the opportunity-to-learn standards, best practices, thematic units, authentic assessment, an interdisciplinary curriculum, school improvement plans, school-to-work opportunities, service learning, family involvement, technology, and inclusion.

By implementing a coordinated school health program, a school directly or indirectly addresses all of the Education Goals 2000 (National Education Goals Panel, 1994). The link with Goal 1—that all children start school ready to learn—is clear. Children cannot start school ready to learn if they do not have proper nutrition, are not fit, or have health problems. Goal 6 calls for all schools to be drug-, violence-, and firearms-free, which contributes to a healthy environment. Health programs such as substance use prevention and pregnancy prevention can contribute to the other goals by keeping more young people in school longer and increasing the percentage of students who graduate from high school. Advocates could use this language to garner support for a coordinated school health program: "A child who is not healthy has difficulty learning; undernourishment affects a child's concentration; medical problems interfere with a child's ability to learn" (National School Boards Association, American Association of School Administrators, American Cancer Society, & National School Health Education Coalition, 1995).

Resiliency and Youth Development

The youth development approach builds on research about resiliency, "a quality in children, who, though exposed to significant stress and adversity in their lives, do not succumb to school failure, substance use, or mental health and juvenile delinquency problems" (Linquanti, 1992). The youth development approach focuses on developing youth with skills and goals; adequate family, peer, and community supports; and opportunities to contribute (Pittman, 1992).

Coordinated school health programs can help students improve their decision-making, planning and goal-setting, communication, and stress-management skills through health education and physical education curricula. The programs can provide additional supports through strong family involvement activities, adequate health services, and appropriate counseling services. Coordinated school health programs develop health-literate youth who are critical thinkers and problem solvers; responsible, productive citizens; self-directed learners; and effective communicators (Joint Committee on National Health Education Standards, 1995).

Community Planning

Community planning embraces the notion that culturally competent health programs addressing the unique needs of the community must involve both representatives from the community that the programs intend to serve and relevant professionals. This is the same approach that schools take in implementing coordinated school health programs. One of the eight program components focuses on family and community involvement (see Chapter 4).

Consolidated Funding Streams

Block grant funding has been increasing in the last few years, and the trend is likely to continue. Block grants are a double-edged sword. They are an example of efforts to consolidate categorical, fragmented federal funds into fewer funding streams and provide a unified structure with more flexibility and less administrative burden. They also, however, fix allocations, decrease accountability, and increase the likelihood of funding cuts. To ensure that schools receive funding allocations, school and district staff responsible for implementing the coordinated school health program must participate in activities such as block grant planning and decision making at the community level.

CONCLUSION

Poor health among America's adolescents has reached crisis proportions (Carnegie Council on Adolescent Development, 1991). Today, a frighteningly large number of youth suffer from depression that could lead to suicide. To cope with life's challenges, more and more young people are turning to substance use. As adolescents get older, they engage in less and less physical activity; many also have eating habits that put them at risk for serious diseases later in life. And many young people cannot access the health and counseling services they need to survive and thrive.

Without their health, young people cannot take full advantage of the school program and become productive adults in tomorrow's world. Many components of a coordinated school health program described in this book are not new. However, few schools fully implement all the components of a coordinated school health program and fewer still coordinate what they do have. Piecemeal approaches to these serious health issues have proved ineffective. The need for coordinated school health programs is clear. By joining forces with each other and with their communities, school and district staff can successfully implement a coordinated school health program that can help ensure that today's young people become productive adults in tomorrow's world.

REFERENCES

Allensworth, D. D., Symons, C. W., & Olds, R. S. (1994). *Healthy Students 2000: An agenda for continuing improvement in America's schools.* Kent, OH: American School Health Association.

Bosworth, K., Gingiss, P. M., Potthoff, S., & Roberts-Gray, C. (1995). *A Bayesian model to predict the success of the implementation of health and education innovations in school-centered programs.* Unpublished manuscript.

Boyer, E. L. (1983). *High school: A report on secondary education in America: The Carnegie Foundation for the Advancement of Teaching.* New York: Harper & Row.

Carnegie Council on Adolescent Development. (1989). *Turning points: Preparing American youth for the 21st century.* New York: Carnegie Corporation.

Carnegie Council on Adolescent Development. (1991). *Fateful choices: Healthy youth for the 21st century.* New York: Carnegie Corporation.

Carnegie Council on Adolescent Development. (1995). *Great transitions: Preparing adolescents for a new century.* New York: Carnegie Corporation.

Centers for Disease Control and Prevention. (1995, March 24). CDC surveillance summaries. *Morbidity and Mortality Weekly Report, 44*(SS-1), 1–56.

Council of Chief State School Officers. (1991). *Beyond the health room.* Washington, DC: Author.

Dryfoos, J. G. (1994). *Full-service schools.* San Francisco: Jossey-Bass.

Healthy People 2000. (1991). National health promotion and disease prevention objectives and healthy schools. *Journal of School Health, 61,* 287–328.

Joint Committee on National Health Education Standards. (1995). *Achieving health literacy: An investment in the future.* Atlanta, GA: American Cancer Society.

Kolbe, L. J., Kann, L., & Collins, J. C. (1993). Overview of the Youth Risk Behavior Surveillance System. *Public Health Reports, 108*(Suppl. 1), 2–10.

Linquanti, R. (1992). *Using community-wide collaboration to foster resiliency in kids: A conceptual framework.* San Francisco: Far West Laboratory for Educational Research and Development.

National Commission on the Role of the School and the Community in Improving Adolescent Health. (1990). *Code blue.* Alexandria, VA: National Association of State Boards of Education.

National Education Goals Panel. (1994). *The national education goals report: Building a nation of learners.* Washington, DC: U.S. Government Printing Office.

National School Boards Association, American Association of School Administrators, American Cancer Society, & National School Health Education Coalition. (1995). *Be a leader in academic achievement.* Alexandria, VA: Authors.

Newman, I. M., & Farrell, K. A. (1995). *Thinking ahead: Preparing for controversy.* Kent, OH: American School Health Association.

Pittman, K. J. (1992, January). *Promoting youth development: Strengthening the role of youth serving and community organizations.* Paper presented at the conference of Partners in People on "A Day to Build Coalitions for Children and Youth," Berkeley, CA.

Rogers, E. M. (1983). *Diffusion of innovations.* New York: Free Press.

U.S. Department of Education & U.S. Department of Health and Human Services. (1994). *Joint statement of school health by the Secretaries of Education and Health and Human Services.* Washington, DC: Office of Disease Prevention and Health Promotion.

The author would like to acknowledge the valuable input and recommendations from the following focus group participants: Lynnanne Baumgardner, school board member, Columbia, Missouri; Matt Benningfield, principal, Louisville, Kentucky; Del Emerson, principal, Lincoln, Nebraska; Helen Guerkink, health education coordinator, Chesterfield, Missouri; Leslie Hogshead, school board member, Ferguson, Missouri; Charles Holliday, principal, Hickman, Kentucky; Royce Holtgrewe, principal, Lincoln, Nebraska; Nancy Karas, principal, Granby, Colorado; Terry Miskell, health coordinator, Montgomery, Alabama; John Osteen, principal, Norfolk, Virginia; and Veronica Smith, principal, Linn, Missouri.

David K. Lohrmann, Ph.D., C.H.E.S.
Susan F. Wooley, Ph.D., C.H.E.S.

3 Comprehensive School Health Education

- o *Classroom instruction that addresses the physical, mental, emotional, and social dimensions of health; develops health knowledge, attitudes, and skills; and is tailored to each age level.*
- o *Designed to motivate and assist students to maintain and improve their health, prevent disease, and reduce health-related risk behaviors.*

No knowledge is more crucial than knowledge about health. Without it, no other life goal can be successfully achieved.
—Ernest L. Boyer (1983, p. 304)

Today, hundreds of thousands of children and adolescents across the United States are becoming health literate through regular participation in school-based comprehensive health education. In addition to learning to use information gathering, problem solving, and other skills to manage health problems they already face, these young people know how to avoid both health problems that present an immediate threat, such as unintentional injury due to car crashes or HIV infection, and those that pose a greater threat during their adult years, such as cancer and heart disease.

Schools have an enormous potential for helping students develop the knowledge and skills they need to be healthy and achieve academically. Since comprehensive school health education occurs within the context of education and learning, it contributes to the broader mission of schools. Moreover,

Health Is Academic: A Guide to Coordinated School Health Problems. Edited by Eva Marx and Susan Frelick Wooley, with Daphne Northrop. New York: Teachers College Press, 1998. ISBN 0-8077-3713-5 (pbk.), ISBN 0-8077-3714-3 (cloth). Prior to photocopying items for classroom use, please contact the Copyright Clearance Center, Customer Service, 222 Rosewood Dr., Danvers, MA 01923, USA, tel. (508) 750-8400. © 1998 Education Development Center, Inc. All rights reserved.

there is broad agreement that schools should accept responsibility for providing health education for young people. A national survey conducted by The Gallup Organization in 1994 found that a majority of school administrators, students, and their families support comprehensive school health education. In fact, a majority of parents and administrators surveyed believed that adolescents should be taught more health information and skills in schools, and 55% of the students surveyed said that schools should spend more time on health education than on subjects such as English, math, and science.

Education reformers, including business leaders, want schools to produce graduates who can contribute to national productivity (Secretary's Commission on Achieving Necessary Skills, 1992; Wentworth, undated). As a recent analysis showed, school health education can contribute to productivity through cost containment. The analysis estimated that for every dollar spent on high-quality, multicomponent health education delivered in a school, society saves more than $13 in direct costs, such as medical treatment for preventable diseases, addiction counseling, alcohol-related motor vehicle injuries, and drug-related crime, and indirect costs, such as lost productivity due to premature death and social welfare expenditures associated with teen pregnancy (CDC, 1997b).

Several large-scale studies of comprehensive health education curricula have found that high quality health education contributes to significant improvements in students' health knowledge, skills, and practices (Connell, Turner, & Mason, 1985; Walter, Vaughan, & Wynder, 1989; Errecart et al., 1991). Recent reviews of several studies found that curricula can positively affect students' health-related behaviors. (Dusenbury & Falco, 1995; Kirby et al., 1994). Effective curricula share eight characteristics; they

- Are research-based and theory-driven.
- Include basic, accurate information that is developmentally appropriate.
- Use interactive, experiential activities that actively engage students.
- Provide students an opportunity to model and practice relevant social skills.
- Address social or media influences on behaviors.
- Strengthen individual values and group norms that support health-enhancing behaviors.
- Are of sufficient duration to allow students to gain the needed knowledge and skills.
- Include teacher training that enhances effectiveness.

In addition, a study by Louis Harris and Associates (1988) found that benefits of curricula increase when students receive at least three consecutive years of high-quality health instruction.

Both Drug Strategies, a nonprofit group based in Washington, D.C., and the Centers for Disease Control and Prevention (CDC) have identified curricula that have been shown to reduce risk behaviors among youth. Drug Strategies published a directory of substance abuse prevention curricula that have a high probability of reducing tobacco, alcohol, and other drug use among young people (Dusenbury & Lake, 1996). CDC's Research to Classroom project identifies curricula that show credible evidence of positively affecting specific risk behaviors among school-aged youth (http://www.cdc.gov/nccdphp—Research to Classroom Project, Comprehensive School Health Education in Comprehensive Approaches). So far CDC has identified curricula for sexuality education and for tobacco use prevention.

Many schools throughout the country are providing health education. The School Health Policies and Programs Study (SHPPS), a national study of secondary schools in the United States (Kann et al., 1995), found that

- 97% of middle/junior high and senior high schools require instruction in health topics, and many provide instruction through a required course.
- Required health courses last one semester in 44% of all middle/junior high and senior high schools and for an entire school year in 20% of these schools.
- The topics most likely to be included in such courses are alcohol and other drug use prevention (90%), HIV prevention (86%), tobacco use prevention (86%), disease prevention and control (84%), nutrition and healthy eating (84%), STD prevention (84%), human growth and development (80%), human sexuality (80%), personal health (79%), and physical activity and fitness (78%) (Collins et al., 1995).

Despite the potential for positively affecting children's lives and widespread public support, and the societal benefits, few schools offer truly comprehensive health education. Although many school districts provide instruction in a variety of health topics, health education often is not taught at every grade, is not of sufficient duration to affect student health practices (Connell, Turner, & Mason, 1985), and is taught by teachers who lack professional preparation in health education (Collins et al., 1995).

ESSENTIAL FUNCTIONS OF COMPREHENSIVE
SCHOOL HEALTH EDUCATION

The intent of comprehensive school health education is to motivate students to maintain and improve their health, prevent disease, and avoid or reduce health-related risk behaviors. It also provides students with the knowledge and skills they need to be healthy for a lifetime. To achieve these goals, schools must *select or develop* and then *implement* a curriculum. Curriculum selection or development involves delineation of the content and skills that students must learn at each grade level and how often and for what duration the curriculum will be delivered. Implementation requires acceptance of the curriculum by the school community (school staff, students' families, and other interested community members); teacher training accompanied by ongoing follow-up support; procurement and distribution of materials; management of family and community linkages, training, and logistical support (Ames, 1994; Marx & Northrop, 1995); and periodic program evaluation (Iverson, 1994). Both phases are discussed below.

Curriculum Selection and Development

Most schools and districts have established a process for reviewing and selecting curricula and textbooks. By making curricular decisions at the school or district level, as opposed to leaving such decisions to individual teachers, schools help ensure that curricula address essential skills and do not have redundancies or gaps. Broader involvement in curriculum selection produces a stronger overall program.

Health education has traditionally been organized around broad content areas (Joint Committee on Health Education Terminology, 1991; National Professional School Health Education Organizations, 1984; School Health Education Study, 1967):

- personal health
- family health
- community health
- environmental health
- growth and development/sexuality
- mental and emotional health
- injury prevention and safety
- nutrition
- prevention and control of disease
- prevention of substance use and abuse

In the past, health education curricula typically contained independent instructional units, each addressing one of these health content areas (Pollock, 1987). Organizing curricula in this way tended to result in an emphasis on health *facts* rather than functional health *information* and the ability to *use essential skills* for adopting, practicing, and maintaining healthy behaviors. More recently, effective curricula have focused on learning critical health skills such as communication, stress management, decision making, and goal setting (Fetro, 1992). The rationale for the focus on skills is derived

FIGURE 3.1. National Health Education Standards

The National Health Education Standards state that students will:

- Comprehend concepts related to health promotion and disease prevention.
- Demonstrate the ability to access valid health information and health-promoting products and services.
- Demonstrate the ability to practice health-enhancing behaviors and reduce health risks.
- Analyze the influence of culture, media, technology, and other factors on health.
- Demonstrate the ability to use interpersonal communication skills to enhance health.
- Demonstrate the ability to use goal-setting and decision-making skills to enhance health.
- Demonstrate the ability to advocate for personal, family, and community health.

Source: Joint Committee on National Health Education Standards, 1995.

from health education theory (Kolbe, Iverson, Kreuter, Hochbaum, & Christensen, 1981; Lohrmann, Gold, & Jubb, 1987; Wooley, 1995) and is supported by research that has demonstrated the effectiveness of skills-based curricula in influencing students' health attitudes and practices (Botvin, Baker, Dusenbury, Botvin, & Diaz, 1995; Dusenbury & Falco, 1995; Kirby et al., 1994).

Standards-Based Health Curriculum.   In 1995, the Joint Committee on National Health Education Standards released National Health Education Standards (Figure 3.1) that were informed by health education theory and practice as well as curriculum frameworks and standards from several states. The national standards are compatible with the Goals 2000: Educate America Act (National Education Goals Panel, 1994) and provide a bridge to Healthy People 2000: National Health Promotion and Disease Prevention Objectives (Public Health Service, 1991).

State education agencies and local school districts can use the national standards as a framework for decisions about which lessons, strategies, activities, and types of assessment to include in a health education curriculum. Health education curricula based on the national standards can foster universal health literacy—"the capacity of an individual to obtain, interpret, and understand basic health information and services and the competence to use such information and services in ways that are health-enhancing" (Joint Committee on National Health Education Standards, 1995). The national standards also contribute to four broadly accepted educational outcomes. They prepare students to be critical thinkers and problem solvers; responsible, productive citizens; self-directed learners; and effective communicators (Boyett & Conn, 1991; Secretary's Commission on Achieving Necessary Skills, 1991). Health education curricula based on the national standards contribute to the mission of education by encouraging students to use technology to access information and use language arts, science, and mathematics skills in a health context. Moreover, standards-based health education provides students opportunities to learn and practice the speaking and listening skills as well as conflict resolution skills that they need to function effectively in school, in social settings, at home and later, in the workplace. In other words, health education has the potential to improve the academic achievement of children and adolescents as well as their health status.

Accompanying each standard are performance indicators that define what students should know and be able to do at grades 4, 8, and 11. The standards and performance indicators address students' knowledge of health content and the processes and skills involved in healthful living. Implicitly or explicitly, the standards and performance indicators include the traditional health content areas as well as the six risk behaviors that CDC has identified as the greatest contributors to illness and death (Kolbe, 1990). A model showing this relationship appears as Figure 3.2. Suggestions for addressing specific risk behaviors appear in guidance documents CDC has produced on tobacco use and addiction (CDC, 1994), physical activity (CDC, 1997a), healthy eating (CDC, 1996), and AIDS education (CDC, 1988).

If state education agencies and local school districts use the national standards and performance indicators as a guide, the health curricula that result from their efforts will be more likely to have the following elements, which are characteristic of effective, comprehensive school health education programs:

- A developmentally and age-appropriate, planned scope and sequence of instruction from pre-kindergarten through twelfth grade, with a minimum of 50 hours of instructional time annually (Connell, Turner, & Mason, 1985; American Association of School Administrators, 1991; National School Boards Association, 1991).
- An organizing framework based on the National Health Education Standards to ensure that all performance indicators are addressed at the appropriate grade level (American Cancer Society, 1992).

FIGURE 3.2. Standards-Based Health Education Curriculum

Tobacco use
Poor eating habits
Physical inactivity   **Health Risks**
HIV, STDs, and unintended pregnancy
Abuse of alcohol and other drugs
Unintentional and intentional injuries

Mental health
Consumer health
Personal health
Family health
Community health
Environmental health
Growth and development

**Explicit or
Implicit Topics**

Understand disease prevention & health promotion concepts

Be able to access health information, products, & services

Practice health-enhancing behaviors

Analyze influences on health

Use interpersonal communication skills

Use goal-setting and decision-making skills

Advocate for health

Standards

- Health content and skills introduced in the early grades and reinforced in later grades (Joint Committee on National Health Education Standards, 1995).
- Student assessments that measure skill acquisition as well as functional knowledge (Joint Committee on National Health Education Standards, 1995).

In addition, educators must consider the needs of diverse learners, including bilingual students and students with cognitive, physical, and sensory disabilities. Curricula should allow teachers to provide these students with additional time to master course materials, to modify instructional materials as appropriate, or to use different assessments to determine whether diverse learners have attained the national standards.

Curriculum Scope and Sequence.   Figure 3.3 illustrates how the National Health Education Standards can provide a framework for organizing a component of the K–12 curriculum, in this case prevention of alcohol, tobacco, and other drug use. The figure is meant to be illustrative and there-

FIGURE 3.3. Preventing Alcohol, Tobacco, and Other Drug Abuse (ATOD): Application of National Standards

				NATIONAL STANDARD			
Grades	Understand Disease Prevention & Health Promotion Concepts	Be Able to Access Health Information, Products & Services	Practice Health-Enhancing Behaviors	Analyze Influences on Health	Use Interpersonal Communication Skills	Use Goal-Setting & Decision-Making Skills	Advocate for Health
Direct instruction focusing on:							
K–4	Impact of ATOD abuse on families Health impact of ATOD use	Proper use of medications	Poison prevention Stress management strategies Personal responsibility	Influence of family, culture, school, and media on health behavior	Appropriate expression of emotions Attentive listening Refusal skills	Practice in making decisions about health issues Predicting the impact of not smoking on health Setting and working toward goals	Supporting others in making positive health choices Working cooperatively with others
5–8	Health impact of ATOD use Short-term benefits of nonuse Impact of ATOD abuse on families	School and community mental health and substance abuse services Positive alternative activities Proper use of medications	Relationships of ATOD use to accidental injury Poison prevention Stress management strategies Personal responsibility Analysis of personal risk for addiction Development of injury prevention strategies	Influences on use and nonuse of ATOD Analysis of advertising messages Prevalence of ATOD use Social norms	Attentive listening Refusal skills Avoidance skills	Applying decision making to ATOD issues Potential for dependence based on family history Decision making when something does not go as planned	Supporting school and community prevention efforts Supporting others in making positive health choices Working cooperatively with others

9–12	Short-term health impact of ATOD use Long-term health consequences of ATOD use Short-term benefits of nonuse Impact of ATOD abuse on families Impact of ATOD abuse on society	School and community mental health and substance abuse services Positive alternative activities Proper use of medications	Relationships of ATOD use to unintentional injury, especially in car crashes Stress management strategies Role of individual responsibility Analysis of personal risk for addiction Development of injury prevention strategies	Influences on use and nonuse of ATOD Analysis of advertising messages Prevalence of ATOD use Social norms	Attentive listening Refusal skills Avoidance skills	Applying decision making to ATOD issues Potential for dependence based on family history Legal consequences of ATOD use Financial issues Occupational concerns Adult roles and responsibilities Lifelong health plan that addresses use/nonuse of ATOD including medications	Supporting school and community prevention efforts Supporting others in making positive health choices Working cooperatively with others

Integration of health content into other courses

5–12	English literature selections about effects of ATOD abuse in different contexts Social and legal issues in social studies class Family impact in family living class	Use of technology to access and critique information about ATOD from multiple sources in science class	Alcohol use and driving in driver education class	Writing assignments on community and social implications of ATOD use in English and social studies classes	Debates and panel discussions on ATOD issues in English and social studies classes Development of a multimedia presentation in art class for use in school and in the community	Pledge to abstain from use of ATOD Setting goals in career education class	Launching a nonuse pledge campaign Project Graduation Establishment of a SADD chapter School-wide peer programs

fore does not include all the knowledge and skills that students should acquire. Some topics appear at more than one grade level either because they are phased in over time (i.e., introduced, then emphasized and reinforced) or because instruction becomes more sophisticated as students mature.

Student Assessment. As is true for all academic content areas, determining students' level of achievement is an important component of comprehensive school health education. An effective health education curriculum includes multiple assessment strategies designed to determine what students know and what they can do.

A curriculum based on the National Health Education Standards requires teachers to rely heavily on assessment strategies through which students contribute to a process and, in many cases, create a product or participate in a performance (Ferrara & McTighe, 1992; Lohrmann, 1993; Rose, Gallup, & Elam, 1997). For example, to address the performance indicator for grade 8 that "students will analyze how messages from media and other sources influence health behaviors," students could work in groups to demonstrate their understanding of print advertising techniques. Individually or in groups, students could analyze tobacco advertisements and identify the techniques tobacco manufacturers use to convince people to buy cigarettes. The result of the analysis could be a written report, a visual report such as a videotape or a poster, or a class presentation. As a follow-up activity, students could develop advertisements incorporating persuasive techniques to convince their peers not to smoke.

To help schools and teachers assess students' performance on competencies set out in the national standards, the Council of Chief State School Officers coordinated the Health Education State Collaborative on Assessment and Student Standards (SCASS) project to develop an assessment system. These assessments include selected response items and performance-based assessments, such as tasks, events, and student portfolios, with rubrics that are consistent with the national standards (P. Plofchan, personal communication, September 29, 1997).

Curriculum Implementation

Implementing the curriculum that has been developed or selected is the second step in bringing comprehensive school health education to the classroom. Implementation and maintenance of a curriculum require a variety of resources such as staff time, money, and logistical support (Anderson & Portnoy, 1989; Gingiss & Hamilton, 1989; Goodman, Tenney, Smith, & Steckler, 1992; Rohrbach, Graham, & Hansen, 1993; Smith, Steckler, McCormick, & McLeroy, 1995). A plan for implementation includes objectives, time lines, staffing, and a budget with identified funding sources (Marx & Northrop, 1995).

Successful implementation efforts share several characteristics: strong leadership that includes an advocate or champion, a school health team, and administrative sanction; a stable environment that supports health education as an instructional priority and integral part of the academic program; adequate and ongoing professional development that accommodates new teaching technologies and staff turnover; and a system for monitoring health education efforts that includes student assessment (Smith, Steckler, McCormick, & McLeroy, 1995).

Leadership. Without the strong commitment to health education on the part of school board members, administrators, and students' families, successful implementation is unlikely. School boards need to set policy and give direction that conveys a commitment to comprehensive school health education. Building and district-level administrators need to make clear their expectation that health education will be taught; support inclusion of health education in the school curriculum; provide teachers access to the training, equipment, and materials needed to deliver the curriculum; allocate sufficient time for teachers to provide meaningful instruction; and monitor to assess how well health education is being taught. Finally, family members can reinforce and expand on the health messages students learn at school by discussing health-related behaviors and topics with their children at home.

Strong leadership is especially important in today's school environment. Public schools are under attack by groups and individuals who feel that education is not an appropriate role for the government (Simonds, 1993/1994). Because health education addresses controversial and personal topics and because some people do not view health education as a core academic subject, school health education is sometimes a focus of such attacks (Johnson & Immerwahr, 1994). In addition, some mistakenly perceive comprehensive health education as only a "cover" for sexuality education and HIV/AIDS prevention education. If controversy arises in a community, school board members' support for teachers and administrators who provide health education, especially those who are dealing with sensitive topics such as human sexuality and HIV/AIDS education, is critical. Students' families can also be an important source of support in times of controversy.

A Stable Environment. Frequent turnover and reassignment of staff and administrators can divert energy from curricular matters and create a vacuum of experienced staff. When health instruction has a place in the overall school curriculum, effective implementation is more likely—even in the midst of staff turnovers and other disruptions.

Schools can offer health education in stand-alone courses, integrate health topics with other subjects, or both. Health educators have traditionally favored health-specific lessons and courses. However, advances in knowledge about how children and adolescents learn have led educators in all disciplines to support "connecting the curriculum" through thematic integration across content areas (Caine & Caine, 1991; Fogarty, 1991). Yet when health topics are infused into other content areas, they are likely to be taught for only one class period (Collins et al., 1995), whereas those taught in a health education class both cover greater depth and continue over several class periods. Thus, while integration of health information and skills, such as communication, negotiation, and refusal, into other subjects should not replace stand-alone health courses, such integration can extend and reinforce the health education curriculum in important ways.

Professional Development. As in many subject areas, the prevailing strategies for teaching health education are still lecture, use of videotape, and reading assignments. Although students will learn facts about health through such strategies, it is less likely that they will learn the skills necessary for practicing healthy behaviors. Professional development activities for health education teachers need to focus on teaching strategies that both actively engage students and facilitate their mastery of critical health information and skills. Through interactive training that includes modeling, practice, and feedback of teaching skills, teachers can hone their skills and learn to use effective teaching strategies such as cooperative learning, peer-led instruction, skills demonstration and practice, and service learning (Dusenbury & Falco, 1995; Ross, Leupker, Nelson, Saavedra, & Hubbard, 1991).

WHO IMPLEMENTS THE ESSENTIAL FUNCTIONS?

Parents and other family members are children's first and foremost health educators. In addition, young people in the United States receive health messages from a variety of sources: their friends; the media; manufacturers, through billboards and other forms of advertising; and the government, through public mandates such as smoke-free buildings and restrictions on the sale of tobacco products to minors. The primary responsibility for planned, sequential school health education, however, resides with teachers. In most elementary schools, *classroom teachers* provide health instruction, along with instruction in language arts, math, science, social studies, and other subjects. Only three states require elementary school teachers who teach health to have certification (Collins et al., 1995). Sometimes a *school nurse* will provide formal classroom instruction; however, it is not likely that a school nurse who has many nonteaching duties will be able to provide comprehensive health education to every class in a school.

Some secondary schools have separate health courses; others have "infused" health content into other academic areas. Among the *health education classroom teachers* interviewed in a national survey (Collins et al., 1995), 5.4% of those who taught a separate health course majored in health education, and less than 1% (0.6%) of those who taught an infused course had a degree in health education. The major most frequently cited by those who taught a separate course was health and physical education (28%). The most popular major among those teaching infused courses was biology or another science (32%). Thirty-six percent of the teachers of separate courses and 56% of those who taught infused classes had not majored in a health-related subject.

Although 69% of the states require health education certification for secondary-level health teachers, compliance appears lacking. The survey found that only 46% of lead health education teachers were certified by their state in either health or health and physical education. Forty-eight percent of classroom teachers who taught a separate course had state certification in health or health and physical education, whereas only 9% of those who taught infused courses had such certification.

Almost 80% of the lead health education teachers surveyed had taught or coordinated health education for five or more years, but fewer than 5% majored in health education. Twenty-seven percent majored in physical education, 22% had a dual health and physical education major, 13% majored in biology or another science, and 37% majored in a non-health-related field.

Many school districts have a *health education coordinator,* who ensures that health education is delivered effectively. Responsibilities include coordinating the curriculum selection or development process, staff development, serving as a content expert for teachers, securing and managing resources, coordinating among schools and between schools and the community, and advocating for school health activities. The health education coordinator is frequently the champion whose powers of persuasion and commitment are essential for acceptance of school health education activities. In some districts the coordinator position is full-time; in others, an administrator or a teacher acts in this role on a part-time basis.

Professional development consultants help to ensure that teachers are adequately prepared to provide health education, especially to deliver specific curricula. Consultants can be district-level staff development personnel who are familiar with a curriculum, teachers experienced with a curriculum, state-level professionals, curriculum developers, outside experts with specialized experience, or *university faculty* who teach health education.

Health education is not limited to the classroom. *All school staff* interact with students and have a role in reinforcing lessons learned from the curriculum. They deliver health education to students by modeling healthy (or unhealthy behaviors) and through the style and tone of their daily interactions with students and among themselves.

The role of *students* is also critical. Peers are a powerful source of information (and sometimes misinformation) about health issues and normative behaviors. Some schools have tapped this resource formally by instituting peer programs and training peer leaders to provide accurate health information and serve as referral sources when needed. Peer programs run the gamut from peer helper arrangements to peer educators and tutors (Berkin, 1994). Some involve same-age peers, while others match high school students with elementary school students. Adult mentors, most often school counselors or classroom teachers, supervise peer programs.

Research on the effectiveness of peer programs has demonstrated their effectiveness for peer leaders. The data for recipients, however, are inconclusive, perhaps because programs vary in intent, duration of contact, and the amount and intensity of training of peers (Milburn, 1995).

WHO SUPPORTS THOSE PROVIDING COMPREHENSIVE SCHOOL HEALTH EDUCATION?

Numerous national health, health education, education, parent, and youth advocacy organizations actively support comprehensive school health education. (See Chapter 12 for a full discussion.) The American Cancer Society (1992), with the participation of representatives of 37 other national organizations, developed an action plan for institutionalizing comprehensive school health education in the United States. Development of the National Health Education Standards sprang directly from that action plan.

Many other individuals and groups also support comprehensive school health education, such as medical professionals, public health officials, parent groups, and voluntary health organizations, but some become vocal only when a community faces controversy. A wide variety of local, state, and national organizations that identify as their mission the health and well-being of children and youth will advocate for school health education when asked (Patten, 1994). Many of the organizations listed in Appendix 1 of this volume provide information and support for school health education.

Two organizations—the American Association for Health Education (AAHE) and the American School Health Association (ASHA)—provide professional support specifically for those teaching health in schools. The membership of AAHE includes health educators in school, university, community, worksite, and health care settings as well as physical educators assigned to teach health. The membership of ASHA includes school- and university-based health educators as well as school nurses and physicians.

Other organizations support various school staff who have direct responsibility for health education. The American Association of School Administrators, the National Association of State Boards of Education, and the National School Boards Association provide materials and technical assistance to school administrators and school board members to help them promote school health education and develop supportive policies. The Association for Supervision and Curriculum Development's Health in Education Network provides professional support for those responsible for coordinating school health education and related school health activities. Some teachers' organizations, such as the National Education Association and the American Federation of Teachers, provide professional development opportunities related to school health for their members.

INTEGRATING COMPREHENSIVE SCHOOL HEALTH EDUCATION WITH THE OTHER COMPONENTS OF A COORDINATED SCHOOL HEALTH PROGRAM

Comprehensive school health education has much to contribute to the other seven components of a coordinated school health program. The health education teacher or coordinator generally has access to a great deal of health information and can be a resource for other staff. If a school or district has a health education coordinator, the coordinator often has the important role of coordinating and advocating for all the components, either independently or as staff to the Healthy School Team (see Chapter 2).

Comprehensive school health education can benefit greatly from input by the staff responsible for the other components. As participants in a Healthy School Team, administrators, staff, family and community members, and students all contribute to the successful implementation of this program component and its integration with the other components. The willingness of health education and other school staff to function as a team and communicate effectively is critical for effective collaboration. Following are examples of such collaboration.

It is normal for people of any age—and especially young people—to be anxious about discussing personal health issues with a health provider. By offering *health services* staff—including school nurses, school-based clinic staff, school mental health personnel, student assistance program staff, and clinicians from the community—an opportunity during a health class to describe the services they can provide, health education teachers increase the likelihood that students will seek out needed health services. And health education teachers, along with all other teachers and school staff, can promote student health by referring students to health services or *counseling, psychological, and social services* staff. In addition, school counseling personnel often coordinate student support programs, such as informal and organized peer support, peer mediation, and student-planned, school-wide prevention activities. Some counselors coordinate programs in which students facilitate health education classroom activities for their peers or for younger students.

The *schoolsite health promotion* program provides an excellent opportunity for student, staff, and community interactions concerning health-promoting behaviors. Staff who participate in schoolsite health promotion activities such as physical fitness, nutrition, smoking cessation, and weight loss programs are more likely to advocate for comprehensive health education and to reinforce health messages in their interactions with students. Health education teachers often support schoolsite health promotion efforts by participating in their planning and implementation or by serving as a resource for program coordinators. Committees of students and staff members can plan and implement activities that bring together students and staff, such as fun runs, after-school sports clubs, and health fairs.

Health education and *physical education* both address the importance of physical activity, nutrition (related to performance), stress management, disease prevention (particularly heart disease and cancer), safety, self-esteem, and body image. There are many ways to coordinate the health education curriculum and the physical education curriculum and thereby ensure that the lessons taught in the two components complement and reinforce each other. For example, the health teacher can define target heart rate and teach why it is important, how to take a pulse rate, and how to compute target heart rate. By having students get into the habit of monitoring their pulse rate during exercise and comparing it with their target heart rate on a regular basis, the physical education teacher can build on this learning.

School *nutrition services* professionals can offer health teachers advice about nutrition education content and suggest experiential activities. In some schools, the school food service director teaches nutrition in the classroom. By making the school kitchen and cafeteria a laboratory in which students can learn about nutrition, healthy eating habits, and safe food handling, nutrition services staff can reinforce health education messages. Even serving nonfat (skim) and low-fat milk in the cafeteria can demonstrate a commitment to a healthier diet and reinforce the health education curriculum. Health education teachers can create opportunities for students to suggest menus to nutrition services staff, determine the nutrient content in foods that might be included in the school lunch menu, and work with nutrition services staff to plan nutritious, culturally diverse meals that appeal to student tastes.

As part of the health education curriculum, students could survey food preferences and eating habits in the school cafeteria. The cafeteria can be an art gallery for sharing students' nutrition-related health education projects with the entire school community.

When students put into practice health education lessons about how to express feelings appropriately, communicate persuasively, resolve conflicts nonviolently, and manage stress effectively, they contribute to a *healthy school environment.* In addition to helping create a healthy psychosocial environment, students can apply injury prevention knowledge and skills to help create a safer, healthier physical environment by reporting broken equipment and other physical hazards. A school environment that supports messages learned in health class in turn enhances the effectiveness of the health education curriculum. For example, a school policy banning tobacco use for staff and students alike reinforces tobacco avoidance messages.

Important linkages can also be created between health education and *families and communities.* Research has shown that adolescent health behaviors are more positive in communities that model, support, and expect healthy behaviors (Blythe, 1992). The opportunities for family and community support are limitless. For example, students benefit tremendously when school health educators collaborate with staff from community health promotion programs and other community planning efforts to provide high-quality programs for children and youth, including service learning opportunities. Examples of school and community health education coordination include sharing information between school and community health educators, working with pediatricians and family practitioners in the community so that they can highlight relevant topics during students' appointments, organizing health fairs that draw on school and community resources, and working together on communitywide health promotion efforts directed at school-aged youth, such as bicycle rallies, blood drives, and walk-a-thons.

Family members can become active on school health advisory committees, and lend their support to school health education planning efforts. They can also serve as guest speakers when they have special expertise on a particular health topic or as chaperones for field trips to local hospitals, clinics, and other health-related sites. Health educators can include parents more directly by giving students homework assignments that require them to interact with their families (see Chapter 4). To keep families current on and involved in the health education curriculum, schools could offer parent education programs focusing on topics that parallel those in the classroom curriculum. Finally, producing special publications that suggest ways families can support and model what their children are learning in the health education classroom is another effective strategy for involving families.

ACTION STEPS FOR IMPLEMENTING COMPREHENSIVE
SCHOOL HEALTH EDUCATION

The Joint Committee on National Health Education Standards (1995), when it developed the national standards specifying student outcomes, recognized that agencies, ranging from schools to national organizations, would need to create and sustain supportive programs and policies if students were to achieve the national standards. Consequently, as a companion to the national standards, the Joint Committee developed "Opportunity to Learn Standards" outlining steps that local education agencies, communities, state education and health agencies, institutions of higher education, and national organizations should take.

Actions for Schools and Districts

The actions recommended for schools and districts fall into four broad categories: curriculum planning and development, curriculum implementation, teacher qualification and preparation, and assessment and evaluation. Additional detailed guidance is available from other sources (see, for example, Marx & Northrop, 1995).

Curriculum Planning and Development

1. Increase community awareness of and support for comprehensive school health education by:
   • Designating a comprehensive school health education coordinator.
   • Establishing a comprehensive health education advisory committee (or a comprehensive health education subcommittee of a broader Healthy School Team) that includes parent representation and reflects the diversity of the community.
   • Providing awareness sessions for the school board, curriculum planning committee, school staff, and community members.
2. Assess student health needs, interests, strengths, and cultures during health education curriculum planning.
3. Develop a plan for funding, selecting or developing, implementing, and assessing a comprehensive health education curriculum through a collaborative process that involves school personnel, students, families, related community agencies, and businesses. The process might include reviewing a variety of published curricula and selecting one for implementation (for a review of selected curricula, see Education Development Center, Inc., 1995, or Dusenbury & Lake, 1996) or, if resources permit, drawing on professional educators to develop the curriculum. In either case, the curriculum must reflect community standards. The plan should address both

the inclusion of health education content in health classes and the integration of health education across the overall curriculum.

4. Review and revise school policies and enforcement strategies regularly to ensure a climate that encourages and reinforces health literacy.

Curriculum Implementation

1. Provide adequate support for implementation, including financial resources and staff time.
2. Establish a system to ensure materials distribution, professional development for teachers, and student assessment.
3. Provide a minimum of 50 hours of health education instruction at every grade level to give all students the time needed to learn health skills and habits for a lifetime. Determine the amount of time needed to deliver the curriculum at each grade level and inform teachers of the minimum amount of instructional time they should devote to health education.
4. Use information technologies in the health education curriculum and make technology accessible to students during instruction and when they work on out-of-school assignments.
5. Encourage team building and collaborative curriculum planning between health education teachers and their colleagues in other subject areas and between elementary teachers who teach different grades.
6. Implement a variety of strategies that foster family involvement in students' health education.

Teacher Qualification and Preparation

1. Select teachers who are academically prepared and qualified specifically in health education and who can use both active teaching strategies and authentic assessment strategies in delivering health education.
2. Hire certified health educators to teach health at the secondary school level.
3. Provide ongoing professional development opportunities and incentives for teachers to maintain and upgrade their knowledge and skills.
4. Expect even highly experienced teachers to attend professional development on newly adopted curricula so they can become fully aware of the curriculum's philosophy, organization, and assessment strategies and the unique preparations needed to implement specific lessons.
5. Provide ongoing professional development opportunities and incentives for the administrators, board members, and other staff responsible for implementation.
6. Provide follow-up booster sessions and ongoing technical assistance.

Assessment and Evaluation

1. Include process evaluation procedures in the curriculum implementation plan. If the curriculum is not being implemented as designed, identify barriers to implementation and initiate strategies to get the implementation plan back on track.
2. In addition to routine, ongoing assessment, plan strategies for measuring student knowledge and skills at grades 4, 8, and 11. Assess the quality of curriculum implementation and individual student performance.
3. Work collaboratively with internal and external evaluation researchers.

Actions for Universities and State- and National-Level Organizations

The following actions are adapted from the Opportunity-To-Learn Standards for Health Education (Joint Committee on National Health Education Standards, 1995) and *Strengthening Comprehensive School Health Education: Process Evaluation Manual* (Centers for Disease Control and Prevention, 1998).

1. Support and implement policies and plans that include health education as a core academic subject, mandate adequate instructional time, and are consistent with the National Health Education Standards.
2. Provide or advocate for adequate financial support for implementation.
3. Require certification in health education for those teaching health education at the secondary level and some course work in health for those teaching at the elementary level.
4. Provide preservice and in-service professional preparation, booster sessions, and technical assistance to prepare school administrators, teachers, and other staff to support and teach health education.
5. Develop guidelines and materials to assist schools with implementation and assessment.
6. Support the use of information technologies to deliver health instruction and the preparation of teachers to apply these technologies.
7. Conduct or support continued research in health education.
8. Devote adequate resources, including personnel, to provide technical assistance and material support to schools that implement comprehensive school health education.
9. Establish, maintain, and utilize communication systems for ensuring that schools have access to current information, technical support, and training opportunities.

CONCLUSION

School health education is not new. It has existed in one form or another since the establishment of public schools. The SHPPS results provide evidence that school leaders are beginning to acknowledge the importance of health education as never before (Kann et al., 1995). Yet the systematic implementation and maintenance needed to make a real difference for all students is lacking in most schools. Many education decision makers have not made health education an integral part of the curriculum, hired qualified teachers, or provided adequate financial support.

The dawning of a new millennium presents a chance to seize this unrealized opportunity. As revealed by the recent public opinion poll sponsored by the American Cancer Society (The Gallup Organization, 1994), broad-scale support for comprehensive school health education exists among parents, school administrators, and students. Moreover, the National Health Education Standards provide a well-conceived framework for state education agencies, local school districts, and local school professionals to use in the development and implementation of high-quality, effective curricula.

Leaders in government, education, and business at all levels have made a commitment to ensure that all children receive a world-class education. This commitment will be fulfilled only if all children have the opportunity to become truly health literate.

REFERENCES

American Association of School Administrators. (1991). *Healthy kids for the year 2000: An action plan for schools.* Arlington, VA: Author.

American Cancer Society. (1992). *National action plan for comprehensive school health education.* Atlanta, GA: Author.

Ames, E. E. (1994). Instructional planning for health education. In P. Cortese & K. Middleton (Eds.), *The comprehensive school health challenge: Promoting health through education* (Vol. 1, pp. 121–144). Santa Cruz, CA: ETR Associates.

Anderson, D. M., & Portnoy, B. (1989). Diffusion of cancer education into schools. *Journal of School Health, 59*(5), 214–217.

Berkin, B. J. (1994). Peer education: Students helping students. In P. Cortese & K. Middleton (Eds.), *The comprehensive school health challenge: Promoting health through education* (Vol. 2, pp. 709–741). Santa Cruz, CA: ETR Associates.

Blythe, D. (1992). *Healthy communities, healthy youth: How communities contribute to positive youth development.* Minneapolis, MN: Search Institute/Lutheran Brotherhood.

Botvin, G. J., Baker, E., Dusenbury, L., Botvin, E. M., & Diaz, T. (1995). Long-term follow-up results of a randomized drug abuse prevention trial in a white middle-class population. *JAMA, 273*(14), 1106–1112.

Boyer, E. L. (1983). *High school: A report on secondary education in America: The Carnegie Foundation for the Advancement of Teaching.* New York: Harper & Row.

Boyett, J. H., & Conn, H. P. (1991). *Workplace 2000: The revolution reshaping American business.* New York: Dutton.

Caine, R. N., & Caine, G. (1991). *Making connections: Teaching and the human brain.* Arlington, VA: Association for Supervision and Curriculum Development.

Centers for Disease Control and Prevention. (1988). Guidelines for effective school health education to prevent the spread of AIDS. *Morbidity and Mortality Weekly Report, 37*(S-2), 1–14.

Centers for Disease Control and Prevention. (1994). Guidelines for school programs to prevent tobacco use and addiction. *Morbidity and Mortality Weekly Report, 43*(RR-2), 1–18.

Centers for Disease Control and Prevention. (1996). Guidelines for school health programs to promote lifelong healthy eating. *Morbidity and Mortality Weekly Report, 45*(RR-9), 1–41.

Centers for Disease Control and Prevention. (1997a). Guidelines for school and community programs to promote lifelong physical activity among young people. *Morbidity and Mortality Weekly Report, 46*(RR-6), 1–36.

Centers for Disease Control and Prevention. (1997b). *Is school health education cost-effective?: An exploratory analysis of selected exemplary components.* Unpublished manuscript, Division of Adolescent and School Health.

Centers for Disease Control and Prevention. (1998). *Strengthening comprehensive school health education: Process evaluation manual.* Atlanta, GA: Author.

Collins, J. L., Small, M. L., Kann, L., Pateman, B. C., Gold, R. S., & Kolbe, L. J. (1995). School health education. *Journal of School Health, 65*(8), 302–311.

Connell, D. B., Turner, R. R., & Mason, E. F. (1985). Summary of findings of the school health education evaluation: Health promotion effectiveness, implementation, and cost. *Journal of School Health, 55*(8), 316–321.

Dusenbury, L., & Falco, M. (1995). Eleven components of effective drug abuse prevention curricula. *Journal of School Health, 65*(10), 420–425.

Dusenbury, L., & Lake, A. (1996). *Making the grade: A guide to school drug prevention programs.* Washington, DC: Drug Strategies.

Education Development Center, Inc. (1995). *Choosing the tools: A review of selected K–12 health education curricula.* Newton, MA: Author.

Errecart, M. T., Walberg, H. J., Ross, J. G., Gold, R. S., Fiedler, J. L., & Kolbe, L. J. (1991). Effectiveness of teenage health teaching modules. *Journal of School Health, 61 (special insert)* (1), 26–30.

Ferrara, S., & McTighe, J. (1992). Assessment: A thoughtful process. In A. Costa, J. Bellanca, & R. Fogarty (Eds.), *If minds matter: A foreword to the future* (Vol. 2, p. 368). Palatine, IL: Skylight Publishing.

Fetro, J. V. (1992). *Personal & social skills: Understanding and integrating competencies across health content.* Santa Cruz, CA: ETR Associates.

Fogarty, R. (1991). *The mindful school: How to integrate the curricula* (Vol. 5). Palatine, IL: Skylight Publishing.

The Gallup Organization. (1994). *Values and opinions of comprehensive school health education in U.S. public schools: Adolescents, parents, and school district administrators.* Atlanta, GA: American Cancer Society.

Gingiss, P. L., & Hamilton, R. (1989). Teacher perspectives after implementing a human sexuality education program. *Journal of School Health, 59*(10), 427–431.

Goodman, R. M., Tenney, M., Smith, D. W., & Steckler, A. (1992). The adoption process for health curriculum innovations in schools: A case study. *Journal of Health Education, 23*(4), 215–220.

Iverson, D.C. (1994). Program evaluation versus research: More differences than similarities. In P. Cortese & K. Middleton (Eds.), *The comprehensive school health challenge: Promoting health through education* (Vol. 2, pp. 575–590). Santa Cruz, CA: ETR Associates.

Johnson, J., & Immerwahr, J. (1994). *First things first: What Americans expect from the public schools.* New York: Public Agenda.

Joint Committee on Health Education Terminology. (1991). Report of the 1990 Joint Committee on Health Education Terminology. *Journal of Health Education, 22*(2), 97–108.

Joint Committee on National Health Education Standards. (1995). *Achieving health literacy: An investment in the future.* Atlanta, GA: American Cancer Society.

Kann, L., Collins, J. L., Pateman, B. C., Small, M. L., Russ, J. G., & Kolbe, L. J. (1995). The School Health Policies and Programs Study (SHPPS): Rationale for a nationwide status report on school health programs. *Journal of School Health, 65*(8), 291–293.

Kirby, D., Short, L., Collins, J., Rugg, D., Kolbe, L., Howard, M., Miller, B., Sonenstein, F., & Zabin, L. (1994). School-based programs to reduce sexual risk behaviors: A review of effectiveness. *Public Health Reports, 109*(3), 339–360.

Kolbe, L. J. (1990). An epidemiological surveillance system to monitor the prevalence of youth behaviors that most affect health. *Health Education, 21*(6), 44–48.

Kolbe, L. J., Iverson, D.C., Kreuter, M. W., Hochbaum, G., & Christensen, G. (1981). Propositions for an alternate and complementary health education paradigm. *Health Education, 12*(3), 24–30.

Lohrmann, D. K. (1993). Overview of curriculum design and implementation. In B. S. Mahoney & L. K. Olsen (Eds.), *Health education teacher resource handbook: A practical guide for K–12 health education* (pp. 35–58). Millwood, NY: Kraus International Publications.

Lohrmann, D. K., Gold, R. S., & Jubb, W. H. (1987). School health education: A foundation for school health programs. *Journal of School Health, 57*(10), 420–425.

Louis Harris and Associates, Inc. (1988). *Health: You've got to be taught: An evaluation of comprehensive health education in American public schools.* New York: Metropolitan Life Foundation.

Marx, E., & Northrop, D. (1995). *Educating for health: A guide to implementing a comprehensive approach to school health education.* Newton, MA: Education Development Center, Inc.

Milburn, K. (1995). A critical review of peer education with young people with special reference to sexual health. *Health Education Research: Theory & Practice, 10*(4), 407–420.

National Education Goals Panel. (1994). *The National Education Goals Report: Building a nation of learners.* Washington, DC: U.S. Government Printing Office.

National Professional School Health Education Organizations. (1984). Comprehensive school health education. *Journal of School Health, 54*(8), 312–315.

National School Boards Association. (1991). *School health: Helping children learn.* Alexandria, VA: Author.

Patten, M. M. V. (1994). Dealing with controversy in the school health program. In P. Cortese & K. Middleton (Eds.), *The comprehensive school health challenge: Promoting health through education* (Vol. 2, p. 962). Santa Cruz, CA: ETR Associates.

Pollock, M. (1987). *Planning and implementing: Health education in schools.* Palo Alto, CA: Mayfield Publishing Company.

Public Health Service. (1991). *Healthy People 2000: National health promotion and disease prevention objectives—Full report, with commentary.* Washington, DC: U.S. Department of Health and Human Services, Public Health Service publication (PHS) 91–50212.

Rohrbach, L. A., Graham, J. W., & Hansen, W. B. (1993). Diffusion of a school-based substance abuse prevention program: Predictors of program implementation. *Preventive Medicine, 22,* 237–260.

Rose, L. C., Gallup, A. M., & Elam, S. M. (1997). The twenty-ninth annual Phi Delta Kappa/Gallup Poll of the public's attitudes toward public schools. *Phi Delta Kappan, 79*(1), 41–56.

Ross, J. G., Leupker, R. V., Nelson, G. D., Saavedra, P., & Hubbard, B. M. (1991). Teenage health teaching modules: Impact of teacher training on implementation and student outcomes. *Journal of School Health, 61*(1), 31–34.

School Health Education Study. (1967). *Health education: A conceptual approach to curriculum design.* St. Paul: Minnesota Mining and Manufacturing Company.

Secretary's Commission on Achieving Necessary Skills. (1991). *What work requires of schools: A SCANS report for America 2000.* Washington, DC: U.S. Department of Labor.

Secretary's Commission on Achieving Necessary Skills. (1992). *Learning a living: A blueprint for high performance.* Washington, DC: U.S. Department of Labor.

Simonds, R. L. (1993/1994). A plea for children. *Education Leadership, 51*(4), 12–15.

Smith, D. W., Steckler, A. B., McCormick, L. K., & McLeroy, K. R. (1995). Lessons learned about disseminating health curricula to schools. *Journal of Health Education, 26*(1), 37–43.

Walter, H. J., Vaughan, R. D., & Wynder, E. L. (1989). Primary prevention of cancer among children: Changes in cigarette smoking and diet after six years of intervention. *Journal of the National Cancer Institute, 81,* 995–999.

Wentworth, E. (undated). *Agents of change: Exemplary corporate policies and practices to improve education.* Washington, DC: Business Roundtable.

Wooley, S. F. (1995). Behavior mapping: A tool for identifying priorities for health education curricula and instruction. *Journal of Health Education, 26*(4), 200–206.

Pauline Carlyon, M.S., M.P.H.
William Carlyon, Ph.D.
Alice R. McCarthy, Ph.D.

4 Family and Community Involvement in School Health

- Partnerships among schools, families, community groups, and individuals.
- Designed to share and maximize resources and expertise in addressing the healthy development of children, youth, and their families.

Our most successful students in school are those from better functioning families, students who attend schools where there is home-school social congruence, and students whose schools have not developed a culture of failure.
—(Comer, Haynes, & Joyner, 1996, p. 7)

If educators view children simply as students, *they are likely to see the family as separate from the school. That is, the family is expected to do its job and leave the education of children to the schools. If educators view students as* children, *they are likely to see both the family and the community as partners with the school in children's education and development.*
—(Epstein, 1995, p. 701)

At the center of school, family, and community partnerships is the student. Functioning, supportive families and social support within communities contribute to students' success. When children feel val-

Health Is Academic: A Guide to Coordinated School Health Problems. Edited by Eva Marx and Susan Frelick Wooley, with Daphne Northrop. New York: Teachers College Press, 1998. ISBN 0-8077-3713-5 (pbk.), ISBN 0-8077-3714-3 (cloth). Prior to photocopying items for classroom use, please contact the Copyright Clearance Center, Customer Service, 222 Rosewood Dr., Danvers, MA 01923, USA, tel. (508) 750-8400. © 1998 Education Development Center, Inc. All rights reserved.

ued, they are more likely to develop important skills, avoid risk behaviors, and remain in school (Epstein, 1995). Students feel competent and do well in school when:

- Their communities have accessible resources and supportive networks and involve students in community services.
- Their families seek preventive care, value and encourage education, spend time with their children, and have clear expectations.
- Schools involve families and students and encourage the development of positive behaviors.
- Schools, families, and communities deliver clear, consistent messages (Hawkins, Catalano, & Miller, 1992).

By contrast, students are less likely to succeed when communities are economically deprived, disorganized, and lack opportunities for employment or youth involvement; when families do not set clear expectations, monitor children's behavior, or model appropriate behaviors; and when schools present a negative climate and do not involve students and their families (Hawkins, Catalano, & Miller, 1992).

The school, the family, and the community each has its own unique resources; each can reach students in ways the others cannot; and each influences young people's behaviors in different ways. Together, as participants in a coordinated school health program, they can provide an environment in which students can learn and mature successfully. This chapter discusses the roles of families as partners with schools in support of coordinated school health programs, ways that schools can support partnerships with families and other relevant community participants, how families and community members can participate in all aspects of a coordinated school health program, and ways national and state decision makers can support family and community involvement in coordinated school health programs. The chapter uses the terms "family" and "parent" interchangeably to refer to primary caregivers, whether they are single parents, birth parents, foster or adoptive parents, guardians, or grandparents.

ESSENTIAL FUNCTIONS OF FAMILY AND COMMUNITY INVOLVEMENT IN SCHOOL HEALTH

Families and communities can support each other and contribute to the success of coordinated school health programs by:

- providing time, experience, and resources
- supporting student involvement in activities that support health
- ensuring that students and their families receive needed health services
- planning jointly to develop relevant and appropriate messages and services
- delivering clear, consistent messages that support health, include high but attainable expectations, and offer appropriate role modeling
- sharing facilities and encouraging participation by all relevant individuals and groups (Blank & Danzberger, 1994; Howell, Bibeau, Mullen, Carr, & McCann, 1991; National Association of State Boards of Education, 1992).

Figure 4.1 illustrates how one school, family, and community partnership created conditions for students to thrive personally and academically. Parents, as students' primary teachers and role models, have a direct caregiving role. They are also members of their larger community, where they can participate in improving the welfare and achievement of youth. This section first addresses family involvement and its challenges and then considers involvement of other members of the community.

Involving Families

Most families want to be involved in their children's education in meaningful ways that not only enhance the school's activities but also contribute positively to their own health knowledge and behaviors (Birch, 1996). "When parents are involved, children do better in school and go to better schools" (Henderson, 1987). When schools have good relationships with parents, parents are more likely to cooperate with school health efforts. Good school and family relationships also lay the groundwork in the home and the community for an environment that models and reinforces classroom learning (NCPIE, 1995b). In addition, when parents are comfortable with the school and communicate regularly, they are more likely to understand and support school health programs (Marx & Northrop, 1995).

There are many ways that families and schools can work together to support coordinated school health programs.

Provide Time, Expertise, and Resources.   When students receive homework that requires interaction with their families, both students and schools benefit from the expertise residing in families. When teachers inform parents about upcoming study units, and send home weekly materials including family-based activities that enhance classroom work, families can not only

FIGURE 4.1. A Partnership in Action

Prevention of educational problems begins at birth, not on the first day of school. That is the philosophy that led Matt Benningfield to create the Byck Cradle School in Louisville, Kentucky. The way to promote the health of students and families in the school's inner-city neighborhood, he realized, was to start working with families before their children started school. Nurses, physicians, medical students, police officers, dentists, counselors, parents, hospitals, a local university, and a host of other community organizations provide an impressive array of health and education services that address all eight components of the Cradle School's coordinated health program. Medical and health care services such as immunizations, health screenings, and physical exams are available as well. A school-based family resource center provides social and legal services, transportation, and child care.

The Cradle School program encourages positive parent-child relationships, promotes parental understanding of child development, provides learning activities and experiences for children and families, encourages a positive home-school working relationship, and provides an environment for practicing readiness skills for a positive transition to kindergarten. One to two hours a week, preschool-age children and their parents attend school together and participate in activities that develop the children's language, critical thinking, and social skills. Byck's program focuses on training parents as educators and provides them with help on nutrition, safety, hygiene, and wellness topics. Parents learn to read and talk with their children, make and play educational games, and foster their children's language skills and mathematical understanding through home activities.

"People say Byck Cradle School brings out the best in parents," said one parent. "But what it really does is show parents that the best has always been within us. We just need some help to find it!" (Byck Cradle School, 1995)

reinforce messages but also alert schools to family and community resources that could enrich the curriculum. Surveys are another way that schools and parent organizations can identify expertise, talents, and other resources that families can offer the school or a classroom. Families could organize recreational activities, such as after-school programs, or manage a school room reserved for family activities. When sending home assignments, teachers need to consider cultural differences and that some issues (sexuality, for example) may be sensitive. Family health beliefs and practices sometimes differ from those taught in school, and family priorities and communication styles might also differ from those of the predominant school culture.

Support Student Involvement. Families can encourage student participation in school health activities through conversations with their children. They can also support activities by arranging transportation and assisting with projects such as fund-raising events that make special undertakings possible. In turn, schools can strengthen student involvement by supporting their families. For example, schools can make available family support services that assist families with health, nutrition, and other services; offer workshops on child and adolescent development; provide information on school involvement and health issues (Bridge Communications, 1996); conduct home visits and neighborhood meetings that help families understand schools and schools understand families; offer family-centered recreational opportunities; and provide facilities or child care for family support groups that bring families together to help each other.

Ensure That Students Receive Needed Health Services. Schools conduct routine health screenings and notify families of conditions that require follow-up. Although families are responsible for obtaining medical, preventive health, and mental health care for their children, sometimes families need the support of the school to fulfill these responsibilities. Whether they are unable to obtain the services their children need because of financial limitations, inability to take time from work, lack of transportation, lack of familiarity with the health care system, language barriers, or other circumstances, families generally will welcome help from the school. Schools can provide families with information on community health, recreation, social support, and other services and can work with community agencies, organizations, and businesses to locate needed resources. If children must take medications or schedule medical appointments during the school day, families and schools can work together to ensure that students receive needed care with minimum disruption to the child's education.

Participate in Joint Planning. Family members can provide valuable insights into community norms, cultural sensitivities, and student needs. As members of school governance and advocacy groups—such as parent organizations, advisory councils, and committees—and district-level councils, they can influence the development of health-related activities. Parents can also identify, build links among, and integrate community and school-based resources and services that strengthen programs, family practices, and student learning and development.

Deliver Consistent Messages. School-to-home and home-to-school communications about school programs and student progress help ensure the delivery of consistent messages. Parents are children's first and most powerful teachers and most important role models. Parents influence students' behaviors through their own lifestyles, provide support for student learning, and present a family perspective on sensitive topics. Through their involvement in schools and reinforcement of the school program by their words and actions, parents can augment the school's efforts to maximize student achievement and academic success, provide an orderly environment, and contribute to the expectation of excellence from students and staff (Squires et al., 1983).

Share Facilities.   Some schools have become centers for a full range of services that families support and use. In some districts opening school facilities to families and the community during off-school hours has improved home and school relations and provided opportunities for family involvement in the school program. A family or parent center at a school provides a welcoming place for families as well as a location for families to plan and carry out a variety of family and community activities (Davies, 1996).

Challenges to Family Involvement

Although the benefits of family involvement are clear, it is not always easy for schools to involve families. A number of challenges can impede family involvement, but they are not insurmountable.

Valuing Diversity.   Students' families represent different cultures, social classes, races, ethnic groups, family structures, and sexual orientations. To tap the energies and creativity of families, schools must respect and build on the unique qualities and interests of all. This means avoiding language that reinforces stereotypes, not identifying people by their race or ethnicity, and making special efforts to include discussions of other lifestyles in written and oral lessons. When school staff remember and respect families' unique backgrounds and beliefs, they demonstrate that they honor all families and welcome their involvement.

Overcoming Language Barriers.   English is not the primary language spoken in many students' homes. In some urban districts, as many as 80 languages are spoken. When all communications with families are in English, families might feel left out. Schools can overcome language barriers by employing one or more staff members fluent in the major languages spoken by families, by translating materials, or by locating publications in appropriate languages. Peer educator programs, that train family members to deliver workshops for and work with other families of the same culture, are another way schools can overcome language and other cultural differences. A peer educator program in New York City succeeded in combating distrust, en-

FIGURE 4.2. Family Liaisons Strengthen Family Involvement

Incomplete homework, hungry or sleepy students, and poorly attended school conferences prompted staff at Timber Lane Elementary School in Fairfax County, Virginia, to develop a program that could strengthen the school's relationship with the community's Spanish- and Vietnamese-speaking families. The program matches community liaisons with parents from the same linguistic and cultural backgrounds. With language and cultural barriers reduced, liaisons are able to discuss health and education issues with parents, help link families to school and community services, work with families to strengthen their parenting skills, and identify opportunities for families to benefit the school by volunteering. The liaisons meet frequently with principals, teachers, counselors, the school psychologist, the school nurse, and parent organizations to strengthen family and school connections (Halford, 1996).

hancing communication, and increasing family involvement in school activities. Figure 4.2 discusses a Fairfax County, Virginia, program to involve Spanish- and Vietnamese-speaking families.

Adjusting to Grade Level Differences. As children get older, their desire to participate in family-centered activities and their interest in involving their families in their day-to-day lives change. The challenge for schools is working with students and their families to find appropriate ways of involving families at each level. At the elementary level, for example, family members might assist with classroom lessons or accompany students on field trips. Parents of older students might plan and participate in after-school activities or attend workshops on health-related issues with their children. Schools can also assist parents of adolescents by helping them understand that adolescents continue to listen to their parents even as they struggle to become more independent (Massachusetts Department of Education, 1996b).

Improving Access. Families that lack transportation or child care are often unable to participate in school-sponsored events, especially when a school is not neighborhood-based. In addition, many parents work during school hours and cannot attend daytime school activities and conferences. By scheduling events in the evening or offering a variety of times and locations for family participation, school can reach out to these parents.

Reducing Distrust or Discomfort.   School staff sometimes assume incorrectly that parents who are not involved in school do not want to be. The fact is that almost all parents care about their children and want to help them succeed. The reasons parents are not involved vary. Some parents distrust schools because of their own negative experiences as students or their feelings of inadequacy as parents. Other parents lack reading or language skills needed to communicate effectively with school personnel. Some parents view teachers and school administration as authority figures and hesitate to ask questions. Still others lack the confidence or social skills to learn about school operations or teachers' expectations. To make it easier for these parents to become involved, teachers, administrators, and other school staff need to make every effort to welcome parents and show respect for their concerns. In addition, schools can institute home-visiting or outreach programs that could convey this respect and allow parents to develop positive relationships with school staff in the comfort of their own environments.

Addressing Family Health Choices.   In some families, adults engage in unhealthy behaviors such as smoking, excessive drinking, or poor dietary habits and view school discussions of risk behaviors as criticism. By tailoring health messages to encourage positive health choices without condemning those who make other choices, schools can make discussions of health topics less threatening. Teachers also can help students understand that some health choices, such as smoking, are difficult to change and teach students how to communicate their concern about parents' risky behaviors without criticism.

Accommodating Differing Views.   Some families disagree with or do not understand the purposes of a school health program. Schools often can head off controversy by communicating openly about various aspects of the coordinated school health program, anticipating concerns and making every effort to accommodate them, and addressing criticism as soon as it arises. Schools should have policies for addressing controversies that give parents opportunities to air their concerns. Controversy can provide a chance to involve parents who might not otherwise participate. If school staff show they value the suggestions of parents and community members and respond positively and respectfully (Newman & Farrell, 1991), controversy can become an important opportunity for learning.

Involving the Community

School-community partnerships have contributed to the success of coordinated school health programs across the country. Communities expect schools and families to prepare students to become healthy, productive citizens. Communities in turn have a responsibility to join with schools and families in support of efforts—such as coordinated school health programs—that can help achieve this goal.

School-community partnerships can exist at many levels. Individuals in the community, individual community groups, or coalitions of community groups can form partnerships with schools. Some partnerships focus on one school; others are district-wide (Epstein, 1995; Howell et al., 1991; Kane, 1993; Siri, 1994). Partnerships can be informal, such as an organization providing materials or a speaker for a health education class, or formal, such as a contract to provide health services. Formal arrangements can also include many configurations that schools or districts might have or create—Healthy School Teams (see Chapter 2), task forces, or action teams; district advisory committees; integrated services systems; school development programs; full-service schools; and school and community collaboratives. These partnerships can incorporate all the components of a coordinated school health program or a few. If the school health focus is but one activity within the larger mission of the partnership, a subcommittee often takes responsibility for school health-related activities. If partnerships do not specifically address coordinated school health programs, school health advocates work to make school health a priority within the partnership. Schools and communities often have several types of partnerships that can complement and reinforce each other.

To be successful, school and community partnerships must:

- Have clear, concise responsibilities and expectations for each participant.
- Allow for flexibility in organization and implementation, taking into account the diversity of students and their families, differing capacities and interests of community organizations, and the varied needs of participants and beneficiaries.
- Acknowledge that partnerships require a time commitment and that initial gains and benefits are likely to be small.
- Provide appropriate training for teachers, administrators, and community members (NASBE, 1992).

Communities can work with schools in essentially the same ways as families. However, the resources, mechanisms, and details differ.

Provide Time, Experience, and Resources. Community agencies and organizations have a host of materials and resources that can enhance a school's health program, such as publications, speakers, special demonstrations, facilities and equipment, and funding. Businesses can "adopt a school" or give employees release time so they can volunteer for school health-related work in the school or community. Representatives of community organizations and businesses can serve as members of school councils or school health advisory committees. Businesses, colleges, and universities can award grants or waive tuition for teachers who wish to further their professional growth and development.

Establishing new initiatives or strengthening existing ones generally requires money. Schools that have a coordinator—a staff member from the school, a person from another community agency, or a volunteer—who devotes time to family and community involvement activities need to support that position. That support includes salaries for paid staff and space and basic resources, such as mail and phone services for workers, whether paid or volunteer. To strengthen community involvement in a school's health program, schools and communities can redirect existing resources by redefining job responsibilities, relocating staff to shared space, consolidating special funds that can support coordinated activities, or targeting resources that are being used for more diffuse activities. Schools can also take steps to secure new funding (Melaville & Blank, 1993).

Federal, state, and local programs that mandate, request, or support family involvement—such as Title I, Title II, Title VII of the Goals 2000 (Improving America's Schools Act)—are possible sources of funding to support staff development for school, family, and community partnerships; establish demonstration programs; or cover other partnership expenses. Potential local sources of funds for a school's partnership programs include donations from businesses that have formed partnerships with a school, school discretionary funds, and special funding-raising events (Epstein, 1995). Education reform initiatives in some states, such as Kentucky and Tennessee, include financing for school-linked family support activities (Farrow, 1994).

Much current financing is earmarked for addressing specific problems, often of specific populations. Some creative managers have combined funding from a number of sources to build a program that blends services, such as basic health services (funded by a Maternal and Child Health block grant), case management for high-risk youth (funded by Child Protective Services), substance abuse prevention (funded by the Drug-Free Schools program), and after-school remediation and cultural enrichment (funded with Title 1 money) (Dryfoos, 1994).

In some cases, community members work with school personnel to design programs and pursue financing from local or national foundations or local health departments. In other situations, foundations or state agencies have offered incentive grants or seed money for development of school and community partnership activities (Dryfoos, 1994). Communities In Schools programs receive financing through a combination of corporate, foundation, and individual donors. Local Education Funds raise money from the philanthropic community as well as from individuals and small businesses to provide grants for pilot programs or to leverage change.

Occasionally, community members offer resources for a purpose that is not compatible with a school's adopted program. For example, donated materials might not fit with an established curriculum or might endorse a commercial product. A school and community advisory committee might serve as a clearinghouse for offers of materials and other resources and, if necessary, suggest alternative uses or substitutions for the donation.

Support Student Involvement. Student community service programs are another tool for linking schools and communities with school health efforts. In several cities, Boys and Girls Clubs work with schools to develop peer leadership programs for substance abuse or HIV prevention. Internships that help students apply health learning in the workplace and explore health careers are another example of how communities support school health activities. Through organizations such as Communities In Schools, community members serve as mentors and positive role models for students. The FYI Youth program provides young people with information about programs, services, opportunities, and caring adults available to them and their peers. Some communities implement YOUTHLINEs, 24-hour telephone hot lines staffed by trained youth who offer callers support and advice, put them in touch with crisis intervention services, and inform them about appropriate community services.

Ensure That Students and Families Receive Health Services. Institutions and agencies that have the welfare of young people as their mission can join forces to use their resources more effectively. Many communities have developed school-based or school-linked integrated systems that bring together service providers, families, school staff, and other community members to form collaboratives (see Chapter 8). They differ in participants, organizational structure, funding sources, and breadth of reach but all have a common vision (Institute for Educational Leadership, 1994; Melaville & Blank, 1993).

The New Beginnings program in San Diego is an example of such a collaborative. At startup it used three trailers, or "portable classrooms," on the grounds of Hamilton Elementary School to provide services for children and families in the community. Representatives of several agencies worked together to broker or provide services, including school registration, immunizations, and counseling, that meet the full range of family needs. The program has expanded to several other schools, where it offers a service mix tailored to the specific needs of each local community.

Walbridge Caring Communities, based in an elementary school and a nearby church in St. Louis, Missouri, aims to keep children in school and increase their success by providing services and connecting families in a fragmented, crime-ridden neighborhood. A partnership of state agencies and a foundation spent six months identifying an appropriate director to work with the community. The school principal, the school community coordinator, the director, and a canvassing crew conducted a door-to-door survey of family needs and priorities, meetings to discuss neighborhood concerns, and interviews with teachers to identify student needs. California's Healthy Start Program has a similar perspective and approach.

Communities In Schools, Inc. (CIS) is a national network of partnerships that connect communities' health, education, and human resources with schools to help young people learn, stay in school, and prepare for life. Each local CIS project is an independent corporation led by a board of directors representative of the community. Community service providers are relocated to the schools to work alongside teachers, volunteers, and mentors. There they can better support students and their families and form one-on-one relationships with students. CIS's Teen Health Corps trains high school students to plan and conduct school and community health activities and teach their peers leaders about healthy behaviors.

Participate in Joint Planning.   Schools, families, students, and community members and agencies can participate in community planning initiatives to help ensure that communities address the needs of young people in a coordinated way. Schools can also create advisory groups of community members along with school staff, students, and families. Such groups can provide direction to a school's and community's health program by assessing present practices, exploring and organizing new activities or programs, and evaluating progress.

Deliver Consistent Messages.   Although families are important role models for young people, they are not the only influences. The outside community influences youth as well. Mass media images can have a particularly powerful effect on young people. By presenting healthy models the media can discourage youth from engaging in unhealthy behaviors and activities, such as smoking, driving without a safety belt, and engaging in early or unprotected sexual activity. When workplaces and other public buildings create smoke-free spaces, they create a healthier environment and also send a nonsmoking message to children and youth.

Share Facilities. Although schools by themselves do not have the capacity to deliver all the services required to address the physical, emotional, social, and intellectual needs of students and their families, there nonetheless are important ways in which schools can help their communities meet those needs. A full-service school in Manatee County, Florida, exemplifies this approach (Chervin & Northrop, 1994). When the bell rings at the end of the school day, supervised after-school activities, such as performing and martial arts, scouts, and tutoring begin. A van parked on the school lot offers free immunizations and extensive health screenings to children. Through its vocational education program, the school helps parents on public assistance prepare for the workforce. Parenting classes help parents develop skills needed to effectively communicate with their children and helping them with homework. A full-time nurse, contracted through the local hospital, provides (with family-style pot-luck suppers) classes on childbirth, nutrition, parenting, and child development. A counselor provides individual and family counseling. Two social workers arrange for free day care and transportation to all school activities, make home visits, follow up on referrals, arrange for Meals on Wheels and distribution of food baskets prepared by local churches, guide families applying for government assistance, and alert community voluntary agencies about the needs of families.

The partnership works both ways. A school's physical education or staff wellness program can use nearby community recreation facilities. A museum can coordinate health-related exhibits with teachers and provide materials for classroom use.

PARTICIPANTS IN SCHOOL PARTNERSHIPS WITH FAMILIES AND COMMUNITIES

Partnerships that help children and youth maintain their health, achieve academically, and become productive citizens involve multiple players with a range of interests and expertise. The effort to involve families in school health programs will be most successful if all members of the school community participate—parents and other caregivers, teachers, counselors, psychologists, nurses, other pupil services personnel, food services personnel, custodians, and bus drivers. Some schools give a school member or parent responsibility for day-to-day management of family-centered activities.

The school principal or chief administrator is a key player. In schools where family partnerships flourish, the principal has usually taken the first steps toward better communication and collaboration (Davies, 1996). Administrators set the tone for how staff communicate with families, and how parent volunteers are involved and acknowledged.

   Participants in partnerships involving the larger community will vary depending on the scope of the effort, the structure and politics of the community, and the availability of interested and capable people. Participants might include:

- *Students and their families.* The ultimate beneficiaries of coordinated school health programs, they represent a wide variety of strengths, needs, and viewpoints.
- *School decision makers,* including principals, district-level administrators, and school board members. They control what happens at the school level. Without their participation and commitment, sustained implementation rarely occurs (Smith, Steckler, McCormick, & McLeroy, 1995).
- *Professionals* in the areas of health, education, and social services; law enforcement and juvenile justice; and youth service, including recreation, sports, and entertainment. They understand first hand the daily needs and crises of students and families and the strengths and weaknesses of support systems and are responsible for providing services to schools as well as the larger community.
- *Leaders of neighborhood and community-based organizations.* They bring the perspective of the community and can marshal support for partnership efforts.
- *Local leaders of business and industry.* They bring fiscal and systems management expertise and can help generate resources.
- *Faculty of local colleges and universities.* They have research capacities and expertise. In addition, they provide professional preparation and staff development for current school staff and school health leaders.
- *Elected officials,* including school board members, city council members, and the mayor. They influence funding and policy decisions and, through their leadership, can strengthen community support.
- *Representatives of voluntary, civic, advocacy, and service organizations.* These organizations often have as their mission promotion of various aspects of community welfare and include in their membership a broad spectrum of the community. Many are affiliates of national organizations (see Chapter 12) that provide resources, public relations, and other expertise (Seffrin, 1994). Some have training capacities that can support coordinated school health programs. Organizational volunteers are frequently trained by professional staff and supported by a national network. Senior citizens are an important and frequently underutilized resource.
- *Media representatives.* They inform the public, influence public opinion, and frame debate. Their coverage of school health issues can affect public understanding and garner support for collaborative decisions and activities.

- *Clergy.* The majority value education and are committed to social welfare. In addition, they are important spokespeople for and links to communities with diverse values (Comprehensive Health Education Foundation, 1995).
- *Foundation staff.* Through their funding decisions, they can become powerful allies for developing coordinated school health programs.
- *Labor union leaders.* They represent the interests of many school employees, service providers, and caregivers and parents who are affected by school activities.
- *Representatives of nonprofit providers, insurance companies, and hospitals.* These institutions control the provision of many services through their staffing and funding policies, are potential sites for programs, and employ experts who can assist in implementation.
- *Leaders of organizations that represent ethnic and cultural groups.* They bring the perspectives of their constituencies and ensure representation of the interests of students from minority populations.

NATIONAL AND STATE SUPPORT FOR FAMILY/COMMUNITY INVOLVEMENT

Many of the community members just discussed are affiliated with national organizations. State chapters often support members through workshop and professional development opportunities, materials development, advocacy, and conferences. National and state agencies and organizations promote family and community involvement through words, actions, materials, and funds. See Chapters 11 and 12 for in-depth discussions of the support that state and national organizations can provide to coordinated school health programs.

One way that national organizations and federal agencies support family and community involvement in coordinated school health programs is through positive statements and supportive statutes and regulations. The following examples are illustrative.

- Goal 8 of the National Education Goals (National Education Goals Panel, 1994) calls for every school to promote partnerships that will increase parental involvement and participation in promoting the social, emotional, and academic growth of children. It bids states to establish policies for assisting schools and districts with programs for increasing these partnerships, schools to actively engage parents and families in a partnership that supports children's academic work at home and shared educational decision making at school, and parents and families to help ensure adequate support for schools and hold students, schools, and teachers to high standards of accountability.

- Head Start and Title I of the Improving America's Schools Act both require parent involvement with community resources and school personnel
  in planning, designing, and implementing programs for improving student
  performance. The Department of Justice provides technical assistance to
  state and local education agencies on safety, discipline, violence, and drug
  prevention. The Department of Agriculture has an initiative that encourages family involvement in ensuring healthy meals at home and in school
  (U.S. Department of Education, 1994).
- The policy statements of numerous national leadership organizations emphasize "comprehensive, sustained, and early involvement of parents" (Cavazos, 1989, pp. 16–17). In 1988, the Council of Chief State School Officers'
  theme was early childhood and family education. The National Association of State Boards of Education issued a report (NASBE, 1988) that rec-
  ommends recognizing parents as essential partners in the education of their
  children and another (NASBE, 1992) that details steps for establishing
  partnerships.
- The National Governors' Association's 1991 report on education featured
  parent involvement among seven highlighted state policy initiatives.
- The Committee for Economic Development in 1985 recommended parent
  education; school-based management in which school staff, parents, and
  students share decision making and accountability for results; and business
  support for parent involvement in their children's education.
- The National Coalition for Parent Involvement in Education (1995a),
  which includes member organizations representing education, business, re-
  ligion, military, youth groups, retirees, colleges and universities, and others,
  has as its mission "to advocate the involvement of parents in their children's
  education and to foster relationships between home, school, and community that can enhance the education of all our nation's young people."
- The National PTA (1992) adopted a position statement that supports family and community involvement in schools efforts to improve children's
  health (Figure 4.3).

National organizations also provide technical assistance to train school
and community coordinators, school staff, and community members. For example, through its training institute Communities In Schools trains teachers,
school administrators, social service providers, and leaders in business and
government to support community partnerships that link schools and community resources. The Public Education Network provides technical assistance to community organizations that identify resources to support local
education, including coordinated school health programs. Finally, the U.S.
Centers for Disease Control and Prevention provides technical assistance

FIGURE 4.3. *Statement of the National PTA Supporting Family and Community Involvement*

National PTA believes that health is based on the quality of life of the whole child—emotional, intellectual, physical, social, and spiritual. All elements must be considered before optimum health can exist. National PTA recognizes that:

- Social changes have produced major health problems among our children that have directly impacted on schools and their ability to teach.
- Academic achievement and student self-esteem and well-being are inextricably intertwined.
- Responsibility for the emotional, intellectual, physical, and social health of children is that of the whole community and all of its institutions.
- After the home, the school is often best positioned to serve as the community's center for meeting the needs of the whole child.

Source: National PTA, 1992.

and materials on community planning to improve health promotion efforts (Centers for Disease Control and Prevention, 1995).

State agencies also support family and community involvement—by issuing policy statements and guidelines, establishing statewide school health coalitions, providing information and training on school health issues to families and communities, developing assessment and monitoring systems, providing grants to projects that involve families and communities in school health activities, conducting awareness campaigns, and making competencies for working with families a credentialing requirement for teachers and other school staff.

Two examples of state programs are those in Texas and West Virginia. The Texas Department of Health (1996) collaborates with the Texas Cancer Council and the state's Regional Education Service Centers to promote school health by staffing each of the 20 centers with a school health specialist. The specialists provide training, workshops, and technical assistance to school districts; assist schools in locating resources for health programs and activities; and act as catalysts for school and community collaboration by enlisting the support of community groups and raising awareness of school health issues. By building coalitions, forging public and private partnerships, and heightening community awareness, these school health specialists link school personnel with state, regional, and local resources.

As part of its school reform movement, West Virginia enacted legislation establishing Local School Improvement Councils. The West Virginia Department of Education and the West Virginia Educational Fund joined forces to encourage the councils to support healthy schools. Among the agencies' efforts was a statewide conference to educate council members on the need for coordinated school health programs.

INTEGRATING FAMILY AND COMMUNITY INVOLVEMENT IN SCHOOL HEALTH WITH THE OTHER COMPONENTS OF A COORDINATED SCHOOL HEALTH PROGRAM

Families, other community members, and community organizations can support and, in turn, be supported by all the other components of a coordinated school health program. Experiences in California and Massachusetts suggest ways of linking family and community members in school health activities (California Department of Education, 1994; Massachusetts Department of Education, 1996a & b).

- *Physical education* staff can encourage family, student, and school staff involvement in health clubs, sports leagues, hiking groups, fund-raising walks, runs, and cycling events, and programs sponsored by local parks or recreation programs. Families can help children become involved in everyday physical activities that increase their health and fitness, such as shoveling snow, walking to the store, riding a bicycle to school, and doing yard work. Schools can make their facilities available for fitness classes, swimming, and other family activities.
- *Nutrition services* staff can send home information about upcoming breakfast and lunch menus, along with nutrition-related news and healthy, easy-to-prepare recipes. Family members who work in the food industry can promote healthier food products throughout the community. Parents can read food labels to compare nutritional values with their children and modify family recipes in keeping with nutrition guidelines for fats, sodium, and sugar.
- *Health promotion* for school staff can invite interested parents to participate in activities, including fitness and smoking cessation programs. Local fitness centers can offer health-risk appraisals for groups and special exercise sessions for families and school staff.
- The coordinated school health program can encourage students to see the connections between the *environment,* both in and out of school, and health. Schools can support a healthy community environment by encouraging student and family involvement in recycling programs, helping fami-

lies reduce air pollution by organizing carpools, and working with communities to provide foot or bicycle paths. Students can support the *community* by volunteering in hospitals, collecting and distributing food for homeless shelters, and visiting nursing homes. Some schools award credit toward graduation for community service. Safety-related community agencies such as emergency services, law enforcement, and fire protection can teach students, families, and school staff first-aid techniques and cardiopulmonary resuscitation and provide information and training on ways to maintain a safe and healthy school environment.

- *Health and physical education teachers* can send health and exercise tips home with students. Families can discuss these tips along with newspaper articles and television reports that reinforce classroom health messages. Grocery stores can provide nutrition information and preparation tips that help students apply nutrition concepts they learn at school. Museums and libraries can feature health exhibits and make health-related materials available to students and families.

- *School health services staff* can hold screening fairs that might identify students' health problems, such as vision and hearing difficulties, recurrent infections, and chronic conditions, that families might otherwise not recognize. Schools can work with families and health care providers to make arrangements for students with special health problems to receive needed services during school hours. Through community-wide planning, health services providers can work with schools to ensure service availability and access.

- School counselors can identify students' needs for *psychological, counseling, and social services,* refer families to appropriate community service providers, and collaborate with families and community mental health providers to address students' problems.

These types of activities, of course, do not happen without considerable thought, effort, and coordination. Comer's School Development Model (Comer, Haynes, & Joyner, 1996) offers a school-based approach for integrating parents into activities that promote the health and educational achievement of students. Dr. James Comer, a psychiatrist at Yale University, developed the model, which schools throughout the country have adopted. The model involves three teams. A School Planning and Management Team led by the principal includes representatives of teachers, parents, and support staff. It develops and monitors a plan for meeting academic, social climate, and staff development goals. A Parent Team reaches out to parents who have had little involvement with their children's education through PTA and PTO meetings, social events, and other school functions. Some parents serve as volunteers or paid assistants in the school library, cafeteria, and classrooms.

The Parent Team selects parents to serve on the School Planning and Management Team. The Student and Staff Support Team consists of school staff with expertise in child development and mental health: the school psychologist, guidance counselor, school nurse, special education teacher, attendance officer, pupil personnel workers, and other appropriate staff. It meets weekly to address schoolwide climate and psychosocial issues and individual student concerns. It supports parents, teachers, and other staff through facilitating interactions, consultations, workshops, and policy recommendations.

ACTION STEPS FOR IMPLEMENTING FAMILY AND COMMUNITY INVOLVEMENT IN SCHOOL HEALTH

Schools, communities, families and parent organizations, colleges and universities, and state and national organizations can all support family and community involvement in coordinated school health programs.

Schools

To enhance family involvement in school health activities, schools can:

- Communicate their commitment to family involvement through supportive mission and policy statements.
- Encourage staff to create an environment that is accepting of family involvement by welcoming visits from family members, to be available to speak with families at convenient times, and to schedule school events to accommodate a variety of family schedules.
- Acknowledge families as partners of teachers and other staff by providing opportunities for family members to express their concerns and to share in solutions.
- Involve parents and other family members in planning, curriculum, and policy development, and decision making related to school health.
- Reinforce understanding and trusting relationships with parents and help to ensure parental support through efforts such as encouraging teachers to incorporate at-home activities in school assignments.
- Give parental participation a high priority, including giving teachers and staff the time and resources to develop and implement family involvement activities.
- Provide training to develop staff skills for collaboration.
- Invite family participation. A survey in the Oakland County, Michigan schools (Bridge Communications, 1995) revealed that one of the main rea-

sons parents and guardians did not help with health education at school was that no one had ever asked them for help.

- Evaluate family involvement activities and adapt them if they are not meeting their objectives (Birch, 1996).
- Establish frequent, clear communications with families (Bridge Communications, 1996) by informing them of their children's successes as well as problems and using a range of printed materials, phone calls, parent breakfasts, and regular conferences.

Families and Parent Organizations

To enhance school health activities, families can:

- Encourage their children's healthy behaviors by praising appropriate behaviors, guiding them toward television programs and books that communicate health-enhancing values important to the family, and acting as positive health role models for their children.
- Encourage their children to adopt good physical activity and eating habits, for example, by keeping fresh fruits available for snacks, taking walks or riding bicycles as a family, and limiting television time.
- Work to provide for children's physical and mental health services by cooperating with schools and others in the community to identify appropriate providers, arrange for getting children to appointments (including working with the school to minimize disruption of the child's academic program), and seek financial assistance when necessary.
- Learn about and reinforce the skills and messages in their children's health and physical education curricula and, if they are uncomfortable with a message, discuss their concerns with school decision-makers.

Parent organizations can:

- Determine what components of a coordinated school health program exist in their children's school and work with the school and others in the community to strengthen weak components or establish those that are missing.
- Distribute notices and handouts at markets, clinics, community centers, and religious institutions to inform families and other community members about health issues and garner broader community support.

Community Members

To enhance school health activities, community members can:

- Learn more about their local school's health program, especially components that particularly interest them.

- Advocate for school health programs by speaking at community forums, writing letters to the editors of local newspapers, and updating organizations to which they belong.
- Meet with school personnel to determine what support (materials, expertise, time) they can offer to advance the school's or district's health objectives.
- Serve on a school-community committee to coordinate resources, activities, and services for a coordinated school health program or a particular component.
- Encourage radio and cable television stations to interview family members, students, school staff, and individuals in the community who are involved in coordinated school health programs or to feature successful programs or activities that inform the community and reinforce health messages.
- Deliver health messages that are consistent with the messages of the school health program.
- Identify appropriate funding sources and raise funds to support the school health program.
- Nurture relationships between schools and community organizations that can provide young people with the physical and mental health services they need to be healthy, develop normally, and achieve academically.

Joint Actions by Schools, Families, and Others in the Community

The initiator of a partnership among schools, families, students, community members, and community organizations can be a school principal or health coordinator, a school health team, a parent, a district superintendent, a school board member, a community-based organization, a health department, or a concerned citizen. Regardless of who the initiators are, they must take the following action steps.

- *Identify or establish a core group.* Schools can participate in, consult with, or seek advice from an existing school and community advisory group when determining program needs, planning program direction, seeking resources, and recommending policies (American Cancer Society, 1994). If such a group does not exist, another group—for example, a community coalition for Safe and Drug-Free Schools or a school and business committee studying school reform options—might take on the responsibility. Alternatively, a school can initiate a group. Regardless of the group's origin, it must include representatives of schools and of youth and their families. Chapters 2 and 11 in this volume suggest action steps for establishing coalitions. The American School Health Association, Education Development

Center, Inc., ETR Associates, and Search Institute are a few of the many organizations that can offer information on how to establish such a group.

- *Identify a coordinator for school and community health.* An individual, a council, or a team can manage a school and community collaboration. However, a paid coordinator with adequate space in either a school facility or a community agency helps ensure coordination of family, school, and community activities and sustain initiatives (Resnicow & Allensworth, 1996). The coordinator communicates and interfaces with community agencies and other participants; provides periodic updates on progress; and serves as a clearinghouse for resources, activities, issues, and concerns. To be effective, a school health coordinator needs program understanding, programmatic vision, leadership and management skills, program planning and evaluation skills, resource awareness, and communication skills (Davis & Allensworth, 1994). This individual can be an employee of the school, local district, or a community organization, or a parent. In their study of schools that had implemented health education curricula, Smith and others (1995) found that full-time health coordinators who focused both on efforts within the school and external school-centered activities were more effective than either coordinators who had other school respon- sibilities or those who focused exclusively on internal or external coordi- nation.
- *Inventory community needs, resources, and values.* To develop programs that address the needs and values of the community, planners need to know what exists in the school(s) and community, including policies, regulations, and mandates that govern school health activities; ongoing projects and available resources (human, informational, financial, structural); the risk- taking behaviors and health problems of young people; and community concerns and interests that might affect coordinated school health pro- grams. Two ways to conduct this inventory are resource mapping and needs assessment (see Chapters 2 and 7). The needs assessment needs to solicit information from all sectors through questionnaires, formal and informal interviews, and community meetings. During this process, additional play- ers who are interested in becoming involved with a school's health program might emerge.
- *Establish communication mechanisms.* Sharing needs assessment findings or prospective activities with potential collaborators and supporters will broaden support for and understanding of coordinated school health pro- grams. Mechanisms, target audiences, and messages will vary depending on the purpose. For example, a focused effort such as integrating services or establishing a funding network might target selected potential collabora- tors. If the goal is to broaden community support and involvement, a well- publicized community forum might be an appropriate vehicle.

- *Invite participation.* Individuals and groups seeking to become involved in a school health program should feel welcome. Additional players might emerge during the inventory of community resources. Mechanisms should exist to match offers of family or community resources with ongoing programs in the school so they fill gaps rather than duplicate efforts. Some potential participants might need special invitations. A survey sponsored by the National Association of State Boards of Education (Porter/Novelli, 1996) found that corporate managers had not considered participating in school health programs because they had never been asked.
- *Develop an action plan.* Partnerships need goals, objectives, clearly defined tasks and responsibilities, timelines, progress or outcome measures, and strategies for obtaining resources. Guidance is available to help schools and communities plan a health promotion effort (CDC, 1995; Green & Kreuter, 1991).
- *Establish subcommittees.* Because complex tasks are accomplished most effectively by people with the appropriate expertise, the collaboration might choose to organize working groups that represent the components of a coordinated school health program or that address various functions of the plan, such as fund raising or public relations. Each working group might need to perform its own needs assessment, develop its own goals and objectives, and report back to the larger group. Each partner might examine ways of connecting with the organizational goals of other partners. Working groups might find models in other communities useful. The reports and recommendations of the working groups can form the basis for an overall action plan.
- *Implement the plan.* Successful implementation requires effective communication channels, coordination, and follow-through with participants.
- *Measure progress and outcomes.* Evaluations help establish what has happened, suggest adjustments, and plan for the future. Findings can inform the community of progress and convince prospective funders and participants to support future efforts.
- *Celebrate and publicize successes.* The partnership should acknowledge achievements and contributions of individuals and groups to improve the health and educational success of young people.

There are several indications that a partnership is working well:

- It holds regular, well-attended meetings.
- Planned activities address the group's goals.
- The school and community recognize the partnership as a valuable asset in promoting and protecting health.

- The partnership has a positive relationship with the school or district, coalition members, and other collaborators.
- Membership represents all sectors of the community.

Colleges, Universities, and State and National Organizations

There is much that colleges, universities, and state and national organizations can do to support family and community involvement in a school's health program. Many of the action steps suggested here are adaptations of recommendations made for state boards of education and state education agencies (NASBE, 1992).

To demonstrate their commitment, organizations can:

- Develop organizational structures for supporting coordinated school health programs that include staff with responsibility for fostering family and community involvement.
- Meet with families and community groups to encourage their support for coordinated school health programs.
- Include representatives of families and community organizations on school health advisory committees and encourage their participation in public hearings.
- Seek innovative models and exemplary programs that involve families and community agencies in school health activities and publicize their stories.
- Encourage organizational members and staff to become involved in their children's school health programs or to participate in adopt-a-school programs.

To adopt supportive position statements, policies, and standards, organizations can:

- Review programs, standards, and services to identify opportunities for enhancing family and community involvement in coordinated school health programs.
- Designate an office or staff members to develop or review policy, communicate with the field, provide technical assistance, and track and evaluate progress toward involving family and community members in coordinated school health programs.
- Include in standards for accreditation requirements for skills to involve families and seek community input.
- Provide funding for local school health initiatives that include family and community participation.

- Include in education reform grants requirements for community collaboration and family involvement in coordinated school health programs.
- Provide line-item funding for activities that target family and community involvement in coordinated school health programs.

To provide educational opportunities, organizations can:

- Review teacher and administrator certification requirements, professional preparation programs, and staff development activities to ensure that they include skills for involving families and community agencies and resources in coordinated school health programs.
- Train volunteers to advocate for and participate in school and family partnerships and school, family, and community collaborations that support coordinated school health programs.
- Develop training and technical assistance for school staff that supports family and community involvement in coordinated school health programs.
- Include strategies for implementing activities that encourage family and community involvement in school health in professional preparation for school administrators, teachers, counselors, psychologists, social workers, nurses, and others likely to participate in coordinated school health programs.
- Develop interprofessional preservice and inservice programs, including practical field experience, that prepare school health, social services, and human services professionals and educators to collaborate with community agencies.

To encourage more active family and community involvement, organizations can:

- Educate members and constituents about coordinated school health programs and encourage them to become advocates.
- Develop media campaigns that encourage families and other community members to participate in coordinated school health programs.
- Offer grants to strengthen family and community involvement in coordinated school health programs.
- Establish a resource and dissemination center to collect, assess, and share resources that help practitioners network with peers in the community or a directory of consultants experienced in working with young people.
- Sponsor conferences and support publications to disseminate information about exemplary local, state, and national initiatives for enhancing partnerships among schools, families, and other community members.

CONCLUSION

When students enter the school building, they do not leave their assets or their problems and needs at the door. A student preoccupied with physical or mental health problems—such as drug abuse, unplanned pregnancy, gang violence, or family dysfunction—cannot profit from even the best a school has to offer. Schools cannot and should not bear the sole responsibility for the health and welfare of young people. Schools, families, and the community must work together to create school, home, and community climates that include high expectations for young people and a commitment to providing a safe, healthy, supportive environment. With family and community support, coordinated school health programs can help students grow up healthy, achieve academically, and become productive adults.

REFERENCES

American Cancer Society. (1994). *Values and opinions of comprehensive school health education in U.S. public schools: Adolescents, parents, and school district.* Atlanta, GA: Author.

Birch, D. A. (1996). *Step by step to involving parents in health education.* Santa Cruz, CA: ETR Associates.

Blank, M. J., & Danzberger, J. P. (1994). *Developing collaborative community governing bodies: Implications for federal policy.* Washington, DC: Institute for Educational Leadership.

Bridge Communications, Inc. (1995). *Bloomfield Hills School District K–12 health education program evaluation: Highlights of the views of parents, teachers, and support staff.* Birmingham, MI: Author.

Bridge Communications, Inc. (1996). *Healthy teens: Success in high school and beyond.* Birmingham, MI: Author.

Byck Cradle School. (1995). *Dan C. Byck Elementary School, Louisville, Kentucky, Jefferson County Public Schools.* Louisville, KY: Author.

California Department of Education. (1994). *Health framework for California public schools kindergarten through grade twelve.* Sacramento, CA: Author.

Cavazos, L. F. (1989). *Educating our children: Parents and schools together—A report to the president.* Washington, DC: U.S. Department of Education.

Centers for Disease Control and Prevention. (1995). *Planned approach to community health: Guide for the local coordinator.* Atlanta, GA: U.S. Department of Health and Human Services.

Chervin, D. D., & Northrop, D. (1994). *Education and health: Partners in school reform.* Newton, MA: BellSouth Foundation and Education Development Center, Inc.

Comer, J. P., Haynes, N. M., & Joyner, E. T. (1996). The school development program. In J. P. Comer, N. M. Haynes, E. T. Joyner, & M. Ben-Avie (Eds.), *Rallying the whole village: The Comer process for reforming education* (pp. 1–26). New York: Teachers College Press.

Committee for Economic Development. (1985). *Investing in our children: Business and the public schools.* New York: Author.

Comprehensive Health Education Foundation. (1995). *Renewing the partnership: The mainline church in support of public education.* Seattle, WA: Author.

Council of Chief State Officers. (1988). *Early childhood and family education: Foundation for success—A policy statement.* Washington, DC: Author.

Davies, D. (1996, July 10). The 10th school: Where school—family—community partnerships flourish. *Education Week, 15*(40), 44, 47.

Davis, T. M., & Allensworth, D. (1994). Program management necessary component for the comprehensive school health program. *Journal of School Health, 64*(10), 400–404.

Dryfoos, J. G. (1994). *Full-service schools.* San Francisco: Jossey-Bass.

Epstein, J. L. (1995, May). School/family/community partnerships: Caring for the children we share. *Phi Delta Kappan, 76,* 701–712.

Farrow, F. (1994). *Financing school-linked community services and supports.* Washington, DC: American Academy of Pediatrics.

Green, L. W., & Kreuter, M. W. (1991). *Health promotion planning: An educational and environmental approach* (2nd ed.). Mountain View, CA: Mayfield Publishers.

Halford, J. M. (1996). How parent liaisons connect families to school. *Educational Leadership, 53*(7), 34–36.

Hawkins, J. D., Catalano, R. F., & Miller, J. Y. (1992). Risk and protective factors in adolescence and early adulthood. *American Psychological Association Bulletin, 112*(1), 64–105.

Henderson, A. (1987). *The evidence continues to grow: Parent involvement improves student achievement.* Columbia, MD: National Committee for Citizens in Education.

Howell, K., Bibeau, D., Mullen, K., Carr, P., & McCann, K. (1991). *Establishing and maintaining school health advisory councils: A how-to manual for local education agencies.* Raleigh, NC: North Carolina Department of Public Instruction.

Institute for Educational Leadership. (1994). *Linking schools with health and social services: Perspectives from Thomas Payzant on San Diego's new beginnings.* Washington, DC: Author.

Kane, W. M. (1993). *Step by step to comprehensive school health: The program planning guide.* Santa Cruz, CA: ETR Associates.

Marx, E., & Northrop, D. (1995). *Educating for health: A guide for implementing a comprehensive approach to school health education.* Newton, MA: Education Development Center.

Massachusetts Department of Education. (1996a). The FIRST grant: Findings from 30 middle schools on comprehensive health education. Boston: Author.

Massachusetts Department of Education. (1996b, March). *The Massachusetts curriculum frameworks: How adults can help at home and in the community.* Paper presented at the meeting of the University of Massachusetts on New Ways for Families and Schools to Work Together, Boston.

Melaville, A. I., & Blank, M. J. (1993). *Together we can: A guide for crafting a profamily system of education and human services.* Washington, DC: U.S. Department of Education and U.S. Department of Health and Human Services.

National Association of State Boards of Education. (1988). *Right from the start.* Alexandria, VA: Author.

National Association of State Boards of Education. (1992). *Partners in educational improvement: Schools, parents, and the community.* Alexandria, VA: Author.

National Coalition for Parent Involvement in Education. (1995a). *Developing family/school partnerships: A guide for schools and school districts* [brochure]. Washington, DC: Author.

National Coalition for Parent Involvement in Education. (1995b). *Why a coalition for parent involvement?* Washington, DC: Author.

National Education Goals Panel. (1994). *The National Education Goals Report: Building a nation of learners.* Washington, DC: U.S. Department of Education.

National PTA. (1992). *Position statement on comprehensive school health programs.* Chicago: Author.

Newman, I. M., & Farrell, K. A. (1991). *Thinking ahead: Preparing for controversy.* Lincoln, NE: Nebraska Department of Education.

Porter/Novelli. (1996). *Reaching corporations with comprehensive school health messages: Focus groups with corporate employees and in-depth interviews with business leaders* (unpublished). Alexandria, VA: National Association of State Boards of Education.

Resnicow, K., & Allensworth, D. (1996). Conducting a comprehensive school health program. *Journal of School Health, 66*(2), 59–63.

Seffrin, J. R. (1994). Voluntary health organizations: The untapped resource. In P. Cortese & K. Middleton (Eds.), *The comprehensive school health challenge: Promoting health through education* (pp. 861–880). Santa Cruz, CA: ETR Associates.

Siri, D. A. (1994). Community/school partnerships: A vision for the future. In P. Cortese & K. Middleton (Eds.), *The comprehensive school health challenge: Promoting health through education* (pp. 881–897). Santa Cruz, CA: ETR Associates.

Smith, D. W., Steckler, A. B., McCormick, L. K., & McLeroy, K. R. (1995). Lessons learned about disseminating health curricula to schools. *Journal of Health Education, 26*(1), 37–43.

Squires, D. A., et al. (1983). *Effective schools and classrooms: A research-based perspective.* Alexandria, VA: Association for Supervision and Curriculum Development.

Texas Department of Health. (1996). *Healthy children are prepared to learn—School health: Programs in action.* Austin, TX: Author.

U.S. Department of Education. (1994). *Strong families, strong schools: Building community partnerships for learning.* Washington, DC: Author.

Alan Henderson, Dr.P.H., C.H.E.S.
Daryl E. Rowe, Dr.P.H., R.E.H.S.

5 A Healthy School Environment

- *The physical, emotional, and social climate of the school.*
- *Designed to provide a safe physical plant as well as a healthy and supportive environment that fosters learning.*

L itter was almost everywhere in the Palmer School yard: blown up against chain-link fences, overflowing from trash bins, and collecting in stairwells; graffiti defaced the doors. But on a Monday after school vacation, the grounds were raked, the trash emptied, and the doors newly painted. The first annual Clean-up Day was a resounding success. The spruced-up property was not the only reward. The school exuded a new sense of community, born of shared rakes, casual conversations, and concrete accomplishments; and the principal was determined to make it last.

The scenario just described highlights the importance of perhaps the least acknowledged but most pervasive aspect of school life—a school's environment. A school's environment is the thread that connects the multitude of activities on a campus. In many respects this thread is almost invisible, yet everyone experiences its influence. As the Palmer School's students, staff, and community members discovered, positive social relationships and attitudes about school are as important to the environment as are safe and well-kept buildings and grounds. A safe, clean, and well-maintained school with a positive psychosocial climate and culture can boost student and staff self-esteem and health as well as students' educational achievement.

The environment includes physical and aesthetic qualities as well as psy-

Health Is Academic: A Guide to Coordinated School Health Problems. Edited by Eva Marx and Susan Frelick Wooley, with Daphne Northrop. New York: Teachers College Press, 1998. ISBN 0-8077-3713-5 (pbk.), ISBN 0-8077-3714-3 (cloth). Prior to photocopying items for classroom use, please contact the Copyright Clearance Center, Customer Service, 222 Rosewood Dr., Danvers, MA 01923, USA, tel. (508) 750-8400. © 1998 Education Development Center, Inc. All rights reserved.

chosocial culture and climate. A school's physical environment includes the school building and the surrounding grounds. It includes physical conditions such as noise, temperature, and lighting as well as physical, biological, or chemical agents. Some factors that influence the physical environment are the architecture and age of the school building and the neighborhood surrounding the school (Hathaway, 1995; Rowe, 1987). Figure 5.1 provides more details about the composition of the physical environment.

The psychosocial environment encompasses the attitudes, feelings, and values of students and staff. Physical and psychological safety, positive interpersonal relationships, recognizing the needs and successes of the individual, supporting and building self-esteem in students and staff, and support for learning are all part of the psychosocial environment. Factors that influence the psychosocial environment include the organization of a school and the nature of its policies, procedures, and practices, as well as the consistency of their enforcement.

Basic factors that affect other sectors of society also affect school environments. These basic factors include the economy; social, cultural, and religious influences; predominant occupations and businesses; geography; socioeconomic status of students' families; tax bases; and legal, political, and social institutions. Although these factors have a real and potentially significant effect on school environments, they are beyond the control of the school. They might, however, necessitate adjustments to a school's coordinated school health program.

ESSENTIAL FUNCTIONS OF A HEALTHY SCHOOL ENVIRONMENT

A healthy school environment supports learning and contributes to students' health by:

- minimizing distractions
- minimizing physical, psychological, and social hazards
- creating a climate in which students and school staff do their best work
- expecting that all students can succeed
- implementing supportive policies

Minimizing Distractions

Neither students nor teachers can do their best work in classrooms that are too warm or too cold. Poor lighting or inadequate ventilation can also interfere with learning.

Concerns about potential violence also distract both students and staff

FIGURE 5.1. Aspects of a School's Physical Environment

School grounds include:

- shrubs, trees, and grass
- drainage, sidewalks, fencing, and gates
- access to the school for transportation and emergency purposes

Buildings include:

- stairwells, elevators, and hallways
- bathrooms
- closets
- offices
- health and guidance space
- water supply
- auditorium and theater
- gymnasium and locker room
- cafeteria
- library
- classrooms, laboratories, and shops

Other aspects include:

- materials used in floors, walls, and ceilings
- equipment
- signage
- safety provisions
- handicapped access
- maintenance
- snow and ice removal
- acoustics
- waste disposal
- heating, ventilation, and air conditioning

Source: Hathaway, 1995; Rowe, 1987.

from the business of education. Whether in the hallways or lurking outside the school doors, threats of violence can not only distract students, but can also lead to a fatalism that any future orientation in education is pointless: "Why study if I am not going to live to graduate?"

Minimizing Physical, Psychological, and Social Hazards

Almost one out of every two public school buildings in the country contains an environmental hazard, such as asbestos, peeling lead-based paint, radon gas, lead-contaminated water, or biologically contaminated heating and ventilating systems (Kowalski, 1995). When schools reduce or eliminate preventive maintenance, costs are higher in the end. Indoor air contamination might require evacuation of buildings. Delays in renovation result in more deterioration of school facilities and increased costs when funds eventually become available. Run-down physical plants can result in hazards and associated unintentional injuries at school (Gursley, 1991). Playgrounds, which account for the largest percentage of student injuries at school, need close supervision of children, maintenance of equipment, and use of energy-absorbing materials to cushion the shock of falls from slides, swings, and climbing apparatuses (Children's Safety Network at Education Development Center, Inc., 1997; Rowe, 1987).

Instructional materials can also pose hazards. For example, animals, plants, and microorganisms used in some science instruction can create biological hazards. Children with allergies sometimes have adverse reactions to classroom pets such as rabbits or guinea pigs. Many chemical agents used in science, art, and technology education classes in secondary schools require special handling, storage, and disposal. Pottery and jewelry making can expose students and teachers to lead, silica, and toxic pigments.

Violence, which has become commonplace in our schools, poses other sorts of hazards to both students and staff. In 1995, a survey of U.S. high school students revealed that 4.5% of students had missed at least one day of school in the preceding month because they felt unsafe either being at school or going to or from school (Kann et al., 1996). Black and Hispanic students were significantly more likely than white students to report feeling unsafe. During the same 30-day period, one out of ten students and one out of seven males had carried a weapon to school on one or more days. Moreover, one out of twelve students interviewed reported being threatened or injured with a weapon on school property during the preceding year. One out of six had been in a physical fight on school property, and a third had had property stolen or deliberately damaged on school grounds (Kann et al., 1996). In another study one in three Latinos, one in five African Americans, and one in eight whites reported that gangs operated in their schools in 1989 (Rendon & Hope, 1996).

Creating a Climate in Which Students and School Staff Can Do Their Best Work

Climate is a combination of a school's physical and psychological atmospheres. A school's climate affects students, teachers, administrators, and staff alike. The appearance and condition of a school's facilities and grounds significantly affect experiences during the school day (Corcoran, 1986). Flaking ceilings, graffiti-tainted walls, run-down floors, crumbling sidewalks, debris-strewn playgrounds, and leaky toilets can promote a "Why bother, no one cares" attitude among students. By contrast, schools with aesthetic appeal spur students to take more pride in their education (Brown, 1984). Similarly, an inviting and unhurried climate in a school lunchroom can encourage students to eat nutritious meals and interact positively.

The relationship between a school's physical appearance and its psychological climate is often ignored (Hathaway, 1988). Yet deterioration of morale and performance among both students and teachers often accompanies deterioration of the physical plant and equipment, leading to lowered expectations. Negativism about school sets a tone of low expectations and values about school that exacerbates the situation (Hoy, Tarter, & Bliss, 1990), decreasing the quality of teaching, the extent of learning, school attendance, and the rate of school completion. Such conditions can lead to criticism by parents and community members or, worse, apathy toward the schools, or some combination of both (Hawkins & Overbaugh, 1988).

Considerations of how the physical environment affects teaching and learning must go beyond aesthetics. School size appears to affect students' performance. Smaller organizational units, in which adults and young people know each other by name and look out for one another, foster achievement. Large schools can mitigate the distancing that occurs in large, anonymous settings by creating smaller, more personal units. Such "schools-in-schools" allow for stronger connections among students (O'Neil, 1995). Engaging students actively in their own learning, often by working in small groups, tends to enhance academic achievement. However, a space with poor acoustics or with furniture that does not move can hinder small group work. Where schools do not create opportunities for small group bonding, students often create their own structures that sometimes include gangs.

Decisions based on purely physical considerations can have a psychological impact. For instance, when a school assigns the health class to a corner of the cafeteria, the decision sends the message that health issues are not important.

A school's climate also reflects perceptions of fairness and inclusion. When teachers or administrators enforce school policies unevenly, when teachers feel embattled by labor disputes or criticism from vocal community interest groups, or when students from different cultural backgrounds feel excluded from school activities or social groups, a school's climate is unhealthy.

As adult role models, teachers affect the school's climate. A child's behavior is related to the perceived importance of the behavior among significant adults in the child's life (Henderson, 1993). Students are perceptive observers of adults' practices and often pay more attention to what they see than what they hear. Moreover, the school itself can model a healthy environment. For example, a school that regularly maintains its grounds and physical plant reinforces classroom messages of respecting the environment by recycling or caring for equipment such as athletic or playground structures.

Expecting That All Students Can Succeed

Children learn to adapt to the expectations of those in their social environments at home, in school, and within the community. Part of the psychosocial environment is the belief, or lack thereof, that all students can succeed. Families, schools, and communities that value academic achievement and set high standards for children have higher-achieving students. Ideally, the expectations of students' families and teachers will reinforce instruction, encourage student achievement, and model healthy practices. To ensure healthy development, expectations could include ones related to health behaviors, such as engaging in an active lifestyle; eating well-balanced meals; refraining from alcohol, tobacco, and other active drug use; minimizing risk-taking behaviors; and abstaining from sexual activity.

Conflicting expectations of home and school can produce stressful situations for students (Conners, 1983; Kelley, 1981). Health behaviors constitute an arena where expectations (or role models) at home, in the community, and at school are sometimes in conflict. Differences can arise around food choices; exercise patterns; the acceptance of tobacco, alcohol and other drug use; values placed on various forms of sexual expression; and the use of health products and services. Sometimes schools exhibit conflicting expectations internally, such as when school meal offerings conflict with nutrition education in the classroom or when physical exercise or withholding opportunities for physical activity become punishment for student misbehavior, conflicting with the physical education program's effort to encourage physical activity.

Rapid social change, including demographic and economic transformations, also challenges assumptions and expectations. As the population in the United States ages and diversifies, many school staff find themselves working with students from cultures very different from their own. Their lack of familiarity with other cultures could result in inappropriate expectations.

Implementing Supportive Policies

A healthy school environment depends on policies. Schools that want to minimize hazards and distractions to teaching and learning, create a climate in which students and school staff can do their best work, and expect that all students can succeed will ensure that the necessary policies are in place. Such policies typically cover a broad range of health and safety issues, including bans on firearms and other deadly weapons from the school grounds; prohibition of the possession or use of alcohol, tobacco, and other drugs at school; and the exclusion of people who do not have legitimate school business from the school grounds. Policies for a healthy school environment would also include measures such as the sale of nutritious foods in vending machines, adequate time for meals, not using physical activity as punishment, and allowing families and community groups to use school facilities after hours.

However, adoption of policies does not guarantee their implementation. For policies and procedures to be effective, relevant members of the school community must implement them fairly and consistently. Implementation requires developing protocols, training staff, communicating to everyone at school, and sometimes developing task forces that address specific issues and that involve various participants such as the principal, teachers, students and their families, insurers, risk managers, school health professionals, counselors, and health and social service staff.

Supportive policies contribute to a school's psychological climate and how people value the school. Implementing supportive policies helps establish a normative culture. The observation of appropriate policies and procedures embeds a healthy school environment into a school's organization.

WHO IMPLEMENTS THE FUNCTIONS?

Creating a healthy school environment requires the involvement of virtually everyone in the school—students, administrators, teachers, custodial and maintenance staff, school counselors, school nurses, nutrition services workers. In addition, it needs the involvement of families and often outside environmental, public health, public safety, public welfare, and other community agencies.

If *students* feel no ownership for a school, they will have little or no commitment to preserving the physical environment. Students' interactions with fellow classmates and teachers contributes to the general climate of safety and security at school.

School administrators, of course, have overall responsibility for a school's environment—both the physical and psychosocial aspects. At the district level, *superintendents* have responsibility for complying with laws, rules, and education code sections that affect the school environment. Most larger districts assign responsibility for these areas to one or more district personnel. In many districts, *facilities coordinators, risk managers,* or *environmental health specialists* ensure compliance. Smaller districts that cannot support such specialists sometimes share environmental health specialists with other districts or borrow them from health departments. Some schools engage specialists as consultants rather than hiring them as permanent employees.

Although *principals* typically receive scant preparation to deal with the myriad environmental responsibilities they face (Harris, 1992), they have responsibility for the physical, emotional, social, and educational environment in a school building. Principals often delegate authority for many aspects of the school environment to one or more staff members. Some form teams comprised of faculty, custodial staff, environmental health specialists, risk managers, guidance counselors, secretarial staff, cafeteria and food service personnel, students, nurses, and administrators to collaborate on specific environmental issues or the entire environmental plan. A team approach can enhance accountability for the school environment, improve communication with key stake holders, and help ensure adoption and implementation of supportive policies and procedures. A coordinator, designated by the principal, usually provides leadership and continuity for a team. It is critical that the team act as a team, not as a collection of individuals. When each contributor pursues individual priorities and competes with other team members for limited resources and attention, environmental concerns often remain ignored (Henderson, 1993). The principal's commitment to maintain and improve the environment is key.

Teachers influence the school environment through their efforts to encourage student achievement, thoughtfully designed teaching strategies that take into account the health and safety of students, and careful use of materials for decoration. Science, art, home economics, and technology education teachers have responsibility for handling, storing, and disposing of hazardous substances safely; replacing more hazardous substances with less hazardous ones; and ensuring that students receive proper training in the safe use of hazardous materials as part of carefully constructed, well supervised learning experiences (Rowe, 1987). Industrial arts teachers teach and enforce safety standards for machinery and proper use of personal safety equipment. *Physi-*

cal educators, coaches, and *playground aides* make sure equipment and facilities do not present hazards, require students to use protective equipment, and provide supervision to ensure students' physical and psychological safety.

Creative teachers have even found ways to use environmental problems as learning laboratories. For example, the Los Padillas Elementary School in Albuquerque, New Mexico, was in a community with no municipal sewer (Jesperson, 1995). The school's reliance on two elevated leach fields resulted in groundwater contamination. Led by the primary teacher in the environmental education program, the school developed a wetland to treat wastewater, which had the added benefit of providing a wildlife sanctuary.

School counselors and *other mental health staff* can provide leadership for creating positive psychosocial environments. They can also facilitate conflict resolution to reduce threats of violence. School *nurses* often recognize hazardous conditions as they notice patterns of injury or illness. They have responsibility for implementing and training others in the safe handling of blood and other bodily fluids.

Custodial staff ensure the cleanliness of buildings and use appropriate measures to clean up spills promptly. *Maintenance personnel* inspect and repair equipment and keep grounds in good condition. *Office staff,* who are often the first point of contact in a school, play a key role in setting the psychological climate. They also have responsibility for facilitating communication, ensuring the appropriate and timely referral of reported problems, and handling chemicals used in duplicating in a safe manner. *Bus drivers* and *crossing guards* are responsible for students' safety on the way to and from school. *Food service personnel* are responsible for ensuring safe food handling and creating a pleasant cafeteria environment.

Some specialists have expertise in specific aspects of a school's environment. For example, *environmental health specialists* (registered sanitarians) have training in the safe handling of hazardous materials. Such specialists, whether employed by a school, school district, or local public health agency, are responsible for school environments in at least 35 states (Rowe, 1987). They can help schools identify and find solutions to potential and actual hazards at school sites.

Risk managers ensure that school districts have coverage for claims arising as a result of injuries. They also conduct on-site inspections of facilities to identify potentially hazardous situations and devise corrective measures. They review incident reports and worker's compensation claims, and, if a consistent problem emerges, they might develop appropriate training programs for relevant school staff. They can also inform school administrators of relevant federal and state laws, regulations, and education codes and help them comply.

Architects and *builders* create new school sites and buildings and renovate existing facilities. They work with school boards, administrators, parents, students, and interested community members (Goldburg, 1991; Rydeen, 1993). The constraints within which they work include construction code provisions for new buildings and renovations and available fiscal resources.

Every member of the school community serves as a role model for students by engaging in safe practices and being supportive of fellow staff members as well as students, families, and volunteers. Simple words of thanks or acknowledgment of a job well done help create an environment that inspires people to do their best.

SUPPORT FOR A HEALTHY SCHOOL ENVIRONMENT

School personnel working to create a healthy school environment can get support for their efforts from a variety of sources. *Agencies in the community,* such as law enforcement and public health departments, often lend human resources or expertise. For example, it is common for members of the local police department to participate in school programs on safety.

In addition to local school taxes and state per capita subsidies, most schools receive outside *funding* that could support environmental priorities. Although categorical sources rarely specify environmental considerations, they might support specific environmental improvements, such as a more hygienic kitchen, security measures to eliminate weapons from schools, or ramps for wheelchair accessibility.

Experts in national, state, and academic institutions can establish *guidelines* for safe, supportive school environments. For example, many states' education codes provide guidance for building or renovating schools.

Using these guidelines, national, state, or academic institutions could develop *assessment instruments* to help schools evaluate the health of their environment and set priorities for action. University faculty could help schools by reviewing existing *data* sources and determining what additional data sources are needed, such as student-teacher ratios, distribution of students in the school, standardized test scores, drop out and graduation rates, diversity of educational experiences offered during the school day, unintentional/intentional injuries, and reported health problems. The Youth Risk Behavior Survey, conducted by the Centers for Disease Control and Prevention and many state education agencies, provides profiles of student risk behaviors that might help schools determine priorities (Kolbe, Kann, & Collins, 1993).

Publications produced by both governmental and nongovernmental organizations can also be of great use. For example, the Office of Technology Assessment of the U.S. Congress (1995) has published *Risks to Students in*

School. It describes injuries from play, athletics, transportation, and violence; infectious diseases; and illnesses from school materials, indoor air, and school location. Chapter 12 lists other publications available from governmental and nongovernmental organizations.

Professional organizations that represent people with expertise in various aspects of a healthy school environment can provide training for professionals, establish best practice standards, certify professionals, or consult with school staff who need technical assistance. Many have state and local affiliates that offer resources and professional training. Some of the organizations that can provide these types of support are as follows:

- American Association for Health Education
- American Institute of Architects
- American Public Health Association
- American School Health Association
- Association of School Business Officials International
- Athletic Equipment Managers Association
- National Environmental Health Association
- National Operating Committee on Standards for Athletic Equipment
- National Organization on Legal Problems in Education
- National Safety Council
- National School Boards Association
- National School Transportation Association
- Public Risk Management Association

Chapters 11 and 12 also describe national and state organizations that can support healthy school environment efforts.

INTEGRATING A HEALTHY SCHOOL ENVIRONMENT WITH THE OTHER COMPONENTS OF A COORDINATED SCHOOL HEALTH PROGRAM

A healthy school environment is the framework within which the other seven components of a coordinated school health program operate (Council of Chief State School Officers, 1989) and cements relationships among components. Components' effectiveness depends on a supportive and healthy environment (Allensworth & Kolbe, 1987; Allensworth, Wyche, Lawson, & Nicholson, 1995). The following examples illustrate how a healthy school environment both supports and is supported by the other components.

- *Health education* is more effective when the school and community environment reinforces health messages and concepts. For example, prohibiting tobacco usage on campus by students, faculty, staff, and visitors reinforces the messages about the harmful effects of tobacco that students hear in class.

- In the *physical education program,* replacing old or otherwise unsafe equipment reduces hazards to students and teachers alike (Allen & Johnson, 1995).
- By serving tasty, appealing meals in an aesthetically pleasing environment, *school nutrition services* staff enhance the school climate.
- Environmental sanitation measures that prevent the spread of disease support the efforts of *school health services* staff to prevent and control communicable diseases and injuries at school.
- *Staff health promotion* that raises productivity, decreases absenteeism, and improves staff morale and enthusiasm has a positive effect on the entire school community and the learning process.
- *School counseling, psychological, and social services* specialists can help improve a school's psychosocial climate by designing supportive policies, procedures, and interventions aimed at creating a healthy environment, such as conflict resolution processes for reducing violence at school.
- *Families and other community members* have an important role to play in helping schools to set health-enhancing norms and expectations for students, providing appropriate role models, and identifying and resolving conflicts. In addition, their support for improvements to the school's physical environment is often critical for obtaining resources. By involving students, their families, and communities in clean-up campaigns, schools both improve the school environment and build pride in the school as well as a sense of community.

ACTION STEPS FOR IMPLEMENTING A HEALTHY SCHOOL ENVIRONMENT

Creation of a healthy school environment requires action by school administrators and staff together with students and their families and community members. National and state organizations and institutions of higher education also can take steps to support healthy school environments. As with any school reform, change typically takes years to become incorporated into a school's culture. Through a deliberate process, schools can identify and analyze problems, create thoughtful plans for change, monitor implementation and make modifications as needed, and address new challenges as they arise. A healthy school environment constantly adapts while maintaining focus and direction for a school.

Actions for Schools

In order for a school to create and maintain a physically and psychologically healthy, aesthetically pleasing environment, it must have accurate information, supportive leadership, resources, a plan, and a monitoring system. While not necessarily sequentially, schools need to take, and periodically revisit, all the steps described below.

1. Develop and use a data collection system for assessing and monitoring the school environment.

A data collection system can provide information to help decision makers identify the rationale for creating or adapting policies or procedures, develop the content of these policies and procedures, and determine the effectiveness of their implementation. Many data sources exist but rarely does one person have access to all that are relevant. In some schools, risk management and environmental health professionals have established elements of a data collection system. The records of health services and counseling providers are also likely to supply useful information. A reporting system for school staff to provide data on injuries sustained on school grounds can inform decisions about modifications to the physical environment or adult supervision of student activities. Data on student absenteeism and disciplinary actions can offer clues about the psychosocial environment. Data about a school's policies and procedures can contribute to understanding effective remedies. National- and state-level data from sources such as the Centers for Disease Control and Prevention's Youth Risk Behavior Survey can be useful comparisons. For example, if students' use of alcohol or tobacco far exceeds the state or national averages, a school would want to look closely at such findings. By combining these types of data, school staff assemble a picture of the social structures and interactions and physical conditions that influence students' health and academic achievement.

2. Provide leadership and administrative support for creating and sustaining a healthy school environment.

Leaders who articulate their own commitment to improving the school environment facilitate the process of change. But no leader can do the job alone. Therefore, administrative support includes designating a coordinator for environmental initiatives (Rowe, 1986) and providing the human and financial resources needed for improvements.

3. Create a team to identify needs, set priorities, and identify resources.

The team might be an existing group within the school, such as a school improvement team that focuses on school reform and restructuring or a

Healthy School Team (see Chapter 2) that has responsibility for all components of a coordinated school health program. Alternatively, a separate team could focus on environmental issues; in this case, the team should have liaisons to broader teams. The team's recommendations must reflect the basic values and culture of the school and surrounding community. Its membership should include students and other people with experience in a variety of areas and with broad contacts in the school and the larger community. A team can directly, or through contacts of team members, provide the expertise, materials, time, and funds needed to carry out specific projects.

The team can use the data collected in step 1, best practice standards, and the views of the school community in identifying needs and setting priorities for action. In setting priorities, the team must consider local, state, and national events or conditions. For example, a school's current focus on restructuring might be the framework for addressing environmental issues. Communitywide concerns such as gang activity near the school or circumstances of an individual student such as a disability that needs accommodation might dictate priorities. School leaders often bring a vision of the direction in which they want to lead a school. Whatever their origin, priorities help schools focus energy on needed changes and are essential to start the change process.

Because the environment is so broad, schools could consider one or more elements of the environment as a priority each year. Priority setting will help a team select a few projects that have a good probability of success in creating a healthier school environment.

4. Develop and implement a plan for creating and sustaining a healthy school environment.

A plan details the projects and activities that address each priority, the timetable for completing each activity, and benchmarks to assess progress. A plan also identifies who has responsibility for overall coordination of each activity and for securing funding and other needed resources. By selecting a few projects that have a good probability of success, the team will generate enthusiasm, support, and resources for future projects. In addition, projects that involve a broad spectrum of the school community and that reflect shared values can build support for school health and create a sense of pride in the school.

Generally, the more people who have input into a plan, the better the plan and the better its chances of being implemented. A good plan also allows for contingencies because unanticipated events always occur. Revisiting the plan periodically will allow the team to take advantage of new opportunities or address new concerns.

5. Monitor implementation of the plan as well as the school environment.

Monitoring implementation leads to evaluation of the plan. Evaluation assesses how well projects address the priorities and initiates another cycle of needs assessment, planning, implementation, and evaluation.

Actions for National and State Organizations and Universities

1. Foster collaboration among agencies and organizations with an interest in healthy school environments.

Many groups that are interested in elements of the school environment are unaware of each other and thus pursue their work independently. Groups with compatible interests are sometimes in competition for the same resources of time and money. Collaboration might result in a better outcome for less expense. State school health advisory committees or state coalitions of school health professionals and leaders in the community could serve a coordinating function for groups interested in healthy school environments.

Coordination would help to ensure that initiatives target the broad scope of the environment and that collaborators consider the impact that change in one component might have upon the other components. For example, a campaign encouraging students to wear hats to reduce sun exposure might create hazards for children climbing and hanging on playground equipment.

2. Develop trainings that help environmental specialists and school personnel work together more effectively in school settings.

No national standards define the skills needed by environmental health specialists who work in school settings. In addition to covering the necessary technical expertise, such training could include an introduction to school cultures and cross-training that focuses on collaboration in developing effective environmental programs. At the same time administrators, teachers, and other school staff need training on creating and maintaining healthy physical and psychosocial environments in collaboration with environmental health specialists. State education agencies, local and state affiliates of national professional organizations, and colleges and universities could provide such training as both preservice and in-service programs.

3. Identify and share examples of healthy school environments.

As they work with their constituents, state agencies and professional organizations could look for examples of schools that have created healthy school environments through thoughtful, step-by-step processes. These models could inspire other schools and help them avoid costly and time-consuming trial-and-error methods.

4. Collect data and support research on the status and impact of the school environment.

No data source provides a national overview of school environments. Databases on intentional and unintentional injuries sustained at school are not consistent from state to state. While 10 to 20% of all injuries to children and adolescents occur in and around schools, little research has been conducted regarding serious injuries on school grounds (Children's Safety Network at Education Development Center, Inc., 1997). Data on the condition of the schools' physical plants and the status of school policies related to an improved school environment are not available. Although various organizations and agencies collect data on specific environmental hazards and risks at schools, data collection is often inconsistent and reporting is sporadic, making it difficult to compare data across sites or identify trends.

Scant information exists about the effects of policies, climate, and social relationships on educational achievement. Anecdotes and isolated investigations do not provide sufficient basis for improving school environments. Research would help inform schools' efforts in this area. For example, improved waste disposal methods will reduce hazards and improve health and safety, but their effect on other aspects of the school environment is unknown. A uniform inspection of each school in periodic statewide visits could become a source of such data.

CONCLUSION

In addition to being the locus for education activities, schools are sources of employment, social and health services, cultural opportunities, and recreation and entertainment facilities. They are places that help young people develop into capable adults. Because everyone attends school for a significant period, the school experience shapes an individual's outlook, expectations, relationships, and behavior not only while a student but for a lifetime (Henderson, 1993). The quality of the school experience depends to a large extent on the quality of the school's physical and psychosocial environment.

Creating and sustaining a healthy school environment requires a commitment on the part of school personnel, students and their families, and other community members. As with any systemic reorganization, change takes time, sometimes years. Over time, schools identify problems, then analyze them and make changes. Some innovations become institutionalized, some are modified to better meet a school's unique needs, and some are discarded. Even as schools find successful solutions to one set of problems, they find new challenges that arise. Thus, schools' attention to the healthfulness of their environments evolves and adapts to changing circumstances while never losing sight of their primary focus—educating students.

REFERENCES

Allen, S. K., & Johnson, R. R. (1995). A study of hazards associated with playgrounds. *Journal of Environmental Health, 57,* 23–26.

Allensworth, D. D., & Kolbe, L. J. (1987). The comprehensive school health program: Exploring an expanded concept. *Journal of School Health, 57,* 409–412.

Allensworth, D. D., Wyche, J., Lawson, E., & Nicholson, L. (Eds.). (1995). *Defining a comprehensive school health program: An interim report.* Washington, DC: National Academy Press.

Brown, T. F. (1984). Improving school climate—The symptoms vs. the problem. *NASSP Bulletin, 68*(472), 3–7.

Children's Safety Network at Education Development Center, Inc. (1997). *Injuries in the school environment: A resource guide* (2nd ed.) Newton, MA: Education Development Center.

Conners, D. A. (1983). The school environment: A link to understanding stress. *Theory Into Practice, 22,* 15–20.

Corcoran, T. B. (1986). *Improving the quality of work life in public schools.* Philadelphia: Research for Better Schools, Inc.

Council of Chief State School Officers. (1989). *What are the characteristics and components of effective comprehensive school health programs?* Washington, DC: Author.

Goldburg, B. (Ed.). (1991, April-May). Redesigning schools: Architecture and school restructuring, *Radius, 3,* 1.

Gursley, D. (1991). Warning: Your school may be hazardous to your health. *Teacher Magazine, 2,* 34–45.

Harris, E. L. (1992). A principal and the evolution of a school culture: A case study. *Planning and Changing, 23,* 29–44.

Hathaway, W. E. (1988). Educational facilities: Neutral with respect to learning and human performance? *CEFP Journal, 26,* 8–12.

Hathaway, W. E. (1995). Effects of school lighting on physical development and school performance. *Journal of Educational Research, 88,* 228–242.

Hawkins, H. L., & Overbaugh, B. L. (1988). The interface between facilities and learning. *CEFP Journal, 26,* 4–7.

Henderson, A. C. (1993). *Healthy schools, healthy futures: The case for improving school environment.* Santa Cruz, CA: ETR Associates.

Hoy, W. K., Tarter, C. J., & Bliss, J. R. (1990). Organizational climate, school health, and effectiveness. A comparative analysis. *Educational Administration Quarterly, 26,* 260–279.

Jesperson, K. (1995, Summer). Constructed wetland project is nature's classroom. *Small Flows, 9,* 3.

Kann, L., Warren, C. W., Harris, W. A., Collins, J. L., Williams, B. I., Ross, J. G.,

Kolbe, L. J., & State and Local YRBS Coordinators. (1996). Youth Risk Behavior Surveillance—United States, 1995. In *CDC Surveillance Summaries: Morbidity and Mortality Weekly Report, 45*(SS-4).

Kelley, E. A. (1981). Auditing school climate. *Educational Leadership, 39,* 180–183.

Kolbe, L. J., Kann, L., & Collins, J. L. (1993). Overview of the youth risk behavior surveillance system. *Public Health Reports, 108,* 1.

Kowalski, T. (1995). Chasing the wolves from the schoolhouse door. *Phi Delta Kappan, 76,* 486–489.

Office of Technology Assessment, Congress of the U.S. (1995). *Risks to students in school.* Washington, DC: U.S. Government Printing Office.

O'Neil, J. (1995). On lasting school reform: A conversation with Ted Sizer. *Educational Leadership, 52,* 4–9.

Rendon, L. I., & Hope, R. O. (1996). *Educating a new majority: Transforming America's educational system for diversity.* San Francisco: Jossey-Bass.

Rowe, D. E. (1986). Safety in the science laboratory. *The Georgia Science Teacher, 24*(1), 5–8.

Rowe, D. E. (1987). Healthful school living: Environmental health in the school. *Journal of School Health, 57,* 426–431.

Rydeen, J. E. (1993). Designs for learning. *American School Board Journal, 180,* 34–36.

SUGGESTED ADDITIONAL READING

Allensworth, D. D. (1994). The research base for innovative practices in school health education at the secondary level. *Journal of School Health, 64,*180–187.

Berner, M. M. (1993). Building conditions, parental involvement and student achievement in District of Columbia public school system. *Urban Education, 28,* 6–29.

Bogden, J. F. (nd). *Prevention for a healthy future: The role of schools.* Alexandria, VA: National Association of State Boards of Education.

Boyd, V. (1992). *School context: Bridge or barrier for change?* Austin, TX: Southwest Educational Development Laboratory.

Brubaker, C. W. (1988). These 21 trends will shape the future of school design. *American School Board Journal, 175,* 31–33.

Cardellichio, T. L. (1995). Curriculum and the structure of the school. *Phi Delta Kappan, 76,* 629–632.

Christopher, G. (1988). Does the quality of the school environment affect the quality of our children's education? *CEFP Journal, 26,* 21–23.

Clark, T. A., & McCarthy, D. P. (1983). School improvement in New York City: The evolution of a project. *Educational Researcher, 12*(4), 17–24.

Defriese, G., Crossland, C., Macphail-Wilcox, B., & Sowers, J. (1990). Implementing comprehensive school health programs: Prospects for change in American schools. *Journal of School Health, 60,* 182–187.

Dryfoos, J. G. (1994). *Full service schools.* San Francisco: Jossey-Bass.

DuFour, R. (1995). Restructuring is not enough. *Educational Leadership, 52,* 33–36.

Dwyer, D. C. (1985). *Understanding the principal's contribution to instruction: Seven principals, seven stories.* San Francisco: Far West Laboratory.

Elam, S. M., Rose, L. C., & Gallup, A. M. (1994). The 26th annual Phi Delta Kappa/ Gallup poll on the public's attitudes toward the public schools. *Phi Delta Kappan, 76*(1), 42–56.

Frost, P. J., Moore, L. F., Louis, M. R., Lundberg, C. C., & Martin, J. (1985). *Organizational culture.* Beverly Hills, CA: Sage Publications.

Fruchter, N., Silvestri, K. L., & Green, H. (1985). Public policy and public schools: A training program for parents. *Urban Education, 20*, 199–203.

Fullan, M. G., & Miles, M. B. (1992). Getting reform right: What works and what doesn't. *Phi Delta Kappan, 73*, 745–752.

Fuller, B., & Clarke, P. (1994). Raising school effects while ignoring culture?: Local conditions and the influence of classroom tools, rules, and pedagogy. *Review of Educational Research, 64*, 119–157.

Garmston, R., & Wellman, B. (1995). Adaptive schools in a quantum universe. *Educational Leadership, 52*, 6–12.

Glass, T. E. (1994). Do you know buildings? Facility planning knowledge and skills. *School Business Affairs, 60*, 16–19.

Gonder, P. O., & Hymes, D. (Eds.). (1994). *Improving school climate and culture: AASA critical issues.* Arlington, VA: American Association of School Administrators.

Hoy, W. K., & Feldman, J. A. (1987, Summer). Organizational health: The concept and its measure. *Journal of Research and Development in Education, 20*(4), 30–37.

Kleborg, J. R. (1985). Planning for security. *CEFP Journal, 23*, 18–19.

Kober, N. (1994). *Caring schools, caring communities: An urban blueprint for comprehensive school health and safety.* Washington, DC: Council of Great City Schools.

Lott, J. G. (1995). When kids dare to question their education. *Educational Leadership, 52*, 38–42.

McCormack-Larkin, M. (1985). Ingredients of a successful school effectiveness project. *Educational Leadership, 42*, 31–37.

Melville, B., Brown, D., Segree, W., Paul, T., & Donaldson, A. (1995). Development of a questionnaire for assessing the school environment. *International Quarterly of Community Health Education, 15*, 15–20.

Miller, N. L. (Ed.). (1995). The healthy school handbook. Washington, DC: National Education Association.

Miller, S. K. (1982). School learning climate improvement: A case study. *Educational Leadership, 40*, 36–37.

Mitchell, J. T., & Willover, D. J. (1992). Organizational culture in a good high school. *Journal of Educational Administration, 30*, 6–16.

Newacheck, P. W., & Taylor, W. R. (1992). Childhood chronic illness: Prevalence, severity, and impact. *American Journal of Public Health, 82*, 364–371.

Newmann, F. M., Ruter, R. A., & Smith, M. S. (1989). Organizational factors that affect school sense of efficacy, community and expectations. *Sociology of Education, 62*, 221–238.

Ornstein, A. C. (1994). School finance and the conditions of schools. *Theory Into Practice, 33*, 118–125.

Perreira, C. (1994). Violence in the schools: Can we make them safe again? *Update on Law-Related Education, 18,* 45–48.

Report of the Task Force on Education of Young Adolescents. (1989). *Turning points: Preparing American youth for the 21st century.* Washington, DC: Carnegie Council on Adolescent Development.

Roche, L. M. (1995). Reducing carcinogens in public schools: A non-regulatory approach by a regulatory agency. *Journal of Environmental Health, 57,* 23–26.

Roesner, L. (1995). Changing the culture at Beacon Hill. *Educational Leadership, 52,* 28–32.

Ross, J. G., Einhause, K. E., Hohenemser, L. K., Greene, B. Z., Kann, L., & Gold, R. S. (1995). School health programs and policy study: School health policies prohibiting tobacco use, alcohol and other drug use, and violence. *Journal of School Health, 65*(8), 333–338.

Safe schools: A planning guide for action. (1989). Sacramento, CA: California Department of Education.

Safety initiatives in urban public schools. (1993). Washington, DC: Council of Great City Schools.

Schulz, E. W., Glass, R. M., & Kamholtz, J. D. (1987). School climate: Psychological health and well-being in school. *Journal of School Health, 57,* 432–435.

Smith, W. M., & Andres, R. L. (1989). *Instructional leadership: How principals made a difference.* Alexandria, VA: Association for Supervision and Curriculum Development.

Sydoriak, D. (1993). Designing schools for all kids. *Educational Facility Planner, 31,* 15–17.

Taylor, A., & Gousie, G. (1988). The ecology of learning environments for children. *CEFP Journal, 26,* 23–28.

Toffler, A., & Toffler, H. (1994). *Creating a new civilization: The politics of the third wave.* Atlanta, GA: Turner Publishing, Inc.

Violence in the schools: A national, state, and local crisis. (1994). Albany: New York State Department of Education.

Wilson, C. C., & Wilson, E. A. (Eds.) (1969). *Healthful school environments* (2nd ed.). Washington, DC: National Education Association and American Medical Association.

Vernal D. Seefeldt, Ph.D.

6 Physical Education

- ○ *Planned, sequential instruction that promotes lifelong physical activity.*
- ○ *Designed to develop basic movement skills, sports skills, and physical fitness as well as to enhance mental, social, and emotional abilities.*

Every effort should be made to encourage schools to require daily physical education in each grade and to promote physical activities that can be enjoyed throughout life. (USDHHS, 1996)

From the time of the ancient Greeks and the early Chinese philosophers, educators have recognized that children and youth need physical activity as well as mental pursuits to do their best. Physical education has long been part of the K–12 school curriculum in the United States because of the belief that physical activity is essential for healthy growth and development (McKenzie, 1913; McCurdy, 1920; Brace, 1927; Rogers, 1929; Robinson, 1938; Rarick, 1974; Bailey, Malina, & Mirevald, 1986; Malina, 1992, 1994). Indeed, regular physical activity is associated with many benefits for both physical and mental health (American College of Sports Medicine [ACSM], 1988; Blair, 1995; Dishman, 1995; Fletcher et al., 1992; Pollock, Fergenbaum, & Brechue, 1995; U.S. Department of Health and Human Services [USDHHS], 1991, 1996). People who exercise regularly—children and adults alike—see improvements in blood pressure, depression and anxiety, weight control, and the health of bones, muscles, and joints. Adults who exercise reduce their risk of heart disease, diabetes, high blood pressure, and

Health Is Academic: A Guide to Coordinated School Health Problems. Edited by Eva Marx and Susan Frelick Wooley, with Daphne Northrop. New York: Teachers College Press, 1998. ISBN 0-8077-3713-5 (pbk.), ISBN 0-8077-3714-3 (cloth). Prior to photocopying items for classroom use, please contact the Copyright Clearance Center, Customer Service, 222 Rosewood Dr., Danvers, MA 01923, USA, tel. (508) 750-8400. © 1998 Education Development Center, Inc. All rights reserved.

colon cancer. Lack of physical activity as well as dietary factors contribute to an estimated 300,000 deaths in the United States each year (McGinnis & Foege, 1993).

Schools are uniquely positioned to teach children and youth the benefits of lifetime physical activity because they serve nearly all children and have facilities and equipment as well as staff with the expertise to provide instruction and supervision. Moreover, there is evidence that quality school-based physical education can contribute to the health of children and the adults they will become (American Heart Association, 1995; Pate et al., 1995a)

Periodic reports about the low level of physical fitness among America's youth—beginning as early as the 1950s—spurred many schools to take steps to promote increased physical activity among their students (Kraus & Hirshland, 1953; American Medical Association, 1957; Hunsicker, 1958; Hunsicker & Reiff, 1966; Wilmore, 1982; Lacy & Marshall, 1984; Ross & Gilbert, 1985; Novello, DeGraw, & Kleinman, 1992). Yet, the number of adolescents who participate in daily physical education has declined in recent years, from 42% in 1991 to 25% in 1995 (Centers for Disease Control and Prevention [CDC], 1996). Nearly half of American young people aged 12–21 are not vigorously active on a regular basis. Moreover, moderate to vigorous physical activity declines sharply with age among adolescents (CDC, 1996). Because many of the precursors to unhealthy lifestyles, such as inactivity and poor dietary habits, begin in childhood and are well established by adolescence (McGinnis, 1992), intervention must begin during childhood and continue throughout adolescence. Physical education that emphasizes moderate to vigorous activity can increase students' knowledge about ways to be physically active (Arbeit et al., 1992), the amount of physical activity in physical education classes (Luepker et al., 1996; McKenzie, Sallis, Faucette, Roby, & Kolody, 1993; Simons-Morton, Parcel, Baranowski, Forthofer, & O'Hara, 1991), and students' physical fitness levels (Arbeit et al., 1992; Duncan, Boyce, Itami, & Paffenbarger, 1983; Dwyer, Coonon, Leitch, Hetzel, & Baghurst, 1983; Shephard & Lavallee, 1994a, 1994b; VanDongen et al., 1995).

Recommendations in support of organized physical activity for children come from numerous quarters, including the American Academy of Pediatrics (1987), the American College of Sports Medicine (1988), the American Association of School Administrators (1991), the American Heart Association (Fletcher et al., 1992), the American Medical Association (1994), the Centers for Disease Control and Prevention (1997), the International Consensus Conference on Physical Activity Guidelines for Adolescents (Sallis & Patrick, 1994), and the National Association for Sport and Physical Education (1991, 1992b, 1994; USDHHS, 1991). Figure 6.1 presents a summary of the statements on physical activity, fitness, and health issued by these and other national agencies and organizations. The most specific calls for action

FIGURE 6.1. Pronouncements of Professional Organizations on Physical Activity, Fitness, and Health

Organization	Year	Title of Publication	Purpose or Focus
American Academy of Pediatrics	1987	"Physical Fitness and the Schools"	Urges pediatricians to persuade school boards to maintain or increase physical education programs, with an emphasis on lifetime physical activities.
American College of Sports Medicine	1988	"Physical Fitness in Children and Youth"	Lists eight recommendations for the adoption of lifelong physical activity, with an emphasis on school physical education programs.
American Heart Association	1986	"Coronary Risk Factor Modification in Children: Exercise" (Riopel et al., 1986)	Reviews the ways lifelong physical activity can be initiated in childhood.
American Heart Association	1992	"Benefits and Recommendations for Physical Activity Programs for All Americans" (Fletcher et al., 1992)	Reviews the benefits of physical activity and defines the role of medical professionals, parents, schools, employers, community groups, and the insurance industry in the implementation of exercise programs.
American Heart Association	1995	*Strategic Plan for Promoting Physical Activity*	Identifies physical activity behavior change and knowledge outcomes for youth and educational policy outcomes supporting physical education.
American Medical Association	1994	*Guidelines for Adolescent Preventive Services*	Recommends that pediatricians provide annual health guidance to adolescents about the benefits of exercise and encourage them to engage in safe exercise on a regular basis.

Organization	Year	Title	Description
American Medical Association	1994	"Cardiovascular Health and Diseases in Children: Current Status" (Moller, Taubert, Allen, Clark, & Lauer, 1994)	Outlines the heart health needs of the next generation of young people and describes barriers to progress.
Carnegie Council on Adolescent Development	1989	*Turning Points: Preparing American Youth for the 21st Century*	Advocates fostering the health and fitness of youth as a means of attaining academic success. Targets adolescents who are at risk for failure to achieve their potential.
Centers for Disease Control and Prevention	1997	"Guidelines for School and Community Programs to Promote Lifelong Physical Activity Among Young People"	Makes 10 broad recommendations for school and community health programs to promote lifelong physical activity.
Centers for Disease Control and Prevention and the American College of Sports Medicine	1995	"Physical Activity and Public Health" (Pate et al., 1995a)	Outlines major issues relating physical activity to health and recommends actions for public health agencies, health professionals, communities, educators, individuals, and families.
International Consensus Conference on Physical Activity Guidelines for Adolescents	1994	"Physical Activity Guidelines for Adolescents: Consensus Statement" (Sallis & Patrick, 1994)	Provides age-specific guidelines for adolescents with suggestions for implementation in primary care settings.
Michigan Governor's Council on Physical Fitness, Health, and Sports	1995	*The Importance of Physical Activity for Children and Youth* (Pivarnik, 1995)	Provides the scientific basis for physical activity in childhood and adolescence and advocates policies for families, communities, public health, and schools.
National Association for Sport and Physical Education	1992	*Developmentally Appropriate Physical Education for Children* (1992a)	Provides a rationale for physical education based on developmental age and lists appropriate and inappropriate practices for teachers of physical education.

FIGURE 6.1. Continued

Organization	Year	Title of Publication	Purpose or Focus
National Association for Sport and Physical Education and Council on Physical Education for Children	1994	*Developmentally Appropriate Practices in Movement Programs for Young Children Ages 3–5*	Defines physical activity experiences that are appropriate for young children.
National Association for Sport and Physical Education and Middle and Secondary School Physical Education Council	1995	*Appropriate Practices in Middle School Physical Education*	Defines physical activity experiences that are appropriate for middle school students.
National Heart, Lung, and Blood Institute	1992	"Physical Activity and Cardiovascular Health: Special Emphasis on Women and Youth" (Lenfant, 1992)	Provides the recommendations of 10 working groups on the relationship of physical activity and cardiovascular health in women and youth.
Second International Consensus Symposium on Physical Activity, Fitness, and Health	1994	*Physical Activity, Fitness, and Health: International Proceedings and Consensus Statement* (Bouchard, Shephard, & Stephens, 1994)	Presents evidence from the biological, social, and behavioral sciences on the interactions between physical activity and health.
National Education Goals Panel	1995	*The National Education Goals Report: Building a Nation of Learners*	Advocates access for all young people to school-based health and physical education to promote health and fitness.
U.S. Department of Health and Human Services	1996	*Physical Activity and Health: A Report of the Surgeon General*	Reports that people of all ages can improve their health and quality of life through lifelong, moderate physical activity.
U.S. Department of Health and Human Services, Public Health Service	1991	*Healthy People 2000: National Health Promotion and Disease Prevention Objectives*	Presents 300 measurable health objectives, including seven with direct implications for school-based physical education programs.

FIGURE 6.2. *Healthy People 2000* Objectives with Relevance for the K–12
Physical Education Curriculum

1.3 Increase to at least 30% the proportion of people aged 6 and older who
engage regularly, preferably daily, in light to moderate physical activity
for at least 30 minutes per day.

1.4 Increase to at least 20% the proportion of people aged 18 and older and
to at least 75% the proportion of children and adolescents aged 6
through 17 who engage in vigorous physical activity that promotes the
development and maintenance of cardiorespiratory fitness 3 or more
days per week for 20 or more minutes per occasion.

1.5 Reduce to no more than 15% the proportion of people aged 6 and older
who engage in no leisure-time physical activity.

1.6 Increase to at least 40% the proportion of people aged 6 and older who
regularly perform physical activities that enhance and maintain muscular
strength, muscular endurance, and flexibility.

1.7 Increase to at least 50% the proportion of overweight people aged 12 and
older who have adopted sound dietary practices combined with regular
physical activity to attain an appropriate body weight.

1.8 Increase to at least 50% the proportion of children and adolescents in 1st
through 12th grade who participate in daily school physical education.

1.9 Increase to at least 50% the proportion of school physical education class
time that students spend being physically active, preferably engaged in
lifetime physical activities.

Source: Objectives are excerpted from USDHHS, 1991.

to increase physical activity among young people address public school physical education programs (USDHHS, 1991). *Healthy People 2000,* the national
health objectives of the U.S. Public Health Service (USDHHS, 1991), includes seven objectives that have direct implications for the K–12 physical
education curriculum (Figure 6.2).

There can be no doubt that school-based physical education can make
an important contribution to the health of the next generation of Americans.
The next section reviews the functions of a school-based physical education
program.

ESSENTIAL FUNCTIONS OF PHYSICAL EDUCATION

Standards developed by the National Association for Sport and Physical Education (NASPE) delineate the essential functions of physical education (1995b). According to these standards, physical education should produce students who can

- *Demonstrate competency in many movement forms and proficiency in a few.* Students should acquire competency and proficiency in fundamental and specialized movement skills during childhood and in using these skills as the basis for participation in a variety of physical activities in adulthood.
- *Apply movement concepts and principles to the learning and development of motor skills.* Students should learn to use cognitive information to enhance the learning of movement skills by applying concepts to real-life situations and in the acquisition of new skills.
- *Exhibit a physically active lifestyle.* Students should learn to adopt a physically active lifestyle by participating in a variety of activities in addition to those in physical education classes and should acquire an understanding of the relationship between physical activity and physiological, social, and emotional well-being.
- *Achieve and maintain a health-enhancing level of physical fitness.* Students should learn to design, establish, and maintain an activity program that is sufficient in intensity and duration to acquire an appropriate level of health-related physical fitness—to include cardiorespiratory endurance, muscular strength and endurance, flexibility and body composition—and accept responsibility for leading an active, healthy lifestyle.
- *Demonstrate responsible personal and social behavior in physical activity settings.* Students should learn to recognize and demonstrate responsible personal and social behavior in settings where sport and physical activities are conducted. Responsible personal and social behaviors include engaging in safe practices; adhering to rules and procedures; practicing etiquette, cooperation, and teamwork; displaying ethical conduct; and engaging in positive social interactions.
- *Demonstrate understanding and respect for differences among people in physical activity settings.* Students should develop respect and understanding for differences among individuals in physical activity, including differences in culture, ethnicity, motor performance, disabilities, physical characteristics, race, gender, and socioeconomic status.
- *Understand that participation in physical activity provides opportunities for enjoyment, challenge, self-expression, and social interaction.* Students should develop an awareness of the intrinsic benefits that accompany participation in physical activity.

The standards draw on a history of physical education in the K–12 curriculum that considers what content should be taught, at what grade level, and by whom. NASPE's *Guidelines for Elementary School Physical Education* (1994), *Guidelines for Middle School Physical Education* (1992b), and *Guidelines for Secondary School Physical Education* (1991) support the standards. The standards and associated guidelines address expected student performance at each level, qualifications of teachers, content of the instructional program, facilities and equipment needed, organization and administration of the physical education program, and the relationship of physical education to other programs in the school and community.

The School Health Policies and Program Study (SHPPS) revealed that 94% of states in the U.S. and 95% of school districts require some physical education (Pate et al., 1995b). But because the number of students who engage regularly in active pursuits decreases during adolescence (CDC, 1996), an additional function of physical education must be to make physical activity enjoyable and increase students' feelings of competence for sustained participation in physical activity. Feelings of competence and enjoyment rank high among the reasons why young people engage in organized sports (Biddle & Goudas, 1996; Dempsey, Kimiecik, & Horn, 1993; Ferguson, Yesalis, Pomrehn, & Kirkpatrick, 1989; Kimiecik, Horn, & Shurin, 1996; Reynolds et al., 1990; Tappe, Duda, & Menges-Ehrnwald, 1990; Zakarian, Hovell, Hofstetter, Sallis, & Keating, 1994).

The Centers for Disease Control and Prevention's *Guidelines for School and Community Programs to Promote Lifelong Physical Activity Among Young People* (1997) suggest policies, activities, and instruction that can help schools achieve the essential functions outlined above. The guidelines include ten recommendations for school and community programs that can help young people establish and maintain physical activity:

1. *Policy:* Establish policies that promote enjoyable, lifelong physical activity.
2. *Environment:* Provide physical and social environments that encourage and enable young people to engage in safe and enjoyable physical activity.
3. *Physical education curricula and instruction:* Implement sequential physical education curricula and instruction in grades K–12.
4. *Health education curricula and instruction:* Implement health education curricula that feature active learning strategies and follow the National Health Education Standards (Joint Committee on National Health Education Standards, 1995) and help students develop the knowledge, attitudes, and skills they need to adopt and maintain a healthy lifestyle.
5. *Extracurricular activities:* Provide extracurricular physical activity pro-

grams that offer diverse, developmentally appropriate activities—both competitive and noncompetitive—for all students.

6. *Family involvement:* Encourage parents and guardians to support their children's participation in physical activity, to be physically active role models, and to include physical activities in family events.

7. *Training:* Provide training to enable teachers, coaches, recreation and health care staff, and other school and community personnel to promote enjoyable, lifelong physical activity to young people.

8. *Health services:* Assess the physical activity patterns of young people, refer them to appropriate physical activity programs, and advocate for physical activity instruction and programs for young people.

9. *Community programs:* Provide a range of developmentally appropriate community sports and recreation programs that are attractive to all young people.

10. *Evaluation:* Regularly evaluate physical education instruction, programs, and facilities.

The goals that physical educators have set for the 1990s build on recent scientific evidence of the importance of physical activity for good health and long life and provides direction for reforming physical education curricula (American Academy of Pediatrics, 1987; American College of Sports Medicine, 1988; American Heart Association, 1995; Fletcher et al., 1992; Freedson & Rowland, 1992; McGinnis, Kanner, & DeGraw, 1991; Pate et al., 1995a; Sallis & McKenzie, 1991; Simons-Morton, O'Hara, Simons-Morton, & Parcel, 1987). The goals place a high priority on increasing physical activity among young people and helping them understand the role that activity has in a healthy lifestyle. In this respect physical education has heeded the calls of proponents of physical activity (Simons-Morton, O'Hara, Simons-Morton, & Parcel, 1987; Blair, Clark, Cureton, & Powell, 1989; Corbin, 1986; Freedson & Rowland, 1992) and numerous professional organizations (see Figure 6.1) to address the concerns of public health as well as promote physical competence and performance standards.

These goals represent a shift in emphasis that has far-reaching implications for how schools define and address appropriate physical education. However, the shift away from an emphasis on competitive sports to helping students gain competence in movement skills and an understanding of lifetime physical activity is far from complete. Two nationwide studies of the cardiovascular endurance, muscular endurance, and body composition of school-aged children (Ross & Gilbert, 1985; Ross & Pate, 1987) and the National Children and Youth Fitness Study (NCYFS I and II) revealed that many physical education curricula did not promote achievement of the test items or devote sufficient class time to permit students to reach the desired physical fitness objectives (Ross, Dotson, Gilbert, & Katz, 1985). The more recent School Health Programs and Policies Study (SHPPS) revealed that the activities most commonly included in physical education curricula are competitive team sports such as basketball rather than lifetime physical activities such as aerobic dance (Pate et al., 1995b).

The NCYFS I and II and SHPPS studies point to a need for reorienting as well as making changes in the professional preparation of physical education teachers. Although recommended competencies for physical education teachers as well as teacher preparation curricula designed to meet the competencies exist (Corbin, 1990, 1991; NASPE, 1995b), professional development for teachers who currently provide physical education must take place before schools can offer physical education that achieves the essential functions. Supportive materials, procedures, and evaluative components that have evidence of effectiveness are needed to promote widespread change.

WHO IMPLEMENTS PHYSICAL EDUCATION?

NASPE's position papers on elementary (1994), middle (1992b), and secondary school (1991) physical education recommend that those who teach physical education have grade level-specific preparation in the discipline. However, the qualifications and competencies—the certification of teachers in physical education—vary widely from state to state.

At the elementary school level, only eight states require those who teach physical education to have certificates in physical education (Pate et al., 1995b). A survey of elementary schools in California found that specialists taught only 7% of elementary school physical education (Sallis & McKenzie, 1991).

At the secondary school level, SHPPS found that the physical education teaching corps was experienced: 82.8% had taught five or more years. But only 54% of the lead teachers of physical education had majored in physical education. Twenty-four percent had a joint major in health and physical education. Among all secondary teachers responsible for physical education, 74% had certification in either physical education or health and physical education, and the balance had professional preparation in an unrelated discipline (Pate et al., 1995b).

Because schools offer opportunities for students to engage in physical activity outside physical education classes, the playground aides, coaches, and athletic trainers employed by schools also contribute to achieving the essential functions of physical education. Coaches play an important role in promoting physical activity among school-age youth. However, those involved in school-based athletics have rarely collaborated or cooperated with those involved in community-based athletics, even when both groups serve the same clients and use the same facilities (Ewing, Seefeldt, & Brown, 1997). Similarly, although physical educators teach fundamental movement and motor skills, they are conspicuously absent in the administration, supervision, and coaching of community-based youth sports where young people use those skills.

Most coaches of youth sports are people who volunteer when their own children participate. The lack of trained adult coaches and the attrition of parent-as-coach in youth sports provide opportunities for physical education specialists in schools to educate volunteer coaches to help ensure that all the organized physical activities for young people are safe, enjoyable, and healthful. *Quality Standards for Athletic Coaches* (NASPE, 1995c), which delineates competencies to coach at various levels of sport involvement, might serve as a useful guide for both educating volunteer coaches and selecting athletic coaches for schools.

In selecting physical educators, school administrators might consider not only applicants' certification but also the accreditation of the degree program from which applicants graduated. The National Council for the Accreditation of Teacher Education (NCATE) works with the National Association for Sport and Physical Education (NASPE) to accredit physical education professional preparation programs. NCATE/NASPE's 25 curricular requirements for accreditation of basic programs of teacher preparation in physical education reflect NASPE's national standards for physical education (1995a) and for beginning physical education teachers (1995b). However, only a small proportion of degree-granting institutions seek NASPE/NCATE accreditation (Young, 1996).

WHO SUPPORTS PHYSICAL EDUCATION?

The most longstanding and prominent national organization for professional physical education teachers and other professionals concerned with physical activity is the National Association for Sport and Physical Education (NASPE). NASPE is the only national association that has as a primary responsibility the promotion of physical education in the pre-K–12 grades. NASPE's parent organization, the American Alliance for Health, Physical Education, Recreation, and Dance (AAHPERD), is comprised of six national associations, of which NASPE is the largest, and six regional associations.

Several other national organizations work to promote physical activity in educational settings: the National Association of Physical Education in

Higher Education (NAPEHE), the American College of Sports Medicine (ACSM), and the National Association of Governor's Councils on Physical Fitness and Sports. As its name suggests, NAPEHE is involved in issues directly related to physical education in colleges and universities. ACSM is a research-based professional organization that focuses on physical education, exercise physiology, and sports medicine. ACSM's journal, *Medicine and Science in Sports and Exercise,* and other journals such as *Pediatric Exercise Science* and AAHPERD's *Research Quarterly for Exercise and Sport* are good sources of information about research on physical activity and health among children and adolescents, factors influencing physical activity among young people, and interventions to promote physical activity among youth. The National Association of Governor's Councils on Physical Fitness and Sports serves as the parent organization for more than 30 state and territorial Governor's Councils on Physical Fitness and Sports.

Three federal agencies actively promote physical activity in educational settings: the National Center for Chronic Disease Prevention and Health Promotion of the Centers for Disease Control and Prevention (CDC); the National Heart, Lung, and Blood Institute of the National Institutes of Health (NIH); and the President's Council on Physical Fitness and Sports. CDC provides scientific and technical leadership and assistance to states, national organizations, and professional groups to promote physical activity. Its support includes involving researchers and professional organizations in the preparation and dissemination of reports and guidelines, such as *Physical Activity and Health: A Report of the Surgeon General* (USDHHS, 1996) and *Guidelines for Schools and Community Programs to Promote Lifelong Physical Activity Among Young People* (CDC, 1997). CDC also provides limited funding to 13 states for development of an infrastructure for coordinated school health programs that include physical education. In addition, CDC awards grants to national organizations that promote key physical activity messages to children and sponsors the Physical Activity and Nutrition Project for Adolescents (PAN project). Finally, CDC has established the Youth Risk Behavior Surveillance System to survey physical activity among adolescents and the School Health Policies and Programs Study to monitor coordinated school health programs that include physical education.

The NIH supports research on efficacy of school efforts to increase physical activity and other activities that reduce cardiovascular risk factors (Luepker et al., 1996). The President's Council on Physical Fitness and Sports advises the president and the secretary of health and human services on matters involving physical activity, physical education, physical fitness, and sports that enhance and improve health. The council enlists the support of individuals, civic groups, businesses, voluntary organizations, and others in its efforts.

INTEGRATING PHYSICAL EDUCATION WITH THE OTHER COMPONENTS
OF A COORDINATED SCHOOL HEALTH PROGRAM

Physical education shares with the other components of a coordinated school health program the roles of addressing the current needs of students and developing skills, values, and knowledge to sustain behaviors that promote health, such as physical activity. This shared concern for students' well-being can be the basis for collaboration among numerous professionals in school and community settings. Among the potential collaborators are health educators, physical educators, nurses, physicians, school counselors, classroom teachers, athletic directors, recreation directors, dietitians, athletic trainers, coaches, family members, food-service personnel, and staff of community programs that serve young people.

When all school staff broaden their perspectives and integrate their work with others, student health, including physical activity, can become a priority within a school. CDC's *Guidelines for School and Community Programs to Promote Lifelong Physical Activity Among Young People* (1997) suggest broad strategies for a coordinated effort to increase the physical activity levels of young people. There are many ways the physical education component of a coordinated school health program can benefit from and contribute to the other components. Teaching movement and sport skills, as well as involving students in health-related physical activities within the school setting, is the province of professional physical educators, athletic coaches, and designated classroom teachers. Health education and physical education curricula overlap when they explore the health benefits of physical activity and include behavioral skills such as decision making, planning, and problem solving related to physical activity. In addition, both seek to enhance students' self-confidence and self-esteem. Coordinated curriculum planning between health educators and physical educators could maximize scarce curricular time in each discipline and ensure that the content in one class supports and reinforces that in the other (CDC, 1997). In addition, other content areas can highlight physical activity through classroom activities. Art projects can create bumper stickers with physical education messages or teach sculpture of the human body's muscle structure; writing projects can focus on athletes or on fitness themes; math projects can teach students to calculate calories, heart rate, and fat grams; and science classes can include the study of body chemistry (Berryman & Breighner, 1994).

When physical activities occur beyond the bounds of scheduled classes or athletic events, or when the required expertise exceeds the competence of the physical education specialist, collaboration with other professionals will increase the effectiveness of a school's physical education. Such collaboration could prove effective in developing students' skills for adopting and maintaining lifelong physical activity (health education); helping students realistically assess and evaluate weight gain or loss, performing physical examinations required for students' participation in sports, developing exercise prescriptions for students with special needs, and treating activity-related injuries (health services); helping troubled students regain emotional stability (counseling, psychological, and social services); addressing issues related to risk management, legal liabilities, insurance, and discipline (school environment); attending to prevention and care of injuries (environment and health services); and providing foods that meet athletes' special needs (nutrition services). In each of these situations, physical education can benefit from a well-defined, stable, functional network of professional partners whose common goal is the promotion of lifelong physical activity.

Physical educators, in turn, have expertise that can be useful to those with primary responsibility for other components of a school health program. For example, physical educators can help *school nutrition services* staff design interventions for students and staff who are struggling to manage their weight. Because students often turn to physical education teachers or coaches for help with personal problems, physical educators can be an important source of referrals for students needing *counseling, psychological, or social services.* Physical activity can, in turn, contribute to improved mental health. Physical educators also have an important role to play in *health promotion for staff.* By encouraging other school staff to participate in physical activities at school, physical educators contribute to the health of both staff members and the students for whom they are role models.

Physical educators can contribute to *a healthy school environment* by refusing to use physical activity as a disciplinary tool (CDC, 1997). They also play a key role in ensuring safe and hazard-free spaces and facilities for physical activity. A Healthy School Team (see Chapter 2) can be the forum in which physical educators coordinate these activities with other school staff.

There are many opportunities for *family and community involvement.* Perhaps most importantly, families serve as role models and sources of support and encouragement for physical activity (Anderssen & Wold, 1992; Biddle & Goudas, 1996; Butcher, 1985; Freedson & Evenson, 1991; Garcia et al., 1995; McMurray et al., 1993; Perusse, Tremblay, LeBlanc, & Bouchard, 1989; Reynolds et al., 1990; Sallis, Patterson, Buono, Atkins, & Nader, 1988; Sallis et al., 1992; Stucky-Ropp & DiLorenzo, 1993; Zakarian, Hovell, Hofstetter, Sallis, & Keating, 1994). By involving their children in family activities that include physical activity, such as family hikes or bicycling, several times a week, parents can build healthy habits at home and reinforce the messages about physical activity their children hear at school. Family members also can support the development of appropriate physical education opportunities by learning about the school's physical education program and insisting that schools provide developmentally appropriate physical activities for all students. They can work with school personnel and community members to develop community standards that require volunteer coaches to become educated about safe practices and ways to make physical activity enjoyable for all young people (NASPE, 1995a). They can also work with schools to develop family fitness fairs to demonstrate the school's commitment to fitness and give community members an opportunity to enjoy the school's facilities. For their part, schools can ensure that before- or after-school physical activity opportunities involve not only students and school staff but families and other members of the community as well.

Community organizations and facilities, such as parks and recreation departments, religious organizations, YWCAs and YMCAs, Boys and Girls Clubs, public and private gymnasiums, golf courses, tennis courts, swimming pools, and private health clubs, can complement and supplement school efforts to increase the activity level of students and their families. Approximately 38 million children and youth participate annually in community-sponsored youth sports (Ewing, Seefeldt, & Brown, 1997), and another 5.8 million in interscholastic athletics (National Federation of State High School Associations, 1995). Thus, nearly 70% of the children and youth in the United States between the ages of 6 and 18 participate in at least one organized sport each year (Seefeldt & Ewing, 1992). However, the attrition rate in sports participation reaches 75% by age 15. Although there are many reasons why young people stop participating, an increased emphasis on competition in lieu of developing physical and social skills can often dampen students' interest and enjoyment (Ewing & Seefeldt, 1988).

There are many ways community-based organizations can help to combat this trend toward declining participation. They can expand their efforts to recruit and accommodate all segments of the population—ethnic minorities, the poor, and people with physical or cognitive disabilities. Youth agencies and recreation centers can support schools' efforts to increase physical activity among youth by providing opportunities for students to develop an interest and become skilled in tennis, swimming, and softball, activities that can be pursued at all stages in life. They can tailor their physical activity programs to the needs and skill levels of participants, especially children and adolescents, rather than adopting the one-program-suits-all approach. They also can hire competent instructors who are certified in the specific activities they teach. Community organizations can also offer a mix of competitive and noncompetitive programs. In addition, they can work with *school health services* personnel and community physicians in counseling young people about the value of increasing their physical activity levels.

There is much that school-based physical educators can do to enhance community programs and ensure that their activities complement those sponsored by the school. They can become involved with the governing bodies that control youth sports and recreation programs in the school and community to ensure that the health and safety of young people are the foremost concerns of administrators and coaches. They can help recruit coaches, secure funds, and identify facilities so that school and community youth sports and recreation programs become an extension of the school's physical education program and have sufficient resources to accommodate the needs and interests of all children. Finally, physical educators can serve as a community resource for information about programming that promotes lifelong physical activity.

ACTION STEPS FOR IMPLEMENTING PHYSICAL EDUCATION

The prevalence of sedentary living among people of all ages and segments of American society and its effects on health and well-being suggests the need for a multifaceted offensive (Kolbe & Newman, 1984; Ward & Bar-Or, 1986; King, 1991; Booth, Bauman, Oldenburg, Owen, & Magnus, 1992; Kuntzleman & Reiff, 1992; Moller, Taubert, Allen, Clark, & Lauer, 1994; Blair, 1995), as does the fact that millions of Americans have tried and rejected activity programs (Hart Research and Associates, 1993). Involving more Americans, especially young people, in lifelong physical activity requires support from school administrators and collaboration with the other components of a coordinated school health program.

Action Steps for Schools

School administrators can take the following steps, consistent with *Guidelines for School and Community Programs to Promote Lifelong Physical Activity Among Young People* (CDC, 1997), to ensure that schools do their part to prepare physically educated citizens:

- Provide effective, enjoyable instructional programs of physical education, preferably daily, for all students in kindergarten through grade 12.
  —Have a written physical education curriculum with objectives stated as outcomes. The content should reflect the health-related concerns of the local community and mesh with instruction in health and other content areas. The curriculum should be developmentally sequenced and the content should be consistent with the national standards for physical education (NASPE, 1995a).

—Ensure that the focus of physical education classes is on generating the knowledge, motor skills, behavioral skills, positive attitudes, and confidence that students need to engage in lifelong activity.

—Allocate sufficient class time to accomplish physical education objectives.

—Ensure teacher-student ratios for physical education classes that are comparable to those for other subjects.

—Monitor classes regularly, paying attention to students' safety and enjoyment levels.

- Offer programs that meet the needs of special populations.
  —Provide modified physical education to students with low levels of fitness, physical or cognitive disabilities, or chronic health conditions.
  —Teach fundamental movement skills that prepare children to learn the sports and physical activities of their culture.

- Ensure that qualified staff deliver physical education programs.
  —Hire professionals who are competent to teach the knowledge, motor, and behavioral skills needed for participation in lifelong physical activity and who can instill the positive attitudes and confidence needed to engage in lifelong physical activity.
  —Provide staff development opportunities to improve the delivery of physical education.

- Develop and enforce policies that support physical education.
  —Make physical education compulsory for all students, even those who participate in band, chorus, cheerleading, interscholastic sports, or other extracurricular programs.
  —Do not usurp physical education spaces and facilities for other events.
  —Discourage using or withholding physical activity as a disciplinary tool.
  —Provide opportunities for students to develop appropriate levels of health-related physical fitness.
  —Review policies periodically and make revisions and improvements as necessary.
  —Identify physical activity and health education standards developed by professional organizations and build them into policy.

- Create an environment that supports physical activity as part of a coordinated school health program (Kane, 1993).
  —Give students opportunities to engage in healthy behaviors, including physical activity, before, during, and after school hours.
  —Reward students and school staff who engage in healthy behaviors.

—Encourage all school staff to serve as role models for a physically active lifestyle.

—Make available to teachers, other school staff, and community personnel the equipment and training they need to provide activity opportunities for all students, including those with unique needs.

—Maintain up-to-date profiles on students' health status that include physical, social, and emotional fitness.

—Use posters and videos, drawing on student work when possible, to build awareness of the academic, mental, and physical benefits of physical education.

—Facilitate communication and collaboration between physical educators and those with primary responsibility for other academic areas and other components of a coordinated school health program.

• Involve families and communities in the promotion of physical activity.

—Work with families and others in the community to develop awareness of the need for physical activity.

—Encourage physical education teachers to form partnerships with families for the promotion of lifelong physical activity.

—Provide physical education homework that students can do with their families.

—Encourage community organizations to use school facilities for physical activity during nonschool hours.

—Encourage physical education teachers to work closely with community organizations to integrate physical education and physical activity programs.

—Build partnerships with local businesses to publicize the benefits of physical activity and physical education programs.

• Systematically assess physical education programs and outcomes and use the results for program improvement.

Action Steps for State and National Organizations and Institutions of Higher Education

Broad-based state and national efforts must reinforce the messages about physical activity that students get in school. The federal government, volunteer health organizations, philanthropic foundations, firms that specialize in medical research and development, state health and education departments, and the professional preparation and research arms of colleges and universities all have a role to play. National and state groups and colleges and universities can:

- Promote physical activity as a measure to prevent chronic disease.
- Collaborate with local agencies to share best practices and effective solutions.
- Develop and disseminate assessment systems that individuals can use to determine their health status.

State organizations, businesses, and governments can:

- Allow third-party reimbursement for health care providers who regularly assess and counsel children and their families about physical activity.
- Provide incentives through health insurance and employee wellness programs to students and school staff who engage in active lifestyles.
- Assess outcomes in physical education as routinely as other subject matter areas.
- Develop state guidelines that recommend the frequency, duration, and quality of offerings in physical education.
- Hold schools accountable for state guidelines on quality physical education.
- Provide staff development opportunities to improve the delivery of physical education.
- Adopt and enforce certification requirements that are consistent with national standards for those who teach physical education (NASPE, 1995b).
- Ensure the quality of school buildings and facilities used for students' and school staff's physical activities and provide funds for construction of safe facilities for physical activity.

Colleges and universities can:

- Refine and enhance the quality of preservice and inservice education that addresses physical education as a component of a multidisciplinary coordinated school health program.
- Seek accreditation by the National Council for the Accreditation of Teacher Education for programs that prepare physical educators for schools.
- Help schools design and assess physical education offerings.
- Conduct research that can inform and support school physical education.

National organizations, foundations, and the federal government can:

- Fund research that targets physical activity for young people.
- Include in the health care reform agenda incentives for participation in physical activity.

CONCLUSION

Physical education is an indispensable component of school programs and one that can improve public health (McGinnis, Kanner, & DeGraw, 1991; Morris, 1991; Nelson, 1991; Pate, Corbin, Simons-Morton, & Ross, 1987). Based on the undisputable evidence that a healthy body promotes a healthy mind, many schools have acknowledged their responsibility to encourage lifetime physical activity among young people. Those that are having the greatest success have implemented physical education as part of a coordinated school health program, require students to engage in daily physical activity, and have put in place programs that support the objectives of *Healthy People 2000* (USDHHS, 1991) and follow *CDC's Guidelines for School and Community Programs to Promote Lifelong Physical Activity Among Young People* (1997). These and other tools exist for schools to use. It is up to schools to provide the commitment to the health of the next generation.

REFERENCES

American Academy of Pediatrics. (1987). Physical fitness and the schools. *Pediatrics, 80*(3), 449–450.

American Association of School Administrators. (1991). *Healthy kids for the year 2000: An action plan for the schools.* Arlington, VA: Author.

American College of Sports Medicine. (1988). Physical fitness in children and youth. *Medicine and Science in Sports and Exercise, 20*(4), 422–423.

American Heart Association. (1995). *Strategic plan for promoting physical activity.* Dallas, TX: Author.

American Medical Association. (1957). Fitness of American youth. *JAMA, 165,* 54–55.

American Medical Association. (1994). *AMA Guidelines for Adolescent Preventive Services (GAPS): Recommendations and rationale.* A. B. Elster & N. J. Kuznets (Eds.). Baltimore, MD: Williams & Wilkins.

Anderssen, N., & Wold, B. (1992). Parental and peer influences on leisure-time physical activity in young adolescents. *Research Quarterly for Exercise and Sport, 63*(4), 341–348.

Arbeit, M. L., Johnson, C. C., Mott, D. S., Harsha, D. W., Nicklas, T. A., Webber, L. S., & Berenson, G. S. (1992). The Heart Smart cardiovascular school health promotion: Behavior correlates of risk factor change. *Preventive Medicine, 21,* 18–32.

Bailey, D. A., Malina, R. M., & Mirevald, R. L. (1986). Physical activity and growth of the child. In F. Falkner & J. Tanner (Eds.), *Human growth: Vol. 2. Postnatal growth, neurobiology* (pp. 147–170). New York: Plenum Press.

Berryman, J. C., & Breighner, K. W. (1994). *Modeling healthy behavior: Actions and attitudes in schools.* Santa Cruz, CA: ETR Associates.

Biddle, S., & Goudas, M. (1996). Analysis of children's physical activity and its association with adult encouragement and social cognitive variables. *Journal of School Health, 66*(2), 75–78.

Blair, S. (1995). Exercise prescriptions for health. *Quest, 47,* 338–353.

Blair, S. N., Clark, D. B., Cureton, K. J., & Powell, K. E. (1989). Exercise and fitness in childhood: Implications for a lifetime of health. In C. V. Gisolfi, & D. L. Lamb (Eds.), *Perspectives in exercise science and sports medicine: Vol. 2. Youth, exercise and sport* (pp. 401–430). Indianapolis, IN: Benchmark Press.

Booth, M., Bauman, A., Oldenburg, B., Owen, N., & Magnus, P. (1992). Effects of a national mass-media campaign on physical activity participation. *Health Promotion International, 7,* 241–247.

Bouchard, C., Shephard, R. J., & Stephens, T. (Eds.). (1994). *Physical activity, fitness, and health: International proceedings and consensus statement.* Champaign, IL: Human Kinetics.

Brace, D. K. (1927). Measurement of achievement in physical education. *American Physical Education Review, 32*(8), 563–568.

Butcher, J. (1985). Longitudinal analysis of adolescent girls' participation in physical activity. *Sociology of Sport Journal, 2,* 130–143.

Carnegie Council on Adolescent Development. (1989). *Turning points: Preparing American youth for the 21st century.* New York: Carnegie Corporation.

Centers for Disease Control and Prevention. (1996, September 27). CDC Surveillance Summaries, 1995. *Morbidity and Mortality Weekly Report, 45* (SS-4).

Centers for Disease Control and Prevention. (1997). Guidelines for school and community programs to promote lifelong physical activity among young people. *Morbidity and Mortality Weekly Report, 46* (RR-6), 1–36.

Corbin, C. B. (1986). Fitness is for children: Developing lifetime fitness. *Journal of Physical Education, Recreation, and Dance, 57,* 82–84.

Corbin, C. B. (1990). The evolving undergraduate major. In C. B. Corbin & H. Eckert (Eds.), *The academy papers: The evolving body of knowledge* (No. 23, pp. 1–4). Champaign, IL: Human Kinetics.

Corbin, C. B. (1991). A multidimensional, hierarchical model for physical fitness: A basis for integration and collaboration. *Quest, 43,* 296–306.

Dempsey, J. M., Kimiecik, J. C., & Horn, T. S. (1993). Parental influence on children's moderate to vigorous physical activity participation: An expectancy-value approach. *Pediatric Exercise Science, 5,* 151–167.

Dishman, R. K. (1995). Physical activity and public health: Mental health. *Quest, 47,* 362–385.

Duncan, B., Boyce, W. T., Itami, R., & Paffenbarger, N. (1983). A controlled trial of a physical fitness program for fifth grade students. *Journal of School Health, 53*(8), 467–471.

Dwyer, T., Coonan, W. E., Leitch, D. R., Hetzel, B. S., & Baghurst, R. A. (1983). An investigation of the effects of daily physical activity on the health of primary school students in South Australia. *International Journal of Epidemiology, 12,* 308–313.

Ewing, M., & Seefeldt, V. (1988). *Participation and attrition patterns in agency-*

sponsored and interscholastic sports. North Palm Beach, FL: Sporting Goods Manufacturers Association.

Ewing, M., Seefeldt, V., & Brown, T. (1997). *Role of organized sport in the education and health of American children and youth.* New York: Carnegie Corporation.

Ferguson, K. J., Yesalis, C. E., Pomrehn, P. R., & Kirkpatrick, M. B. (1989). Attitudes, knowledge, and beliefs as predictors of exercise intent and behavior in schoolchildren. *Journal of School Health, 59*(3), 112–115.

Fletcher, G. F., Blair, S. N., Blumenthal, J., Caspersen, C., Chaitman, B., & Epstein, S. (1992). Benefits and recommendations for physical activity programs for all Americans: A statement for health professionals by the Committee on Exercise and Cardiac Rehabilitation, American Heart Association. *Circulation, 96,* 340–344.

Freedson, P. S., & Evenson, S. (1991). Familial aggregation in physical activity. *Research Quarterly for Exercise and Sport, 62*(4), 384–389.

Freedson, P. S., & Rowland, T. (1992). Youth activity versus youth fitness: Let's redirect our efforts. *Research Quarterly for Exercise and Sport, 63,* 133–136.

Garcia, A. W., Norton Broda, M. A., Frenn, M., Coviak, C., Pender, N.J., & Ronis, D. L. (1995). Gender and developmental differences in exercise beliefs among youth and prediction of their exercise behavior. *Journal of School Health, 65*(6), 213–219.

Hart Research and Associates. (1993, October 15–20). *American attitudes toward physical activity & fitness: A national survey.* Peter D. Hart research material survey. Washington, DC: Author.

Hunsicker, P. A. (1958). First tabulations from the AAHPERD physical fitness, test battery. *Journal of Health, Physical Education and Recreation, 29,* 24–25.

Hunsicker, P. A., & Reiff, G. G. (1966). A survey and comparison of youth fitness, 1958–1965. *Journal of Health, Physical Education, and Recreation, 37,* 23–25.

Joint Committee on National Health Education Standards. (1995). *National health education standards: Achieving health literacy. An investment in the future.* Atlanta, GA: American Cancer Society.

Kane, W. M. (1993). *Step by step to comprehensive school health: The program planning guide.* Santa Cruz, CA: ETR Associates.

Kimiecik, J. C., Horn, T. S., & Shurin, C. S. (1996). Relationships among children's beliefs, perceptions of their parents' beliefs, and their moderate-to-vigorous physical activity. *Research Quarterly for Exercise and Sport, 67*(3), 324–336.

King, A. C. (1991). Community interventions for promotion of physical activity and fitness. *Exercise and Sport Sciences Reviews, 19,* 211–257.

Kolbe, L., & Newman, I. (1984). The role of school health education in preventing heart, lung and blood diseases. *Journal of School Health, 54,* 15–26.

Kraus, H., & Hirshland, R. P. (1953). Muscular fitness and health. *Journal of Health, Physical Education, and Recreation, 24,* 17–19.

Kuntzleman, C. T., & Reiff, G. (1992). The decline of American children's fitness levels. *Research Quarterly for Exercise and Sport, 63,* 107–111.

Lacy, E., & Marshall, B. (1984). Fitness program: An answer to physical fitness improvement for school children. *Journal of Physical Education, Recreation and Dance, 55,* 18–19.

Lenfant, C. (1992). Physical activity and cardiovascular health: Special emphasis on women and youth. *Medicine and Science in Sports and Exercise, 24,* S191.

Luepker, R. V., Perry, C. L., McKinlay, S. M., Nader, P. R., Parcel, G. S., Stone, E. J., Webber, L. S., Elder, J. P., Feldman, H. A., Johnson, C. C., Kelder, S. H., & Wu, M. (1996). Outcomes of a field trial to improve children's dietary patterns and physical activity: The Child and Adolescent Trial for Cardiovascular Health (CATCH). *JAMA, 275*(10), 768–776.

Malina, R. M. (1992). Physical activity and behavioral development during childhood and youth. In N. G. Norgan (Ed.), *Physical activity and health* (pp. 101–120). London: Cambridge University Press.

Malina, R. M. (1994). Physical activity: Relation to growth, maturation and physical fitness. In C. Bouchard, R. Shephard, & T. Stephens (Eds.), *Physical activity, fitness and health: International proceedings and consensus statement* (pp. 918–930). Champaign, IL: Human Kinetics.

McCurdy, J. H. (1920). Physical efficiency as a national asset. *American Physical Education Review, 25,* 101–106.

McGinnis, J. M. (1992). The public health burden of a sedentary lifestyle. *Medicine and Science in Sports and Exercise, 24*(Suppl.), S196–S200.

McGinnis, J. M., & Foege, W. H. (1993). Actual causes of death in the United States. *JAMA, 270,* 2207–2212.

McGinnis, J. M., Kanner, L., & DeGraw, C. (1991). Physical education's role in achieving the national health objectives. *Research Quarterly for Exercise and Sport, 62,* 138–142.

McKenzie, R. R. (1913). The influence of exercise on the heart. *American Journal of the Medical Sciences, 145,* 69–75.

McKenzie, T. L., Sallis, J. F., Faucette, N., Roby, J. J., & Kolody, B. (1993). Effects of a curriculum and inservice program on the quantity and quality of elementary physical education classes. *Research Quarterly for Exercise and Sport, 64*(2), 178–187.

McMurray, R. G., Bradley, C. B., Harrell, J. S., Bernthal, P. R., Frauman, A. C., & Bangdiwala, S. I. (1993). Parental influences on childhood fitness and activity patterns. *Research Quarterly for Exercise and Sport, 64*(3), 249–255.

Moller, J., Taubert, K., Allen, H., Clark, E., & Lauer, R. (1994). Cardiovascular health and diseases in children: Current status. *Circulation, 89,* 923–930.

Morris, H. H. (1991). The role of school physical education in public health. *Research Quarterly for Exercise and Sport, 62,* 143–147.

National Association for Sport and Physical Education. (1991). *Guidelines for secondary school physical education.* Reston, VA: AAHPERD Publications.

National Association for Sport and Physical Education. (1992a). *Developmentally appropriate physical education for children.* Reston, VA: AAHPERD Publications.

National Association for Sport and Physical Education. (1992b). *Guidelines for middle school physical education.* Reston, VA: AAHPERD Publications.

National Association for Sport and Physical Education. (1994). *Guidelines for elementary school physical education.* Reston, VA: AAHPERD Publications.

National Association for Sport and Physical Education. (1995a). *Moving into the future: National standards for physical education.* St. Louis: C. V. Mosby.

National Association for Sport and Physical Education. (1995b). *National standards for beginning physical education teachers.* Reston, VA: AAHPERD Publications.

National Association for Sport and Physical Education. (1995c). *Quality standards for athletic coaches.* Reston, VA: AAHPERD Publications.

National Association for Sport and Physical Education and the Council on Physical Education for Children. (1994). *Developmentally appropriate practices in movement programs for young children ages 3–5.* Reston, VA: AAHPERD Publications.

National Association for Sport and Physical Education and Middle and Secondary School Physical Education Council. (1995). *Appropriate practices in middle school physical education.* Reston, VA: AAHPERD Publications.

National Education Goals Panel. (1995). *The national education goals report: Building a nation of learners.* Washington, DC: U.S. Government Printing Office.

National Federation of State High School Associations. (1995). *Summary: 1994–95 Athletic Participation Survey.* Kansas City, MO: National Federation of State High School Associations.

Nelson, M. (1991). The role of physical education and children's activity in the public health. *Research Quarterly for Exercise and Sport, 62,* 148–150.

Novello, A. C., DeGraw, C., & Kleinman, D. V. (1992). Healthy children ready to learn: An essential collaboration between health and education. *Public Health Reports, 107,* 3–10.

Pate, R. R., Corbin, C. B., Simons-Morton, B., & Ross, J. G. (1987). Physical education and its role in school health promotion. *Journal of School Health, 57,* 445–450.

Pate, R. R., Pratt, M., Blair, S. N., Haskell, W. L., Macera, C. A., Bouchard, C., Buchnere, D., Ettinger, W., Heath, G. W., King, A. C., Kriska, A., Leon, A. S., Marcus, B. H., Morris, J., Paffenbarger, R. S., Jr., Patrick, K., Pollock, M. L., Rippe, J. M., Sallis, J., & Wilmore, J. H. (1995a). Physical activity and public health: A recommendation from the Centers for Disease Control and Prevention and the American College of Sports Medicine. *JAMA, 273*(5), 402–407.

Pate, R. R., Small, M. L., Ross, J. G., Young, J. C., Flint, K. H., & Warren, C. W. (1995b). School physical education. *Journal of School Health, 65,* 312–318.

Perusse, L., Tremblay, A., LeBlanc, C., & Bouchard, C. (1989). Genetic and environmental influences on level of habitual physical activity and exercise participation. *American Journal of Epidemiology, 129*(5), 1012–1022.

Pivarnik, J. (1995). *The importance of physical activity for children and youth.* Lansing, MI: Michigan Governor's Council on Physical Fitness, Health, and Sports.

Pollock, M. L., Fergenbaum, M. S., & Brechue, W. F. (1995). Exercise prescription for physical fitness. *Quest, 47,* 320–337.

Rarick, G. L. (1974). Exercise and growth. In W. Johnson & E. Buskirk (Eds.), *Science and medicine in exercise and sport* (2nd ed., pp. 306–321). New York: Harper & Row.

Reynolds, K. D., Killen, J. D., Brown, S. W., Maron, D. J., Taylor, M. D., Maccoby, N., & Farquhar, J. W. (1990). Psychosocial predictors of physical activity in adolescents. *Preventive Medicine, 19,* 541–551.

Riopel, D., Boerth, R., Coates, T., Henneken, C., Miller, W., & Weidman, W. (1986).

Coronary risk factor modification in children: Exercise. Dallas, TX: American Heart Association.

Robinson, S. (1938). Experimental studies in physical fitness in relation to age. *Arbeitsphysiology, 10,* 251–323.

Rogers, F. R. (1929). *Educational objectives in physical education.* New York: A. S. Barnes and Co.

Ross, J. G., Dotson, C. O., Gilbert, G. G., & Katz, S. J. (1985). What are kids doing in school physical education? *Journal of Physical Education, Recreation, and Dance, 77,* 73–76.

Ross, J. G., & Gilbert, G. G. (1985). The national children and youth fitness study. A summary of findings. *Journal of Health, Physical Education, Recreation, and Dance, 56,* 44–51.

Ross, J. G., & Pate, R. R. (1987). The National Children and Youth Fitness Study II: A summary of findings. *Journal of Health, Physical Education, Recreation, and Dance, 58,* 51–56.

Sallis, J. F., Alcaraz, J. E., McKenzie, T. L., Hovell, M. F., Kolody, B., & Nader, P. R. (1992). Parental behavior in relation to physical activity and fitness in 9-year-old children. *American Journal of Diseases of Children, 146,* 1383–1388.

Sallis, J. F., & McKenzie, T. L. (1991). Physical education's role in public health. *Research Quarterly for Exercise and Sport, 62,* 124–137.

Sallis, J. F., & Patrick, K. (1994). Physical activity guidelines for adolescents: Consensus statement. *Pediatric Exercise Science, 6,* 302–314.

Sallis, J. F., Patterson, T. L., Buono, M. J., Atkins, C. J., & Nader, P. R. (1988). Aggregation of physical activity habits in Mexican-American and Anglo families. *Journal of Behavioral Medicine, 11*(1), 31–41.

Seefeldt, V., & Ewing, M. (1992). *An overview of youth sports in the United States.* Washington, DC: Carnegie Council on Adolescent Development.

Shephard, R. J., & Lavallee, H. (1994a). Changes of physical performance as indicators of the response to enhanced physical education. *Journal of Sports Medicine and Physical Fitness, 34*(4), 323–335.

Shephard, R. J., & Lavallee, H. (1994b). Impact of enhanced physical education on muscle strength of the prepubescent child. *Pediatric Exercise Science, 6,* 75–87.

Simons-Morton, B. G., O'Hara, N. M., Simons-Morton, D. G., & Parcel, G. S. (1987). Children and fitness: A public health perspective. *Research Quarterly for Exercise and Sport, 58,* 295–303.

Simons-Morton, B. G., Parcel, G. S., Baranowski, T., Forthofer, R., & O'Hara, N. M. (1991). Promoting physical activity and a healthful diet among children: Results of a school-based intervention study. *American Journal of Public Health, 81*(8), 986–991.

Stucky-Ropp, R. C., & DiLorenzo, T. M. (1993). Determinants of exercise in children. *Preventive Medicine, 22,* 880–889.

Tappe, M. K., Duda, J. L., & Menges-Ehrnwald, P. (1990). Personal investment predictors of adolescent motivational orientation toward exercise. *Canadian Journal of Sport Sciences, 15*(3), 185–192.

U.S. Department of Health and Human Services. (1991). *Healthy people 2000: Na-*

tional health promotion and disease prevention objectives. Washington, DC: U.S. Department of Health and Human Services, Public Health Service. DHHS Publication No. (PHS) 91-50212.

U.S. Department of Health and Human Services. (1996). *Physical activity and health: A report of the Surgeon General.* Atlanta, GA: U.S. Department of Health and Human Services, Centers for Disease Control and Prevention, National Center for Chronic Disease Prevention and Health Promotion.

VanDongen, R., Jenner, D. A., Thompson, C., Taggart, A. C., Spickett, E. E., Burke, V., Beilin, L. J., Milligan, R. A., & Dunbar, D. L. (1995). A controlled evaluation of a fitness and nutrition intervention program on cardiovascular health in 10- to 12-year-old children. *Preventive Medicine, 24,* 9–22.

Ward, D., & Bar-Or, O. (1986). Role of the physician and physical education teacher in the treatment of obesity at school. *Pediatrician, 13,* 44–51.

Wilmore, J. (1982). Objectives for the nation: Physical fitness and exercise. *Journal of Physical Education, Recreation and Dance, 53,* 41–43.

Young, J. (1996). National Association for Sport and Physical Education, Reston, VA (Personal communication).

Zakarian, J. M., Hovell, N. F., Hofstetter, C. R., Sallis, J. F., & Keating, K. J. (1994). Correlates of vigorous exercise in a predominately low SES and minority high school population. *Preventive Medicine, 23,* 314–321.

Howard Adelman, Ph.D.

7 School Counseling, Psychological, and Social Services

○ Activities that focus on cognitive, emotional, behavioral, and social needs of individuals, groups, and families.
○ Designed to prevent and address problems, facilitate positive learning and behavior, and enhance healthy development.

School systems are not responsible for meeting every need of their students. But when the need directly affects learning, the school must meet the challenge. (Carnegie Council on Adolescent Development, 1989, p. 61)

The number of young people experiencing serious problems that interfere with their learning and performance at school continues to grow. Between 12% and 22% of all children suffer from a diagnosable mental, emotional, or behavioral disorder, and relatively few receive mental health services (Costello, 1989; Hoagwood, 1995). The picture is even bleaker when considering all young people experiencing psychosocial problems, whom Joy Dryfoos (1990) describes as being "at risk of not maturing into responsible adults." The number deemed "at risk" in many schools serving low-income populations exceeds the 50% mark.

Harold Hodgkinson (1989), director of the Center for Demographic Policy, estimates that 40% of students are in "very bad educational shape" and "at risk of failing to fulfill their physical and mental promise." Many live in inner cities or impoverished rural areas or are recently arrived immigrants.

Health Is Academic: A Guide to Coordinated School Health Problems. Edited by Eva Marx and Susan Frelick Wooley, with Daphne Northrop. New York: Teachers College Press, 1998. ISBN 0-8077-3713-5 (pbk.), ISBN 0-8077-3714-3 (cloth). Prior to photocopying items for classroom use, please contact the Copyright Clearance Center, Customer Service, 222 Rosewood Dr., Danvers, MA 01923, USA, tel. (508) 750-8400. © 1998 Education Development Center, Inc. All rights reserved.

For the most part, the problems they exhibit in school are attributable to conditions they bring with them when they enter kindergarten—conditions associated with poverty, difficult and diverse family circumstances, lack of English language skills, violent neighborhoods, physical and emotional problems, and inadequate health care (Knitzer, Steinberg, & Fleisch, 1990).

Most school administrators, board members, teachers, parents, and students realize that, for students to benefit from their schooling, society must address social, emotional, and physical health problems and other major barriers to learning (Carlson, Paavola, & Talley, 1995; Dryfoos, 1994; Knitzer, Steinberg, & Fleisch, 1990; Mintzies & Hare, 1985; Tyack, 1992). Counseling, psychological, and social services are *essential* for youngsters experiencing severe and pervasive problems. These problems include

- *inadequate basic resources* such as food, clothing, housing, and a sense of security at home, school, and in the neighborhood
- *psychosocial problems* such as difficult relationships at home and at school; emotional upset; language problems; sexual, emotional, or physical abuse; substance abuse; delinquent or gang-related behavior; psychopathology
- *stressful situations* such as being unable to meet the demands made at school or at home, inadequate support systems, and hostile conditions at school or in the neighborhood
- *crises and emergencies* such as the death of a classmate or relative, a shooting at school, or natural disasters such earthquakes, floods, or tornadoes
- *life transitions* such as the onset of puberty, entering a new school, and changes in life circumstances (moving, immigration, loss of a parent through divorce or death)

Counseling, psychological, and social service interventions not only provide programs and services to address barriers to student learning, they also focus on enhancing healthy psychosocial development for all students (Conoley & Conoley, 1991; Freeman & Pennekamp, 1988; Gibson & Mitchell, 1990; Holtzman, 1992). Such interventions encompass concern for the development of

- responsibility and integrity
- self esteem
- social and working relationships
- self evaluation and self direction
- temperament
- personal safety and safe behavior
- health maintenance

- effective physical functioning
- careers and life roles
- creativity

ESSENTIAL FUNCTIONS OF SCHOOL COUNSELING, PSYCHOLOGICAL, AND SOCIAL SERVICES

In an ideal world, communities and schools would be safe places, and everyone's basic economic and other survival needs would be met. In such a world, schools would have the resources and staff would have the training opportunities necessary to ensure success for all. Unfortunately, the world we live in is far from ideal. Schools increasingly find that counseling, psychological, and social service interventions are essential for their efforts to reduce dropouts, substance abuse, gang activity, teen pregnancy, and many other problems. Indeed, every day in every school teachers ask for help in dealing with a host of problems facing students.

The specific functions of a counseling, psychological, and social services component to minimize barriers to student learning and promote students' healthy psychosocial development fall into three broad categories:

- *Direct services and instruction*
  —Crisis intervention and emergency assistance
  —Assessment of individuals, groups, classrooms, and school and home environments
  —Treatment, remediation, and rehabilitation (individual and group counseling, student assistance programs, pre-referral interventions)
  —Accommodations to allow for differences and disabilities
  —Transition and follow-up (orientations, social support for newcomers, education and support for families accessing services, follow-through)
  —Primary prevention including enhancement of wellness (guidance counseling; training and coordination of peer mediators and counselors; development and implementation of health and violence-reduction curricula; advocacy; liaison between school and home; gang, delinquency, and safe-school programs; conflict resolution)
  —Multidisciplinary teamwork and consultation to enhance direct service impact
  —Training across disciplines to enhance the skills of teachers and others who work directly with students
- *Developing systems, programs, services, and resources*
  —Needs assessment, gatekeeping, referral, triage, and case monitoring and management

—Coordination of activities
—Mapping and enhancing resources and systems
—Monitoring and evaluating interventions
—Advocacy for programs, services, and standards of care
—Public relations
—Obtaining financial resources for specific services and large programs
—Developing new approaches
• *Connecting school and community resources*
—Increasing the responsiveness of community agencies to referrals from the school
—Creating formal linkages among programs and services
—Reaching out to families that resist involvement in schooling

The services can focus on one individual (for example, counseling for a student who is a substance abuser), a small group (for example, a support group for students whose parents have divorced recently), or the entire student body (for example, a school-wide substance abuse prevention program). Some services are preventive, promoting healthy psychosocial development before problems arise. Others represent interventions in early or late stages of problems, including responding to crises. The activities can occur in a private office on or off school grounds, a school clinic or family resource center, a classroom, a school-linked neighborhood setting, an auditorium, or a student's home.

Regardless of where they occur, the interventions usually involve one or more of the following activities:

• supplying information (printed materials, use of media and advanced technology, directions for obtaining assistance, a telephone information line)
• performing an assessment
• providing skills development activities and formal instruction (instruction in career opportunities; drug and sexuality education; parenting classes; social, performance, and transition skill development)
• mobilizing and enhancing support for students (student and family support groups; adopt-a-student programs; opportunities for positive roles through serving the school and community)
• connecting students with employment, recreational, and enrichment opportunities
• strengthening programs by contributing to system change (participation on school improvement teams)

School-affiliated counseling, psychological, and social work specialists bring an in-depth understanding of psychosocial, developmental, and cultural factors affecting students' functioning. These professionals can help other school staff assist students with mild to moderate learning, behavior, and emotional problems in ways that contribute to growth. Their specialized knowledge and skills also can contribute to solutions for school-wide problems.

The practice of counseling, psychological, and social work specialists generally follows basic intervention guidelines that include

- finding a balance between approaching each problem as if it were unique and addressing underlying factors that are common to many problems
- tailoring interventions to the needs, motivations, and capabilities of the individual
- using the least intervention needed—least restrictive, most nonintrusive intervention required to address problems and accommodate diversity
- designing comprehensive, integrated approaches
- basing priorities on students' needs, not service providers' preferences

Effective counseling, psychological, and social services can reduce problem referrals, increase the efficacy of mainstream and special education programs, and enhance instruction and guidance that fosters healthy development. An extensive literature reports positive outcomes for counseling, psychological, and social service interventions available to schools.[1]

WHO IMPLEMENTS THE SCHOOL COUNSELING, PSYCHOLOGICAL, AND SOCIAL SERVICES FUNCTIONS?

Counseling, psychological, and social services professionals, such as counselors, psychologists, psychiatrists, psychiatric nurses, social workers, have established roles with respect to promoting students' psychosocial development, addressing barriers to their learning, and enhancing the well-being of students, families, and school staff. However, activities that address barriers to learning and enhance healthy development are not the sole province of these specialists. All of the following people also can play a role:

- Related therapists (art, dance, music, occupational, physical, speech-language-hearing, and recreation therapists; psychodramatists)
- Health professionals (nurses, physicians)
- Instructional professionals (health educators, other classroom teachers, special education staff, resource staff)

- Administrative staff (principals, assistant principals)
- Students, including trained peer counselors
- Family members
- School aides, clerical and cafeteria staff, custodians, bus drivers, para-professionals, recreation personnel, volunteers, and professionals-in-training

Most districts employ specialists who provide counseling, psychological, or social services. Increasingly, some schools or districts also are using specialists employed by other public and private agencies, such as health departments, hospitals, and community-based organizations, to provide mental health and social services to students, their families, and school staff.

Pupil Services Personnel

Professionals employed by schools to provide services are often called pupil services personnel. Pupil services professionals include school counselors, psychologists, social workers, and nurses; occupational and physical therapists; special educators; speech-language pathologists; audiologists; therapeutic recreation specialists; and art, music, and dance therapists. Many schools and districts treat the work of such professionals as desirable but not essential—referring to counseling, psychological, and social services as "auxiliary" or "support" services. All too often these personnel are among those deemed dispensable as school budgets tighten. As a result, although some areas of specialty have increased their numbers, overall staffing of pupil services in most districts has been cut back significantly in recent years (Gibelman, 1993).

Few schools come close to having a potent approach for addressing psychosocial barriers to learning and enhancing healthy development for the majority of students. In most states, elementary schools are fortunate if they have a day a week from professionals such as a school counselor, nurse, psychologist, or social worker. Middle and high schools tend to have more diverse practitioners assigned for more days. Federal and state mandates often determine the number of pupil services professionals that schools or districts employ. Funding for compensatory interventions, special education, and other categorical programs can enable schools to afford more services. However, such funding comes with a cost—namely, an overemphasis on services for those who qualify for categorical programs. Schools that have school-based or school-linked health clinics or participate in school-community collaborations usually can offer students a broader range of mental and social services. In most schools and numerous communities, however, many types of personnel and forms of therapy simply are not available to students. Most schools offer only bare essentials. Too many schools cannot even meet students' basic mental health needs. Primary prevention often is only a dream.

In 1994, 84% of middle/junior high schools and 89% of high schools in the United States provided individual counseling; 61% of middle/junior high schools and 59% of high schools provided some type of group counseling (Small et al., 1995). Yet schools generally employ or contract relatively few counseling, psychological, and social services specialists. In a sample of 482 districts of varying sizes in 45 states, 55% had counselors, 41% had psychologists, 21% had social workers, and 2.1% had psychiatrists (Davis, Fryer, White, & Igoe, 1995). Some student-practitioner ratios are staggering: Nationwide, there is one school psychologist or school social worker for every 2500 students and one school counselor for every 1000 students (Carlson, Paavola, & Talley, 1995). When one considers the fact that more than half of the students in many schools are encountering major barriers that interfere with their functioning, such ratios inevitably mean that a large number of students who need help desperately are receiving no assistance at all.

The trend toward fewer pupil services personnel and smaller budgets has many negative effects. Competition for limited resources increases, and collaboration and participation of pupil services personnel in shared governance and planning is hampered. This contributes to the problem of ad hoc, fragmented services and delivery systems and to the lack of a cohesive policy vision for addressing barriers to learning and enhancing healthy student development. As school districts move to decentralize authority, cut costs, and become involved with managed care, various specialists' roles and their involvement in school governance and collective bargaining will probably change. This realignment will play a major role in determining how many pupil services personnel a school or district employs (Hill & Bonan, 1991; Streeter & Franklin, 1993).

Although professional preparation differs for counselors, psychologists, and social service providers, these professionals have many similar skills and can address many of the same tasks. Some of these include team building, program planning, crisis intervention and counseling, building community support, assessing students, and making appropriate referrals. They also share a whole-child orientation and knowledge of healthy development. School nurses and other school personnel also quite often address psychosocial and mental health concerns (see Chapter 8, Figure 8.3).

School-Community Collaborations

Initiatives to restructure community health and human services have fostered the concept of school-linked services and contributed to the burgeoning of school-based and school-linked health clinics (Carnegie Council on Adolescent Development, 1988; U.S. Department of Education, 1995). The term *school-linked* describes off-campus services provided by a community-based organization that has formal ties to a school. Often these services are offered in a special facility near the school site. *School-based* refers to activity provided on a school campus, sometimes by personnel from a community-based organization, sometimes by school district personnel. The terms encompass two dimensions: (a) where services and programs are located and (b) who owns them.

Some schools engage in relationships with public and private community agencies as part of an effort to use existing resources to serve greater numbers better. States such as California, Florida, Kentucky, Missouri, New Jersey, and Oregon have launched statewide initiatives with this purpose in mind (First, Curcio, & Young, 1994; Palaich, Whitney, & Paolino, 1991). Such school-community collaborations, often described as providing wrap-around services and one-stop shopping, are increasingly housed in a family service or resource center at or near a school (Dryfoos, 1993, 1994, 1995). Figure 7.1 illustrates how one school enhanced its services by combining school-based and school-linked interventions.

As of 1994, more than 600 health clinics at or linked to schools were providing both physical and mental health services (Advocates for Youth, 1994; Dryfoos, 1994; Robert Wood Johnson Foundation, 1993). Current estimates place the figure at over 900 (Making the Grade, 1996). Although concerns about teen pregnancy and a desire to increase access to physical health care for underserved youth initially prompted the establishment of many of these clinics, they soon found it essential to address mental health and psychosocial concerns as well (Taylor & Adelman, 1996). The need to provide both physical and mental health services reflects two basic realities. First, physical complaints are often rooted in psychological problems. Second, as many as half of all students come to clinics primarily for help with nonmedical concerns, such as peer and family relationship problems, emotional distress, problems related to physical and sexual abuse, and concerns stemming from the use of alcohol and other drugs (Adelman, Barker, & Nelson, 1993; Anglin, Naylor, & Kaplan, 1996; Center for Reproductive Health Policy Research, 1989; Robert Wood Johnson Foundation, 1989). However, given the limited number of staff at such clinics and in the schools, the demand for psychosocial interventions quickly outstrips the resources available.

Collaborations between school and community providers can improve students' access to services and stimulate strong support from families, the community, and students. Available evidence suggests that such collaborations might be successful and cost-effective over the long run (Knapp, 1995). Projects such as New Jersey's School-Based Youth Services Program, the Healthy Start Initiative in California, the Beacons Schools in New York, and

FIGURE 7.1. Toward the Full Service School Model

A middle school initiated integrated health and social services as part of a comprehensive effort to improve instruction and upgrade the school's facilities and environment. The school—which already employed a school psychologist (part-time), nurse, three migrant education aides, and a supervisor—made agreements with community-based agencies to bring additional practitioners to the campus, including a mental health professional, a part-time student assistance counselor, and a DARE police officer. At first, the increase in services was fragmented and poorly coordinated.

Drawing on grant support, the school formed an interagency case management team and established an on-site center for primary health and dental care. Most of the grant support was used as salaries for a project coordinator who oversees the case management team, a neighborhood services worker who facilitates school and service provider linkages, and a youth development worker responsible for peer programs and linking students to community youth-serving programs.

Service providers meet regularly to share information about clients. A worker is assigned to follow up on each student and family. A coordinating council composed of an equal number of parents and school and agency staff members oversees the initiative.

The center provides the following services:

- mental health counseling
- substance abuse prevention and treatment
- family support and parenting education
- health and dental screening and assessment
- child welfare services
- academic support and tutoring
- information and referral

Referrals are made for:

- dental treatment
- health services
- extensive mental health services
- food, clothing, and housing assistance

Acting as the lead agency, the school creates partnership agreements with other agencies. As a result of these efforts, the school has enhanced existing services and added new ones.

Source: Adapted from Dryfoos, 1994

nationwide programs such as Communities In Schools and the New Futures Initiative show promise (Knapp, 1995). When such projects place staff at schools, underserved and hard-to-reach populations have easier access to services. Such efforts also often encourage schools to open their doors in ways that enhance family involvement in activities such as social support networks for new students and families, parent peer education, and school governance—activities that help create a psychological sense of community (see Chapter 4). Moreover, school-community collaborations can reduce redundancy and improve outcomes by enhancing coordination and case management. The widespread attention given to school-community collaborations has led some policy makers, particularly those interested in trimming school budgets, to believe that community providers are a sufficient resource to address barriers to learning. Such views ignore the value of school-owned and -operated resources and the importance of restructuring these resources as part of school reform. These views also cause some school specialists to feel that their skills are discounted and their jobs threatened, contribute to tension between school-employed specialists and their counterparts in community-based organizations, and undermine school-community collaboration. In fact, in many locales the combined assets of the community and the school are woefully inadequate (Koyanagi & Gaines, 1993), and the resources of both school and community are needed to complement and support each other.

NATIONAL AND STATE SUPPORT FOR SCHOOL COUNSELING, PSYCHOLOGICAL, AND SOCIAL SERVICES

Support for counseling, psychological, and social services interventions in schools exists in national and state legislation and statements by government officials and associations of school administrators (see Chapter 12). Yet mental health and social services, like some other components of school health programs, do not have high status in either the educational hierarchy or many current health care reform initiatives. Several recent measures seek to improve the situation.

At the federal level, to build state capacity to improve school health programs, the Centers for Disease Control and Prevention (CDC) initiated funding to support collaboration between state health and education agencies through a formal administrative link (Kolbe, 1993). In addition, through a CDC-funded project that led to the development of this book, Education Development Center, Inc., worked with national organizations and state and local education and health agencies to advance school health programs that include integrated pupil personnel services. A provision of the Improving

America's Schools Act allows school districts that seek to coordinate services, including mental health and social services, to tap some of their federal funding from the U.S. Department of Education for coordination of services. And, of course, several branches of the U.S. Department of Health and Human Services are involved in research and practice that benefits psychological, counseling, and social services in schools. For example, in 1995 the Office of Adolescent Health (Public Health Service, Health Resources and Services Administration, Maternal and Child Health Bureau) undertook a major initiative to enhance mental health in schools. As a first step, two national training and technical assistance centers and five state projects were established and are already pursuing a wide range of activities designed to improve how schools address barriers to learning and enhance healthy development. Many states, counties, and philanthropic foundations also have initiatives aimed at stimulating school-community collaborations and enhancing service integration.

Several national associations and local affiliates represent counseling, psychological, and social services specialists working in or with schools. A coalition of national associations created an umbrella organization to provide leadership in the field of student support services. The National Alliance of Pupil Service Organizations (NAPSO) encompasses 22 associations and more than 2½ million school professionals.[2] Other membership groups represent professionals concerned with mental health and special education, social problems such as poverty and violence, and specific populations such as individuals with learning disabilities or young people at risk for drug abuse. Many of these national organizations have state and local affiliates or counterparts. These many professional organizations constitute a significant segment of the multifaceted and often competing forces shaping national and state social and mental health-related policies (Dwyer, 1995; Gibelman, 1993). Their interests include the professional preparation of specialists, professional certification or licensure, standards for good practice, and advancing the state of the art. These organizations also advocate for members and for the services and programs their members provide.

INTEGRATING SCHOOL COUNSELING, PSYCHOLOGICAL, AND SOCIAL SERVICES WITH THE OTHER COMPONENTS OF A COORDINATED SCHOOL HEALTH PROGRAM

Personnel providing counseling, psychological, and social services in schools—whether employed by the school or not—need to coordinate with each other and work toward integrated activity. They also need to collaborate with personnel who represent the other components of a coordinated school health program. Opportunities for collaboration arise daily. For example, a school social worker can advise the school nurse about family problems that interfere with a student's receiving needed medical care. A school psychologist can review the mental health unit of a health education curriculum or teach conflict resolution skills to a health class. The school counselor can consult with the physical educator about a student who cuts class because she is embarrassed to change clothes in the locker room. School counselors, psychologists, and social workers can play a key role in creating a healthy psychosocial environment at school and in involving families in their children's learning. To improve the learning environment, they can work with other school staff on class management, conflict resolution, and discipline. They can even counsel teachers whose personal problems become barriers to students' learning.

As necessary as such collaborative efforts are, they do not represent a sufficient approach to enhancing students' psychosocial development and removing barriers to learning. That important goal can only be achieved through systemic reforms that ensure movement away from fragmented interventions to coordinated ones and from narrowly focused, problem-specific, and specialist-oriented services to comprehensive, general, programmatic approaches.

Because most schools do not have cohesive policies for addressing psychosocial barriers to learning and enhancing healthy student development, most school health and human service programs (as well as compensatory and special education programs) are developed and function in relative isolation. This fragmentation results in waste and reduced effectiveness. Many factors contribute to this problem, including funding that is earmarked for narrowly defined categories of students, such as students enrolled in special and compensatory education; school policies that treat health and social service activity as a low priority; and competition among pupil services personnel.

In general, the tendency is to rely on narrowly focused, short-term, cost-intensive interventions that serve a small proportion of students in a noncomprehensive way. For example, in some schools a student identified as at risk for dropout, suicide, and substance abuse might be involved in three independent counseling programs. The result is disjointed advocacy and planning and fragmented service provision (Adler & Gardner, 1994; Kahn & Kamerman, 1992; U.S. General Accounting Office, 1993).

A comprehensive, integrated system, by contrast, can coordinate, reintegrate, and redeploy resources, incorporating the functions described earlier in this chapter (see the section, "Essential Functions of Counseling, Psychological, and Social Services"). Figure 7.2 outlines a continuum of programs and services that ranges from primary prevention to early-after-onset inter-

FIGURE 7.2. Continuum of Community-School Interventions

Intervention Continuum	*Programs and services aimed at system changes and individual needs*
Primary prevention	Programs and services to protect, promote, and maintain public health to foster opportunities, positive development, and wellness:

- economic enhancement of those living in poverty (e.g., work/welfare programs)
- safety (e.g., lead abatement programs)
- physical and mental health (e.g., healthy start initiatives, immunizations, dental care, substance abuse prevention, violence prevention, health/mental health education, sexuality education and family planning, recreation, social services to access basic living resources)

Preschool-age support and assistance to enhance health and psychosocial development:

- education and social support for parents of preschoolers
- quality day care
- quality early education
- appropriate screening and improvement of physical and mental health and psychosocial problems

Early-after-onset interventions

Early-schooling interventions:

- orientations and welcoming and transition support into school and community life for students and their families (especially immigrants)
- support and guidance to minimize school adjustment problems
- quality early education that includes physical and health education delivered in an environment that enhances self-esteem and learning
- accommodations and related services for students with special education needs

FIGURE 7.2. Continued

Intervention Continuum	Programs and services aimed at system changes and individual needs
Early-after-onset interventions	• parent involvement in problem solving • comprehensive and accessible psychosocial and physical health services (including a focus on community and home violence and other problems identified through community needs assessments) Ongoing regular support: • preparation and support for school and life transitions • teaching "basics" of support and remediation to regular teachers, other available resource personnel, peers, and volunteers • parent involvement in problem solving • resource support for parents in need (including help finding work, legal aid, and English and citizenship classes) • comprehensive and accessible psychosocial and physical and mental health interventions (including health and physical education, recreation, violence reduction programs, and peer counseling) • academic guidance and assistance • emergency crisis prevention and response mechanisms Interventions prior to referral for intensive and ongoing targeted treatments: • multidisciplinary team work, consultation, and staff development • short-term specialized interventions (including resource teacher instruction and family mobilization; student assistance programs; and programs for suicide prevention, pregnant minors, substance abusers, gang members, and other potential dropouts)

(continues)

Figure 7.2. Continued

Intervention Continuum	Programs and services aimed at system changes and individual needs
Treatment for severe or chronic problems	Intensive treatments: • referral, triage, placement guidance and assistance, case management, and resource coordination • family preservation programs and services • special education and rehabilitation • dropout recovery and follow-up support • services for severe or chronic psychosocial, mental, and physical health problems

ventions to treatments for severe problems. The continuum underscores that a comprehensive approach requires a range of interventions focused on individuals, families, and environmental systems; connections among these interventions; and linkages for extended periods of time (Adelman & Taylor, 1993a, 1993b). Such an approach includes peer- and self-help strategies and applies a holistic and developmental orientation.

Schools can use four strategies to move toward a coordinated, comprehensive approach: (1) map and analyze resources and needs, (2) coordinate and enhance resources, (3) balance specialist and generalist perspectives, and (4) integrate activity to address barriers to learning with instruction and school management reforms.

Map and Analyze Resources and Needs

Mapping resources consists of identifying what exists at a site, for example, by compiling a list of existing programs and services to support students, families, and staff and outlining referral and case management procedures (see Chapter 2). Resource mapping augments a needs assessment that determines the unmet needs of students, their families, and school staff. For example, as a first step in its extensive restructuring of health and human services, the Los Angeles Unified School District mapped and analyzed existing resources at school sites and for complexes of schools. Through this process, the district identified redundant and nonproductive programs and clarified program strengths and weaknesses, including coordination and resource needs. Based on the findings, schools can set priorities and redesign interventions to enhance outcome efficacy (Los Angeles Unified School District, 1995).

In a nutshell, resource mapping can help schools identify more cost-effective ways to use available resources. Some schools devote almost 40% of their resources to functions other than regular instruction (Tyack, 1992). If redeployed effectively, these resources can go a long way to address unmet needs. With funding for reform so hard to come by, resource mapping and analyses leading to resource deployment holds the answer to the ever-present question, Where will we find the funds?

Coordinate and Enhance Resources

A *Resource Coordinating Team* can be an effective mechanism for coordinating and enhancing resources at a school site (Adelman, 1993; Rosenblum, DiCecco, Taylor, & Adelman, 1995). Such a team brings together representatives of all major programs and services that address barriers to learning and healthy development—school counselors, psychologists, nurses, social workers, health educators, special education staff, bilingual program coordinators, physical educators, nutrition services staff, front office staff, site administrators, classroom teachers, caregivers, and older students. It also includes representatives from community agencies that are significantly involved at a school. (A somewhat different but related type of school-based team is the Healthy School Team described in Chapter 2.) Such a team sometimes can be created by broadening the scope of student study teams, teacher assistance teams, or crisis teams.

A Resource Coordinating Team differs from teams created to review individuals; its focus is on managing and enhancing systems to coordinate, integrate, and strengthen interventions. It can weave together *all* programs for addressing barriers to learning and enhancing healthy development (including but not limited to the eight components of school health programs). Such a team (1) conducts resource mapping and analysis with a view to improving coordination; (2) ensures that effective systems for referral, case management, and quality assurance are in place; (3) establishes appropriate procedures for program management and for communication among school staff and with the home; and (4) suggests ways to reallocate and enhance resources, such as clarifying which activities particular staff could address most appropriately, which resources could be put to better use, and which services other school district or community entities could provide.

Properly constituted, trained, and supported, such school-site teams can complement the work of the site's governance body by providing on-site overview, leadership, and advocacy for activities to address barriers to learning and enhance healthy development. A liaison between the team and the school's governing and planning bodies can help ensure the maintenance, improvement, and increased integration of essential programs and services in the total school program.

Because they often deal with the same families and link with the same community resources, complexes of schools—for example, a high school and its feeder middle and elementary schools—need to work collaboratively. A Complex Resource Coordinating Council brings together representatives from each school's Resource Coordinating Team to facilitate coordination and equity among schools drawing on the same school district and community resources (Adelman, 1993; Rosenblum, DiCecco, Taylor, & Adelman, 1995). As noted in Chapter 2, there is also a need for such a coordinating body at the district level. In districts with only one high school, a single resource coordinating team at the district level might be sufficient.

Balance Specialist and Generalist Perspectives

Generalists, cross-trained specialists, and properly trained paraprofessionals and nonprofessionals bring important perspectives and abilities for addressing the common factors underlying many student problems. Consequently, a comprehensive, integrated approach requires balancing specialist-oriented activity with a generalist perspective (Henggeler, 1995). Two principal factors shape the specialized approaches that currently dominate psychosocial interventions in schools. The first involves regulations and guidelines, such as legislative mandates to provide compensatory and special education programs and categorical programs to address social problems such as substance abuse, gang and on-campus violence, and teen pregnancy. The other shaping force is the prevailing academic preparation of specialists, which focuses on specialized intervention models. In some localities these factors are easing. Flexibility is increasing in the use of some categorical funds and temporary waivers from regulatory restrictions are not uncommon. To diminish the impact of specialized academic training, several universities are experimenting with collaborative interprofessional programs and cross-disciplinary training for those who plan to work with school-aged youth (Adelman & Taylor, 1994; Hooper-Briar & Lawson, 1994; Lawson & Hooper-Briar, 1994; Lipsky & Gartner, 1992; Meyers, 1995; Young, Gardner, Coley, Schorr, & Bruner, 1994).

Integrate Activities to Address Barriers to Learning with Instruction and School Management Reforms

Despite awareness of the many barriers to learning, school reformers tend to concentrate on improving instruction and school management, ignoring the programs and services needed to address barriers to students' learning. The concept of an "enabling component" (Adelman, 1996a; Adelman & Taylor, 1994) that the New American Schools' Learning Center Model illustrates helps correct this oversight and is essential in any effort to reform and restructure schools. As the Learning Center utilizes it, this model guides daily operations and continuing evolution (Learning Center Model, 1995). The three- rather than two-faceted framework consists of the instruction and curriculum component, the management and governance component, and the enabling component, which are essential, complementary, and overlapping. The enabling component weaves together all relevant school, community, and home resources through policy reform and system restructuring. This process begins with reorganizing school-owned activities, such as pupil services and special and compensatory education programs, and expands to integrating school and community resources. As a result, it encompasses the type of integrated health and social services described as the full-service school model (Dryfoos, 1994)—and goes beyond it (Adelman, 1996b).

By ensuring that school reform fully integrates a focus on addressing barriers to learning and enhancing healthy development, the enabling component responds to a wide range of psychosocial factors interfering with school learning and performance. The broad-based programmatic efforts cluster into six interrelated areas:

- enhancing classroom-based efforts to enable learning
- providing prescribed student and family assistance
- responding to and preventing crises
- supporting transitions
- increasing home involvement in schooling
- reaching out to develop greater community involvement and support (including a focus on volunteers).

In an enabling component, the content of each of the six intervention areas guides program planning, implementation, evaluation, personnel development, and stakeholder involvement. The intent is to weave together a continuum of programs (from primary prevention to treatment of chronic problems) and a continuum of interveners, advocates, and sources of support (e.g., peers, parents, volunteers, nonprofessional staff, professionals-in-training, professionals). It is the scope of this activity that underscores the necessity for developing formal mechanisms to ensure long-lasting interprogram collaboration (e.g., cooperation, coordination, and where viable, integration). Collaboration is essential for:

- restructuring existing resources to enhance efficacy in pursuing the six intervention areas

- ensuring coordination
- expanding resources through direct linkages between school and community programs
- increasing integration of resources (school, community, and home)
- integrating the enabling, instructional, and management components.

A Family Resource Center provides a focal point and hub for the entire enabling component, as well as for specific services and programmatic activity. A computerized system to organize information, aid case management, and link students and families to referrals supports integration as well as discrete services. Inclusion of an enabling component recognizes that schools committed to the success of all children must involve an array of activities designed to enable learning and teaching and address barriers.

The eight-component coordinated school health program model and the enabling component concept both represent efforts to establish a broad, unifying focus around which to improve policy formulations for addressing barriers to learning and enhancing healthy student development.

ACTION STEPS FOR IMPLEMENTING SCHOOL COUNSELING, PSYCHOLOGICAL, AND SOCIAL SERVICES

Achievement of institutional changes that move toward a comprehensive, integrated approach requires a sophisticated and appropriately financed process for getting from here to there. Restructuring on a large scale involves substantive organizational and programmatic change at many levels. Although this point seems self-evident, its implications are often ignored (Adelman & Taylor, 1997; Argyris, 1993; Barth, 1990; Connor & Lake, 1988; Fullan & Stiegelbauer, 1991; Knoff, 1995; Replication and Program Services, 1993; Sarason, 1996).

Reform requires establishment of new collaborative arrangements and redistribution of authority and power. Reform requires providing adequate support in the form of time, space, materials, and equipment—not just initially but over time—to those who operate critical mechanisms. Appropriate incentives, including safeguards, must exist for those undertaking the tasks. Persons already highly motivated and competent to enter into collaborative working relationships must guide a process that (1) creates readiness for the needed changes by increasing interest and consensus for a comprehensive approach to addressing barriers to learning and enhancing healthy development, (2) establishes a policy framework that recognizes the approach as a primary and essential facet of school activity, and (3) ensures there are effective leadership and organizational mechanisms for carrying out policy commitments.

Actions for Local Schools

Key stakeholder groups (teachers, other school employees, administrators, school board members, students, families) must clearly establish through policy reformulation, organizational restructuring, and daily actions their strong commitment to addressing barriers to learning and enhancing healthy development. The following are examples of arenas for action:

- *Mission statement.* Revise the school's mission statement to include a comprehensive focus and a high priority on addressing barriers to learning and enhancing healthy development. The revision process must include developing stakeholder consensus for the mission.
- *Organizational restructuring.* Ensure the assignment of a site leader and the creation of a steering group to plan and oversee the policy commitments and systemic changes. In turn, the site leader and steering group can establish and train a school-level team to take responsibility for (1) mapping and analyzing resources; (2) phasing in reorganization of programs and services; (3) reaching out to other schools, the district, and community resources; and (4) establishing systems for improving quality, maintaining momentum for reform, and conducting ongoing renewal. From among this leadership group, designated individuals can carry out specific functions related to daily communication, coordination, and problem solving. To guarantee appropriate representation related to site decision making, one or more persons from this leadership cadre should serve on the school's governance and planning bodies.
- *Map and analyze resources.* Provide a sound basis for redesigning programs and services by mapping and analyzing current resources, focusing on resources for:
  —enhancing classroom efforts to enable learning
  —providing prescribed student and family assistance
  —responding to and preventing crises
  —supporting transitions
  —increasing home involvement in schooling
  —reaching out to the community to increase its involvement and support
- *Staff development.* Increase the amount of staff development devoted to strategies for addressing barriers to learning and enhancing healthy development. Currently, almost none of a teacher's inservice focuses on improving classroom approaches to addressing mild to moderate learning and behavior problems. Paraprofessionals, aides, and volunteers working in

classrooms receive little or no formal training or supervision. Cross-disciplinary training for specialists is rare. Specialists need time to learn more about strategies related to each of the six areas outlined above. Then they must be given a role in providing inservice for teachers and others at the school site so that a wider range of effective strategies can be developed. Release time and appropriate incentives are essential to encourage participation.

Actions for School Complexes and Districts to Support Local Schools

Schools operate within a context established by feeder schools and district policy. Thus, there must be a focus on policy reformulation and organizational restructuring to establish a strong commitment to addressing barriers to learning and enhancing healthy development. This involves ensuring that (1) the stated mission at all levels reflects this commitment, (2) the organizational structure includes the necessary leadership to plan and oversee policy commitments and systemic changes, (3) coordinating bodies are established for complexes of schools and the district as a whole to map and analyze resources and participate in setting priorities and redeploying resources for systemic change, and (4) appropriate staff development and other capacity building is planned and carried out.

In addition, most schools will need the support of a change agent in planning and implementing systemic changes. Current school restructuring efforts demonstrate that pupil services personnel can fulfill this role after special training in facilitating organizational change (Early Assistance for Students and Families Program, 1995). Not only does their previous training make them especially suited to carry out such functions, but pupil services personnel's status as insiders can minimize negative reactions their school and district colleagues might direct at outside reformers.

Actions for State and National Organizations and Institutions of Higher Education to Support Local Schools

State and national groups and institutions of higher education can aid the efforts of schools to promote counseling, psychological, and social services by fostering and supporting

- establishment of a broad unifying concept that can help increase policy support and guide research and practice related to addressing barriers to student learning and enhancing healthy development, including an increased emphasis on prevention

- development of interagency collaborative agreements
- establishment of incentives for systemic changes to develop comprehensive, integrated approaches
- provision of opportunities to learn more about concepts and strategies for addressing barriers to learning and enhancing healthy development
- adoption of cross-disciplinary perspectives and integrated practices

CONCLUSION

Effective counseling, psychological, and social services for children, youth, their families, and school personnel benefit not only schools but also society as a whole. Schools benefit from better student functioning, increased attendance, and less teacher frustration; society benefits from reduced health and welfare costs, unemployment, and use of emergency services. Establishment of comprehensive, integrated approaches to addressing barriers to student learning and enhancing healthy development can increase such benefits. However, as this chapter stresses, fundamental policy and systemic changes at multiple levels must occur before this can happen. Although such changes are never easy, given the unsatisfactory nature of the status quo, the choice is an easy one.

NOTES

1. For example, see Bond & Compas, 1989; Borders & Drury, 1992; Brindis, Morales, McCarter, Dobrin, & Wolfe, 1993; Christopher, Kurtz, & Howing, 1989; Cohen & Fish, 1993; Dryfoos, 1990; Durlak, 1995; Henggeler, Schoenwald, Pickrel, & Rowland, 1994; Kazdin, 1993; Kirby et al., 1994; Knoff & Batsche, 1995; Larson, 1994; Mintzies & Hare, 1985; Mitchell, Seligson, & Marx, 1989; Orr, 1987; Price, Cowen, Lorion, Ramos-McKay, & Hutchins, 1988; Schorr, 1988; Slavin, Karweit, & Madden, 1989; Slavin, Karweit, & Wasik, 1994; Thomas & Grimes, 1995; Weissberg, Caplan, & Harwood, 1991; Weisz & Weiss, 1993.

2. The alliance currently consists of the American Art Therapy Association, American Counseling Association, American Dance Therapy Association, American Occupational Therapy Association, American Physical Therapy Association, American Psychological Association, American Psychological Association Division of School Psychology, American School Counselor Association, American Society of Allied Health Professionals, American Society of Group Psychotherapy and Psychodrama, American Speech-Language-Hearing Association, Council of Directors of School Psychology Programs, Council for Exceptional Children, National Association for Music Therapy, National Association of College Admissions Counselors, Na-

tional Association of Pupil Services Administrators, National Association of School Nurses, National Association of School Psychologists, National Association of Social Workers, National Association of State Consultants for School Social Work, National Education Association, and National Recreation and Parks Association.

REFERENCES

Adelman, H. S. (1993). School-linked mental health interventions: Toward mechanisms for service coordination and integration. *Journal of Community Psychology, 21,* 309–319.

Adelman, H. S. (1996a). *Restructuring support services: Toward a comprehensive approach.* Kent, OH: American School Health Association.

Adelman, H. S. (1996b). Restructuring education support services and integrating community resources: Beyond the full service school model. *School Psychology Review, 25,* 431–445.

Adelman, H. S., Barker, L. A., & Nelson, P. (1993). A study of a school-based clinic: Who uses it and who doesn't? *Journal of Clinical Child Psychology, 22,* 52–59.

Adelman, H. S., & Taylor, L. (1993a). *Learning problems and learning disabilities: Moving forward.* Pacific Grove, CA: Brooks/Cole.

Adelman, H. S., & Taylor, L. (1993b). School-based mental health: Toward a comprehensive approach. *Journal of Mental Health Administration, 20,* 32–45.

Adelman, H. S., & Taylor, L. (1994). *On understanding intervention in psychology and education.* Westport, CT: Praeger.

Adelman, H. S., & Taylor, L. (1997). Toward a scale-up model for replicating new approaches to schooling. *Journal of Educational and Psychological Consultation, 8,* 197–230.

Adler, L., & Gardner, S. (Eds.). (1994). *The politics of linking schools and social services.* Washington, DC: Falmer Press.

Advocates for Youth. (1994). *School-based and school-linked health centers: The facts.* Washington, DC: Author.

Anglin, T. M., Naylor, K. E., & Kaplan, D. W. (1996). Comprehensive, school-based health care: High school students' use of medical, mental health, and substance abuse services. *Pediatrics, 97,* 318–330.

Argyris, C. (1993). *Knowledge for action: A guide to overcoming barriers to organizational change.* San Francisco: Jossey-Bass.

Barth, R. S. (1990). *Improving schools from within: Teachers, parents, and principals can make a difference.* San Francisco: Jossey-Bass.

Bond, L., & Compas, B. (1989). (Eds.). *Primary prevention in the schools.* Newbury Park, CA: Sage.

Borders, L. D., & Drury, S. M. (1992). Comprehensive school counseling programs: A review for policymakers and practitioners. *Journal of Counseling & Development, 70,* 487–498.

Brindis, C., Morales, S., McCarter, V., Dobrin, C., & Wolfe, A. (1993). *An evaluation study of school-based clinics in California: Major findings, 1986–1991.* San Francisco: University of California, Institute for Health Policy Studies.

Carlson, C., Paavola, J., & Talley, R. (1995). Historical, current, and future models of schools as health care delivery settings. *School Psychology Quarterly, 10,* 184–202.

Carnegie Council on Adolescent Development. (1988). *Review of school-based health services.* New York: Carnegie Foundation.

Carnegie Council on Adolescent Development. (1989). *Turning Points: Preparing American Youth for the 21st Century.* Washington, DC: Author.

Center for Reproductive Health Policy Research, Institute for Health Policy Studies, University of California—San Francisco. (1989). *Annual report: Evaluation of California's comprehensive school-based health centers.* San Francisco: Author.

Christopher, G. M., Kurtz, P. D., & Howing, P. T. (1989). Status of mental health services for youth in school and community. *Children and Youth Services Review, 11,* 159–174.

Cohen, J. J., & Fish, M. C. (1993). *Handbook of school-based interventions: Resolving student problems and promoting healthy educational environments.* San Francisco: Jossey-Bass.

Connor, P. E., & Lake, L. K. (1988). *Managing organizational change.* New York: Praeger.

Conoley, J. C., & Conoley, C. W. (1991). Collaboration for child adjustment: Issues for school and clinic-based child psychologists. *Journal of Consulting and Clinical Psychology, 59,* 821–829.

Costello, E. J. (1989). Developments in child psychiatric epidemiology. *Journal of the American Academy of Child and Adolescent Psychiatry, 28,* 836–841.

Davis M., Fryer, G. E., White S., & Igoe, J. B. (1995). *A closer look: A report of select findings from the National School Health Survey 1993–1994.* Denver: Office of School Health, University of Colorado Health Sciences Center.

Dryfoos, J. G. (1990). *Adolescents at risk: Prevalence and prevention.* London: Oxford University Press.

Dryfoos, J. G. (1993). Schools as places for health, mental health, and social services. *Teachers College Record, 94,* 540–567.

Dryfoos, J. G. (1994). *Full-service schools: A revolution in health and social services for children, youth, and families.* San Francisco: Jossey-Bass.

Dryfoos, J. G. (1995). Full service schools: Revolution or fad? *Journal of Research on Adolescence, 5,* 147–172.

Durlak, J. A. (1995). *School-based prevention programs for children and adolescents.* Thousand Oaks, CA: Sage Publications.

Dwyer, K. P. (1995). Government relations. In A. Thomas & J. Grimes (Eds.), *Best practices in school psychology—III* (pp. 91–100). Washington, DC: National Association for School Psychologists.

Early Assistance for Students and Families Program. (1995). *Guidebook.* Los Angeles: University of California-Los Angeles, School Mental Health Project, Department of Psychology.

First, P. F., Curcio, J. L., & Young, D. L. (1994). State full-service school initiatives: New notions of policy development. In L. Adler & S. Gardner (Eds.), *The politics of linking schools and social services* (pp. 63–74). Washington, DC: Falmer Press.

Freeman, E. M., & Pennekamp, M. (1988). *Social work practice: Toward a child, family, school, community perspective.* Springfield, IL: Charles Thomas Pub.

Fullan, M. G., & Stiegelbauer, S. (1991). *The new meaning of educational changes* (2nd ed.). New York: Teachers College Press.

Geiger, K. (1995). L.A.'s kids courageous. *United Teacher, 26,* 14, 19.

Gibelman, M. (1993). School social workers, counselors, and psychologists in collaboration: A shared agenda. *Social Work in Education, 15,* 45–53.

Gibson, R. L., & Mitchell, M. H. (1990). *Introduction to counseling and guidance* (3rd ed.). New York: Macmillan.

Henggeler, S. W. (1995). A consensus: Conclusions of the APA Task Force report on innovative models of mental health services for children, adolescents, and their families. *Journal of Clinical Child Psychology, 23,* 3–6.

Henggeler, S. W., Schoenwald, S. K., Pickrel, S. G., & Rowland, M. D. (1994). The contribution of treatment outcome research to the reform of children's mental health services: Multisystemic therapy as an example. *Journal of Mental Health Administration, 21,* 229–239.

Hill, P., & Bonan, J. (1991). *Decentralization and accountability in public education.* Santa Monica, CA: Rand.

Hoagwood, K. (1995). Issues in designing and implementing studies of non-mental health care sectors. *Journal of Clinical Child Psychology, 23,* 114–120.

Hodgkinson, H. L. (1989). *The same client: The demographics of education and service delivery systems.* Washington, DC: Institute for Educational Leadership. Inc./ Center for Demographic Policy.

Holtzman, W. H. (1992). Community renewal, family preservation, and child development through the School of the Future. In W. H. Holtzman (Ed.), *School of the Future* (pp. 3–18). Austin, TX: American Psychological Association and Hogg Foundation for Mental Health.

Hooper-Briar, K., & Lawson, H. (1994). *Serving children, youth and family through interprofessional collaboration and service integration: A framework for action.* Oxford, OH: Danforth Foundation and Institute for Educational Renewal, Miami University.

Kahn, A., & Kamerman, S. (1992). *Integrating service integration: An overview of initiatives, issues, and possibilities.* New York: National Center for Children in Poverty.

Kazdin, A. E. (1993). Adolescent mental health: Prevention and treatment programs. *American Psychologist, 48,* 127–141.

Kirby, D., Short, L., Collins, J., Rugg, D., Kolbe, L., Howard, M., Miller, B., Sonenstein, F., & Zabin, L. S. (1994). School-based programs to reduce sexual risk behaviors: A review of effectiveness. *Public Health Reports, 109,* 339–360.

Knapp, M. S. (1995). How shall we study comprehensive collaborative services for children and families? *Educational Researcher, 24,* 5–16.

Knitzer, J., Steinberg, Z., & Fleisch, B. (1990). *At the schoolhouse door: An examination of programs and policies for children with behavioral and emotional problems.* New York: Bank Street College of Education.

Knoff, H. M. (1995). Best practices in facilitating school-based organizational change and strategic planning. In A. Thomas & J. Grimes (Eds.), *Best practices in school psychology—III* (pp. 239–252). Washington, DC: National Association of School Psychologists.

Knoff, H. M., & Batsche, G. M. (1995). Project ACHIEVE: Analyzing a school reform process for at-risk and underachieving students. *School Psychology Review, 24*, 579–603.

Kolbe, L. J. (1993). An essential strategy to improve the health and education of Americans. *Preventive Medicine, 22*, 544–560.

Koyanagi, C., & Gaines, S. (1993). *All systems fail.* Washington, DC: National Mental Health Association.

Larson, J. (1994). Violence prevention in the schools: A review of selected programs and procedures. *School Psychology Review, 23*, 151–164.

Lawson, H., & Hooper-Briar, K. (1994). *Expanding partnerships: Involving colleges and universities in interprofessional collaboration and service integration.* Oxford, OH: Danforth Foundation and Institute for Educational Renewal, Miami University.

Learning Center Model. (1995). *A design for a new learning community.* Los Angeles: Los Angeles Educational Partnership.

Lipsky, D. K., & Gartner, A. (1992). Inclusive education and school restructuring. In W. Stainback & S. Stainback (Eds.), *Controversial issues confronting special education: Divergent perspectives* (2nd ed., pp. 3–15). Boston: Allyn and Bacon.

Los Angeles Unified School District. (1995). *Plan for restructuring student health and human services.* Los Angeles: Author.

Making the Grade, George Washington University. (1996, Fall). School-based health centers continue to grow. *Access to Comprehensive School-Based Health Services for Children and Youth* (pp. 1–2). Washington, DC: Author.

Meyers, J. C. (1995). Financing strategies to support innovations in service delivery to children. *Journal of Clinical Child Psychology, 23*, 48–54.

Mintzies, P. M., & Hare, I. (1985). *The human factor: A key to excellence in education.* Silver Spring, MD: National Association of Social Workers.

Mitchell, A., Seligson, M., & Marx, F. (1989). *Early childhood programs and the public schools: Promise and practice.* Dover, MA: Auburn House.

Orr, M. (1987). *Keeping students in school: A guide to effective dropout prevention programs and services.* San Francisco: Jossey-Bass.

Palaich, R. M., Whitney, T. N., & Paolino, A. R. (1991). *Changing delivery systems: Addressing the fragmentation in children and youth services.* Denver, CO: Education Commission of the States.

Price, R. H., Cowen, E. L., Lorion, R. P., Ramos-McKay, J., & Hutchins, B. (Eds.). (1988). *Fourteen ounces of prevention: A casebook of exemplary primary prevention programs.* Washington: American Psychological Association.

Replication and Program Services, Inc. (1993). *Building from strength: Replication as a strategy for expanding social programs that work.* Philadelphia: Author.

Robert Wood Johnson Foundation. (1989). *Annual report.* Princeton, NJ: Author.

Robert Wood Johnson Foundation. (1993). *Making the grade: State and local partnerships to establish school-based health centers.* Princeton, NJ: Author.

Rosenblum, L., DiCecco, M. B., Taylor, L., & Adelman, H. S. (1995). Upgrading school support programs through collaboration: Resource coordinating teams. *Social Work in Education, 17,* 117–124.

Sarason, B. (1996). *Revisiting "The culture of school and the problem of change."* New York: Teachers College Press.

Schorr, L. B. (1988). *Within our reach: Breaking the cycle of disadvantage.* New York: Doubleday.

Slavin, R., Karweit, B. J., & Madden, N. (Eds.). (1989). *Effective programs for students at risk.* Boston: Allyn & Bacon.

Slavin, R., Karweit, N., & Wasik, B. (1994). *Preventing early school failure: Research on effective strategies.* Boston: Allyn & Bacon.

Small, M. L., Majer, L. S., Allensworth, D. D., Farquhar, B. K., Kann, L., & Pateman, B. C. (1995). School health services. *Journal of School Health, 65,* 319–326.

Streeter, C. L., & Franklin, C. (1993). Site-based management in public education: Opportunities and challenges for school social workers. *Social Work in Education, 15,* 71–81.

Taylor, L., & Adelman, H. S. (1996). Mental health in the schools: Promising directions for practice. In L. Juszczak & M. Fisher (Eds.), *Health care in schools. A special edition of Adolescent Medicine: State of the Art Reviews, 7,* 303–317.

Thomas, A., & Grimes, J. (Eds.). (1995). *Best practices in school psychology—III.* Washington, DC: National Association of School Psychologists.

Tyack, D. B. (1992). Health and social services in public schools: Historical perspectives. *The Future of Children, 2,* 19–31.

U.S. Department of Education. (1995). *School-linked comprehensive services for children and families: What we know and what we need to know.* Washington, DC: Author.

U.S. General Accounting Office. (1993). *School-linked services: A comprehensive strategy for aiding students at risk for school failure* (GAO/HRD-94–21). Washington, DC: Author.

Weissberg, R. P., Caplan, M., & Harwood, R. L. (1991). Promoting competent young people in competence-enhancing environments: A systems-based perspective on primary prevention. *Journal of Consulting and Clinical Psychology, 59,* 830–841.

Weisz, J. R., & Weiss, B. (1993). *Effects of psychotherapy with children and adolescents.* Newbury Park, CA: Sage.

Young, N., Gardner, S., Coley, S., Schorr, L., & Bruner, C. (1994). *Making a difference: Moving to outcome-based accountability for comprehensive services.* Falls Church, VA: National Center for Service Integration.

Paula Duncan, M.D., F.A.A.P.
Judith B. Igoe, R.N., M.S., F.A.A.N.

8 School Health Services

○ *Preventive services, education, emergency care, referral and management of acute and chronic health conditions.*
○ *Designed to promote the health of students, identify and prevent health problems and injuries, and ensure care for students.*

*I*t is Monday morning, the reception area of the school health center is crowded, and the school nurse and the health assistant are busy. Lisa is waiting to have a cut on her hand checked and discuss some questions. As she waits, her eyes wander to a poster advertising the school's student health fair and screenings for cholesterol, fitness, and stress. "I wonder if they do drug testing?" she asks herself.

John has come for his seizure medication. He usually comes at noon, but because his mother forgot to get his prescription refilled, he did not take his prescribed doses last evening or this morning. The school nurse must contact his mother and alert the teacher to watch for seizure activity.

The school nurse must leave in 15 minutes to meet with the principal and the social worker for an interview with a nurse practitioner who has applied for a position in the Get Well, Stay Well primary health care center that will open soon. The new venture is sponsored jointly by one of the hospital networks in town and the school system, with the endorsement of the school and community health advisory board. The school nurse is hopeful that this center will be able to directly manage some of the health problems that are interfering with the attendance of students with special health care needs and provide care to students whose medical problems might otherwise go untreated.

Also in the waiting room is Roberta, a sophomore who is visibly pregnant.

Health Is Academic: A Guide to Coordinated School Health Problems. Edited by Eva Marx and Susan Frelick Wooley, with Daphne Northrop. New York: Teachers College Press, 1998. ISBN 0-8077-3713-5 (pbk.), ISBN 0-8077-3714-3 (cloth). Prior to photocopying items for classroom use, please contact the Copyright Clearance Center, Customer Service, 222 Rosewood Dr., Danvers, MA 01923, USA, tel. (508) 750-8400. © 1998 Education Development Center, Inc. All rights reserved.

Together Roberta, her mother, and the school nurse have worked out prenatal care at a nearby community health center. Four student peer educators who will start youth service work soon are also in the health center. Their mentor, the school health educator, is due shortly. Her goal for this youth service project is to stem the alarming increase in eating disorders among students by providing more nutritional and stress management information to students.

The waiting room is a warm and caring environment. Music plays softly from a radio, school announcements over the loud speaker are understandable but not blaring, and the general atmosphere reflects the concern people have for one another, students and staff alike. The telephone rings. It is the receptionist for Metro Help, the community agency from which speech, physical, and occupational therapies are contracted. The caller confirms a school health services team meeting scheduled later in the week.

Suddenly, the school health center door flies open. "Help! Come quick!" shouts Jim, the security guard. Heads turn, pulse rates shoot up, and conversations stop in mid-sentence as everyone waits for Jim to continue. "I need the school nurse immediately in the cafeteria," he says. The emergency side of school health services will be put to the test.

School health centers are busy places that do important work. Some students must take medicines, others experience acute illness, and still others have special health needs. Behavioral and health problems of school-age young people often hinder their ability to learn. Growing numbers of young people in the United States today have health conditions that affect their school attendance and classroom performance. The extent of physical, emotional, psychological, and social problems present in some student populations is so great that the primary mission of the school—education—cannot proceed if these pathologies are not addressed (Carnegie Council on Adolescent Development, 1989).

School health services contribute to goals of both the education system and the health care system. Students with special education needs frequently also have health and human services needs (Klerman, 1988), and schools are logical settings to provide these services in an integrated fashion (Committee on School Health, 1993; Dryfoos, 1994; Lear, 1996; Santelli, Morreale, Wigton, & Grason, 1996). Because most children older than five years attend school, schools are particularly ideal places to provide preventive services such as mass screenings for vision and hearing. In addition, many schools offer health and social services that help overcome troublesome health care access issues and fill gaps in the health care system in communities where community-based health services are limited or unavailable to many students, especially those who are poor and uninsured. The provision of such services illustrates a public commitment to achieving minimum health standards for all social groups during a time when many students have no other opportunity to obtain such services (Solloway & Budetti, 1995). Moreover, preventive health services provided through schools, coupled with health education and counseling that promote healthy lifestyles and self-sufficiency, can help contain health care costs (U.S. Department of Health and Human Services, 1991).

Public support for school health services is evident. Over the last 10 years education and health leaders have supported an agenda for improved health services for adolescents. The education goals for the year 2000 (National Education Goals Panel, 1994) as well as other education initiatives concentrate on coordination and collaboration of health, education, and social services for young people within and outside the school organization. Reports of the National Association of State Boards of Education (1996) and the American Medical Association (National Commission on the Role of the School and the Community in Improving Adolescent Health, 1990), the Carnegie Foundation (Carnegie Council on Adolescent Development, 1990), the Robert Wood Johnson Foundation (1995), the American Nurses Association (1991), the National Nursing Coalition for School Health (1995a), and the Ad Hoc Working Group on Integrated Services (1996) have advocated strengthening school health services (Igoe & Giordano, 1992). In 1993, the Phi Delta Kappa/Gallup Poll of attitudes toward the public schools found that a majority of the American public would like public schools to provide student health services. And 91% of respondents to a 1995 poll by the same groups considered "servicing the emotional and health needs of students" an important function of schools (Elam & Lowell, 1995).

Two recent studies, the School Health Policies and Programs Study (SHPPS) (Small et al., 1995) and the National School Health Survey (Davis, Fryer, White, & Igoe, 1995), documented the health services that school districts provide. The National School Health Survey found that 85% of all public school systems offer some health services. SHPPS, which examined health policies for grades K–12 and service delivery for junior high/middle schools and high schools found that about half of the states require schools to offer school health nurse services. Of all the school districts examined, 74% had a person responsible for directing or coordinating school health services. Of the junior high/middle schools and high schools surveyed, 86% reported providing some type of health services. Sixty-six percent of the junior high/middle schools had a health services facility, and of this group, 89% had a health room, 8% had a school-based health center, and 2% had a school-linked clinic.

Federal law requires schools to serve all students, making it incumbent on schools to provide health services that allow disabled children to attend school. To comply with the Individuals with Disabilities Education Act of 1990 and its predecessor, the Education for all Handicapped Children Act of 1973, schools have had to provide individual health care for qualifying students since 1974. In 1994, 44% of secondary schools in the United States developed individualized health plans as part of individualized education plans for students with special needs (Small et al., 1995).

State mandates for school health services also influence the health services local school systems offer. For example, 51% of all states do not allow students to attend school without proper immunizations (or signed refusal). More than a third allow students to attend school as long as they are properly immunized within a specified number of days of entering (Small et al., 1995). Ninety percent of states recommend that districts and schools have procedures to keep confidential the health status of HIV-infected students and staff; 86% of states require that districts and schools have policies to ensure the safe handling of body fluids that could transmit infectious diseases. Another factor that influences schools to offer health services is the need to ensure the safety of students and provide needed care in cases of emergency.

Health services that schools provide, in partnership with community resources, can benefit children and youth in a number of ways. Children and youth will:

- come to school healthy and ready to learn, thus reducing barriers to their learning and enhancing their learning potential (Institute of Medicine, 1997)
- be safe from major injuries caused by hazards or violence (Education Commission of the States, 1996)
- have a primary provider for preventive medical and dental services (American Medical Association, 1994; Casamassimo, 1996; National Center for Education in Maternal and Child Health, 1994)
- receive needed nutrition and mental health, substance abuse, sexual abuse, and other counseling services (Knitzer, Steinberger, & Fleisch, 1990).

ESSENTIAL FUNCTIONS OF SCHOOL HEALTH SERVICES

The working group of national organizations that informed the development of this chapter identified core health services that every school should provide:

- screening, diagnostic, treatment, and health counseling services
- referrals and linkages with other community providers
- health promotion and injury and disease prevention education

The health services schools provide beyond the core services will depend on other resources in the community as well as students' health needs.

Screening, Diagnostic, Treatment, and Health Counseling Services

Screening, diagnostic, treatment, and health counseling services respond to medical emergencies, identify and address health problems, protect students through immunizations, and enable students with special needs to participate in classes. They require record maintenance and management to ensure proper documentation and follow-up care.

Urgent and Emergency Care. Emergency situations that require special procedures and appropriately trained staff include severe allergic reactions; drug overdoses; choking; suicide attempts; trauma related to violence; and serious injuries due to unintentional causes, including sports-related injuries. The National School Health Survey found that 99% of schools surveyed offered first aid. Similarly, 99% of the junior high/middle schools and high schools the SHPPS surveyed offered first aid; moreover, in 54% of these schools, staff held certification from the Red Cross or another agency.

Timely Identification of and Appropriate Intervention for Health Problems. Common health problems that students either bring to school or develop while at school include infections, injuries, asthma, and emotional difficulties. If not attended to promptly, these problems can lead to absence from school and, in extreme cases, failure in school.

Mandated and Necessary Screenings for All Students. Screenings help identify problems, such as vision and hearing deficits that can interfere with learning (Young, 1986). Eighty-seven percent of the schools that participated in the National School Health Survey offered some type of screening services (Davis, Fryer, White, & Igoe, 1995). According to SHPPS, 95% of school districts require schools to conduct screening for vision and hearing; a much smaller percentage—only 40%—require schools to screen for blood pressure (Small et al., 1995). Often, both schools and well-child primary health care programs offer vision and hearing screenings, some have expressed concern about possible duplication of effort. However, schools should not discontinue screenings unless a community-based approach ensures screening for all children.

In some schools specially trained nurses perform Early and Periodic Screening, Diagnosis, and Treatment (EPSDT) physicals for students with no other source of well-child health care. The focus of such screenings is on referral and treatment for identified health problems.

Assistance with Medication During the School Day. Some children with special health needs, for example, asthma, attention deficit hyperactivity disorder, epilepsy, require regular medications during the school day. Other students require medications occasionally, for example, antibiotics, anti-inflammatories, for other health problems. The process of dispensing medications to students requires careful documentation and appropriate supervision. If students, for example, those with asthma, carry their medication with them and self-administer it, they must have preparation for this responsibility (Small et al., 1995).

Almost all school districts (97%) require documentation before school staff, including nurses, can give medications to students. Ninety percent require written permission from a parent, and 81% require instructions from a physician. Eighty-nine percent of these school district's policies on medication address medicines that students bring to school (Small et al., 1995).

Health Services for Children with Special Health Needs. Scientific advances along with federal law and school reform have made it possible for many students with chronic conditions such as diabetes, cancer, arthritis, severe asthma, emotional disorders, and post-traumatic head injuries to attend neighborhood schools. Schools must plan and deliver such students' medications, special treatments, supplies, and equipment in consultation with their families and physicians. Seventy-five percent of the schools that participated in the National School Health Survey have a health component in the Individualized Education Plan (IEP) for students assigned for special education services, and 58% provide case management of chronic health problems (Davis, Fryer, White, & Igoe, 1995). Half the school districts that participated in the survey provide complex nursing care. Of the junior high/middle schools and senior high schools in the SHPPS sample, 40% provide complex nursing care to special needs students. School health nurses provide this care in two-thirds of the schools, and teachers provide the care in 12%.

Health Counseling. Health services providers can provide information and counseling about healthy and safe lifestyle choices and risk reduction that can motivate students to take responsibility for their safety and health. Health counseling services for students with health problems discovered during screening, diagnosis, or treatment might address cigarette smoking, use of alcohol and other illicit drugs, HIV/AIDS, unintentional injuries, eating disorders, adjustment to puberty and adolescence, hypertension, immunization status, or health-related learning disorders. Pregnant students and those with sexually transmitted diseases and other complex health problems often face severe emotional and physical challenges for which they need special health counseling.

Health Promotion, Prevention Education, and Preventive Services

Activities to promote health that are carried out by school health services providers can help students, their families, and school staff identify and minimize health risks and adopt good health habits, such as wearing seat belts, eating nutritious foods, practicing safer sexual behaviors, and managing stress (Igoe, 1993). These activities can be designed for individuals, for groups or classrooms, or for the entire student body. Nurses, social workers, health educators, and clinic aides often make classroom presentations that contribute to the prevention of high-risk behaviors and promote healthy lifestyles. They share this responsibility with staff working in other components of a coordinated school health program. Effective schoolwide efforts include posters, displays and special projects, announcements over the public address system or via e-mail, articles in the school newspaper, and special events such as health fairs.

Preventive health services include activities such as providing immunizations and dental sealants. Schools in states that require students to be immunized for certain communicable diseases must check appropriate immunizations. For example, many states have enacted highly specific regulations specifying immunizations required for school attendance and the records that schools must maintain (Small et al., 1995). School immunization clinics are most often held in areas that serve students with poor access to preventive health care, in response to the outbreak of an infectious disease, or following release of a new vaccine. Many school immunization projects are collaborations with community public health agencies or community health centers (Davis, Fryer, White, & Igoe, 1995).

Referrals to and Linkages with Other Community Providers

Careful assessment of and appropriate intervention at school for students' seemingly minor health complaints can reduce unnecessary absences. School health services personnel often identify underlying health problems and, when necessary, provide appropriate and timely referrals to their community health care providers or school-based health centers for further diagnosis and treatment.

School health services staff also can work with families and social services agencies to facilitate access to primary health care services. Frequently students with physical health problems also have underlying emotional disorders (Starfield, 1992). For example, a youth who complains of abdominal discomfort or always feels ill might suffer from an eating disorder or need referral for psychiatric services. By providing links to community health services (such as private providers, public health clinics, community health centers, dental services, or mental health services) or school-based health centers, school health services staff can help students obtain needed care, particularly for services not available on site.

WHO IMPLEMENTS THE ESSENTIAL FUNCTIONS OF SCHOOL HEALTH SERVICES?

The range of activities that falls under the rubric of school health services requires the involvement of a variety of professionals, including school nurses, physicians, dentists, dental hygienists, counselors, psychologists, social workers, and other pupil services personnel such as occupational therapists, physical therapists, and speech pathologists. Over 50% of school districts in the United States hire or contract with registered nurses or counselors, 55% hire or contract with counselors, 40% with psychologists, and 21% with social workers (Davis, Fryer, White, & Igoe, 1995). On average, the 11.6% of districts that hire or contract for physicians' services engage a physician for 5.6 hours a week. Forty-three percent of districts employ speech pathologists, 19% employ occupational therapists, and 14% employ audiologists, reflecting the importance placed on services for children with special needs.

Figure 8.1 provides a more in-depth look at health services providers in schools based on a survey of U.S. school districts. Although several types of service providers, including dentists, dental hygienists, and athletic trainers were not included in the survey, they also provide valuable health services in some schools (Davis, Fryer, White, & Igoe, 1995).

Due to budgetary constraints, many school districts, especially those with a student enrollment exceeding 2,500, have expanded school health services by hiring school health assistants. The same school personnel survey revealed that 29% of districts use school health assistants, who work under the close supervision of school nurses. School health assistants provide first aid for minor injuries, administer medications, screen students for lice, perform clerical duties, and maintain immunization records (Fryer & Igoe, 1996).

Another approach some schools are taking to deliver school health ser-

FIGURE 8.1. Staffing Patterns in School Health Programs

Position	% of all districts that have the position	Average number of full-time equivalents
Audiologist	14	0.2
Counselor	55	3.1
Dietitian	14	0.1
Hazardous waste specialist	4	0.1
Health promotion specialist	4	0.0
Licensed practical nurse	9	0.2
Nutritionist	3	0.0
Occupational therapist	19	0.2
Paraprofessional	20	0.7
Physical assistant	3	0.1
Physical therapist	15	0.2
Physician	12	0.1
Psychiatrist	2	0.0
Psychologist	41	0.9
Registered nurse	57	2.3
Risk manager	7	0.1
Social worker	21	0.4
Speech pathologist	43	1.2

Source: Adapted from Davis, Fryer, White, & Igoe, 1995

vices is to contract with one or more community agencies. Although contracting appeals to some administrators as one less burden on a school, contracting can result in a loss of control over the program, less coordination with other components of a school's health program, and deterioration in the quality of service (Igoe, 1995). Administrators would be well advised to consider both sides of the issue carefully before deciding to contract for health services.

A common perception is that fiscal restraint in school districts has led to a reduction in the number of nurses and other school health services personnel. However, 16% of respondents to the health services personnel survey indicated that the nursing staff was larger in 1993 than in 1990, 75% said the nursing staff was the same size, and only 9% reported that the nursing staff was smaller. During the same period the number of school health assistants increased in 22% of the responding districts and stayed the same in 72%. Over 30% of the reporting school districts added social workers, counselors, and health educators. The number of physicians employed in school health also increased (Davis, Fryer, White, & Igoe, 1995). But even so, the SHPPS study found that only 32% of junior high/middle schools and senior high schools have a ratio of 1 nurse per 750 students, as recommended by the National Association of School Nurses (Nancy Brener, Centers for Disease Control and Prevention, personal communication, May 27, 1997).

Credentials for School Health Services Personnel

Most professions that provide health services require a license and/or a certificate. A license is a legal credential that establishes that an individual has the basic competencies/requirements for generalized practice in a discipline (for example, nursing, medicine, dentistry). A certificate is another form of credential that signifies individuals are prepared to function in a designated role (for example, school nursing). Certificates and certification come from both national sources (for example, professional certification boards for different disciplines) and state agencies (for example, a state education agency). Certificates indicate general expertise in a discipline, such as a certified social worker, or a setting such as a certified school social worker.

Licensure and certification requirements for school health services personnel vary from state to state. When hiring school nurses and physicians, it is important to establish that they are licensed by the appropriate state regulatory board and have met state requirements for certification. Some states also have licensure requirements for psychologists, social workers, occupational and physical therapists, dental hygienists, and speech therapists and pathologists.

School systems might need certified personnel to access certain resources. For example, in some states certified school nurses are the only nurses in schools who are eligible for third-party reimbursement for services provided to students with special health care needs.

Paraprofessionals are the most recent members of the school health services team (Fryer & Igoe, 1996). Consequently, many states have not established a credentialing requirement for paraprofessionals (Task Force on Unlicensed Assistive Personnel, 1994). Determining whether a state has established a minimum standards requirement for the educational preparation and functions of paraprofessionals is the school's responsibility. Determining the qualifications of applicants for paraprofessional positions is particularly critical when they will provide clinical services to students, particularly those with special health care needs. When a school hires a paraprofessional, the school health services staff should provide supervision. School administrators need to know the process of delegating.

School administrators need job descriptions and credential requirements for all the members of a school's health services team to plan, recruit, and evaluate performance. The state education agency can supply this informa-

FIGURE 8.2. Major Areas of Responsibility for Professional Support Personnel

- *Planning/Preparation*—Designing activities that change the program or its implementation.
- *Intervention*—Delivering services to improve skills/functional abilities or inform recipients.
- *Consultation*—Collaborating with school personnel and/or parents to assist with and coordinate the delivery of services to students.
- *Staff Development*—Facilitating the staff's achievement of desired professional goals.
- *Liaison/Coordinator*—Coordinating information and program delivery within the school and between the school and its major constituents.
- *Assessment/Evaluation*—Gathering and interpreting data from individuals, groups, or programs to evaluate needs/performance.
- *Administration/Management*—Organizing, directing, or coordinating programs that include responsibility for budgeting, staffing, reporting, and other similar activities.
- *Professional Responsibilities/Development*—Developing and improving individual competence and skills and delivering service consistent with professional standards.

Source: Stronge, Helm, & Tucker, 1995

tion. Administrators should establish a tracking mechanism to ensure that all staff keep their credentials current.

Clarifying the Roles of School Health Services Providers

A lack of clarity about the roles of the various school health service providers can result in underutilization of staff, duplication of services, or turf wars among providers. To help schools avoid such situations, Stronge, Helm, and Tucker (1995) assessed the roles of support personnel in educational settings, including school nurses, psychologists, and counselors, and developed an "areas of responsibility" framework (see Figure 8.2) that provides a useful approach for identifying the core attributes of the role of each school health services staff member and delineating the similarities and differences between the various role functions. Districts using this framework asked school health service providers to identify their job responsibilities using the categories in the table. The school health team (consisting of various disciplines such as nurses, physicians, counselors, psychologists, hygienists, paraprofessionals, and occupational, physical, and speech therapists) reviewed completed forms looking for areas of overlap and uniqueness.

Education Development Center, Inc., with a group of school nurses, school counselors, school psychologists, and school social workers representing national professional organizations[1] used a similar process to develop the chart in Figure 8.3. This figure represents this interdisciplinary group's perceptions of their professions' work relative to schools. Health services and mental health professionals in school, district, and other groupings could replicate this activity to clarify roles within their own settings.

Choosing the Most Appropriate Option for Meeting Students' Health Services Needs

For students to benefit from health services, schools and communities need to work together to ensure the availability of age-appropriate health services. All schools should provide a core of health services and links to community providers. Many schools expand beyond the core services to ensure that other needed services (most often mental, behavioral, and primary health care services) are available to all students. In assessing which additional health services schools will provide, school and community professionals, students, and parents must consider students' health and educational needs as well as the availability of appropriate community health services. Anecdotal reports from school nurses throughout the country suggest that the move to managed care and other health care reforms has not solved the problem of access to health care. Students' health problems continue to interfere with their learning. School health services personnel continue to need places to refer students for diagnosis and treatment (Davis, Fryer, White, & Igoe, 1995).

The school health services component of a coordinated school health program can provide a range of services that address health needs: core services only, core services plus expanded health services, and services through school-based or school-linked health centers. An increasing number of schools are choosing the expanded services, the school-based center, or the school-linked health center options, often in partnership with local health departments, community health centers, and other community agencies. School personnel, students and their families, and community providers need to participate in assessment, planning, and implementation to determine which option best utilizes the strengths of both school and community resources to meet the health needs of students. The availability of community-based providers and their interest in participating in the assessment process and coordinating their services with the school's services often influences the choice.

FIGURE 8.3. The Big Picture: Partners at the Table

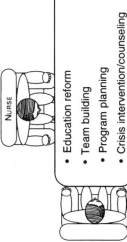

NURSE

- Apply clinical nursing knowledge and assessment skills to determine student health needs, interventions, and expected outcomes.
- Educate school community to the nature and educational relevance of disabling health conditions.
- Develop individual health care plans that focus on restoring health, promoting wellness, and minimizing/removing health barriers to learning.
- Create, disseminate, and monitor school health practices and protocols.

COUNSELOR

- Serve as school-based coordinator of comprehensive developmental guidance and integrated counseling services.
- Coordinate post-secondary educational and school-to-work transition programs.
- Broker resources for education/academic curricula and program information.
- Provide initial access point to on-site individual and group counseling in academic, personal, social/emotional, and career areas for entire school population.

Center table:

- Education reform
- Team building
- Program planning
- Crisis intervention/counseling
- Whole child development
- Community support building
- Assessment and referral
- School community wellness

PSYCHOLOGIST

- Apply learning theory for individuals and groups to improve instruction.
- Coordinate and evaluate plans for needs unique to individuals with special learning/behavior problems.
- Promote the use of psychology theory/practice in curriculum development, including sports and athletics.
- Design, implement, and analyze research studies/school programs.
- Provide psychotherapeutic interventions, including psychotherapeutic crisis interventions.

SOCIAL WORKER

- Apply an ecological perspective to psychosocial assessments that link home, school, and community factors affecting learning.
- Provide case management services to mobilize and coordinate resources for students and families.
- Take social action to create comprehensive community resources for students and families.
- Use dynamics of family systems to develop effective strategies for families of high-risk students.

Core Services Only Model. When a community assessment demonstrates that the majority of students have access to health care from community providers, a high quality core student health services model might be the appropriate choice. In this model, a school has the services of a nurse and provides special health services, such as speech or physical therapy, for students entitled to such services through federal legislation; counselors and psychologists employed by the school tend to devote their time to academic advising and testing, and provide some personal counseling and support groups within the school. For other needs, including primary health care, dental care, and behavioral problems, schools refer students to community resources.

Core Plus Expanded School Health Services Model. When students are unable to access community-based services or communities lack providers, schools sometimes provide services in addition to the core services. Assistance for students' behavioral, mental health, and substance abuse treatment needs are the most common additional services offered. The focus is on identification of problems and referral to community providers with most primary care continuing to be provided in the community. In other cases, specially educated nurses perform EPSDT physicals in school for students with no other source of well-child care. Schools either employ professionals to provide the services or contract with community providers or agencies. Ideally, school-employed professionals and community professionals work together as part of an interdisciplinary team.

School-Based Health Centers. More than 900 schools use school-based health centers to provide primary care services for a select group of the school population, especially students who need a variety of health services (Making the Grade, 1996). The National Health & Education Consortium defines a school-based student health center as "a health center *located in a school or on school grounds* that provides, at a minimum, on-site primary and preventive health care, mental health counseling, health promotion, referral and follow-up services for young people enrolled" (1995, p. 2, emphasis added). Some school-based health centers are components of larger organizational units such as family resource centers. Others are part of the Communities In Schools initiative, in which health center personnel from a variety of community agencies come to the school (Cities in Schools, 1991).

School-Linked Health Centers. Some school systems use a school-linked student health center, defined as a health center located *beyond school property* that serves one or more schools. The center may also serve young people from the area who are not students. Services include, but are not limited to, primary health care, screening and treatment, mental health counseling, health promotion, referral and follow up. The center usually has formal or informal ties to the schools—including accepting referrals from school personnel, providing priority appointments for students, marketing the services of the center in the school and/or offering classroom health education. A formal letter of agreement may or may not exist between the health center and the school. (National Health & Education Consortium, 1995, pp. 2–3, emphasis added)

INTEGRATING SCHOOL HEALTH SERVICES WITH THE OTHER COMPONENTS OF A COORDINATED SCHOOL HEALTH PROGRAM

Most school health services staff recognize the importance of coordinating with those responsible for the other seven components of the coordinated school health program to improve health outcomes for students. Yet, only one-third of school districts have done needs assessments and engaged in formal processes to design their school health services (Davis, Fryer, White, & Igoe, 1995). Planning for school health services, as well as for each of the other components of a coordinated school health program, should involve health professionals from the school and the community, school administrators, and students and their families and should occur as part of planning for an overall school health program.

Two groups are important to these efforts: a Healthy School Team (see Chapter 2) and an interdisciplinary school health services team. Members of the Healthy School Team usually include representatives from the school (the interdisciplinary school health team coordinator, representatives of those responsible for each component of a coordinated school health program, administrators, teachers, and students and their families), community health care providers (medical, dental, mental health), school-based student health center providers, hospitals, human services agencies (including public health, social services, child protection), and community government (including law enforcement). Functions of the Healthy School Team include recommending ways to strengthen school health services and coordinate students' access to medical, dental, and mental health services. Activities could include designing and completing a community/school assets inventory and needs assessment for preventive, therapeutic, and rehabilitative services (see the discussion of resource mapping in Chapter 2). In some communities a district-level advisory committee is responsible for these activities.

There should also be an interdisciplinary school health services team, comprised of the professionals who deliver health services on site in schools. The teams might include, when available, school nurses, school health assistants, school counselors, school psychologists, school social workers, school physicians, substance abuse counselors (student assistant program staff), physical therapists, and speech therapists. In many schools these professionals already work together; the creation of a formalized team with identified leadership could facilitate their efforts. A school health services coordinator, chosen from this core membership, can provide leadership and represent the team on the Healthy School Team or district advisory committee. With the coordinator's leadership, the interdisciplinary health services team would

- Oversee implementation of the school health services plan.
- Coordinate school health services with the other components of the school health program.
- Coordinate school health services with community-based medical and mental health providers, community health centers, school-based or school-linked health center staff (if one exists), and local public health officials.
- Coordinate the school's health services with those of the district.

The team should involve student and family representatives to work with school and community health service providers in the planning, operation, and evaluation of services as well as in developing the necessary policy framework. Policies might address issues such as confidentiality of health information as well as broader concerns such as infection control procedures.

If the coordinator also has responsibility for other components of a coordinated school health program, the health services component is more likely to be integrated into the larger program. For example, in a school where there is no family liaison or environmental specialist for health issues, the health coordinator sometimes oversees these activities (Resnicow & Allensworth, 1996). If the health coordinator is not a health care provider, a physician or a nurse with consultation from a physician must have direct responsibility for the delivery of a school's health services.

School health services team members can work with members of the other components of a coordinated school health program in many ways. A school physician can consult on or teach the communicable disease unit for a *health education* class. *Physical education* teachers can help the physical therapist design appropriate activities for students with physical limitations. Athletic trainers can work with *nutrition services* staff to coordinate athletes' special dietary needs. School nurses can coordinate the *staff wellness* program together with those who provide *counseling, psychological, and social services.*

The health coordinator could use student health records to identify health problems related to the *school environment* and suggest corrective actions.

Because of their role in facilitating students' access to primary health care for treatment and prevention services, school health services staff have the additional challenge of integrating their services with those of community-based primary care providers and, where they exist, school-based health centers. School health services personnel can facilitate partnerships with community agencies to better meet the health needs of students. In schools where a community-based provider serves as a school consultant, that person can be responsible for much of the liaison work. Public health staff can coordinate access to community human services providers. School links with public health staff have resulted in combined efforts to address screening, immunization, safety, and access-to-care issues. Many school nurses have developed formal and informal relationships with community pediatricians, family practice physicians, nurse practitioners, and physician assistants, who provide valuable consultation on the care of children with special health needs and schoolwide health and health policy issues. School nurses can involve community health service providers in the planning, operation, and evaluation of services as well as in developing policies to support them (see Chapter 4).

WHO SUPPORTS THOSE PROVIDING SCHOOL HEALTH SERVICES?

Financial Support

Historically, schools have paid the cost of school health services. Some local education agencies have supported school health services by providing building space for a health center or providing salary and benefits for school nurses. Beginning in the 1980s, some schools discovered how to access other sources of funding. For example, some school districts pay for services that directly influence learning, while public health agencies pay for school-based health promotion and services related to controlling infections and communicable diseases and preventing injuries. Sometimes insurance companies, health maintenance organizations, Medicaid, or other third-party sources provide some financial support for optional services such as primary care (Meeker, DeAngelis, Berman, Freeman, & Oda, 1986).

Several states use state revenues to fund school health services (Making the Grade, 1995). Others use discretionary federal block grant funding to support school health services. One primary source of federal funding is Title V of the Social Security Act (more commonly referred to as the Maternal and Child Health Block Grant). The Preventive Health Services Block Grant and the Social Services Block Grant are other potential sources of federal support.

The Health Resources and Services Administration provides funding through the Healthy Schools, Healthy Communities grant program to demonstration sites that provide preventive health services for students. The Universal Access to Immunizations Program, administered by the Centers for Disease Control and Prevention, provides immunizations through health care facilities and schools at a nominal cost to children not covered by private insurance.

Financial support available through Medicaid reimbursement is an increasing source of funding for school health services. The Health Care Financing Administration's *Medicaid and Schools: A Technical Assistance Guide* (U.S. Department of Health and Human Services, in press) is a useful source of information on Medicaid funding. The Individuals with Disabilities Education Act of 1997 (IDEA) allows the use of federal Medicaid funding for children with special education needs; Medicaid payment is permitted through a child's Individualized Education Plan or an Individualized Family Service Plan. A school can also bill Medicaid if it is an eligible provider and serves children under the Early and Periodic Screening, Diagnosis, and Treatment (EPSDT) Program. Medicaid/EPSDT funds a broad range of medically necessary health care services including physical and mental health assessments, immunizations, laboratory tests, and dental and vision services.

Title I of the Improving America's Schools Act of 1995 (IASA) provides flexible formula grant funding from the U.S. Department of Education's Office of Elementary and Secondary Education for state education agencies to help disadvantaged students meet high standards. Schools may use Title I funds to provide student health services and education that addresses the social, emotional, and physical health and safety of students. Under Title IV, Safe and Drug-free Schools and Communities, of the same act, state education agencies, governors' offices, and local education agencies receive funds for drug- and violence-prevention programs that may include drug prevention education, counseling, rehabilitation referral, or integrating the delivery of services. Other revenue sources administered by the U.S. Department of Education include Title III, Amendments to Other Acts, Part B—Education for Homeless Children and Youth; and Title I, Prevention and Intervention Services for Youth Who are Neglected and Delinquent or At Risk of Dropping Out. Schools may use these funds to support activities such as counseling, social work, and psychological services; drop-out prevention programs; and before- and after-school programs.

Recognizing the need to identify funding sources that support all components of a coordinated school health program, the Centers for Disease

Control and Prevention has established the School Health Finance Project. Information about funding sources is available on the Internet at http:www.cdc.gov/nccdphp/dash.

Other Types of Support

Putting the Pieces Together: Comprehensive Schooling Strategies for Children and Families (U.S. Department of Education, 1996) outlines ways federal and state officials, communities, and private agencies can work together to set and achieve benchmarks for improving student well-being. The Working Group on Comprehensive Services, a panel created by and staffed by the U.S. Department of Education, prepared the report to study ways to achieve "shared accountability" for the healthy development of children and youth. The report's recommendations assume the availability of school health services.

Most states and districts take some action to increase the likelihood that schools follow policies and guidelines relative to school health. For example, 69% of states provide training for school staff on infection control guidelines, 86% distribute such guidelines to school staff, and 48% of states and 55% of districts monitor compliance with such guidelines (Small et al., 1995).

Because of their shared focus on prevention and health outcomes, partnerships between managed care organizations and schools are growing (Making the Grade, 1996). Managed care organizations often are interested in supporting schools' efforts in the areas of preventive services, early identification of problems, and health promotion activities.

Along with states, districts, and local communities, many national organizations also support school health services and school health services professionals (Figure 8.4). Several of these organizations have developed excellent recommendations related to school health services. The National Health & Education Consortium's publication, *School Nursing: Trends for the Future,* which addresses trends in nursing such as the need for a baccalaureate degree, state graduate-level curricula certification mechanisms, and clinical supervision by masters-level clinicians (Passarelli, 1993). The National Association of School Nurses makes available policy papers on education, certification, and supervision of school nurses and provides guidance on policies for HIV-infected students and staff. The National Nursing Coalition for School Health (1995b) has published an article on national issues and priorities that includes recommendations for standards and discusses legal and ethical concerns, preservice and inservice professional collaboration, research, and financing. The American Academy of Pediatrics has identified the knowledge and skills that pediatricians need to provide quality

FIGURE 8.4. Selected National Organizations that Support School Health Services Professionals

Advocates for Youth
Ambulatory Pediatric Association
American Academy of Child and Adolescent Psychiatry
American Academy of Family Practice
American Academy of Pediatrics
American Medical Association
American Nurses Association
American Public Health Association
American School Health Association
Association of Maternal and Child Health Programs
National Assembly on School-Based Health Care
National Association of Pediatric Nurse Associates and Practitioners
National Alliance of Pupil Services Organizations (and its member
     organizations)
National Association of Community Health Centers
National Association of School Nurses
National Association of State School Nurse Consultants
National Education Association
National Safety Council
Robert Wood Johnson Foundation

school health and has also issued a comprehensive manual on school health (Committee on School Health, 1993).

The American School Health Association's (1995) *Guidelines for Comprehensive School Health Programs* includes recommendations on school health services policy and administrative support, student services, physician and nursing standards, and professional development. Publications issued by Making the Grade, a program funded by a grant from the Robert Wood Johnson Foundation (1995), have also outlined recommendations for school-based health centers. The School Health Policy Initiative (Brellochs & Fothergill, 1995) analyzed school-based primary care services and worked with national organizations to develop model policies.

The 1994 National Consensus Building Conference on School-Linked Integrated Service Systems (Ad Hoc Working Group on Integrated Services, 1994), attended by more than 50 child-serving national organizations, developed several principles to guide further action. These include the following:

- the formation of interdisciplinary teams and partnerships
- development of operating systems and techniques that facilitate inter-disciplinary interagency coordination
- continued attention to resource needs.

ACTION STEPS FOR IMPLEMENTING SCHOOL HEALTH SERVICES

Implementation of school health services as part of a coordinated school health program requires actions at the local level and support at the national and state levels. School health services will look different from one school district to another, depending upon the needs of the students, school characteristics, and community resources. Community members, parents, and students can help school professionals determine needs and resources for ensuring provision of essential school health services.

Action Steps for Schools and Communities

- Form a Healthy School Team with representatives from the school (the interdisciplinary school health team coordinator, representatives of those responsible for each component of a coordinated school health program, administrators, teachers, and students and their families), community health care providers (medical, dental, mental health), school-based student health center providers, hospitals, human services agencies (including public health, social services, child protection), and community government (including law enforcement).
- Establish an interdisciplinary school health services team comprised of well-qualified, appropriately educated health providers. The team can have different configurations but should include school nurses, health assistants, nurse practitioners, and physicians in partnership with school counselors, school psychologists, and school social workers. This team could function as a subcommittee of the Healthy School Team and could be school-based or districtwide.
- Identify a school health services coordinator from among the team's membership to allocate services efficiently and to link the work of this team to the people responsible for the other components of a coordinated school health program in the school or district.
- Map health care resources and student access to health care. The team should assess the availability of primary care, dental care, emergency medical care, and other services such as behavioral and drug and alcohol services for students.
- Use the results of mapping to identify the most appropriate school health services configuration. A coordinated school/community health care deliv-

ery system will differ from one district to another depending on students' needs, school characteristics, and community resources. Matching characteristics of community resources to student needs and assets informs the choice of the system best suited for each community: core services only, core with expanded services, school-based health center, school-linked health center.

- Establish a continuous quality management program with student and parent input. As part of this program, develop a data management system to evaluate the provision of school health services and link school health services to community services to avoid duplication. In addition, the program needs a short- and long-term financial plan for health services. The plan should begin with a simple per-pupil-per-day cost analysis and expand to investigate all possible funding sources. The Healthy School Team should help develop solid financial support for these community-oriented school health services.

Action Steps for National and State Organizations and Universities

- Establish certification processes and educational opportunities that can prepare diverse school health professionals to function effectively as members of interdisciplinary, results-oriented teams.
- Develop and disseminate guidelines, best practices, and model policies for school health services that focus on a range of service delivery models.
- Provide technical assistance and position statements that support the development of a coordinated service system.
- Provide data, funding, training, and statistical support for mapping and community assessment.
- Educate staff to help schools blend funding streams, accept consolidated applications and reports from communities, establish program objectives, and ensure that new initiatives relate to and build on each other.
- Conduct or fund research that examines the impact of school health services on student well-being and academic performance.

CONCLUSION

All too many students come to school today with health needs that interfere with their ability to learn and to reach their full potential. Although parents and other caregivers have primary responsibility for the health care their children receive, schools also have responsibility for promoting the well-being of students. Schools and families must work together to ensure that students receive the services they need, whether at school or through other resources in the community.

Many professionals representing a diversity of disciplines provide health services to children, youth, and their families. To fully meet students' needs,

> representatives of all health services, from primary care to specialized services for children with disabilities, must come together and form a single cohesive strategy. School health services must respond to the identified needs of children in the community, and they must do so in an organized approach that builds on carefully developed ties to community-based services as well as fully integrated partnerships among those who provide care within the school setting. Only in that way can school-based health services play an effective role in the future of child health care in the United States. (Lear, 1996, p. 178)

NOTE

1. American Psychological Association, American School Counselor Association, National Association of School Nurses, National Association of School Psychologists, National Association of Social Workers.

REFERENCES

Ad Hoc Working Group on Integrated Services. (1994). *Integrating education, health, and human services for children, youth, and families: Systems that are community-based and school-linked.* Washington, DC: American Academy of Pediatrics.

Ad Hoc Working Group on Integrated Services. (1996). *Moving from principles to practice: A resource guide.* Washington, DC: American Academy of Pediatrics.

American Medical Association. (1994). *Guidelines for Adolescent Prevention Services (GAPS): Recommendations and rationale.* Baltimore, MD: Williams & Wilkins.

American Nurses Association. (1991). *Nursing's agenda for healthcare reform.* Kansas City, MO: Author.

American School Health Association. (1995). *Guidelines for comprehensive school health programs.* Kent, OH: Author.

Brellochs, C., & Fothergill, K. (1995). *Ingredients for success: Comprehensive school-based health centers* (A special report on the 1993 national work group meetings). Bronx, NY: School Health Policy Initiative, Montefiore Medical Center, Albert Einstein College of Medicine.

Carnegie Council on Adolescent Development. (1989). *Turning points: Preparing American youth for the 21st century. Report of the Task Force on Education of Young Adolescents.* Washington, DC: Author.

Carnegie Council on Adolescent Development. (1990). *Turning points: Preparing*

American youth for the 21st century: Recommendations for transforming middle schools. Washington, DC: Author.

Casamassimo, P. (Ed.). (1996). *Bright futures in practice: Oral health guide.* Arlington, VA: National Center for Education in Maternal and Child Health.

Cities in Schools. (1991). *Cities in schools: Turning children around.* Alexandria, VA: Author.

Committee on School Health, American Academy of Pediatrics. (1993). *School health: Policy and practice.* Elk Grove Village, IL: American Academy of Pediatrics.

Davis, M., Fryer, G. E., White, S., & Igoe, J. B. (1995). *A closer look: A report of select findings from the National School Health Survey 1993–1994.* Denver: Office of School Health, University of Colorado Health Sciences Center.

Dryfoos, J. (1994). *Full-service schools: A revolution in health and social services for children, youth, and families.* San Francisco, CA: Jossey-Bass.

Education Commission of the States. (1996). *Youth violence: A policymaker's guide.* Denver, CO: Author.

Elam, S., & Lowell, C. R. (1995). The 27th annual Phi Delta Kappa/Gallup poll of the public's attitudes toward the public schools. *Phi Delta Kappan, 77*(1), 44.

Fryer, G. E., & Igoe, J. B. (1996). Functions of school nurses and health assistants in U.S. school health programs. *Journal of School Health, 66*(2), 55–58.

Igoe, J. B. (1993). Healthier children through empowerment. In J. W. Barnett & J. M. Clark (Eds.), *Research in health* (pp. 145–153). London: Macmillan.

Igoe, J. B. (1995). *Is contracting an option? Office of School Health report.* Denver: University of Colorado Health Sciences Center.

Igoe, J. B., & Giordano, B. (1992). *Expanding school health services to service families in the 21st century.* Washington, DC: American Nurses Publishing.

Institute of Medicine. (1997). *Schools and health: Our nation's investment.* D. Allensworth, E. Lawson, L. Nicholson, & J. Wyche (Eds.). Washington, DC: National Academy Press.

Klerman, L. (1988). School absence—A health perspective. *Pediatric Clinics of North America, 35,* 1253–1269.

Knitzer, J., Steinberger, A., & Fleisch, B. (1990). *At the schoolhouse door: An examination of programs and policies for children with behavioral and emotional problems.* New York: Bank Street College of Education.

Lear, J. G. (1996). School-based services and adolescent health: Past, present and future. In L. Juszczak & H. Fisher (Eds.), *Adolescent medicine: State of the art reviews* (pp. 163–180). Philadelphia: Haneley and Belfus, Inc.

Making the Grade, George Washington University. (1995). *Issues in financing school-based health centers: A guide for state officials.* Washington, DC: Author.

Making the Grade, George Washington University. (1996, Fall). School-based health centers continue to grow. *Access to comprehensive school-based health services for children and youth* [newsletter] (pp. 1–2). Washington, DC: Author.

Meeker, R. J., DeAngelis, C., Berman, B., Freeman, H. E., & Oda, D. (1986). A comprehensive school health initiative. *Image: Journal of Nursing Scholarship, 18*(3), 86–91.

National Association of State Boards of Education. (1996). *Someone at school has AIDS: A complete guide to education policies concerning HIV infection.* Alexandria, VA: Author.

National Center for Education in Maternal and Child Health. (1994). *Bright futures: Guidelines for health supervision of infants, children, and adolescents.* Arlington, VA: Author.

National Commission on the Role of the School and the Community in Improving Adolescent Health. (1990). *Code blue: United for healthier youth.* Alexandria, VA: National Association of State Boards of Education and American Medical Association.

National Education Goals Panel. (1994). *The National Education Goals Panel report: Building a nation of learners.* Washington, DC: U.S. Government Printing Office.

National Health & Education Consortium. (1995). *Starting young: School-based health centers at the elementary level.* Washington, DC: Author.

National Nursing Coalition for School Health. (1995a). School health nursing services: Exploring national issues and priorities. *Journal of School Health, 65*(9), 370–385.

National Nursing Coalition for School Health. (1995b). Issues, priority actions, and possible means to implement priority actions. *Journal of School Health, 65*(9), 381–383.

Passarelli, C. (1993). *School nursing: Trends for the future.* Washington, DC: National Health & Education Consortium.

Resnicow, K., & Allensworth, D. (1996). Conducting a comprehensive school health program. *Journal of School Health, 66*(2), 59–63.

Robert Wood Johnson Foundation. (1985). *Special report: National school health services program.* Princeton, NJ: Author.

Santelli, J., Morreale, M., Wigton, A., & Grason, H. (1996). School health centers and primary care for adolescents: A review of the literature. *Journal of Adolescent Health, 18,* 357–366.

Small, M. L., Majer, L. S., Allensworth, D. D., Farquhar, B. K., Kann, L., & Pateman, B. C. (1995). School health services. *Journal of School Health, 65*(8), 319–325.

Solloway, M. R., & Budetti, P. P. (Eds.). (1995). *Child health supervision: Analytical studies on the financing, delivery, and cost-effectiveness of preventive and health promotion services for infants, children, and adolescents.* Arlington, VA: National Center for Education in Maternal and Child Health.

Starfield, B. (1992). Child and adolescent health status measures. In R. E. Berman (Ed.), *The future of children: U.S. health centers for children. 2*(2)(pp. 25–39). Los Altos, CA: Center for the Future of Children, David and Lucille Packard Foundation.

Stronge, J. H., Helm, V. M., & Tucker, P. D. (1995). *Evaluation handbook for professional support personnel: School counselors, school psychologists, school nurses, and library media specialists.* Kalamazoo, MI: The Evaluation Center, Western Michigan University.

Task Force on Unlicensed Assistive Personnel. (1994). *Registered professional nurses and unlicensed assistive personnel.* Washington, DC: American Nurses Publishing.

U.S. Department of Education. (1996). *Putting the pieces together: Comprehensive schooling strategies for children and families.* Washington, DC: Author.

U.S. Department of Health and Human Services. (1991). *Healthy people 2000: National health promotion and disease prevention objectives.* Washington, DC: U.S. Department of Health and Human Services, Public Health Service. DHHS Publication No. (PHS) 91–50212.

U.S. Department of Health and Human Services, Health Care Financing Administration. (in press). *Medicaid and schools: A technical assistance guide.* Washington, DC: U.S. Government Printing Office.

Young, B. S. (1986, January). *A study of visual efficiency necessary for beginning reading.* Paper presented at the annual meeting of the Southwest Regional Conference of the International Reading Association, San Antonio, TX. (ERIC Document Reproduction Service No. ED 26B498).

Dorothy Caldwell, M.S., R.D., L.D.
Marion Nestle, Ph.D., M.P.H.
Werner Rogers, Ed.D.

9 School Nutrition Services

○ *Integration of nutritious, affordable, and appealing meals; nutrition education; and an environment that promotes healthy eating behaviors for all children.*

○ *Designed to maximize each child's education and health potential for a lifetime.*

L earning to eat and eating to learn are opportunities that schools can provide today's students to help them maximize education achievements, develop healthy lifestyles, and lower their risk of chronic disease. The first National Education Goal recognizes that nutrition is an essential first step toward learning readiness. It calls for children to receive "the nutrition and health care needed to arrive at school with healthy minds and bodies" (National Education Goals Panel, 1992). Even moderate undernutrition or hunger can reduce children's cognitive development and school performance (American Dietetic Association, 1990; Center on Hunger, Poverty, and Nutrition Policy, 1993; National Health & Education Consortium, 1993). Yet hunger is no stranger to millions of children in the United States (Community Childhood Hunger Identification Project, 1991). About 1% of elementary school-age children and 2 to 4% of teenage girls show evidence of iron-deficiency anemia (Dallman, Looker, Carroll, & Johnson, in press). Children with iron-deficiency anemia score lower on a wide range of tests, including developmental scales, intelligence tests, and tasks of specific cognitive function (Pollitt, 1994).

Children's brain function, and consequently school performance, is also

Health Is Academic: A Guide to Coordinated School Health Problems. Edited by Eva Marx and Susan Frelick Wooley, with Daphne Northrop. New York: Teachers College Press, 1998. ISBN 0-8077-3713-5 (pbk.), ISBN 0-8077-3714-3 (cloth). Prior to photocopying items for classroom use, please contact the Copyright Clearance Center, Customer Service, 222 Rosewood Dr., Danvers, MA 01923, USA, tel. (508) 750-8400. © 1998 Education Development Center, Inc. All rights reserved.

diminished by *short-term* or periodic hunger or malnutrition caused by missing or skipping meals (Pollitt, 1995). Well-nourished elementary school children perform better on cognitive tests when they have eaten breakfast than when they have skipped breakfast (Pollitt, Leibel, & Greenfield, 1981; Pollitt, Lewis, Garza, & Shulman, 1982–1983). A study of low-income elementary students found that participants in the School Breakfast Program had greater improvements in standardized test scores and lower rates of tardiness and absenteeism than comparable nonparticipants (Meyers, Sampson, Weitzman, Rogers, & Kayne, 1989). Surveys have shown that 12% of all students skip breakfast, 7% skip lunch (Devaney, Gordon, & Burghardt, 1995), and 40% of 8th- and 10th-grade students eat breakfast on two or fewer days of the week (American School Health Association [ASHA], Association for the Advancement of Health Education [AAHE], & Society for Public Health Education [SOPHE], 1989).

Generally, young people have unhealthy eating habits. More than 84% of young people exceed national recommendations for total fat intake (Lewis, Crane, Moore, & Hubbard, 1994), more than 90% exceed recommendations for saturated fat intake, and less than 21% eat the recommended five or more daily servings of fruits and vegetables (Krebs-Smith et al., 1996).

Along with mental functioning, diet is linked to a number of physical health problems of childhood and adolescence including obesity (Troiano, Flegal, Kuczmarski, Campbell, & Johnson, 1995), anorexia, bulimia (American Psychiatric Association, 1994), and dental caries (Public Health Service, 1991). Approximately 11% of today's youth aged 6 to 17 are seriously overweight, twice the rate in the 1960s (Troiano et al., 1995). Young people who are seriously overweight have higher rates of elevated blood cholesterol levels (Kikuchi et al., 1992) and high blood pressure (Shear, Freedman, Burke, Harsha, & Berenson, 1987). Furthermore, seriously overweight children and adolescents experience psychological stress, are often excluded from peer groups and discriminated against by adults, and have a poor body image and low self-esteem (Wadden & Stunkard, 1985). As many as 3% of adolescent and young adult females are anorexic or bulimic (American Psychiatric Association, 1994). These eating disorders can cause many severe complications, and mortality rates for these disorders are among the highest for any psychiatric disorder (Herzog & Copeland, 1985). More than half of school-age youth have dental caries (National Institute of Dental Research, 1989), and an estimated 50 million hours of school absences are due to dental problems or dental visits (Gift, Reisine, & Larach, 1992).

Diet is a known risk factor for many health problems of adulthood, including coronary heart disease, stroke, and cancer, the three leading causes of death in the United States (Committee on Diet and Health, 1989). Diet and sedentary lifestyles combined are second only to tobacco use as contributors to death (McGinnis & Foege, 1993). Diet is also linked to hypertension, which affects one in four adults (National High Blood Pressure Education Program, 1993) and osteoporosis, which affects more than 25 million people in the United States (National Institutes of Health Consensus Development Panel on Optimal Calcium Intake, 1994). Since some of the physiological processes related to these health problems start in childhood (National Heart, Blood, and Lung Institute, 1991) and dietary patterns tend to be established early in life (Kelder, Perry, Klepp, & Lytle, 1994), initiatives that promote healthy eating and physical activity patterns during childhood and adolescence can promote healthy growth and development, prevent some of the leading causes of illness and death, decrease health care costs, and improve long-term quality of life.

It is unrealistic to hold schools alone accountable for improving students' eating behaviors; eating habits are shaped by a variety of powerful influences, including the family, sociocultural and economic factors, the food industry, and the mass media (Crockett & Sims, 1995; Institute of Medicine, 1997). However, schools are a critical part of the social environment that shapes young people's behaviors. Helping students gain the knowledge, attitudes, and skills they need to develop healthy eating patterns is an important challenge for schools and communities. School nutrition is a critical component of a coordinated school health program. The record shows that school-based programs can improve students' eating habits (Contento et al., 1995a; Edmundson et al., 1996).

ESSENTIAL FUNCTIONS OF SCHOOL NUTRITION SERVICES

The essential functions of a school nutrition program are to provide:

- Access to a variety of nutritious, culturally appropriate foods that promote growth and development, pleasure in healthy eating, and long-term health, as well as prevent school day hunger and its consequent lack of attention to learning tasks
- Nutrition education that empowers students to select and enjoy healthy food and physical activity
- Screening, assessment, counseling, and referral for nutrition problems and the provision of modified meals for students with special needs.

There is no single model for the effective delivery of school nutrition services and education. All schools need to provide a basic level of support for each of the three essential functions; the specific services and education offered for each function will vary from school to school depending on the needs and priorities identified in the school and the community. For school nutrition services to carry out the functions, schools must create a school environment that provides opportunities and reinforcement for healthy eating and physical activity, must have the support of students' families and the larger community, must integrate nutrition services into the coordinated school health program, and must gain the cooperation of all school staff. The following discussion of each essential function of school nutrition services provides information to help with program planning and implementation.

Access to Nutritious, Culturally Appropriate Foods

Students are more inclined to eat nutritious foods when meals are affordable and meet students' tastes and when the school cafeteria environment is pleasant and relaxed. Meals provided through the National School Lunch Program (NSLP) and the School Breakfast Program (SBP) are affordable and planned to appeal to students. They provide sufficient food for students to avoid hunger during the day and improve their total nutrient intake. Research by the U.S. Department of Agriculture shows that the average lunch of students who participated in the NSLP provided at least one-third of the Recommended Dietary Allowance (RDA)[1] for food energy and key vitamins and minerals. Lunches of nonparticipants, by contrast, averaged less than one-third of the RDA for food energy, vitamin A, vitamin B-6, calcium, iron, and zinc (Gordon, Devaney, & Burghardt, 1995). Breakfasts of SBP participants exceed the goal of 25% of the RDA for food energy, whereas those of nonparticipants average only 19%. Compared with breakfasts of nonparticipants, breakfasts of SBP participants contain significantly more calcium, phosphorus, magnesium, thiamin, and riboflavin (Gordon, Devaney, & Burghardt, 1995). In addition, overall nutrient intake of SBP participants is better than that of nonparticipants (Nicklas, Weihang, Webber, & Berenson, 1993).

The problem, however, is that too few students take advantage of these programs. Although the NSLP is available to 92% of all students and more than 25 million students participate on average every school year, more than 40% of students make other choices with no nutrition standards (Gleason, 1995). Students with ample money often select a la carte foods, and many students who cannot afford a complete lunch of a la carte foods either skip lunch or select snacks from the a la carte program, vending machines, or snack bars. Poor eating among students has a snowball effect. As declining numbers of students select school meals for their lunch, perceived peer approval for choosing school meals decreases and the number of students who either skip meals or make poor food choices increases.

Although about half of all students attend schools that offer breakfasts through the SBP, only 19% of these students eat a school breakfast on a given day. Nationwide, about 10% of students participate in the SBP (Gleason, 1995). The number of schools that offer the SBP has almost doubled in the past 10 years, and 71.4% of schools that offer the NSLP also offer the SBP (Food Research and Action Council [FRAC], 1996). Students from low-income families are more likely to participate in the SBP than are students from families with higher incomes (Gleason, 1995). In 1990, 4.2 million students who were eligible for free meals—26% of all students eligible—did not apply (Abt Associates, 1990). Many of these students cite the stigma associated with free meals.

Health Promotion and Disease Prevention. In recent years, the focus of school meals has increasingly emphasized not only hunger and nutrient deficiency issues but also health promotion and disease prevention. The potential of school lunch and breakfast programs to contribute to healthy eating patterns is recognized in *Healthy People 2000* objective 2.17: "Increase to at least 90 percent the proportion of school lunch and breakfast services and child care food services with menus that are consistent with the nutrition principles in the Dietary Guidelines for Americans" (Public Health Service, 1991, p. 126). The USDA requires that school lunch and breakfast menus be consistent with the Dietary Guidelines for Americans (DGAs)[2] and meet one-third and one-fourth, respectively, of the RDA for key nutrients (USDA, 1995c). Like previous editions, the 1995 Dietary Guidelines emphasize balance and variety; an adequate consumption of grain products, vegetables, fruits, and calcium-rich foods; moderate consumption of sugar, salt, and sodium; and low consumption of fat, saturated fat, and cholesterol. The guidelines also stress balancing food consumption and physical activity for weight control (U.S. Department of Agriculture [USDA] & U.S. Department of Health and Human Services [HHS], 1995) and the importance of learning to enjoy healthy eating (USDA, 1995c).

Participation in the NSLP helps students meet some of the DGAs. Compared with nonparticipants, NSLP participants drink more milk and fewer soft drinks; eat more fruits and vegetables; and eat fewer cakes, cookies, salty snacks, and candies at lunch (Gordon & McKinney, 1995). However, NSLP participants consume more fat, saturated fat, and sodium at lunch than recommended and more than nonparticipants consume (Gordon, Devaney, & Burghardt, 1995). Many school meals need to have reduced amounts of fat and sodium and students need to learn to eat healthier. Recent initiatives that promote student acceptance and help foodservice managers reduce the fat and sodium content of school meals while maintaining or improving the taste and acceptability of the food appear later in this chapter.

Marketing Good Nutrition.   Improving the nutritional quality of school meals will have little effect if students do not eat the school meals. People eat food for enjoyment, and food choices depend on history, culture, and environment as well as on energy and nutrient needs (USDA, 1995c). Students are more likely to select and eat school meals when they meet students' taste and cultural preferences and are served in a supportive school environment (USDA, 1994a). A comfortable and attractive social environment also contributes to establishing healthy eating patterns among students (Crockett & Sims, 1995). Federal recommendations include environmental factors such as adequate time and space for students to eat meals in a pleasant and safe environment (Centers for Disease Control and Prevention [CDC], 1996) and policies that will improve the cafeteria environment (Child Nutrition Program Rule, 1995).

To improve student perceptions of school meals and compete with the fast-food restaurants whose products are being sold increasingly in schools, schools have developed in-house food brands; implemented restaurant-type menus; established food courts, portable food bars, and cart systems; employed chefs to improve the visual and sensory elements of food presentations; and increased a la carte offerings (American Dietetic Association, 1991; Pilant, 1994; Snyder, Lytle, Pellegrino, Anderson, & Selk, 1995). In addition, schools have used social marketing techniques to enhance the image of school meals, increase student demand for healthy foods, and solicit suggestions from their student customers on how to make school meals more appealing (Pilant, 1994; School Food Service Foundation, 1994).

School nutrition services should address all the food available at school, not only school meals. This includes a la carte items and food served in snack bars and vending machines; as classroom snacks; and at parties, special events, athletic competitions, fund raisers, and meetings of the parent association. Nutrition services staff can help schools set policies that require healthy choices wherever food is served in schools (CDC, 1996) and minimize the availability of snack foods high in fat, sodium, or sugar.

Program Management Tasks.   A fully functioning school nutrition services component of a coordinated school health program must maintain management procedures that ensure the delivery of high quality school food services (American School Food Service Association [ASFSA], 1995), including supervision to ensure that policies and procedures comply with state and federal regulations and local needs; maintenance of a management information system; preparation of budgets and ongoing review of financial and management practices; recruitment, hiring, and supervision of qualified personnel; and implementation of staff development activities.

Financing. Eighty-three percent of middle/junior and senior high schools surveyed recently expected their nutrition services to make enough money to cover their costs, excluding salaries, and among this group 29% expected the school foodservice to earn money in excess of costs (Pateman et al., 1995). School-wide support for the provision of affordable, nutritious school meals in supportive school environments should encourage decisions based on total program goals, rather than finances alone (Institute of Medicine, 1997; Story, Hayes, & Kalina, 1996).

Nutrition Education

Changing family structures, increasing autonomy of children in making food decisions, aggressive food advertising targeted to children, and the unhealthy eating habits of most young people underscore the need for sound nutrition education (Crockett & Sims, 1995). Well-designed and effectively implemented school-based nutrition education helps students improve their nutrition knowledge, attitudes, and behaviors. Nutrition education is likely to be most effective when it is behaviorally oriented and emphasizes primarily skills needed to adopt and maintain specific healthy eating behaviors (for example, eating less fat, eating more fruits and vegetables). Nutrition education that focuses narrowly on transmitting nutrition information typically produces gains in knowledge but has little effect on behavior (Contento et al., 1995a; Lytle & Achterberg, 1995). The coordination of classroom and cafeteria learning experiences promotes opportunities to practice skills and reinforce attitudes needed for behavioral change.

For efficiency as well as effectiveness, nutrition education should be part of sequential, comprehensive health education that connects personal behaviors and health and supports the National Health Education Standards (Joint Committee on National Health Education Standards, 1995). Unhealthy eating behaviors are often interrelated with other health risk factors and respond to the same behavior change techniques as other health education content areas (CDC, 1996) (see Chapter 3). In addition, nutrition education can enhance and be reinforced by integration into the lesson plans of other school subjects, such as mathematics, language arts, and social studies (Bagby, Campbell, & Achterberg, 1993).

The Centers for Disease Control and Prevention has identified the characteristics of nutrition instruction that are most likely to be effective. According to CDC, such instruction features:

- Behaviorally focused content that is developmentally appropriate and culturally relevant
- Active, participatory learning strategies

- Fun activities
- Repeated opportunities for students to taste foods that are low in fat, sodium, and added sugars and high in vitamins, minerals, and fiber
- Positive, appealing aspects of healthy eating patterns
- The benefits of healthy eating behaviors in the context of what is already important to students
- "Social learning" (Perry, Baranowski, & Parcel, 1990) techniques such as role modeling, providing incentives, enhancing students' self-confidence in their ability to make dietary changes, developing social resistance skills, working to overcome barriers to behavior change, and goal setting.

Healthy People 2000 objective 2.19 calls for at least 75% of the nation's schools to "provide nutrition education from preschool through 12th grade, preferably as part of quality school health education" (Public Health Service, 1991, p. 127). Almost 70% of states and just over 80% of districts require that schools offer nutrition education as part of a required course. In fact, 84% of middle/junior and senior high schools provide nutrition education. In more than 70% of health education classes at this level, teachers include content on choosing healthy meals and snacks, and in more than half they cover Five a Day,[3] the Dietary Guidelines, and preparing healthy meals and snacks (Collins et al., 1995).

Despite the prevalence of nutrition education, however, concern exists about the quality of nutrition education taught in U.S. schools. Often, nutrition education occurs haphazardly or through one-shot, isolated units (Lytle & Achterberg, 1995). Curricula and instructional materials that feature a cognitive-oriented approach are still all too common. Perhaps worse still, many teachers provide outdated information. A 1994 study found that more than two-thirds of health education teachers in middle school and junior and senior high school classrooms taught their students about the four food groups, a concept that leading nutrition education authorities no longer use (Collins et al., 1995). Finally, there is also concern about the lack of coordination between classroom nutrition education and foodservice staff. Although this was the underlying goal of the U.S. Congress in establishing the Nutrition Education and Training Program, funding for this program has been low and inconsistent and effective coordination remains an unmet goal in many schools (USDA, 1993).

Screening, Assessment, Counseling, and Referral

Nutrition screening, performed by trained professionals using reliable, appropriately targeted diagnostic procedures can identify individual children and populations at risk (American Dietetic Association, 1996b). Nutrition assessment and counseling by qualified professionals can assist children and their families, as well as school foodservice staff, to adjust dietary intake and identify resources to meet specific health needs. Collaboration among professionals, such as physicians, school nutrition staff, public health nutritionists, school nurses, health educators, coaches, consulting dietitians, and college and university faculty, provides support and reinforcement.

Federal legislation and regulation require schools to provide special meals at no additional charge to children who have in the school file medical certification that disabilities restrict their diet (USDA, 1995b). Schools also may provide or arrange for special nutrition services for nonhandicapping conditions, such as obesity and eating disorders.

Ten to 15% of children have special health care needs, and an estimated 40% of these children have a nutrition problem (Alabama State Department of Education, 1993). The Individuals with Disabilities Education Act of 1990 requires that schools develop Individual Education Plans (IEPs) with measurable goals and objectives for students with disabilities. If a nutrition problem exists, modifications in the foodservice program should become part of the IEP (USDA, 1995b). School districts that do not have staff with appropriate training and time to perform this function need to arrange for and monitor the provision of modifications by qualified nutrition professionals in the community (Yadrick & Sneed, 1993).

The cost of the food for special meals for children with disabilities is comparable to that of regular school meals; however, labor and administrative expenses make these meals more costly (Conklin & Nettles, 1994). Potential sources of funding for special meals include special education funds and Medicaid. To ensure that schools can deliver nutrition screening, assessment, and counseling on a continuing basis, schools need to find ways of reimbursing health care providers and other resources.

IMPLEMENTING SCHOOL NUTRITION SERVICES

Implementing school nutrition services requires competent people backed by adequate resources. Resources can come from national, state, and district levels.

Who Implements Nutrition Services?

All the essential functions of school nutrition services require cooperation among foodservice staff, teachers, school administrators, students, families, health services staff, counselors, psychologists, and social workers. Nutrition directors, managers, and assistants have primary responsibility for providing adequate and appropriate foods. Nutrition directors and managers also ensure the provision of special services. Classroom teachers and health educators have primary responsibility for nutrition education.

Foodservice Staff. School nutrition services require competent district-level nutrition directors and school-level managers with strong financial and program management skills as well as the ability to coordinate instruction with teachers and serve as members of a Healthy School Team (see Chapter 2). USDA, which administers child nutrition programs, has no educational requirements for program directors or managers. Only about 10% of states have state certification for district-level directors, and about 6% have state certification for school-level managers (Pateman et al., 1995). About 20% of states offer certification for district-level directors and school-level managers (Pateman et al., 1995). More than 27,000 directors and managers hold voluntary certification from the American School Food Service Association's (ASFSA) national certification program (personal communication, ASFSA, November 14, 1996).

Only 18% of all states require foodservice directors and managers to acquire appropriate continuing education units (CEUs) to retain state certification (Pateman et al., 1995). In-service training, however, is widely available and utilized by foodservice staff. All states and more than three-fourths of school districts offered in-service training on at least one foodservice topic during the two years prior to a 1994 survey. Seventy-seven percent of middle school and junior and senior high school foodservice managers received some type of foodservice training during the same time period. Training focused most often on food preparation, food safety, making school meals more appealing, and marketing nutrition and school meals (Pateman et al., 1995).

As for the educational attainment of district-level nutrition directors, 16% have a graduate degree, 23% have a college degree, 20% have completed some college courses, 38% have a high school diploma or a general equivalency diploma (GED), and 3% have less than a high school education (Sneed & White, 1993). Only 3% are registered dietitians (Pateman et al., 1995). Of school-level managers, 1% have a graduate degree, 6% have a college degree, 21% have completed some college courses, 63% have a high school diploma or a GED, and 8% do not have a high school diploma (Sneed & White, 1993).

More than one in four managers and directors have worked in food service for more than 21 years, indicating that large numbers of managerial staff are approaching retirement (National Food Service Management Institute [NFSMI], 1993). Recruitment and retention of qualified staff will offer challenges and opportunities for schools in the next decades.

Teachers.   A 1994 survey of teachers who taught required health education classes at the middle school and junior and senior high school level revealed that only 5% had majored in health education, 28% had a joint major in health and physical education, and 36% had majored in a non-health-related field. Forty-eight percent of these teachers were state-certified in health education or health and physical education. Eighty percent of lead health education teachers had received four or more hours of in-service training on one or more health topics in the two years prior to the survey; in the same period, only 14% had received in-service training related to dietary behaviors and nutrition (Collins et al., 1995).

In elementary schools, classroom teachers usually provide health instruction, including nutrition education. Only 5% of states require health education certification for elementary school teachers who teach health education (Collins et al., 1995).

Who Provides Support?

The U.S. Department of Agriculture (USDA); the National Food Service Management Institute (NFSMI), which USDA funds; and the American School Food Service Association (ASFSA) provide a variety of technical assistance, training, and resources for school foodservice programs. (See Chapters 11 and 12 for discussions of national- and state-level support for school health programs.)

USDA Assistance.   USDA's Team Nutrition aims to improve the health and education of children by creating innovative public and private partnerships that promote food choices for a healthful diet through the media, schools, families, and the community. Team Nutrition helps children and their families expand the variety of foods in their diet; add more fruits, vegetables, and grains to the foods they already eat; and construct a diet lower in fat. Through this project, USDA offers training and technical assistance materials for foodservice staff and nutrition education materials for students, their families, and educators. The assistance and materials help schools meet the School Meals for Healthy Children Initiative.

USDA also provides training and technical assistance to school nutrition programs in each state through its Nutrition Education and Training Program, established by the U.S. Congress to ensure that schools use child nutrition programs as learning laboratories. The nutrition education materials for teachers, parents, and students and in-service training materials for foodservice personnel that individual states or consortiums of states develop are shared through USDA's Food and Nutrition Information Center of the National Agricultural Library. The center serves as a repository and lending library for food and nutrition topics, including information on foodservice and classroom instructional materials. The center maintains a variety of electronic access points for the full texts of its bibliographies, resource lists, and fact sheets. Databases include Food and Nutrition Software and Multimedia Programs, Foodborne Illness Educational Materials, and Hazard Analysis Critical Control Points Training Programs and Resources. Additional information is available on human nutrition, nutrition education, foodservice management, and other topics. The center provides technical assistance by telephone (301-504-5719) and e-mail (fnic@nal.usda.gov). Its World Wide Web address is http://www.nal.usda.gov/fnic/. The center also has developed the Healthy School Meals Resource System, which has a web address of http://schoolmeals.nal.usda.gov:8001.

National Food Service Management Institute (NFSMI). The NFSMI organizes teleconferences and training workshops on topics such as meal planning, procurement, and food preparation practices. The organization also manages a clearinghouse for dissemination of its research studies, reports, and videos (Martin, 1993). To help schools comply with requirements for serving students with special needs, the NFSMI conducts national surveys, disseminates training materials, and supports regional training for school nutrition staff (Alabama State Department of Education, 1993; Conklin & Nettles, 1994; Horsley, Allen, & White, 1989; NFSMI, 1994; Yadrick & Sneed, 1993). A help desk provides assistance to child nutrition professionals in all areas of foodservice management; it can be accessed by telephone at 1-800-943-5463 or by e-mail at yhfline@olemiss.edu.

American School Food Service Association (ASFSA). The ASFSA sponsors conferences and seminars and provides technical assistance materials on school nutrition issues. *Keys to Excellence* (ASFSA, 1995), a guide to assist schools in achieving nutrition goals at the administrative, managerial, and operational levels, is one resource. The ASFSA also provides technical assistance to schools and districts that seek to establish nutrition advisory councils. *The ASFSA Connection,* an on-line network at http://www. asfsa.org, provides information on regulations and legislation, sources of technical assistance, professional development opportunities, economic research, discussion groups, forums, and electronic links to other sites on the World Wide Web. The public component of *The ASFSA Connection* has specific categories for students, parents, and teachers.

Other Assistance. The School Food Service Foundation's (SFSF) *Target Your Market* training program (1994) helps school nutrition staff increase student demand for healthy foods, using social marketing techniques. Two other SFSF training programs, *Healthy E.D.G.E.* and *Trimming the Fat,* are in wide use by schools seeking to help students meet the Dietary Guidelines for Americans. The SFSF also provides scholarships for continuing education as well as undergraduate and graduate study in the foodservice field.

Other training programs for making school meals healthier include the American Cancer Society's *Changing the Course* program and the American Heart Association's *Hearty School Lunch* program. Many state education agencies have also developed or adapted Dietary Guidelines training programs for local staff. The National Heart, Lung, and Blood Institute (NHLBI) offers materials developed as part of *Eat Smart,* the school foodservice component of the Child and Adolescent Trial for Cardiovascular Health (CATCH). CATCH significantly reduced the fat content of school meals without a decrease in the rate of student participation in school meals (Luepker et al., 1996). The NHLBI also offers CATCH curricular materials to integrate with *Eat Smart* (Resnicow, Robinson, & Frank, 1996). Information on innovative school-based initiatives that promote increased consumption of fruits and vegetables is available from the National Cancer Institute's Five a Day for Better Health Program (Havas et al., 1995). CDC's Division of Adolescent and School Health provides guidance on developing coordinated school health programs. Nutrition education curricula and materials also are available from voluntary organizations such as the American Cancer Society, American Dietetic Association, American Health Foundation, and American Heart Association. Many corporations in the food industry and commodity organizations also produce nutrition education materials. However, many of these commercial materials favor specific products, which might pose a concern for school officials. Schools need to have a policy to review and screen such materials.

INTEGRATING SCHOOL NUTRITION SERVICES WITH THE OTHER COMPONENTS OF A COORDINATED SCHOOL HEALTH PROGRAM

A school nutrition service can most effectively fulfill its three functions as an integrated component of a coordinated school health program. Integration can provide critical support for healthy eating from multiple sectors of the school community. Moreover, students are more likely to make healthy eating choices when they receive consistent, reinforcing messages from a number of credible sources within an environment that encourages healthy choices. When nutrition services staff work with other school staff, families, and community members, services are also more efficient and effective. Collaboration is also a visible demonstration of the connection between nutrition and academic performance.

Despite these benefits, collaboration between foodservice personnel and other school staff is more the exception than the rule. A 1994 survey (Pateman et al., 1995) found that only about one-third of foodservice managers at middle schools and junior and senior high schools had organized health-related activities or projects in the prior two years. Less than 9% had collaborated on such activities with health education teachers; 10% had collaborated with physical education staff; 16% had collaborated with parent, teacher, or student organizations; and 25% had collaborated with community organizations. Similarly, health education, physical education, and health service staffs reported organizing fewer joint activities or projects with foodservice staffs than with any other school health component staff (Collins et al., 1995; Pate et al., 1995; Small et al., 1995).

The integration of nutrition services into the coordinated school health program can best begin with collaboration between the classroom and the cafeteria. The cafeteria provides a setting where students can practice the healthy eating skills taught in *health education* and other classes, which makes it a learning laboratory. As one long-time advocate for strong school nutrition programs commented,

> Nothing we teach about nutrition in the classroom is going to have any effect at all if it is flatly contradicted by experience. . . . The lunchroom must become part of the classroom—a place where respect for food is modeled; where the elements of a rational health-promoting diet are served and where the complex interrelationships between energy, food, and the environment are taken account of. Make no mistake, a great deal more than hunger is at stake in the lunchroom. (Gussow, 1977)

Foodservice managers can further reinforce classroom lessons by:

- Offering specific foods that coincide with lesson themes (for example, whole wheat rolls can complement lessons about fiber).
- Displaying nutrition information about available foods.
- Giving students a tour of the cafeteria kitchen and showing them techniques for preparing low-fat meals.
- Involving students in planning menus and preparing recipes.

Foodservice managers and health educators can also work together to plan and implement special learning activities, such as taste-testing parties, nutrition displays at school health fairs, and poster contests that challenge students to depict healthy diets.

Another natural collaboration is between foodservice managers and *physical education* staff. Nutrition and physical education staff can plan lessons and activities that teach students about the importance of good nutrition and physical activity as linked components for an overall healthy lifestyle. Nutrition services personnel can include physical activity messages in all their educational activities. Physical education teachers and athletic team coaches are important role models who can influence young people through healthy eating advice and behavioral modeling. A positive example of the effectiveness of this collaboration is provided by the health education, physical activity, and foodservice interventions of the Child and Adolescent Trial for Cardiovascular Health (Luepker et al., 1996).

Since *families* play such an important role in shaping their children's eating behaviors, nutrition services personnel can involve and educate parents and other family members by sending home foodservice menus with educational messages, inviting families to eat lunch or breakfast at school with their children, making presentations at meetings of parent associations and civic clubs, working with teachers and students to develop nutrition education events for families, and soliciting regular input from parents on foodservice menus and recipes. A valuable resource for involving families is *Food, Family, and Fun: A Seasonal Guide to Healthy Eating* (USDA, 1996). The guide includes 50 healthy, tasty recipes and highlights family nutrition education activities and ways to involve children in healthy eating and cooking at home.

School nutrition services can also benefit from collaboration with *community organizations,* such as voluntary health organizations, local health departments, and hospitals. These organizations can provide schools with guest speakers, educational materials, targeted interventions, and nutrition counseling and treatment services. Coordinating school nutrition education efforts with ongoing community-based nutrition education campaigns can enhance their impact (Kelder, Perry, Lytle, & Klepp, 1995). For example, schools can coordinate their nutrition education efforts with powerful community-based campaigns such as the American Dietetic Association's (1996a) *Child Nutrition and Health Campaign,* which emphasizes the importance of starting the day with a good breakfast, being physically active, and having positive adult role models.

The importance of adult role models is a key reason for coordinating nutrition services with *health promotion for staff* activities. When school staff improve their eating habits, they tend to teach effective nutrition education lessons and to model healthy eating behaviors (Baranowski, Hearn, & Baranowski, 1995; Johnson, Powers, Bao, Harsha, & Berenson, 1994). When foodservice staff contribute to health promotion for staff activities, other school staff often perceive school meals more positively and are more motivated to encourage students to participate in school meal programs.

When nutrition services are coordinated with the *health services* and the *counseling, psychological, and social services* components of the coordinated school health program, students receive reinforcement for nutrition education messages and supportive services to deal with nutritional problems. Collaboration with school nutrition experts can encourage school counselors and nurses to provide nutrition information and advice as part of their overall efforts to help students meet their potential for good health and educational achievement. Nutrition services personnel can provide counselors and nurses with educational materials, referral sources, and advice on how to address particular nutrition issues, such as eating disorders or diabetes. Counselors and nurses can work with nutrition services personnel to plan meals for students with special dietary needs.

Finally, all school personnel can foster a healthy *school environment* by supporting policies that ensure a variety of healthy food choices wherever food is available in the school. They can help create a social environment that favors healthy eating by involving the entire school community in efforts that promote good nutrition. An example of the team approach to school nutrition is Arkansas's *Health Action Teams* (Arkansas Department of Education, 1995), which typically consist of the school's principal, physical education and health teachers, foodservice manager, school nurse, counselor, custodian, a cafeteria aide, and a parent. Team members work together to analyze school-specific issues related to nutrition and physical activity, establish goals, and develop initiatives for improving school nutrition services and promoting healthy eating among students.

To give nutrition services the visibility and importance they merit within the school community, foodservice managers need to play an active role on school planning committees and, in particular, on school health committees. One-third of all school districts have a district-wide school health advisory council that addresses policies and programs related to health education. Almost all of these councils include teachers, parents, and administrators as members, while about half have health care providers, counselors, school board members, students, and representatives of religious organizations as members. Only 8% of these school health advisory councils, however, include foodservice staff (Collins et al., 1995).

ACTION STEPS FOR IMPLEMENTING SCHOOL NUTRITION SERVICES

Schools, as well as national, state, and local organizations, can take steps to implement school nutrition services that promote healthy eating. Chapter

2 discusses action steps that schools and school districts can take to implement a coordinated school health program.

Schools

Schools will be most successful in improving the eating behaviors of young people and their potential for learning and good health if they implement the recommendations in CDC's "Guidelines for School Health Programs to Promote Lifelong Healthy Eating" (1996). The CDC guidelines feature recommendations related to seven different areas:

- school policy on nutrition
- a sequential, coordinated curriculum
- appropriate and fun instruction for students
- integration of school foodservice and nutrition education efforts
- staff development
- family and community involvement
- program evaluation

Schools and districts can take eight action steps to implement these recommendations.

1. *Establish a coordinating group to assess school nutrition needs and develop a strategic plan for addressing those needs.* Such a group should include school foodservice staff, students, administrators, faculty, parents, and community members. An existing group such as a Healthy School Team (see Chapter 2), a subgroup of that team, or a separate group with links to the larger school health team could fill this role.

   As teams of staff, parents, and other community members work together to assess school nutrition needs, opportunities for collaboration related to school nutrition issues will surface. A Pennsylvania school district that used a team approach succeeded in increasing student and staff participation in school meals, reversing financial losses, and energizing staff with optimism and excitement for their work (Caldwell, 1994).

   USDA promotes a team approach in its *Team Nutrition Schools* program, which involves more than 15,000 schools. USDA assistance through this program includes training for foodservice managers in being effective team members, which can help them contribute to the success of this initiative. In addition, the American School Food Service Association's (1995) self-assessment guide, *Keys to Excellence: Standards of Practice for Nutrition Integrity,* can help nutrition teams develop and monitor strategic plans.

FIGURE 9.1. The Role of Nutrition

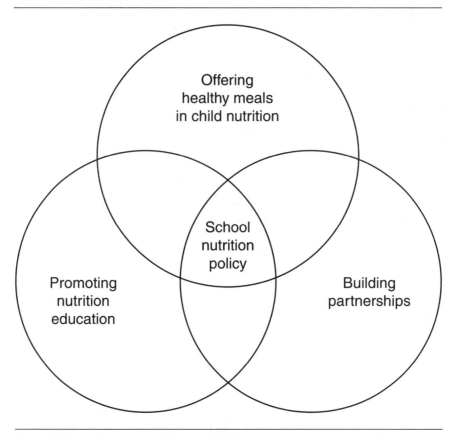

Offering
healthy meals
in child nutrition

School
nutrition
policy

Promoting
nutrition
education

Building
partnerships

Source: California Department of Education (1995)

2. *Develop and implement policies consistent with the strategic plan that reflect healthy eating as a high priority in the school.* The school foodservice and nutrition conceptual framework developed by the California Department of Education (1995) (Figure 9.1) illustrates the key role of policy in school nutrition services. Schools and districts need to establish policies that ensure a variety of healthy eating choices instead of high-fat, high-sodium, high-sugar alternatives wherever food is available in schools. The policies should apply to school meals and a la carte items; classroom snacks and party foods; and food sold in vending machines, at school stores, at snack bars, at sporting events and other special activities, and as part of fund-raising activities (CDC, 1996). Policies also should prohibit fund-raising

activities that involve the sale of low-nutritive snacks during lunch hours, establish clear nutrition standards for any fast-food restaurants that propose selling food at school, and eliminate the use of food to punish or reward students.

Policies should also promote universal access to healthy meals (ASFSA, 1992, 1993; American Dietetic Association, Society for Nutrition Education, & American School Food Service Association, 1995; Nestle, 1992; USDA, 1994a; White, 1994). In 1992, a past president of the Council of Chief State School Officers said that everything is in place to implement a successful universal school nutrition program—except the policy (Rogers, 1992).

CDC's (1996) "Guidelines for School Health Programs to Promote Lifelong Healthy Eating" provide guidance for policy development and content (1996). Another resource is the American School Food Service Association's (1994) nutrition integrity policy guide, which covers nutrition standards, student preferences, purchasing practices, production methods, professional development of school nutrition staff, team building for school staff and community members, eating environments, foods available in addition to reimbursable meals, and positive supervision and role modeling.

3. *Ensure adequate funding for school meal programs.* Many communities that once supported school nutrition services with local resources now require such services to be financially self-sufficient and to pay overhead costs to the operating budget (Story, Hayes, & Kalina, 1996). In addition, many schools depend on revenues from the sale of foods that compete with the school lunch and breakfast programs to finance extracurricular activities, playground improvements, and other special projects. In such situations, school nutrition services are under enormous pressures to attract student customers—even if they must compromise the nutritional value of meals or a la carte items (American Dietetic Association, 1991). When profit margins rather than nutrition become the overriding determinant for decisions by nutrition services staff, students get the message that healthy eating is merely a topic for classroom discussion, not an important practice in their daily lives (American Dietetic Association, 1991; Institute of Medicine, 1997).

Just as schools need to find ways to fund nutrition services, they also need to remove the stigma attached to free or reduced-priced meals. As one physician wrote, "To be mean about food is symbolically powerful neglect; to be generous may teach children that their school and society are truly committed to their well-being" (Rush, 1984, p. 364).

4. *Hire qualified school nutrition managers and directors.* To effectively manage all the responsibilities of a modern school food service and play a

leadership role in the coordinated school health program, school nutrition personnel need stronger professional preparation. Leaders in the profession recommend that school nutrition managers have at least an associate degree (a baccalaureate preferred) and that district-level directors have at least a baccalaureate degree (a master's preferred) (American School Health Association, 1995; NFSMI, 1993).

5. *Teach nutrition education as part of behaviorally oriented comprehensive health education, using fun, active learning strategies.* Schools and districts should allot adequate time for nutrition instruction that meets the criteria set forth by CDC (1996).

6. *Ensure that all involved staff have appropriate in-service training.* Schools must be alert to the need for in-service training. Some foodservice personnel lack experience in applying the Dietary Guidelines or in collaborating with other components of the coordinated school health program (Luepker et al., 1996). Some managers need training in marketing school meals and in management techniques. Many teachers who use traditional didactic teaching strategies are not comfortable with the behaviorally oriented, active learning strategies that are more likely to be effective in teaching good eating habits (Killen & Robinson, 1988).

   Training delivered over time, with opportunities for participants to try out newly acquired content between sessions, is more effective than one-shot training sessions no matter how long (Contento et al., 1995b; Gingiss, 1992). To ensure that staff obtain the training they need, schools must provide time, including release time, facilities, and funding for training.

7. *Involve families and community organizations in policy development and program planning.* Family and community involvement can reinforce school-based nutrition education efforts and increase support for policies that promote healthy eating. Parents and representatives of community organizations should play key roles in nutrition planning teams and all major nutrition-related initiatives (see Chapter 4).

8. *Conduct an ongoing assessment of the effectiveness of school nutrition efforts and use the results for planning.* Evaluation helps ensure effective use of scarce resources, documentation of successes, and learning from setbacks. Assessment results can also provide data to support grant applications. Assessment can involve both process evaluation, which examines the implementation of services, and outcome evaluation, which measures results (for example, changes in students' knowledge, attitudes, and in-school eating behaviors) (CDC, 1996). Two USDA publications (1994b, 1995a) offer guidance in conducting such assessments.

Colleges, Universities, and National and State Organizations

Colleges and universities and national and state organizations can take seven steps to support school nutrition services.

1. *Develop or disseminate behaviorally oriented nutrition education curricula, frameworks, and standards that meet the criteria set forth by CDC (1996).*
2. *Require teachers to take a food skills, nutrition, and health course as part of their formal preparation.* As the Committee on Dietary Guidelines Implementation recommended in 1990 (Food and Nutrition Board, 1991), some colleges and universities offer such a course as an elective for undergraduate or graduate credit. In addition to improving teachers' food literacy and knowledge of nutrition, this type of course can promote staff wellness and increase teachers' motivation and confidence to implement nutrition education and be a contributing member of a Healthy School Team. CDC has issued recommendations (1996) that can provide the nucleus for such a course.
3. *Establish educational qualifications for the certification of school district nutrition directors and school foodservice managers that are commensurate with the qualifications for other school personnel with similar levels of responsibility.* All states should establish minimum educational qualifications that ensure staff can meet their important responsibilities. Certification requirements for school nutrition directors and managers should include training for the role they will play as key members of a school health team. Leaders in the profession recommend that school level managers of nutrition services have a minimum of an associate degree with a baccalaureate preferred and that district level directors have a minimum of a baccalaureate degree with a master's preferred (ASHA, 1995; NFSMI, 1993).
4. *Support policy initiatives that promote healthy eating choices wherever food is available in schools.* Although the Center for Science in the Public Interest (1995) and 10 other national organizations have spoken out in favor of national nutritional standards for foods sold in competition with the National School Lunch Program, federal law still assigns state agencies and school food authorities the responsibility for controlling the sale of such foods in competition with lunches and breakfasts served under the program. The only federal restriction is on the sale of foods of "minimal nutritional value" in the foodservice area during meal periods. State and federal agencies and national organizations should join in supporting initiatives to ensure that the nutritional needs of young people take priority over commercial interests (American Dietetic Association, 1991; CDC, 1996; Institute of Medicine, 1997). In addition, colleges and universities

can develop initiatives that help school administrators and parents find healthy snack alternatives (Nicklas et al., 1989).

5. *Ensure adequate funding for school nutrition programs.* Funding streams for school meals have changed dramatically over the years. Taking inflation into account, the school lunch program receives only 58% of the federal funding it received when it was launched in 1946 (Citizen's Commission on School Nutrition, 1990). The reimbursement for meals served to paying students (adjusted for 1992 dollars) is only half its 1978 level (U.S. General Accounting Office [GAO], 1993). Funding from local and state governments has also declined. The concerted efforts of local, state, and federal agencies should provide the financial means to ensure that school meals support the relationship between diet, education, and health (Caldwell, 1995).

6. *Minimize administrative complexities, foster appropriate program standards, and provide maximum flexibility for achieving those standards.* Legislative and regulatory efforts should seek to reduce paperwork and provide seamless program guidelines for nutrition services during the regular school day, as well as in after-school and summer programs. Limiting the expenditure of program resources on unnecessary administrative tasks is essential so that school foodservice and nutrition programs at all levels can focus on meeting the needs of children and families

7. *Support and conduct research that will inform school nutrition programs.* A variety of research could guide the development of school nutrition programs for the twenty-first century. Some topics of interest include:

- The degree to which state and local policy decisions influence student participation in school meal programs.
- The influence of other factors (for example, transportation and class schedules, space and time constraints, marketing techniques and food presentation practices, adult role modeling, peer norms, the availability of fast food) on student eating behaviors and participation in school meal programs.
- The effects of policies that increase healthy eating choices on student eating behaviors and school revenue.
- The effectiveness of specific nutrition education curricula and teacher training activities in improving student eating behaviors.
- The effect of integrating nutrition content into other subject areas on student eating behaviors.

CONCLUSION

Nutrition services personnel need to become more active in organizing health-related activities. Schools will reach their potential for improving students' eating behaviors only when school nutrition services become fully integrated with other components of a coordinated school health program. Schools must do their part to help students understand the benefits of healthy eating patterns and adopt healthy behaviors. By offering a learning laboratory in which students can practice healthy eating, the school nutrition program is a vital component of a coordinated school health program designed to help students lead healthy, happy, and productive lives.

NOTES

1. An RDA specifies the quantity of a nutrient that the average person should consume to maintain health and avoid nutritional deficiencies.

2. The DGAs interpret the RDAs and dietary recommendations for prevention of chronic diseases by suggesting the quantity and types of foods that a person should consume daily to meet the RDAs as well as reduce chronic disease risk factors..

3. Five a Day refers to the National Cancer Institute's recommendations that Americans eat five daily servings of fruits and vegetables to promote good health and prevent chronic diseases.

REFERENCES

Abt Associates. (1990). *Final report: Study of income verification in the National School Lunch Program.* Arlington, VA: Author.

Alabama State Department of Education, Child Nutrition Programs. (1993). *CARE: Special nutrition for kids.* Birmingham, AL: Author.

American Dietetic Association. (1990). Position: Domestic hunger and inadequate access to food. *Journal of the American Dietetic Association, 90,* 1437–1441.

American Dietetic Association. (1991). Position: Competitive foods in schools. *Journal of the American Dietetic Association, 91,* 1123–1125.

American Dietetic Association. (1996a). *Child nutrition and health campaign.* Chicago, IL: Author.

American Dietetic Association. (1996b). Position: Child and adolescent food and nutrition programs. *Journal of the American Dietetic Association, 96,* 913–917.

American Dietetic Association, Society for Nutrition Education, & American School Food Service Association. (1995). School-based nutrition programs and services. *Journal of the American Dietetic Association, 95*(3), 367–369.

American Psychiatric Association. (1994). *Diagnostic and statistical manual of mental disorders* (4th ed.). Washington, DC: Author.

American School Food Service Association. (1992). *Legislative issue paper. Universal vision: America's children ready to learn.* Alexandria, VA: Author.

American School Food Service Association. (1993). *Consensus conference: Building healthy children ready to learn. Executive Summary.* Alexandria, VA: Author.

American School Food Service Association. (1994). *Creating policy for nutrition integrity in schools.* Alexandria, VA: Author.

American School Food Service Association. (1995). *Keys to excellence: Standards of practice for nutrition integrity.* Alexandria, VA: Author.

American School Health Association. (1995). *Guidelines for comprehensive school health programs* (Rev. 2nd ed.) (ASHA Publication No. G011). Kent, OH: Author.

American School Health Association, Association for the Advancement of Health Education, & Society for Public Health Education. (1989). *The National Adolescent Student Health Survey: A report on the health of America's youth.* Oakland, CA: Third Party Publishing.

Arkansas Department of Education. (1995). *Health Action Team training manual.* Little Rock, AR: Author.

Bagby, R., Campbell, V. S., & Achterberg, C. (1993). *Every day, lots of ways: An interdisciplinary nutrition curriculum for kindergarten–sixth grade.* Harrisburg, PA: Pennsylvania State Department of Education.

Baranowski, T., Hearn, M. D., & Baranowski, J. C. (1995). Teach well: The relation of teacher wellness to elementary student health and behavior outcomes: Baseline subgroup comparisons. *Journal of Health Education, 26*(Suppl. 2), S61–S71.

Caldwell, D. (1994, November). Clear vision leads to success: Foodservice strategic planning. *School Business Affairs,* 19–22.

Caldwell, D. (1995). Matching policy to priorities. *School Foodservice & Nutrition, 49*(4), 30–35.

California Department of Education, Nutrition Education and Training Program. (1995). *Eat well, learn well.* Sacramento, CA: Author.

Center for Science in the Public Interest. (1995). *Petition to establish national nutritional standards for foods sold in competition with the national school lunch program and to require vendors to offer discounts to qualifying students.* Submitted to the U.S. Department of Agriculture on March 21, 1995. Washington, DC: Author.

Center on Hunger, Poverty, and Nutrition Policy. (1993). *Statement on the link between nutrition and cognitive development in children.* Medford, MA: Tufts University School of Nutrition.

Centers for Disease Control and Prevention. (1996). Guidelines for school health programs to promote lifelong healthy eating. *Morbidity and Mortality Weekly Report, 45*(RR-9 Whole).

Child Nutrition Programs: School Meals Initiatives for Healthy Children Rule, 7 C.F.R. Parts 210 and 220 (1995).

Citizen's Commission on School Nutrition. (1990). *White paper on school lunch nutrition.* Washington, DC: Center for Science in the Public Interest.

Collins, J. L., Small, M. L., Kann, L., Pateman, B. C., Gold, R. S., & Kolbe, L. J. (1995). School health education. *Journal of School Health, 65,* 327–332.

Committee on Diet and Health, National Research Council. (1989). *Diet and health: Implications for reducing chronic disease risk.* Washington, DC: National Academy Press.

Community Childhood Hunger Identification Project. (1991). *A survey of childhood hunger in the United States.* Washington, DC: Food Research and Action Center.

Conklin, M., & Nettles, M. (1994). *Costs associated with providing school meals for children with special food and nutrition needs.* University, MS: National Food Service Management Institute.

Contento, I., Balch, G., Bronner, Y., Lytle, L., Maloney, S., Olson, C., Swadener, S., & Randell, J. (1995a). The effectiveness of nutrition education and implications for nutrition education policy, programs, and research: A review of research. *Journal of Nutrition Education, 27,* 359.

Contento, I., Balch, G., Bronner, Y., Lytle, L., Maloney, S., Olson, C., Swadener, S., & Randell, J. (1995b). Inservice preparation in nutrition education for professionals and paraprofessionals. *Journal of Nutrition Education, 27,* 347–354.

Crockett, S., & Sims, L. (1995). Environmental influences on children's eating. *Journal of Nutrition Education, 27*(Suppl.), 235–249.

Dallman, P. R., Looker, A. C., Carroll, M., & Johnson, C. L. (in press). Influence of age on laboratory criteria for the diagnosis of iron deficiency and iron deficiency anemia in infants and children. In L. Hallburg (Ed.), *Proceedings of the symposium on iron nutrition in health and disease.* London: John Libbey.

Devaney, B. L., Gordon, A. R., & Burghardt, J. A. (1995). Dietary intakes of students. *American Journal of Clinical Nutrition, 61*(Suppl. 1), 205S–212S.

Edmundson, E., Parcel, G., Feldman, H., Elder, J., Perry, C., Johnson, C., Williston, B., Stone, E., Yang, M., Lytle, L., & Webber, L. (1996). The effects of the child and adolescent trial for cardiovascular health upon psychosocial determinants of diet and physical activity behavior. *Preventive Medicine, 25,* 442–454.

Food and Nutrition Board, Institute of Medicine. (1991). *Improving America's diet and health: From recommendations to action.* Washington, DC: National Academy Press.

Food Research and Action Center. (1996). *School breakfast score card: A status report on the School Breakfast Program* (6th ed.). Washington, DC: Author.

Gift, H., Reisine, S., & Larach, D. (1992). The social impact of dental problems and visits. *American Journal of Public Health, 82*(12), 1663–1668.

Gingiss, P. L. (1992). Enhancing program implementation and maintenance through a multiphase approach to peer-based staff development. *Journal of School Health, 62*(5), 161–166.

Gleason, P. (1995). Participation in the national School Lunch Program and the School Breakfast Program. *American Journal of Clinical Nutrition, 61*(Suppl.), 213–220.

Gordon, A., Devaney, B., & Burghardt, J. (1995). Dietary effects of the national school lunch program and the school breakfast program. *American Journal of Clinical Nutrition, 61*(Suppl.), 221–231.

Gordon, A., & McKinney, P. (1995). Sources of nutrients in students' diets. *American Journal of Clinical Nutrition, 61*(Suppl.), 232–240.

Gussow, J. (1977). *Beyond the school: What else educates? Report of summer institute.* Bellaire, MI: Council of Chief State School Officers.

Havas, S., Heimendinger, J., Damron, D., Nicklas, T. A., Cowan, A., Beresford, S. A. A., Sorensen, G., Buller, D., Bishop, D., Baranowski, T., & Reynolds, K. (1995). Five a day for better health—Nine community research projects to increase fruit and vegetable consumption. *Public Health Report, 110*(1), 68–79.

Herzog, D. B., & Copeland, P. M. (1985). Eating disorders. *New England Journal of Medicine, 313*(5), 295–303.

Horsley, J., Allen, E., & White, P. (1989). *Nutrition management of handicapped and chronically ill school age children: A resource manual for school personnel, families and health professionals.* Richmond: Virginia Department of Health and Virginia Department of Education.

Institute of Medicine. (1997). *Schools and health: Our nation's investment.* D. Allensworth, E. Lawson, L. Nicholson, & J. Wyche (Eds.). Washington, DC: National Academy Press.

Johnson, C. C., Powers, C. R., Bao, W., Harsha, D. W., & Berenson, G. S. (1994). Cardiovascular risk factors of elementary school teachers in a low socioeconomic area of a metropolitan city: The Heart Smart Program. *Health Education Research, 9*(2), 183–191.

Joint Committee on National Health Education Standards. (1995). *National health education standards: Achieving health literacy. An investment in the future.* Atlanta, GA: American Cancer Society.

Kelder, S., Perry, C., Klepp, K., & Lytle, L. (1994). Longitudinal tracking of adolescent smoking, physical activity, and food choice behaviors. *American Journal of Public Health, 84*(7), 1121–1126.

Kelder, S. H., Perry, C. L., Lytle, L., & Klepp, K.-I. (1995). Community-wide nutrition education: Long-term outcomes of the Minnesota Heart Health Program. *Health Education Research, 10,* 119–131.

Kikuchi, D. A., Srinivasan, S. R., Harsha, D. W., Webber, L. S., Sellers, T. A., & Berenson, G. S. (1992). Relation of serum lipoprotein lipids and apolipoproteins to obesity in children: The Bogalusa Heart Study. *Preventive Medicine, 21,* 177–190.

Killen, J. D., & Robinson, T. N. (1988). School-based research on health behavior change: The Stanford Adolescent Heart Health Program as a model for cardiovascular disease risk reduction. In E. Z. Rothkopf (Ed.), *Review of research in education* (Vol. 15; pp. 171–200). Washington, DC: American Educational Research Association.

Krebs-Smith, S. M., Cook, D. A., Subar, A. F., Cleveland, L., Friday, J., & Kahle, L. L. (1996). Fruit and vegetable intakes of children and adolescents in the United States. *Archives of Pediatric and Adolescent Medicine, 150,* 81–86.

Lewis, C. J., Crane, N. T., Moore, B. J., & Hubbard, V. S. (1994). Healthy People 2000: Report on the 1994 nutrition progress review. *Nutrition Today, 29*(6), 6–14.

Luepker, R. V., Perry, C. L., McKinlay, S. M., Nader, P. R., Parcel, G. S., Stone, E. J., Webber, L. S., Edler, J. P., Feldman, H. A., Johnson, C. C., Kelder, S. H., & Wu, M. (1996). Outcomes of a field trial to improve children's dietary patterns and physical activity: The Child and Adolescent Trial for Cardiovascular Health (CATCH). *Journal of the American Medical Association, 275,* 768–776.

Lytle, L., & Achterberg, C. (1995). Changing the diet of America's children: What works and why? *Journal of Nutrition Education, 27*(5), 250–260.

Martin, J. (1993). Child nutrition programs: Legislation. *Topics in Clinical Nutrition, 9*(4), 9–19.

McGinnis, J., & Foege, W. (1993). Actual causes of death in the United States. *Journal of the American Medical Association, 270,* 2207–2212.

Meyers, A., Sampson, A., Weitzman, M., Rogers, B., & Kayne, H. (1989). School Breakfast Program and school performance. *American Journal of Diseases of Children, 143,* 1234–1239.

National Education Goals Panel. (1992). *The national education goals report: Building a nation of learners.* Washington, DC: U.S. Government Printing Office.

National Food Service Management Institute. (1993). *Preparing child nutrition program professionals for the 21st century.* Oxford, MS: Personnel Conference Proceedings.

National Food Service Management Institute. (1994). *Insight: Managing nutrition services for children with special needs.* University, MS: Author.

National Health & Education Consortium. (1993). *Eat to learn, learn to eat: The link between nutrition and learning in children.* Washington, DC: Institute for Educational Leadership.

National Heart, Lung, and Blood Institute. (1991). *Report of the expert panel on blood cholesterol levels in children and adolescents* (NIH Publication No. 91-2732). Bethesda, MD: U.S. Department of Health and Human Services, Public Health Service, and National Institutes of Health.

National High Blood Pressure Education Program. (1993). *Working group report on primary prevention of hypertension.* Bethesda, MD: U.S. Department of Health and Human Services; Public Health Service; National Institutes of Health; and National Heart, Blood, and Lung Institute.

National Institute of Dental Research. (1989). *Oral health of United States children: The national survey of dental caries in U.S. school children: 1986–87. National and regional findings* (NIH Publication No. 89-2247). Bethesda, MD: U.S. Department of Health and Human Services, Public Health Service, National Institutes of Health.

National Institutes of Health Consensus Development Panel on Optimal Calcium Intake. (1994). Optimal calcium intake. *Journal of the American Medical Association, 272,* 1942–1948.

Nestle, M. (1992). Societal barriers to improved school lunch programs: Rationale for recent policy recommendations. *School Food Service Research Review, 16*(1), 5–10.

Nicklas, T., Forcier, J., Farris, R., Hunter, S., Webber, L., & Berenson, G. (1989). Heart Smart School Lunch Program: A vehicle for cardiovascular health promotion. *American Journal of Health Promotion, 4*(2), 91–100.

Nicklas, T., Weihang, B., Webber, L., & Berenson, G. (1993). Breakfast consumption affects adequacy of total daily intake in children. *Journal of the American Dietetic Association, 93,* 886–891.

Pate, R., Small, M., Ross, J., Young, J., Flint, K., & Warren, C. (1995). School physical education. *Journal of School Health, 65,* 312–318.

Pateman, B., McKinney, P., Kann, L., Small, M., Warren, C., & Collins, J. (1995). School health policies and programs study: School food service. *Journal of School Health, 65,* 327–332.

Perry, C. L., Baranowski, T., & Parcel, G. S. (1990). How individuals, environments, and health behavior interact: Social learning theory. In K. Glantz, F. M. Lewis, & B. K. Rimer (Eds.), *Health behavior and health education: Theory, research, and practice* (pp. 161–186). San Francisco: Jossey-Bass.

Pilant, V. (1994). Current issues in child nutrition. *Topics in Clinical Nutrition, 9*(4), 1–8.

Pollitt, E. (1994). Poverty and child development: Relevance of research in developing countries to the United States. *Child Development, 65,* 283–295.

Pollitt, E. (1995). Does breakfast make a difference in school? *Journal of the American Dietetic Association, 95*(10), 1134–1139.

Pollitt, E., Leibel, R., & Greenfield, D. (1981). Brief fasting, stress, and cognition in children. *American Journal of Clinical Nutrition, 34,* 1526–1533.

Pollitt, E., Lewis, N., Garza, C., & Shulman, R. (1982–1983). Fasting and cognitive function. *Journal of Psychiatric Research, 17*(2), 169–174.

Public Health Service. (1991). *Healthy People 2000: National health promotion and disease prevention objectives.* Washington, DC: U.S. Government Printing Office.

Resnicow, K., Robinson, T., & Frank, E. (1996). Advances and future directions for school-based promotion research: Commentary on the CATCH intervention trial. *Preventive Medicine, 25,* 378–383.

Rogers, W. (1992). *School lunch: No side dish.* Speech delivered at a legislative action conference of the American School Food Service Association, Washington, DC.

Rush, D. (1984). The national evaluation of school nutrition programs: Guest editorial. *American Journal of Clinical Nutrition, 40,* 363–364.

School Food Service Foundation. (1994). *Target your market.* Alexandria, VA: Author.

Shear, C. L., Freedman, D. S., Burke, G. L., Harsha, D. W., & Berenson, G. S. (1987). Body fat patterning and blood pressure in children and young adults: The Bogalusa Heart Study. *Hypertension, 9,* 236–244.

Small, M., Majer, L., Allensworth, D., Farquhar, B., Kann, L., & Pateman, B. (1995). School health services. *Journal of School Health, 65,* 319–326.

Sneed, J., & White, K. (1993). Continuing education needs of school-level managers in child nutrition programs. *School Food Service Research Review, 17*(2), 103–108.

Snyder, P., Lytle, L., Pellegrino, T., Anderson, M., & Selk, J. (1995). Commentary on school meals from school food service personnel and researchers. *American Journal of Clinical Nutrition, 61*(Suppl.), 247–249.

Splett, P., & Story, M. (1991). Child nutrition: Objectives for the decade. *Journal of the American Dietetic Association, 1991,* 665–668.

Story, M., Hayes, M., & Kalina, B. (1996). Availability of foods in high schools: Is there cause for concern? *Journal of the American Dietetic Association,* 123–126.

Troiano, R., Flegal, K., Kuczmarski, R., Campbell, S., & Johnson, C. (1995). Overweight prevalence and trends for children and adolescents: The National Health Examination Surveys, 1963–1991. *Archives of Pediatric and Adolescent Medicine, 95*(149), 1085–1091.

U.S. Department of Agriculture, Food and Nutrition Service. (1993). *The strategic plan for nutrition education: Promoting healthy eating habits for our children.* Washington, DC: Author.

U.S. Department of Agriculture. (1994a). *Healthy kids: Nutrition objectives for school meals.* Washington, DC: Author.

U.S. Department of Agriculture, Food and Nutrition Services. (1994b). *Needs assessment guide for the Nutrition Education and Training Program.* Washington, DC: Author.

U.S. Department of Agriculture. (1994c). *USDA Team Nutrition strategic plan for training and technical assistance to achieve healthy school meals. Executive Summary.* Washington, DC: Author.

U.S. Department of Agriculture. (1995a). *Evaluation guide for the Nutrition Education and Training Program.* Washington, DC: U.S. Department of Agriculture, Food and Nutrition Service.

U.S. Department of Agriculture, Food and Consumer Service. (1995b). *Guidance for accommodating children with special dietary needs in the school nutrition program.* Alexandria, VA: Author.

U.S. Department of Agriculture, Agricultural Research Service, Dietary Guidelines Advisory Committee. (1995c). *Report of the Dietary Guidelines Advisory Committee on the dietary guidelines for Americans, 1995, to the Secretary of Health and Human Services and the Secretary of Agriculture.* Washington, DC: Author.

U.S. Department of Agriculture, Food and Consumer Service. (1996). *Food, family, and fun: A seasonal guide to healthy eating, commemorating 50 years of school lunch* (FCS 298). Washington, DC: U.S. Government Printing Office. (001–000–04627–6)

U.S. Department of Agriculture & U.S. Department of Health and Human Services. (1995). *Nutrition and your health: Dietary guidelines for Americans* (4th ed.). Washington, DC: Author.

U.S. General Accounting Office. (1993). *Food assistance: Information on meal cost in the National School Lunch Program* (GAO Publication No. RCED-94–32 BR). Washington, DC: Author.

Wadden, T. A., & Stunkard, A. J. (1985). Social and psychological consequences of obesity. *Annals of Internal Medicine, 103*(6, Pt. 2), 1062–1067.

White, G. (1994). Nutrition integrity defined. *School Food Service Journal, 48*(1), 21–22.

Yadrick, K., & Sneed, J. (1993). *Providing for the special food and nutrition needs of children.* University, MS: National Food Service Management Institute.

John P. Allegrante, Ph.D.

10 School-Site Health Promotion for Staff

○ Assessment, education, and fitness activities for school faculty and staff.
○ Designed to maintain and improve the health and well-being of school staff, who serve as role models for students.

In Battle Creek, Michigan, a staff wellness program reports a significant drop in teacher absences and saves schools $8,000 in costs for substitute teachers (Falck & Kilcoyne, 1984).

In New York City, participants in a health promotion program for school staff emerge with positive attitudes and better morale (Allegrante & Michela, 1990).

Through school-site health promotion programs, school staff from 25 states improve their safety, nutrition, and exercise behaviors (Fetro & Drolet, 1991).

As these examples reveal, school-site health promotion programs for staff (sometimes called "staff wellness programs") can have a profound impact on the health of school faculty and staff. As every school administrator can attest, teachers and staff who are healthy—both emotionally and physically—are an invaluable asset to a school. But schools are not the sole beneficiaries of staff wellness programs. Students, their families, and community members reap significant rewards as well. Students benefit because their teachers are more energetic and are absent less, school employees stay on staff longer, and the school climate is more optimistic

Health Is Academic: A Guide to Coordinated School Health Problems. Edited by Eva Marx and Susan Frelick Wooley, with Daphne Northrop. New York: Teachers College Press, 1998. ISBN 0-8077-3713-5 (pbk.), ISBN 0-8077-3714-3 (cloth). Prior to photocopying items for classroom use, please contact the Copyright Clearance Center, Customer Service, 222 Rosewood Dr., Danvers, MA 01923, USA, tel. (508) 750-8400. © 1998 Education Development Center, Inc. All rights reserved.

(Symons, Cummings, & Olds, 1994). The energy level and outlook of staff are contagious. When teachers are enthusiastic and healthy, they are role models of healthful living, helping to reinforce messages that families communicate to young people (Wolford, Wolford, & Allensworth, 1988). For community members, reduced school costs (e.g., fewer substitutes, lower insurance, decreased turnover expenses) and expanded use of community health resources contribute to more positive, supportive attitudes about school.

As one of the largest employers in the United States—public schools employ more than 2.5 million teachers and more than 2 million others, including school administrators, instructional support staff, and other personnel (National Center for Education Statistics, 1995)—schools are in a unique position to bolster staff health and contribute to the nation's goals for the promotion of health and prevention of disease and disability (Allensworth & Kolbe, 1987; Blair, Piserchia, Wilbur, & Crowder, 1986; Institute of Medicine, 1995; McGinnis & DeGraw, 1991).

A study by the American Association of School Administrators found that one in six school employees has hypertension, one in ten has a problem with alcohol or drugs, and half are likely to be overweight (Wolford, Wolford, & Allensworth, 1988). Teachers and other school employees develop heart disease, cancer, and stroke—the leading causes of premature death and disability among Americans—at rates equal to those of the general population. The direct costs of health care for teachers, and the indirect costs associated with lost productivity due to teacher absenteeism, burnout, and replacement in schools, reflect those of private business and industry.

Recognizing the importance of schools as worksites and that schools are a "natural locus" for educational interventions in health, the surgeon general encouraged the nation's schools to adopt the objectives of *Healthy People 2000,* the national initiative to improve health (U.S. Department of Health and Human Services, 1991). The objectives include 10 worksite health promotion goals that apply to all schools and districts (Symons, Cummings, & Olds, 1994). The goals cover:

- school-site wellness programs
- screenings
- referrals
- treatment and follow-up programs
- safety and injury prevention
- employee assistance programs

Schools have made steady progress in responding to the surgeon general's call for worksite health promotion. In 1991, at least 27 states participated in the National Network of State Conferences for School Worksite Wellness, a coalition of states that have implemented school-site workplace health promotion activities. Of these states, 25 have sponsored statewide conferences to foster implementation of local school-site health promotion activities. Since the first in 1987, more than 30,000 school professionals have attended similar conferences (Davis, Koch, & Ballard, 1991). No data exist for the number of schools that have implemented the programs locally.

ESSENTIAL FUNCTIONS OF SCHOOL-SITE HEALTH PROMOTION FOR STAFF

The essential functions of school-site health promotion for staff are the promotion of physical, emotional, and mental health, as well as the prevention of disease and disability among school employees. Full-scale programs integrate multiple activities with the school's effort to improve student health. Staff wellness programs typically involve one or more of the following activities:

- screening
- education and supportive activities to reduce risk-factors
- organizational policies that promote a healthful and psychologically supportive work environment
- an integrated employee assistance program (O'Donnell, 1985)
- employee health care, including health insurance, managed care organizations, and access to school health services (National Education Association, 1995)

Screening

Screening, early detection, and disease-control activities, by identifying faculty and staff who are at risk for major diseases prior to the onset of symptoms, help raise awareness and motivate action. Many screening programs focus on blood pressure and cholesterol. Screening for cancer—including breast cancer (Goldfein, Schneider, & Allegrante, 1993), colo-rectal cancer, and skin cancer—is increasingly common. Screening also sometimes involves general physical examinations and testing for diseases, such as tuberculosis. Health-risk assessments or appraisals, using questionnaires to evaluate health status and risk for certain diseases, help faculty and staff identify health behaviors they might wish to improve. Health fairs in which community health practitioners participate can be appealing venues for screening activities (Sowers & Sowers, 1986).

Risk-Factor Reduction Education and Activities

Education and activities that reduce individual risk factors and encourage a healthy lifestyle among school staff often focus on:

- stress management
- smoking cessation
- exercise and physical fitness
- alcohol and drug abuse prevention
- nutrition and weight control
- injury prevention
- prenatal education
- medical self-care
- mental health
- HIV/AIDS
- sexually transmitted diseases
- training in first aid and cardio-pulmonary resuscitation

Such activities help faculty and staff develop the knowledge, attitudes, and skills needed to adopt healthy behaviors and become better health care consumers. Offerings can include: basic awareness sessions, sessions on particular health risks, skill development workshops, a health promotion library, and information-sharing activities such as newsletters, videos, and inserts with pay stubs (Sowers & Sowers, 1986). Activities can be for individuals, for small groups, or for teams. Special events such as road races, field days, and team games are sometimes part of risk-factor reduction efforts (Sowers & Sowers, 1986).

Organizational Policies

Policies designed to improve the school climate are an important element of school-site health promotion. Such policies might mandate or prohibit risk behaviors, for example, by prohibiting smoking at school; reduce heath risks by eliminating harmful substances or risks from the school environment, such as asbestos or dangerous equipment; and promote health by modifying the work environment, for example, by replacing soda in school vending machines with fruit juices (Eddy, Fitchugh, Gold, & Wojtowicz,

1996; Michela, Lukaszewski, & Allegrante, 1995; Sloan, 1987; Sloan, Gruman, & Allegrante, 1987).

Employee Assistance Programs

Employee assistance programs (EAPs) staffed by mental health professionals provide confidential counseling and advice to faculty and staff who have physical or mental health problems that affect their job performance and work with youth (Sowers & Sowers, 1986). Such programs have been an important feature of school-site wellness programs for many years. A 1987 study of 91 school districts found that 46 had an EAP. EAPs are typically set up at the district level and serve all school staff. Bargaining units or unions should participate in developing EAPs (Hacker, 1986). EAPs address a range of problems, including alcohol and substance abuse, physical and emotional health, marital and family stress, and financial difficulties. They also assist school staff with personal crises, legal problems, job-related problems, and social adjustment (Norton, 1988).

Confidentiality is an important concern in establishing an EAP. EAPs must safeguard the privacy and job security of staff and avoid the misuse of information on health and other problems that can result in blaming staff with problems or treating them paternalistically (Allegrante, Goldfein, & Sloan, 1995). At the same time, however, there must be a mechanism for addressing abusive or illegal activities that individuals might disclose during EAP sessions.

Because EAPs handle confidential information, the potential for legal claims always exists. To ensure that the operations and practices of an EAP protect employees' legal rights, qualified professionals should provide services in areas that provide privacy.

Health Care

Health insurance that includes dental and vision coverage is part of a full-scale school-site health promotion program (National Education Association, 1995). In addition, school health services such as immunizations and emergency care should be available to staff as well as students.

SOME EXAMPLES OF SUCCESSFUL PROGRAMS

Twenty Years of Team-Building

The first major effort to promote health among teachers as an occupational group was the Seaside Health Education Conference, developed in

Oregon in 1977 (Tritsch, 1991). Conceived as a means to build awareness of the importance of school health education, the Seaside Health Education Conference has emerged as a model for team building that states have used to bring together multidisciplinary teams of superintendents, principals, counselors, nurses, health and physical education teachers, and members of school boards for discussions about health and wellness as a lifestyle and to design, advocate for, and implement school-wide health education and promotion efforts.

The Seaside approach to school-site health promotion emphasizes personal health and building a multidisciplinary team to develop a school health promotion action plan (Tritsch, 1991). The concept now includes a range of topics and formats (Fetro & Drolet, 1991). For example, workshops focus on improving teacher health, reducing health-care costs, and strengthening health instruction for students.

Participation in the Seaside Conference—and in similar conferences—not only improves participants' knowledge, attitudes, and health practices; it also helps diffuse the concept of comprehensive school health education (Drolet & Fetro, 1991; Girvan & Cottrell, 1987; McLeroy, McCann, Smith, & Goodman, 1989). An evaluation of the personal health practices of more than 4,000 participants who had attended 25 state conferences revealed that participation led to statistically significant changes in use of alcohol, tobacco, and other substances as well as in safety, nutrition, and exercise behaviors (Drolet & Fetro, 1993).

Reinforcing Health as a Community Priority

Established with a grant from the W. K. Kellogg Foundation, the Battle Creek, Michigan, Schools Healthy Lifestyles Program was the product of a community-wide effort. Faced with a statewide economic downturn and dwindling funding for school health services in the early 1980s, school leaders in Battle Creek organized a school-site health promotion initiative for faculty and staff as part of an effort to improve the school health program. The school health program focused on developing school staff as role models, improving the health-related behaviors of students, and helping parents, families, and the community to reinforce healthy habits among children. The program included health fairs, health instruction using a model curriculum, and testing students' physical fitness. Health promotion for staff activities emphasized teachers and staff as role models, for example, by walking for physical fitness. The program held competitions among the eight participating school systems to encourage staff in weight loss, aerobic activities, smoking cessation, stress management, and accident prevention. To encourage students and teachers to eat more healthful foods and monitor their progress, the school lunch program added a nutritious salad bar, health education included nutrition education, and the school nurse offered cholesterol testing. In one year, lower staff absenteeism saved Battle Creek schools $8,000 in salaries for substitute teachers (Falck & Kilcoyne, 1984).

Building Teacher Morale

Job stress and burnout are occupational risks associated with teaching in many urban centers (Cedoline, 1982; D'Arienzo, Moracco, & Krajewski, 1982). To reduce absenteeism and improve teachers' morale and job satisfaction as well as their physical and mental health, Paul Viboch, a physical education teacher in Community School District Six in New York, developed the Health Enhancement Program (HEP) in the late 1980s. HEP used four strategies:

- a school-wide orientation to raise awareness about behavioral risk factors for stress-related disease
- a health fair where teachers and staff could undergo medical screenings and health risk appraisals and guidance in correcting unhealthy behaviors
- a group session for feedback on health risk appraisals
- educational offerings on nutrition, fitness, stress management, weight control, and smoking cessation.

In addition, the school implemented recreational activities, such as team volleyball, and contracted with a daily salad delivery service. Teachers College, Columbia University provided technical assistance. A one-year evaluation study funded by the Health Insurance Plan of New York, which also provided funding for program implementation, showed that teachers who participated in HEP viewed their school environment more positively and had higher morale than nonparticipants (Allegrante & Michela, 1990).

Large-Scale Change Using Small Grants

To advance staff health promotion in Vermont's schools, the Vermont School Boards Insurance Trust (VSBIT) initiated the Planned Action Toward Health (PATH) program in 1991. PATH encourages schools to help employees develop healthy lifestyles and become more knowledgeable consumers of health care. The insurance trust funds the program through small competitive grants of up to $500, which schools use for in-service programs, training for health promotion coordinators and teams, after-school programs, the purchase of exercise equipment, and monthly wellness breakfast meetings. A bimonthly wellness newsletter sent to 11,000 school employees provides health-related information, facilitates statewide communication on health topics, and recognizes successful health promotion programs. "The VSBIT PATH program has helped to define our wellness program," said one administrator. "Our program is not elaborate or expensive, yet . . . the entire staff is happier, healthier, and, I think, more productive since we began our quest toward better health." The PATH program demonstrates that even small grants can help launch successful school-site health promotion for staff (Ward & Phillips, 1993).

BENEFITS OF WORKSITE HEALTH PROMOTION PROGRAMS

Worksite health promotion can have an important impact not only on health but on organizational costs as well. More than four dozen studies of health promotion and disease prevention programs at the worksite have found considerable evidence of positive impacts on employees' health behavior and health status. Many of these studies have also found that worksite health promotion programs reduce health care costs and employee absenteeism and improve productivity and morale (Pelletier, 1991, 1993). Many of the benefits seen in business and industry programs are also common to school-site health promotion programs.

Improved Health Behavior and Health Status

School-site health promotion programs have brought about changes in employee health behavior and health status that parallel those at worksites in general. Worksite programs have involved employees in daily physical activity and have helped them successfully control weight and blood pressure, and stop smoking (Alderman, Madhavan, & Davis, 1983; Alderman & Stormont, 1979; Breslow, Fielding, Herrmann, & Wilbur, 1990; Williams & Kubik, 1990; see also Abrams & Follick, 1983; Altman, Flora, Fortmann, & Farquhar, 1987; Brownell, Cohen, Stunkard, Felix, & Cooley, 1984; Shipley, Orleans, Wilbur, Piserchia, & McFadden, 1988). School-site health promotion programs for staff in Michigan (Williams & Kubik, 1990), South Carolina (Maysey, Gimarc, & Kronenfeld, 1988), and Texas (Bishop, Myerson, & Herd, 1988) have improved participants' attitudes, behaviors, and knowledge of health issues. These programs have helped faculty and staff stop smoking, adopt healthful eating behaviors, increase physical activity, and better manage emotional stress.

Reduced Health Care Costs

Worksite health promotion programs also can have positive economic outcomes for schools (Elias & Murphy, 1986; Warner, Wickizer, Wolfe, Schildroth, & Samuelson, 1988). Studies evaluating the impact of such programs in business and industry on employee health care costs found that participation results in fewer hospital admissions and shorter stays (Bly, Jones, & Richardson, 1986), lower medical-claims costs (Fries, Harrington, Edwards, Kent, & Richardson, 1994), and reduced employee health care costs due to disability (Bowne, Russell, Morgan, Optenberg, & Clarke, 1984). Other studies have reported on the cost-effectiveness of programs for blood-pressure control (Erfurt & Foote, 1984), weight loss (Bishop, Myerson, & Herd, 1988), stress management (Pruitt, Bernheim, & Tomlinson, 1991), and smoking cessation in pregnant women (Windsor, Warner, & Cutter, 1988). Although long-term participation by employees in health promotion programs is necessary for employers to realize savings in health care costs, such studies nonetheless demonstrate the potential of worksite health promotion programs to help schools manage their health care costs (Gibbs, Mulvaney, Henes, & Reed, 1985).

Lower Employee Absenteeism and Higher Productivity and Morale

Worksite health promotion in business and industry can reduce absenteeism (Baun, Bernack, & Tsai, 1986; Bertera, 1990; Lynch, Golaszewski, Clearie, Snow, & Vickery, 1990), improve productivity (Leutzinger & Blanke, 1991), and increase morale, job satisfaction, and organizational commitment (Holzbach et al., 1990). Similarly, programs in schools can reduce absenteeism and job stress (Blair et al., 1984; Blair, Smith, & Collingwood, 1986; Falck & Kilcoyne, 1984), improve morale and perceptions of the organizational climate (Allegrante & Michela, 1990), and enhance interest in teaching about health (Drolet & Fetro, 1991; Passwater, Tritsch, & Slater, 1980). For example, a school administrator from Vermont whose school implemented a worksite health promotion program said, "Our school has definitely benefited from our wellness program. Not only are our teachers physically healthier, there is an improved sense of climate and morale since we began the program" (K. Ward, personal communication, August, 1995). In addition, schools that reduce teacher absenteeism find that they save money because they require fewer substitutes.

IMPLEMENTING SCHOOL-SITE HEALTH PROMOTION FOR STAFF

Many schools are in a unique position to implement staff health promotion activities because they have both key facilities and educational resources—classrooms, gymnasiums, swimming pools, weight-training rooms, and athletic fields, as well as professional educators and other skilled staff who can develop and implement such activities. Even the smallest schools and districts have some resources on which they can build, for example, counselors, nurses, physical education teachers, coaches, strong community programs, and publicity professionals (Sowers & Sowers, 1986).

Successful school-site health programs share three features. First, they have a strong *coordinator* and a trained, multidisciplinary team of committed individuals from the school and the community (ideally, as part of a larger school health team). Although almost any member of the school team can serve as coordinator, the individual must be highly motivated; must have skills in program development and evaluation, marketing, communication, and fund-raising; and be able to work well with and motivate others. The best candidates usually are school nurses, physical education teachers, health education teachers, dietitians, school psychologists, social workers, and principals.

Second, leadership *training and teamwork* characterize successful programs. Leadership training is available in states that hold annual statewide school health promotion conferences and workshops. Conference sponsors generally require schools and districts to send teams that include staff and administrators. Leadership training requires local school support and sometimes requires release time for school-based teams to attend workshops, develop action plans, and implement activities. In addition, colleges and universities, recreation facilities, and local affiliates of national organizations such as the American Cancer Society, American Heart Association, and American Lung Association can provide schools with speakers, educational materials, trained volunteers, and other technical assistance that support their school-site health promotion activities. In some communities, insurance companies, religious organizations, and community hospitals and other health-care provider groups support a school's health promotion initiatives.

Third, successful school-site health promotion programs work with both institutions of higher learning and local providers of community medical services, including hospitals, health clinics, and university medical centers.

INTEGRATING SCHOOL-SITE HEALTH PROMOTION FOR STAFF PROGRAMS WITH OTHER COMPONENTS OF A COORDINATED SCHOOL HEALTH PROGRAM

School-site health promotion can most effectively fulfill its functions as an integrated component of a coordinated school health program. Because staff wellness is not typically assigned to any individual, a school health coordinator who works with the total school program can help to ensure that this integration does indeed occur (Resnicow & Allensworth, 1995).

School-site health promotion activities complement activities in the other components of a coordinated school health program. School-site health promotion benefits *comprehensive school health education* because teachers who become interested in their own health tend to take an interest in the health of students and to serve as health role models. Such teachers also usually understand better the health needs of students and are more effective teachers of health. For this reason, many schools launch a health effort by first initiating health promotion for staff, often by sending a team to a wellness conference.

The *school environment* improves when students, staff, and administrators share a concern for physical, mental, and social health. In turn, a safe, healthy school environment supports health promotion. School-site health promotion activities can provide a forum for discussions among school administrators, faculty, and staff about organizational and worksite improvement. One way to integrate staff health promotion activities with activities that improve the school environment is for the school health coordinator to help establish and implement policies that maintain a smoke-free environment at school (Resnicow & Allensworth, 1995).

School-site health promotion programs draw on the facilities and resources of a school's *physical education* program—the gymnasium, swimming pool, weight-training equipment, and athletic field. A school's physical education teaching staff can provide participants in school-site health promotion programs with instruction about physical activity and lifelong fitness as well as organize and lead staff health promotion activities.

School nurses, counselors, psychologists, and social workers can bring important professional expertise to a school-site health promotion program. Nurses can conduct medical screenings and immunizations. Psychologists, counselors, and social workers can provide counseling services and other types of employee assistance. And by helping teachers with classroom management and discipline techniques, they can improve the working conditions for teachers and the learning environment for students.

School-site health promotion programs often include *nutrition education* as part of a broad effort to promote healthy food choices in the school cafeteria and vending machines. School food services can offer meals that appeal to adults as well as students. Furthermore, when teachers eat well-balanced meals at school they set a positive example for students.

Finally, school-site health promotion programs provide an excellent medium for nurturing the bonds between a school and the *community*. With their expertise and facilities, schools serve as a focal point in the community for health promotion (Stokols, Pelletier, Fielding, 1995, 1996). Families can participate with staff in recreational and fitness activities; school staff can use community facilities and services; and community and family members with appropriate expertise can participate in or lead discussions about school safety, physical hazards, organizational climate and morale, job stress, and other topics.

ACTION STEPS FOR IMPLEMENTING SCHOOL-SITE HEALTH PROMOTION FOR STAFF

Schools

Schools as well as national, state, and local district organizations can take steps to implement school-site health promotion programs for staff. Nine steps can guide schools in developing school-site health promotion programs (adapted from McKenzie, 1988).

- *Step 1: Initiate the Idea.* The first step—at either the district or school level—is to convince teachers, staff, and the school board that an investment in the health of faculty and staff is also an investment in students. An argument that focuses on reasonable, feasible targets and accentuates cost-effectiveness can build support.
- *Step 2: Establish a Team.* The team, the Healthy School Team (see Chapter 2) or a subgroup, should involve a wide range of school personnel—teachers, administrators, staff, union representatives, and school board members. By involving staff at all levels, the program is likely to respond to their needs and concerns. The team develops a mission statement, generates ideas, and guides development, implementation, and evaluation of the health promotion program. A coordinator who is excited about staff health promotion, has good people skills, and can implement and institutionalize an initiative should head the team. The team should tap the resources of other schools and local health-related organizations, colleges and universities, and hospitals. Numerous national organizations that specialize in areas covered by worksite health promotion programs also can help (see Chapter 12).

- *Step 3: Assess Needs and Current Activities.* The team should determine the nature of the health problems among school faculty and staff using data on absences and their costs, insurance claims, and health risks. Surveys and interviews can help the team assess morale and determine the types of activities faculty and staff might like, identify potential barriers and problems, and evaluate resources and supports, such as staff available to assist with the program or the support of a union or collective bargaining unit (Sowers & Sowers, 1986).
- *Step 4: Set Goals and Objectives and Develop a Plan.* The goals of a school-site health promotion program can include reducing health care costs, decreasing absenteeism, heightening morale, improving health education, or meeting specific requests of faculty and staff. The objectives should specify anticipated accomplishments, the intended beneficiaries, the cost, and the time frame for implementation. *Objectives can specify the process, impact, or outcome.* For example, the following is a *process* objective:

  > To offer at least two on-site recreational exercise classes for faculty and staff each week during the school year.

  Impact objectives can focus on *knowledge, skills,* or *behavior.* An impact objective focusing *on knowledge*:

  > To increase by 50% the number, of faculty and staff who can identify at least three benefits of regular exercise.

  On skills:

  > To increase by 50% the number of faculty and staff who locate a pulse point and monitor their heart rate before and after exercise.

  On behavior:

  > To increase by 50% the number of faculty and staff who exercise at least three times a week by the end of the school year.

  The following is an *outcome* objective:

  > To decrease by 50% the number of faculty and staff who are sedentary by the end of the school year.

- *Step 5: Identify Materials and Activities.* The educational content, materials, and activities of a school-site health promotion program should meet the needs identified in the needs assessment (Step 3). Activities should respect individual choice and health status and provide flexibility for individuals (Sowers & Sowers, 1986).
- *Step 6: Organize Logistics.* Screenings, education classes, and other activities should fit staff schedules. Facilities also need scheduling. Beginning a school-site health promotion initiative with one or two activities and increasing the number when the program is established, allows the health promotion effort to demonstrate what it can do. Promising more than the program can deliver consistently and successfully can create disappointment and frustration.

- *Step 7: Publicize and Promote the Program.* A catchy title can often help attract support for a program (Sowers & Sowers, 1986). A newsletter, promotional materials, or other regular communication vehicles can help publicize activities and events. Linking school-site health promotion activities to other school events helps build awareness and interest.
- *Step 8: Keep People Involved.* Successful health promotion programs solicit input from participants, build on successes, and respond to evolving needs. Incentives, such as competitions and token rewards, can foster and maintain participation, as can convenient scheduling and even providing snacks and drinks. Community support is likely to increase when activities attract participation of the entire school community.
- *Step 9: Evaluate the Program.* Evaluation should include process, impact, and outcome evaluations. *Process evaluation* measures the quality of the program and the extent of implementation. *Impact evaluation* measures changes in awareness, knowledge, attitudes, skills, behaviors, or school policies. *Outcome evaluation* measures the effect on health status, absenteeism, or productivity. The evaluation should also assess whether the program has met its goals and objectives as well as provide information that can guide improvements.

These nine steps can help guide schools in their efforts. But advocates of school-site health promotion initiatives will face political challenges as well. The future of school-site health promotion will depend on the ability of schools and districts to find funding to support programs and assess their progress. Increasingly, staff skills in marketing, planning, and program evaluation will be critical (Richardson & Bensley, 1991).

Four key concepts offer a guide to future efforts. First, to gain a broader constituency and base of support, school-site health promotion efforts must develop initiatives that go beyond individual-level risk reduction activities (Sloan & Allegrante, 1985). New initiatives might address the health consequences and occupational risks of a rapidly changing economy, diverse family structures, job strain, underemployment, and unemployment due to restructuring. These initiatives can help workers and their families cope with the stress of balancing work and family, including the problem of child care.

Second, improved methods for evaluating the health outcomes and cost-effectiveness of worksite health promotion programs will help schools justify these initiatives in the face of competing priorities and demands. Anecdotal reports of impact and outcomes abound, but only a handful of evaluation studies have generated data that can inform future planning and policy decisions. Larger and more well-designed evaluations of school-site health promotion for faculty and staff are needed to convince state, district, and local school decision makers of the potential benefit. Studies must gather more and better data about the long-term impact of health promotion activities on health status, health care costs, absenteeism costs, productivity, and morale.

Third, school-site health promotion programs can extend their focus to school support staff, including school bus drivers, food-service workers, building custodians, and classroom aides. An increasing number of school staff are of diverse racial and ethnic backgrounds and might have difficulty accessing health services in the community, especially preventive health care.

Finally, school districts, like corporate employers, can integrate health promotion and disease prevention into employee benefit plans and make such efforts compatible with the goals of managed care. Historically, traditional health insurance plans have not provided reimbursement for health promotion and preventive services; however, the trend toward managed care holds the promise of facilitating better access to preventive services for employees and their dependents.

National, State, and Local Organizations

National, state, and local organizations can support school-site health promotion initiatives in a variety of ways:

- Insurance companies and other businesses can offer grants that assist and provide incentives for local schools and districts to develop, implement, and evaluate school-site health promotion programs.
- Community coalitions of schools, businesses, voluntary health organizations, and insurance companies can advocate for and support the development of school-site health promotion for faculty and staff.
- School boards can establish a standing committee to assess employee and school needs, identify resources, and evaluate the impact and outcomes of school-site health promotion efforts.
- National organizations, including those that represent teachers, can identify exemplary models of school-site health promotion and encourage schools to replicate them.
- Teachers unions can examine and monitor the impact of school-site health promotion efforts on health benefits and ensure that such programs meet the needs of all school employees.
- Districts and state education agencies can provide technical assistance, guidelines, resources, and opportunities for networking that will help schools develop plans with measurable goals and objectives for improving faculty and staff health. Such plans, together with policy statements regarding faculty and staff health, can become an integral part of a school's improvement plan.

- States can offer or support statewide conferences that foster development and implementation of school-site health promotion for faculty and staff.
- States can develop guidelines and standards for school-site health promotion for faculty and staff based on model guidelines (Floyd & Lawson, 1992).
- State insurance commissioners, health insurance providers, and managed care representatives can provide economic and other incentives for schools that implement school-site health promotion and preventive health services for faculty and staff.
- State and federal agencies can establish integrated databases that monitor health promotion development, implementation, and evaluation results. Such systems can capture data on participation to inform analyses of the cost-effectiveness and cost-benefit of school-site health promotion for staff.
- Federal agencies can suggest guidelines for assessing the quality and outcome of school-site health promotion for faculty and staff.

More detailed discussion of the support that state and national organizations can provide to coordinated school health programs appears in Chapters 11 and 12.

CONCLUSION

The backdrop for everything that schools are doing today is change: transformations in the national economy; the shifting politics of public spending, school reform, and restructuring; privatization of schools; and health care reform. Schools that approach these developments with optimism and view their employees as resources that strengthen them in times of change will thrive. School-site health promotion for staff initiatives can nurture one of a school's most precious resources: the teachers and staff who instruct, guide, and influence its students. Staff wellness programs have grown in popularity during the last decade and have achieved major successes. These benefits will multiply as more schools launch school-site health promotion programs and coordinate them with the other components of the total school health program.

REFERENCES

Abrams, A. B., & Follick, M. J. (1983). Behavioral weight-loss intervention at the worksite: Feasibility and maintenance. *Journal of Consulting and Clinical Psychology, 51,* 226–233.

Alderman, M. H., Madhavan, S., & Davis, T. K. (1983). Reduction of cardiovascular disease events by worksite hypertension treatment. *Hypertension, 5,* 138–143.

Alderman, M. H., & Stormont, B. (1979). Worksite vs. community-based antihypertensive care: A controlled trial. *Preventive Medicine, 8,* 123.

Allegrante, J. P., Goldfein, K. D., & Sloan, R. P. (1995). Ethical problems and related critical issues in worksite health promotion. In D. M. DeJoy & M. G. Wilson (Eds.), *Critical Issues in Worksite Health Promotion* (pp. 51–70). Boston: Allyn & Bacon.

Allegrante, J. P., & Michela, J. L. (1990). Impact of a school-based workplace health promotion program on morale of inner-city teachers. *Journal of School Health, 60,* 25–28.

Allensworth, D. D., & Kolbe, L. J. (1987). The comprehensive school health program: Exploring an expanded concept. *Journal of School Health, 57,* 409–411.

Altman, D. G., Flora, J. A., Fortmann, S. P., & Farquhar, J. W. (1987). The cost-effectiveness of three smoking cessation programs. *American Journal of Public Health, 77,* 162–165.

Baun, W. E., Bernack, E. J., & Tsai, S. P. (1986). A preliminary investigation: Effect of a corporate fitness program on absenteeism and health care cost. *Journal of Occupational Medicine, 28,* 18–22.

Bertera, R. L. (1990). The effects of workplace health promotion on absenteeism and employment costs in a large industrial population. *American Journal of Public Health, 80,* 1101–1105.

Bishop, N., Myerson, W. A., & Herd, J. A. (1988). The school district for health promotion. *Health Values, 12,* 41–45.

Blair, S. N., Collingwood, T. C., Reynolds, R., Smith, M., Hagen, R. D., & Sterling, C. L. (1984). Health promotion for educators: Impact on health behaviors, satisfaction, and general well-being. *American Journal of Public Health, 74,* 147–149.

Blair, S. N., Piserchia, P. V., Wilbur, C. S., & Crowder, J. H. (1986). A public health intervention model for worksite health promotion. *Journal of the American Medical Association, 255,* 921–926.

Blair, S. N., Smith, M., & Collingwood, T. R. (1986). Health promotion for educators: Impact on absenteeism. *Preventive Medicine, 15,* 166–175.

Bly, J. L., Jones, R. C., & Richardson, J. E. (1986). Impact of worksite health promotion on health care costs and utilization. *Journal of the American Medical Association, 256,* 3235–3240.

Bowne, D. W., Russell, M. L., Morgan, J. L., Optenberg, S. A., & Clarke, A. E. (1984). Reduced disability and health care costs in an industrial fitness program. *Journal of Occupational Medicine, 26,* 809–816.

Breslow, L., Fielding, J., Herrmann, A. A., & Wilbur, C. S. (1990). Worksite health promotion: Its evolution and the Johnson & Johnson experience. *Preventive Medicine, 19,* 13–21.

Brownell, K. D., Cohen, R. Y., Stunkard, A. J., Felix, M. R., & Cooley, N. B. (1984). Weight loss competitions at the worksite: Impact on weight, morale and cost-effectiveness. *American Journal of Public Health, 74,* 1283–1285.

Cedoline, A. J. (1982). *Job burnout in public education: Symptoms, causes, and survival skills.* New York: Teachers College Press.

D'Arienzo, R. V., Moracco, J. C., & Krajewski, R. J. (1982). *Stress in teaching.* Washington, DC: University Press of America.

Davis, T. M., Koch, S., & Ballard, D. J. (1991). The nature of seaside-style health education conferences. *Journal of Health Education, 22,* 73–75.

Drolet, J. C., & Fetro, J. V. (1991). State conference for school worksite wellness: A synthesis of research and evaluation. *Journal of Health Education, 22,* 76–79.

Drolet, J. C., & Fetro, J. V. (1993). State conferences for school worksite wellness: Personal health practices of conference participants. *Journal of Health Education, 24,* 174–183.

Eddy, J. M., Fitchugh, E., Gold, R. S., & Wojtowicz, G. G. (1996). A worksite health promotion model for public schools. *Journal of Health Education, 27,* 48–50.

Elias, W. S., & Murphy, R. J. (1986). The case for health promotion programs containing health care costs: A review of the literature. *American Journal of Occupational Therapy, 40*(11), 759–763.

Erfurt, J. C., & Foote, A. (1984). Maintenance of blood pressure treatment and control programs. *Journal of Occupational Medicine, 26,* 892–900.

Falck, V., & Kilcoyne, M. (1984). A health promotion program for school personnel. *Journal of School Health, 54,* 239–242.

Fetro, J. V., & Drolet, J. C. (1991). State conferences for school worksite wellness: A content analysis of conference components. *Journal of Health Education, 22,* 80–84.

Floyd, J. D., & Lawson, J. D. (1992). Look before you leap: Guidelines and caveats for schoolsite health promotion. *Journal of Health Education, 23,* 74–84.

Fries, J. F., Harrington, H., Edwards, R., Kent, L. A., & Richardson, N. (1994). Randomized controlled trial of cost reductions from a health education program: The California Public Employees' Retirement System (PERS) study. *American Journal of Health Promotion, 8,* 216–223.

Gibbs, J. O., Mulvaney, D., Henes, C., & Reed, R. (1985). Worksite health promotion: Five-year trend in employee health care costs. *Journal of Occupational Medicine, 27,* 826–830.

Girvan, J., & Cottrell, R. (1987). The impact of the seaside health education conference on middle school health programs in Oregon. *Health Education, 18,* 78–82.

Goldfein, K. D., Schneider, W. J., Allegrante, J. P. (1993). Worksite mammography screening: The Morgan Guaranty Trust Company. In J. P. Opatz (Ed.), *Economic impact of worksite health promotion* (pp. 145–158). Champaign, IL: Human Kinetics Publishers.

Hacker, C. (1986). *EAP: Employee Assistance Programs in the public schools.* Washington, DC: National Education Association.

Holzbach, R. L., Piserchia, P. V., McFadden, D. W., Hartwell, T. D., Herrmann, A. A., & Fielding, J. E. (1990). Effect of a comprehensive health promotion program on employee attitudes. *Journal of Occupational Medicine, 32,* 973–978.

Institute of Medicine. (1995). *Defining a comprehensive school health program.* Washington, DC: National Academy Press.

Leutzinger, J., & Blanke, D. (1991). The effect of a corporate fitness program on perceived worker productivity. *Health Values, 15,* 20–29.

Lynch, W. D., Golaszewski, T. J., Clearie, A. F., Snow, D., & Vickery, D. M. (1990).

Impact of a facility-based corporate fitness program on the number of absences from work due to illness. *Journal of Occupational Medicine, 32,* 9–12.

Maysey, D., Gimarc, J. D., & Kronenfeld, J. J. (1988). School worksite wellness programs: A strategy for achieving the 1990 goals for a healthier America. *Health Education Quarterly, 15,* 53–62.

McGinnis, J. M., & DeGraw, C. (1991). Healthy schools 2000: Creating partnerships for the decade. *Journal of School Health, 61,* 292–297.

McKenzie, J. F. (1988). Twelve steps in developing a schoolsite health education/promotion program for faculty and staff. *Journal of School Health, 58,* 149–153.

McLeroy, K., McCann, K., Smith, D., & Goodman, R. M. (1989). The role of a summer institute in the diffusion of comprehensive school health. *Family and Community Health, 12,* 26–39.

Michela, J. L., Lukaszewski, M. P., Allegrante, J. P. (1995). Organizational climate and work stress: A general framework applied to inner-city school teachers. In S. L. Sauter & L. R. Murphy (Eds.), *Organizational risk factors for job stress* (pp. 61–80). Washington, DC: American Psychological Association.

National Center for Education Statistics. (1995). *Statistics in brief.* Washington, DC: U.S. Department of Education, Office of Educational Research and Improvement.

National Education Association. (1995). *National Education Association handbook— 1995–1996.* Washington, DC: Author.

Norton, M. S. (1988). Employee Assistance Programs—A need in education. *Contemporary Education, 60,* 23–26.

O'Donnell, M. P. (1985). *Design of worksite health promotion programs* (2nd ed.). Birmingham, MI: American Journal of Health Promotion.

Passwater, D., Tritsch, L., & Slater, S. (1980). *Seaside Health Education Conference: Effects of three 5-day teacher inservice conferences.* Salem: Oregon Department of Education.

Pelletier, K. R. (1991). A review and analysis of the health and cost-effective outcome studies of comprehensive health promotion and disease prevention programs. *American Journal of Health Promotion, 5,* 311–315.

Pelletier, K. R. (1993). A review and analysis of the health and cost-effective outcome studies of comprehensive health promotion on disease prevention programs at the worksite: 1991–1993 update. *American Journal of Health Promotion, 8,* 350–362.

Pruitt, R. H., Bernheim, C., & Tomlinson, J. P. (1991). Stress management in a military health promotion program: Effectiveness and cost efficiency. *Military Medicine, 156,* 51–53.

Resnicow, K., & Allensworth, D. (1995). Conducting a comprehensive school health program. *Journal of School Health, 66*(2), 59–63.

Richardson, G. E., & Bensley, L. B. (1991). The future of schoolsite health promotion programs. *Journal of Health Education, 22,* 90–93.

Shipley, R. H., Orleans, C. T., Wilbur, C. S., Piserchia, P. V., & McFadden, D. W. (1988). Effect of the Johnson & Johnson Live for Life Program on employee smoking. *Preventive Medicine, 17,* 25–34.

Sloan, R. P. (1987). Workplace health promotion: A commentary on the evolution of a paradigm. *Health Education Quarterly, 14,* 181–194.

Sloan, R. P., & Allegrante, J. P. (1985). Corporate health is more than a robust balance sheet. *Training and Development Journal, 39,* 57–59.

Sloan, R. P., Gruman, J. C., & Allegrante, J. P. (1987). *Investing in employee health: A guide to effective health promotion in the workplace.* San Francisco: Jossey-Bass.

Sowers, J. G., & Sowers, W. D. (1986). *A wellness program for school employees.* Hampton, NH: Sowers Associates.

Stokols, D., Pelletier, K. R., & Fielding, J. E. (1995). Integration of medical care and worksite health promotion. *Journal of the American Medical Association, 273,* 1136–1142.

Stokols, D., Pelletier, K. R., & Fielding, J. E. (1996). The ecology of work and health: Research and policy directions for the promotion of employee health. *Health Education Quarterly, 23,* 137–158.

Symons, C. W., Cummings, C. D., & Olds, R. S. (1994). Healthy People 2000: An agenda for schoolsite health promotion programming. In D. D. Allensworth, C. W. Symons, & R. S. Olds (Eds.), *Healthy Students 2000: An agenda for continuous improvement in America's schools* (pp. 137–144). Kent, OH: American School Health Association.

Tritsch, L. (1991). A look back on the Seaside Conference. *Journal of Health Education, 22,* 70–72.

U.S. Department of Health and Human Services. (1991). *Healthy People 2000: National health promotion and disease prevention objectives.* Pub. No. 91–50212. Rockville, MD: Author.

Ward, K., & Phillips, J. (1993, Fall). Wellness works for Vermont schools. *Wellness Management, 6–7.*

Warner, K. E., Wickizer, T. M., Wolfe, R. A., Schildroth, J. E., & Samuelson, M. H. (1988). Economic implications of workplace health promotion programs: Review of the literature. *Journal of Occupational Medicine, 30,* 106–112.

Williams, P., & Kubik, J. (1990). The Battle Creek (Michigan) schools healthy lifestyles program. *Journal of School Health, 60,* 152–146.

Windsor, R. A., Warner, K. E., & Cutter, G. R. (1988). A cost-effectiveness analysis of self-help smoking cessation methods for pregnant women. *Public Health Reports, 103,* 83–88.

Wolford, C. A., Wolford, M. R., & Allensworth, D. D. (1988). A wellness program for your staff sets a healthy example for students. *American School Board Journal, 175,* 38–40.

Donald Ben Sweeney, M.A.
Patricia Nichols, M.S., C.H.E.S.

The State Role in Coordinated School Health Programs

11

You can't have people in 100,000 different schools and 16,000 different school districts out there, each trying to make collaborative arrangements with eight different [federal] agencies. There must be a strategy for defining the state role, and the role that local agencies will play in relating to all of the schools within their jurisdiction.
—Thomas Payzant, superintendent, Boston Public Schools, and former assistant secretary for elementary and secondary education, U.S. Department of Education (The Policy Exchange, The Institute for Educational Leadership, 1994, p. 26)

In most countries, the national government directs a centralized education system that mandates policies and promulgates curricula. In the United States, responsibility for much education decision making resides at the state level and not with the federal government. While national legislation, policy, and funding influence and support actions at the state and local level, states have crucial roles and responsibilities for the implementation of programs in the schools. At the same time, the advent of site-based management has significantly changed the influence of state government on local school decision making and implementation. State agencies defer to schools that adapt programs to their unique local needs and values. State agencies understand that the best state-level policies, programs, and planning

Health Is Academic: A Guide to Coordinated School Health Problems. Edited by Eva Marx and Susan Frelick Wooley, with Daphne Northrop. New York: Teachers College Press, 1998. ISBN 0-8077-3713-5 (pbk.), ISBN 0-8077-3714-3 (cloth). Prior to photocopying items for classroom use, please contact the Copyright Clearance Center, Customer Service, 222 Rosewood Dr., Danvers, MA 01923, USA, tel. (508) 750-8400. © 1998 Education Development Center, Inc. All rights reserved.

are effective only when transformed by the school or community into a quality school health program that directly affects the life of a child.

No magic formula exists to solve the many problems that threaten the health and welfare of young people. There are, however, many successful approaches that can positively affect children and communities to make them safer, healthier, and more cohesive (National Commission on the Role of the School and Community in Improving Adolescent Health, 1990). This chapter describes state-level government and nongovernment players and the support they provide to school health programs. Also included are other sources of support (e.g., universities, businesses, foundations, media) that function at an intermediate level that falls between the federal and local. These sources are not necessarily statewide but can affect multiple districts or schools. The chapter discusses several approaches that state organizations or other intermediate-level institutions are using, separately or in combination, that can influence the local implementation of coordinated school health programs. The chapter concludes with action steps that state organizations can take to support schools as they implement coordinated school health programs.

STATE-LEVEL GOVERNMENT PLAYERS

The *state legislature* governs all educational matters that do not conflict with federal or state constitutions. While the U.S. Constitution does not mention education, the state constitutions of all 50 states authorize the state legislature to provide for a system of public schools. The state legislature enacts laws that specify how schools should operate. It has the option of delegating authority to local school boards. Legislators establish education- and health-related budgets and programs and introduce resolutions on specific issues. Legislative committees hold public hearings and write bills to provide funds to stimulate new and expanded health education or services. All states have at least one standing legislative committee that addresses education concerns and one addressing health issues (McCarthy, Langdon, & Olson, 1993).

Governors have enormous power to influence coordinated school health programs through their authority to establish advisory councils, appoint agency heads and members to state boards, and propose and veto appropriations bills. They can, for example, encourage state agencies to coordinate health and education efforts or establish a state-level advisory council on school health. A governor can function as the "chief architect, chief executive, and chief communicator" of a state's policy toward children and families (National Governors' Association, 1987, p. 8). In developing state health and education collaboratives one national organization found that working in partnership with the governor's office gave these efforts the status and high-level support needed for successful program development (National Health & Education Consortium, 1995).

State boards of education make policy as prescribed by the legislature. In most states, the governor appoints the board; in other states, the board is elected by popular vote or by representative bodies. Some states prohibit educators from serving on the state board, whereas others mandate that educators fill some board seats. State boards have powers to set statewide curriculum standards, establish requirements for high school graduation, determine qualifications for education personnel, establish testing and assessment programs, establish standards for the accreditation of local school districts and preparation programs for teachers and administrators, administer federal assistance programs, review and approve state education agency budgets, and develop rules and regulations for the administration of state programs (National Association of State Boards of Education, 1995).

In most states, the state board of education appoints a *chief state school officer* (CSSO), typically called the state commissioner or superintendent of education. In other states, the CSSO is elected or appointed by the governor. CSSOs generally have responsibility for supervising the state's public school system, setting the agenda for the department of education, addressing controversies regarding education policies and programs, and proposing legislation. In most states, the qualifications for the CSSO position, such as education, professional experience, and certification, are by legal mandate. In states where the state board of education appoints the CSSO, the board may determine the qualifications (McCarthy, Langdon, & Olson, 1993).

The *state education agency* acts as staff to the CSSO. Some staff have responsibility for specific components of a school health program. For example, every state education agency has a staff member who is responsible for directing or coordinating school health education and a food service director responsible for the school breakfast and lunch programs and other nutrition-related activities. Many agencies also have staff members who focus on physical education and school nurse services (Kolbe et al., 1995).

A *state health official* in each state heads a *state health agency* with a broad range of responsibilities aimed at improving the health status and well-being of all individuals, including children and youth in their state. In most states, the governor appoints the state health official; in other states, the board or an agency commissioner makes that appointment. The state health official can have the title of administrator, assistant secretary, commissioner, director, or secretary (Association of State and Territorial Health Officials [ASTHO], 1995a). State health agencies have varying levels of involvement in school-related activities through their divisions of maternal and child health, health promotion and chronic disease prevention, primary care, and communicable diseases. All perform ten essential public health services (Grason & Guyer, 1995) based upon three core functions—assessment, policy development, and quality assurance (Institute of Medicine, 1997)—to build systems of care for school-aged populations. Public health agency activities that support school health at the community level include providing technical assistance for needs assessments; policy development related to issues such as confidentiality, immunization, and children with special health care needs; training community personnel to screen vision and hearing; funding demonstration projects; and administering Early and Periodic Screening, Diagnosis, and Treatment (EPSDT) and Medicaid programs (Brown & Aliza, 1995). In some states the state health agency operates the local health departments or shares authority with the local governments (ASTHO, 1995b). Some state health agencies have structured their organization to address school health issues specifically. For example, in 1992 the Texas Department of Health, whose health professionals had for years engaged in various topical health programs, established a school health program to address the health needs of students in a coordinated way (Texas Department of Health, 1996).

Other state agencies that address school health issues include social services, highway safety, public welfare, safety and hygiene, environmental protection, agriculture, consumer protection, and mental health. Many provide literature for classroom use, send representatives to speak at awareness or training sessions, provide technical assistance and training, and monitor the implementation of policies and regulations. In Michigan, the departments of social services, mental health, state police, substance abuse, and highway safety joined with the state health and education agencies to develop a system to deliver coordinated school health programs more effectively.

In some states, governors or legislatures create *statewide task forces* that address school health issues. For example, the governor of West Virginia appointed a school health task force comprised of leaders in business, education, government, health care, and community whose recommendations provided a blueprint for the design of coordinated school health programs in the state and led to the appointment of a state-level committee on school health.

State courts sometimes play a role in school health. For example, the Kentucky Supreme Court faulted the public school system for failing to "provide an efficient system of common schools" and directed the state legislature to redesign the system (National Conference of State Legislatures, 1997). The court action resulted in broad-reaching legislation that addressed the physical and emotional needs of students as well as their academic achievement by requiring that children begin school ready to learn, that schools ensure parental and family involvement, and that community services be available to increase the educational capacities of families and schools.

STATE-LEVEL NONGOVERNMENT PLAYERS

Nongovernment organizations at the state level also support school health programs. For example, many national organizations with an interest in school health programs have *state affiliates*. These include associations that represent administrators (American Association of School Administrators, National Association of Elementary School Principals, National Association of Secondary School Principals), teachers (National Education Association), pupil services professionals (American School Counselor Association, National Association of School Psychologists, National Association of Social Workers), medical professionals (American Medical Association, American Nurses Association, National Association of School Nurses), voluntary associations (American Cancer Society, American Heart Association, American Lung Association, American Red Cross), school health and physical education professionals (American Alliance for Health, Physical Education, Recreation, and Dance; American School Health Association), and parents (National PTA). (See Chapter 12 for a description of these and other national organizations and the ways that they and their affiliates promote and support coordinated school health programs.)

Colleges and universities play a vital role in supporting school health programs by preparing most teachers, health professionals, administrators, and other school staff for their professional roles and training graduate students for leadership positions in school health at state and local levels. The degree to which the curriculum prepares teachers to teach health education, health professionals to participate in multidisciplinary teams, and administrators to support coordinated school health programs influences the quality and quantity of school health program implementation. By organizing interdisciplinary programs at both the undergraduate and graduate levels, universities can model collaboration and prepare professionals to work together effectively in schools and communities to address the health needs and concerns of children and their families.

College and university faculty also have substantial expertise that can inform and support a variety of state-level school health activities. Moreover, by establishing student internships in cooperation with state agencies, colleges and universities can both contribute to the ongoing programs and activities of state agencies and groom potential state agency staff.

Some *businesses* realize that school health initiatives support their interests. Businesses are in a position to promote change, can bring a fresh perspective and strong resources to school health efforts, and can help to blend a concern for fiscal responsibility with a focus on human services (National Health & Education Consortium, 1995). In addition, through their participation in business roundtables and other forums, business leaders can provide the impetus for school reform and restructuring. One corporate executive in West Virginia who understood school's potential for preparing a healthy workforce was influential in the governor's decision to establish a statewide task force on school health. His corporation also provided staff and financial support for the promotion and implementation of coordinated school health programs in the state (Marx & Northrop, 1995).

Foundations are an important source of seed money for specific projects. Many focus on children and adolescents or health issues. For example, the Colorado Trust, whose mission is to promote and enhance the health and well-being of the people of Colorado, funds training, technical assistance, and curricular materials to help local school districts adopt and sustain school health education. Through its Making the Grade program, the Robert Wood Johnson Foundation funds state efforts to involve communities in the delivery of comprehensive school-based health services for children in grades K–12. In California, a consortium of foundations funded a nonprofit agency to monitor, evaluate, and provide technical assistance to communities and schools (Dryfoos, 1994).

Media (radio, television, print) have great potential for creating awareness of, interest in, and understanding of coordinated school health programs as they relate to wellness, health promotion, and educational achievement. Their participation can play a major role in educating the public, forming public opinion, and framing debate on issues.

STATE-LEVEL SUPPORT FOR COORDINATED SCHOOL HEALTH PROGRAMS

The work of many state organizations focuses on one or more areas that a national summit of education and health organizations identified as key activities for promoting school health (American Cancer Society, 1993):

- *Policy*—Creating a state infrastructure that links health and education, establishes a stable funding base, and promotes the entire coordinated school health program.
- *Parent, student, and community involvement*—Including representatives on state boards and supporting local advisory councils with training and professional development.
- *Advocacy and awareness*—Developing a statewide marketing plan and conducting program evaluation.
- *Quality programs*—Providing quality teacher training and creating model standards and assessment (Colorado Department of Education, 1995).

Efforts to carry out these key activities include a variety of areas: regulatory functions, standards development, credentialing and licensure, technical support, staff development, materials development, funding, and monitoring and evaluation.

Regulatory Functions

All states have enacted legislation affecting some aspects of school health programs. Some states are directive, whereas others make recommendations. Legislation varies from broad mandates to detailed requirements. State agencies seek a balance between being prescriptive to ensure that certain standards are met and giving communities flexibility to develop programs that match local needs, structures, and resources. Some states' laws require that schools conduct hearing and vision screening and provide follow-up for potential problems. Others require schools to maintain specific health records, to report suspected abuse to appropriate officials, to establish procedures to protect the confidentiality of HIV-infected persons, and to conduct HIV prevention education for students and staff. Some states set staffing ratios, for example, the number of school nurses to enrolled students. Others mandate that districts provide physical education, including programs for students with special needs, or health education that includes particular issues, such as HIV/AIDS, or addresses particular grade levels. The National Conference of State Legislatures (1997) has published a summary of state legislation addressing adolescent health issues.

States also make policy recommendations and provide model policies for implementing health programs in schools. These policies address a broad range of issues such as prohibiting the use of tobacco, alcohol, and other drugs on school grounds, establishing smoke-free environments in schools or drug-free zones in school neighborhoods, and preventing students without proper immunization from attending school.

States also administer a complex set of federal laws, regulations, nonbinding guidelines, and mandated programs. School food services is one federal program for which states are responsible. States are also responsible for managing Title V of the Social Security Act (the Maternal and Child Health Block Grant), which mandates states to develop community-based networks of preventive and primary care for children and adolescents and coordinated care systems for children with special health care needs (Hayes & Walker, 1997). States administer the provisions of the Goals 2000 Educate America Act, which includes a prohibition on smoking in schools. Funding for Safe and Drug-Free Schools is available to governors, state education agencies, and colleges and universities to link state and local efforts for preventing the use of tobacco and other drugs, reducing gang violence, and supporting conflict resolution. Guidelines developed by the Centers for Disease Control and Prevention to prevent the spread of AIDS (1988), to prevent the use of tobacco (1994), and to promote lifelong healthy eating (1996) and physical activity (1997a) inform state education agencies' work with local districts and schools.

Standards Development

Many state agencies set standards for outcomes to ensure that programs meet the needs of children and youth and their families. Many also require or encourage assessments that measure progress that programs are making in meeting outcomes. In some states—for example, Kentucky, New Jersey, Minnesota, and West Virginia—standards take the form of mandates. Other states issue standards as guidelines or recommendations. States sometimes customize the standards developed by national health and education bodies to fit their own needs.

A number of states participate in a State Collaborative on Assessment and Student Standards to develop valid and reliable items that assess whether students meet academic standards in a variety of disciplines and that can strengthen school curricula. Assessments for health education are available at the elementary, junior high/middle, and high school levels. They address the National Health Education Standards (Joint Committee on National Health Education Standards, 1995) and the six health risk behaviors that the Centers for Disease Control and Prevention has identified (Kolbe, Kann, & Collins, 1993). Assessments often encourage teachers to focus on tested areas. States that add health-related items as part of mandated academic testing will in this way show their support for health education as important content on a par with traditional academic subjects such as math, science, and language arts.

Credentialing and Licensure

To ensure the quality of professional services, state agencies often recommend or mandate standards for accreditation, certification, and licensing that influence the preparation and employment of professionals in the state (see also Chapter 8). For example, most state education agencies offer certification in health education and in physical education or combined certification in both. Various state agencies also certify or license school nurses, school counselors, school psychologists, sanitarians, school physicians, among others (Small et al., 1995). States sometimes adapt model certification standards that professional organizations develop or use them to validate their own standards, such as standards developed by the Interstate School

Leaders Licensure Consortium, a consortium of states formed by Council of Chief State School Officers.

The health, education, and social services professions have highly specialized and categorical standards. To attract and retain students, colleges and universities design courses of study that prepare students to meet these professional standards. Unless professional standards include interdisciplinary competencies, education institutions are unlikely to move to develop collaborative programs. One result will be that coordinated school health programs will suffer from a lack of interdisciplinary competencies among school staff. To remedy this situation, state agency personnel responsible for academic and credentialing requirements can work with university faculty and practitioners representing the health, education, and social services professions to devise new standards for professional preparation that include school health and interdisciplinary collaboration.

Technical Support

Both state government agencies and the state-level affiliates of national nongovernment organizations are well positioned to gather, organize, and share the varied resources available both in the state and nationally. They provide technical assistance for local school activities such as program planning and implementation, managing student health records, and applying for grants; develop information or resource clearinghouses; and make referrals to other sources of technical support. State agencies and organizations also assist schools in assessing program gaps and overlaps and charting their progress toward building and institutionalizing a coordinated school health program. By sharing their evaluation expertise with schools and communities, professionals working at the state level not only provide an important service to local implementers but also ensure the use of common measures and the collection of consistent data within the state. In addition, the development of instruments, including those used for evaluation, at the state level is a cost-effective approach to instrument design.

Staff Development

State agencies and organizations offer staff development that prepares practitioners in a variety of skill areas, such as interpreting new legislation; implementing new policies; accessing and managing complex funding, such as Medicaid; and teaching health-related topics. They sponsor conferences and provide opportunities for community providers to network and share resources. Some state education agencies organize annual wellness or health promotion conferences to which they invite teams who develop plans to take back to their schools or districts.

Materials Development

State agencies and organizations, both government and nongovernment, provide resources such as implementation manuals, explanations of legislation and regulations, and resource listings. School districts that lack the time, money, and expertise to develop age-appropriate, accurate materials and interactive curricula for use in schools benefit from the fact sheets, model curricula, guidelines, and frameworks developed by state agencies and organizations. For example, model curricula or frameworks give local districts and schools a starting point on which to build a classroom instructional program that fits the needs of the community. State-level organizations often suggest strategies that schools can use to adapt these materials to increase relevance, ownership, and the likelihood of implementation.

Funding

In education, the saying is "What gets tested, gets taught." In school health, it is "What gets funded, gets attention." Support for various aspects of coordinated school health programs sometimes appears as a line item in a state's budget or as part of an agency's budget. Financial support renewed annually demonstrates the importance of these programs as part of the state's commitment to its children's health. For example, more than half of the states fund one or more school-based or school-linked health clinics often using federal Title V and state matching funds (Brown & Aliza, 1995; Small, Majer, Allensworth, Farquhar, Kann, & Pateman, 1995).

State regulations and guidelines also affect funding for school programs. For example, states can influence course content by allowing districts to use funds allocated to purchase textbooks only for books that meet state criteria.

A commitment to healthy students often requires the blending of funding from several sources (Melaville & Blank, 1993), for example, Medicaid, social services, education, health, law enforcement. By identifying and coordinating existing resources, state agencies can provide the framework for program efforts at the local level. For example, in New Mexico the departments of education and of health together with other youth-serving state agencies used maternal and child health funds and adolescent health funds, among other monies, to support school-based health centers, teen pregnancy prevention efforts, and comprehensive school health education and to encourage local school districts to develop an implementation model that combined these resources (personal communication, K. Meurer, January 1997). The state's Office of School Health invited local school districts to propose innovative approaches to the health needs of students, and the proposals became models for replication in other communities in the state. In Rhode Island the education and public health departments worked with two nongovernment funding sources—the United Way and the Rhode Island Foundation—to establish Child Opportunity Zones. These locally created and controlled entities are housed in schools, where they bring together education, health, and social services resources for students and families.

Many state and federal programs are moving toward fewer funding restrictions. With health and education block grants, state departments of health and of education would administer federally funded programs. The state, rather than the federal government, would set priorities. One result might be more comprehensive approaches to protecting students' health.

Monitoring and Evaluation

To monitor how their resources are being used, determine the progress toward desired outcomes, such as reducing youth's risk behaviors, and identify needed corrective action, state organizations conduct process evaluations. To obtain the data needed for such evaluations, state agencies ask districts, schools, or service providers to complete reports. Frequently, staff of state agencies conduct site visits. Outcome evaluations help state-level organizations measure the impact of programs and determine success in meeting objectives. States use data, such as health status, absenteeism, dropout rate, behavioral measures, and utilization of screening and referral, to establish credibility for programs and set spending priorities. School districts can use these data to promote their own school health agendas to improve students' health.

APPROACHES TO STATE-LEVEL COORDINATION

To support coordinated school health programs state organizations often find that they need to change the way they do business. The three approaches described in this section can help organizations in this process. All require implementing systemic change, sharing or relinquishing control, and learning new ways to approach and solve problems. Each can support and reinforce the others' efforts to promote coordinated school health programs within a state. Because such changes can affect schools and districts, understanding these state-level functions can benefit those at the local level. Briefly, the three approaches are as follows:

- *Development of a state infrastructure.* State organizations collectively build the support systems to plan, implement, and evaluate fully functioning coordinated school health programs. By coordinating new or dedicated resources and using existing resources more efficiently and effectively, state organizations can better help schools to meet the health needs of students and their families.
- *Cooperation in interdisciplinary professional development.* State organizations work together to support professionals working to build coordinated school health programs. Colleges and universities provide professional preparation, and professional organizations provide professional development opportunities for public and private practitioners. Both take an interdisciplinary approach. The provision of interdisciplinary training at the postsecondary level can provide schools with staff prepared to implement coordinated school health programs.
- *Coalition building.* State-level government and nongovernment organizations form coalitions and other alliances to advocate for, share resources and information related to, and coordinate efforts in support of fully functioning coordinated school health programs. State coalitions can help schools obtain support for their school health activities and coordinate their local efforts.

Development of a State Infrastructure

Through a coordinated approach, the impact of the total is greater than the impact of the individual efforts (Dryfoos, 1994). Although many state public health agencies that address child and adolescent issues coordinate their efforts with those of state education agencies at the program level (Brown & Aliza, 1995), most do not have agencywide coordination. To build a state-level infrastructure that supports coordinated school health programs, the staffs of state health and education agencies—along with the staff of other relevant state agencies such as social services, mental health, and environmental health—must work with each other and with nongovernment organizations in the state. Elements that need to be in place to establish and maintain a state-level infrastructure that supports local school health programs include:

- *Leadership and staff commitment.* The heads of state government agencies must make a commitment to support the process of infrastructure development, appoint qualified senior-level personnel to oversee and coordinate a state-level infrastructure, and assign support staff and other needed resources.

- *Interagency cooperation.* State agencies must develop agreements that include jointly prepared implementation plans to coordinate administrative responsibilities and activities among agencies. Midlevel agency staff must meet regularly to maintain momentum.
- *Ongoing monitoring and assessment.* Working within their agencies and with other state organizations, staff must assess the status of available resources and the scope of the health problems of children and youth. Staff must develop and apply impact measures to determine the effects of coordinated school health program activities and the degree to which they reach predetermined objectives.
- *Regulatory support.* State-level decision makers must review, adapt, and adopt legislation, regulations, policies, and procedures to strengthen coordinated school health program initiatives.
- *Collaboration.* Government and nongovernment organizations and coalitions must work together to improve the health of children and youth.
- *Marketing and communication.* Collaborators must develop and apply promotion strategies.
- *Professional preparation.* Colleges, universities, state professional organizations, and state agencies must develop and offer training programs and professional development opportunities to prepare local school staff to provide education and services as part of a coordinated school health program (Centers for Disease Control and Prevention, 1997b).

In some states, the Centers for Disease Control and Prevention (CDC) supports the salaries of senior-level staff in the state education agency and the state health agency who are working together to develop and sustain an infrastructure that supports coordinated school health programs (see Figure 11.1). Through similar partnerships between their departments of education and departments of health, other states should be able to eliminate program gaps and overlaps and provide more effective programming.

Cooperation in Interdisciplinary Professional Development Efforts

Professional Development for Practitioners. Professional development that promotes and strengthens interdisciplinary collaboration and integration of services is a key to the implementation of effective coordinated school health programs. Education Development Center, Inc., along with five national organizations (American Psychological Association, American School Counselor Association, National Association of School Nurses, National Association of School Psychologists, and National Association of Social Workers), developed a training and technical assistance model that in-

FIGURE 11.1. An Example of a State Infrastructure That Supports Coordinated School Health Programs

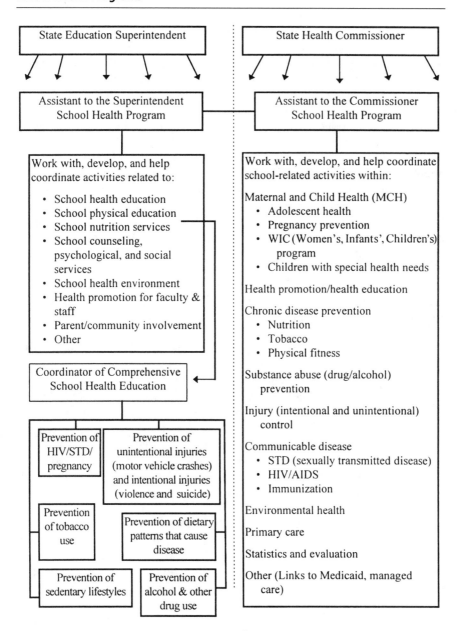

State Education Superintendent

State Health Commissioner

Assistant to the Superintendent
School Health Program

Assistant to the Commissioner
School Health Program

Work with, develop, and help coordinate activities related to:

- School health education
- School physical education
- School nutrition services
- School counseling, psychological, and social services
- School health environment
- Health promotion for faculty & staff
- Parent/community involvement
- Other

Coordinator of Comprehensive School Health Education

Prevention of HIV/STD/ pregnancy

Prevention of unintentional injuries (motor vehicle crashes) and intentional injuries (violence and suicide)

Prevention of tobacco use

Prevention of dietary patterns that cause disease

Prevention of sedentary lifestyles

Prevention of alcohol & other drug use

Work with, develop, and help coordinate school-related activities within:

Maternal and Child Health (MCH)
- Adolescent health
- Pregnancy prevention
- WIC (Women's, Infants', Children's) program
- Children with special health needs

Health promotion/health education

Chronic disease prevention
- Nutrition
- Tobacco
- Physical fitness

Substance abuse (drug/alcohol) prevention

Injury (intentional and unintentional) control

Communicable disease
- STD (sexually transmitted disease)
- HIV/AIDS
- Immunization

Environmental health

Primary care

Statistics and evaluation

Other (Links to Medicaid, managed care)

Adapted from and courtesy of: Department of Adolescent and School Health. National Center for Health Promotion and Disease Prevention. Centers for Disease Control and Prevention.

volves the state affiliates of professional organizations and their counterparts at state agencies (see Figure 11.2).

The model links national, state, and local activities and can start at any level. State organizations as key intermediaries between the national and local levels develop interdisciplinary teams that represent state government agencies and the affiliates of national organizations and include several components of a coordinated school health program. These teams deliver awareness sessions, provide training and technical assistance, and serve as conduits for sharing model policies, materials, and approaches with their counterparts at all levels. The awareness sessions can help gain buy-in by increasing leadership and community understanding of coordinated school health programs, modeling interdisciplinary collaboration, encouraging the development of organizational position statements in support of coordinated school health programs, and promoting the development of similar interdisciplinary teams. At the national level, interdisciplinary teams representing several national organizations can deliver awareness sessions and workshops at meetings for national and state organization leadership. At the state level interdisciplinary teams can support the development of state infrastructure and can train local district staff to implement interdisciplinary programs. Local districts that have developed interdisciplinary teams can help state staff design and deliver training based on "real world implementation" and provide technical assistance for other districts.

Before an interdisciplinary team can provide professional development, team members need to clarify their profession's role in a coordinated school health program. The development of interdisciplinary teams requires each profession to acknowledge that it does not have sole responsibility for addressing the needs of young people and to define its unique contributions. The interdisciplinary team working with Education Development Center, Inc., overcame turf issues and other barriers to collaboration by working together to identify common roles. For the nurses, counselors, social workers, and psychologists participating in this project, the common roles included assessment and referral, crisis intervention and counseling, whole child development, and school community wellness. After agreeing on common roles, team members then separately defined the unique functions of their profession, such as "applying an ecological perspective to psychosocial assessments which link home, school, and community factors affecting learning" for social workers or "applying learning theory for individuals and groups to improve instruction" for school psychologists. (See Figure 8.3 in the chapter on school health services.) Essential to the success of interdisciplinary cooperation for professional development are mutual trust and a shared concern for the welfare of young people.

FIGURE 11.2. Sharing the Vision of a Coordinated School Health Program: Training and Technical Assistance Model

Level	Players	Strategies
National	National and state-affiliate leadership representing organizations that address components of coordinated school health programs and national health and education organizations (both government and nongovernment)	Leaders of organizations increase their understanding of the components of a coordinated school health program. National organizations develop organizational position statements regarding their role in coordinated school health programs. National-level players meet to develop recommendations on their roles in coordinated school health programs. National organizations develop and implement strategies to promote coordinated school health programs.
State	Interdisciplinary state teams representing: • state affiliates of organizations that address components of coordinated school health programs • state education agencies • state health agencies • other state agencies responsible for implementation of components	State teams are trained in their roles as part of a coordinated school health program. State teams strengthen and integrate state-level components that support a coordinated school health program. State teams work with local districts to implement components as part of a coordinated school health program. State teams inform national organizations and receive their support and technical assistance.
Local	Local school districts, schools with site-based management, local health departments, other community agencies, and parents and other concerned citizens	Districts and local providers receive training from interdisciplinary state teams regarding their roles in the implementation of the components of coordinated school health programs. Districts/schools and providers develop and implement coordinated school health programs. Districts/schools and providers share experiences with and receive ongoing support and technical assistance from state teams.

If practitioners are to collaborate and integrate, they must receive preparation. Courses and experiences designed to provide social workers, nurses, health promotion specialists, educators, recreationists, and others (e.g., criminal-juvenile justice, public administration) with a common denominator of vision(s), mission(s), knowledge, values, norms, skills, and language for collaboration and integration are called interprofessional education programs. Like the preparation provided foreign nationals who will enter a new country with unfamiliar cultures, traditions and language, interprofessional education prepares helping professionals for "border crossing". (Lawson & Hooper-Briar, 1994, p. 29)

Preservice Interprofessional Preparation.   Professional preservice and graduate programs typically aim to prepare practitioners for specific service, educating, helping, or care-giving roles. By contrast, interprofessional education programs train professionals to collaborate and thus maximize limited resources and their impact on children, youth, and their families. An example of a successful interprofessional education program is the University of Washington's training for interprofessional collaboration which draws its faculty and students from the graduate schools of education, public health and community medicine, nursing, social work, and public affairs. As the project entered its fifth year, the dean of the school of education was looking for ways to infuse the program's philosophy throughout the university into the training of all principals, counselors, teachers, public health practitioners, and nurses (Cohen, 1996).

Preservice instructors who aim to prepare school personnel to function as effective partners might consider Casto's nine conditions that are necessary to launch and sustain interprofessional education programs (Lawson & Hooper-Briar, 1994):

- a neutral base of operation outside the territory of the participants
- administrative support, such as release time or special organizational structures
- shared interest and commitment of participants
- shared credit with other team members and the program's sponsors
- shared resources
- partnerships with the community
- training in collaborative skills
- replacing hierarchical organizational structures with collaborative ones
- rewards, such as salary increases, favorable tenure, promotion reviews, and institutional funding

State organizations can use a number of strategies in support of interdisciplinary preparation, many of which schools and local districts might find useful as well. They include assembling an interdisciplinary directory of professionals who can provide mentoring, compiling a bibliography of publications about interdisciplinary approaches to professional preparation, publishing related newsletters and journal articles, changing credentialing and licensure requirements to include interdisciplinary competencies, and announcing interdisciplinary professional development opportunities for faculty.

Coalition Building

A coordinated, comprehensive approach to school health programs requires that multiple players with differing viewpoints achieve a shared vision of healthy, academically successful, productive children and youth. A state-level coalition can be a powerful tool for achieving such a shared vision and supporting coordinated school health programs. Coalitions demonstrate to proponents and observers alike the breadth of concern for school health. A broad-based statewide structure that supports school health sends a clear message to local districts and schools about the value of coordination and shared efforts to help children grow up healthy (U.S. Department of Education, 1994).

A coalition is an association of groups and individuals with differing interests who share their resources to accomplish a specific objective that members cannot achieve alone. To succeed members must focus on common concerns and not try to change others' organizational agendas. A well-functioning statewide coalition allows individuals and organizations to concentrate on what they do best and encourages coordination of efforts among all components of a coordinated school health program.

Bringing together the representatives of diverse programs and resources to form a statewide coalition is analogous to constructing a jigsaw puzzle. With luck, all the pieces are there, even if they are not assembled. In most states potential participants can be identified easily—in government agencies, private industry, the legislature, the faith community, voluntary organizations (e.g., state affiliates of the American Cancer Society, American Lung Association, American Heart Association, American Red Cross), civic groups, parent and student organizations, and professional associations such as nurses, pediatricians, dentists, social workers, psychologists, health educators, physical educators, dieticians, and counselors.

The first step in starting a jigsaw puzzle is finding the corners. These cornerstone pieces are the groups and individuals in the state, who, by their history and design, already have an interest in developing and strengthening coordinated school health programs. Sometimes jigsaw puzzle pieces are stuck together. Similarly, existing alliances help organizers piece together whole sections at once.

As with complex jigsaw puzzles, coalitions are not built in one sitting. Different people might work on the problem at various times from unique angles and differing conditions. As with all systems change, coalition building takes time, sometimes years. Discussion of some subjects, such as resource sharing, might have to wait until members establish trusting relationships. One state coalition waited two years before addressing funding issues.

Numerous state and national groups have devised recommendations for coalition building (Allensworth, 1994; American Cancer Society, 1993; National Health & Education Consortium, 1995; Waters & Byrd, 1995). They agree on the importance of taking the following steps:

- *Find partners who share the vision of healthy kids.* The changing political, social, economic, and educational climates have created the opportunity for unique alliances among groups traditionally concerned with the health of children and those not usually involved with such issues.
- *Identify champions.* Successful coalitions include highly placed, well-connected individuals who have made a personal and professional commitment to school health. Champions change over time and vary depending on the issue. Although they might not participate in routine coalition activities, they can be counted on at times of crisis and growth.
- *Develop a common mission and manageable goals and objectives.* For a coalition to flourish, participants must have a clearly articulated vision of the mission, develop ownership of the mission, and agree upon the processes for achieving it.
- *Build on existing strengths and resources.* Tried, tested, and accepted programs are the backbone of support for local coordinated school health programs.
- *Secure funding and other resources.* Resources might include staff time, office and meeting space, supplies, and equipment to support the coalition's work.
- *Develop members' skills.* Collaboration requires resolving conflicts, working in new ways, and understanding other members' areas of specialization.
- *Meet regularly and solve problems one at a time.* Because coalition building is a complex process, patience and persistence are critical.
- *Build public awareness.* Messages that focus on the links between health and student success and the benefits of a coordinated school health program are most likely to win public support.

- *Evaluate efforts.* Activities should fit with the mission and support coalition objectives. Evaluation helps to identify what is working and what needs changing.
- *Rebuild and restructure.* New approaches, new players, and new resources help to keep the coalition dynamic and responsive to local needs.
- *Celebrate and share successes.* Taking time to recognize and reward people and projects that support the coalition's efforts to help young people grow in healthy ways helps to recharge all coalition members.

These steps are equally applicable to coalition building at the local level (see Chapter 2 on local implementation and Chapter 4 on family and community involvement). A state coalition might assist local coalition development to support coordinated school health programs, using these same processes.

The complex integration of many programs and resources requires fundamental change in how participants view their own systems and how they fit into other systems. Successful outcomes require the presence of elements such as vision, skills, incentives, resources, and an action plan (Knoster & Enterprise Group, 1991). When participants do not share and understand a common purpose, confusion is likely to result. When participants do not have the necessary skills, such as small group process, they might experience anxiety. Lack of incentives or a clear understanding of how the proposed changes will benefit participants can slow the change process. Inadequate resources can produce frustration. Without an action plan that includes small, manageable, measurable steps the process can undergo false starts. Figure 11.3 depicts what is likely to occur when one of these ingredients is missing.

STATE-LEVEL ACTION STEPS TO FACILITATE LOCAL IMPLEMENTATION OF COORDINATED SCHOOL HEALTH PROGRAMS

State organizations, both government and nongovernment, can take a number of steps to support coordinated school health programs.

- *Articulate a vision.* A clearly stated vision of what a coordinated school health program is and how it contributes to the health and educational achievement of students gives direction to state-level and statewide efforts.
- *Develop a state-level structure that supports the implementation of coordinated school health programs.* Bringing together key resources, programs, and decision makers within a supportive structure demonstrates that coor-

FIGURE 11.3 Elements for Making Change

Vision	Skills	Incentives	Resources	Action Plan	=	CHANGE

	Skills	Incentives	Resources	Action Plan	=	CONFUSION

Vision		Incentives	Resources	Action Plan	=	ANXIETY

Vision	Skills		Resources	Action Plan	=	SLOW CHANGE

Vision	Skills	Incentives		Action Plan	=	FRUSTRATION

Vision	Skills	Incentives	Resources		=	FALSE STARTS

Source: Knoster, T. & Enterprise Group, Ltd. (1991). System reform for children and their families. Lansing: State of Michigan.

dinated school health programs are a priority and models a collaborative structure for local implementation.

- *Provide financial support for program implementation.* Support for coordinated school health programs needs to be a funding priority. The availability of funding can provide a strong incentive for schools and districts to implement coordinated school health programs.
- *Support or develop coalitions to strengthen coordinated school health programs.* Most states already have a core of organizations that support one or more aspects of school health. Just as many national organizations encourage their state affiliates to participate in school health activities, state-level organizations can encourage their local counterparts to form or participate in local coalitions.
- *Strengthen professional preparation and ongoing development.* The inclusion of an introduction to school health and ways that school health activities support the school culture can strengthen professional preparation for school administrators, teachers, and health care providers. Colleges and universities can develop interprofessional education programs that encourage staff and community members to work together in support of coordinated school health programs
- *Support the employment of professionally prepared and appropriately credentialed staff.* The inclusion of a requirement for preservice preparation that

incorporates education or experience in an interprofessional school health program can strengthen credentialing, licensure, and certification. State accrediting organizations can reexamine requirements that either do not consider the role that school staff may play in a coordinated school health program or that impede collaboration among school staff.

- *Involve local practitioners in state-level planning and program development.* The experiences of personnel who are implementing coordinated school health programs at the school and district levels can inform state efforts in the areas of policy, program, training, technical assistance, and materials development.
- *Develop materials, guidelines, and publications that support program implementation.* The development of materials, guidelines, and publications at the state level results in both uniformity and cost savings. State organizations also often have greater access to research materials than school staff do.
- *Provide data.* Data on health risk behaviors and the incidence of behavior-related disease and death can help to demonstrate the need for coordinated school health programs.
- *Demonstrate program effectiveness.* By working together to evaluate the effectiveness of coordinated school health programs or its components, state agencies and colleges and universities can produce information that will help policy makers make spending decisions and set program priorities.
- *Conduct advocacy and public awareness activities.* State organizations can contact key legislators and conduct public awareness campaigns to promote coordinated school health programs.
- *Model participation in school health-related functions.* State-level policy makers and staff can support school health activities by participating in fitness events, agency-sponsored employee health programs, and forums on school health-related issues.
- *Provide technical assistance and training.* State organizations can provide schools and districts with many types of technical assistance, including a resource and information clearinghouse, information on legislative and regulatory changes, marketing support, and assistance with developing grant applications. State organizations can also offer workshops, conferences, and continuing education to prepare school staff for participation in coordinated school health programs.
- *Develop supportive systems and technological approaches.* Such systems can help minimize administrative complexities and provide data bases for measuring impact, outcomes, and efficiency and effectiveness. Consistent technology across all systems can facilitate communication and networking among school personnel statewide.

• *Regionalize technical assistance and training to facilitate access.* Regional staff can more readily develop ongoing relationships with local implementers and tailor training and technical assistance to local needs.

CONCLUSION

Schools and communities can look to state-level organizations to help them make the best use of resources for carrying out coordinated school health programs. Statewide government and nongovernment organizations can assist local activities by facilitating coordination and providing support such as technical assistance, consultation, and training to schools that want to implement a coordinated school health program. Resources are often available at the state level but applying them in new ways requires that schools have a commitment to the vision of healthy students and an understanding of the programs needed to achieve that vision (Melaville & Blank, 1993). State organizations can help them achieve this.

State-level organizations and local schools must work together because no individual initiative can have the sustained resources or energy to provide a quality program to the multitude of students and families in a state. Organizations collaborating at the state-level demonstrate the benefits of integrating the components of a coordinated school health program and are better prepared to assist schools with their implementation.

REFERENCES

Allensworth, D. (1994). *Building effective coalitions to prevent the spread of HIV: Planning considerations.* Kent, OH: American School Health Association.

American Cancer Society. (1993). *Working together for a future—Comprehensive school health education: Developing a state-level workshop.* Atlanta, GA: Author.

Association of State and Territorial Health Officials. (1995a). *State health official salary survey results.* Washington, DC: Author.

Association of State and Territorial Health Officials. (1995b). *Summary data: State health agency characteristics for U.S. states and territories.* Washington, DC: Author.

Brown, T. W., & Aliza, B. (1995). *A changing epidemic: How state Title V programs are addressing the spread of HIV/AIDS in women, children, and youth.* Washington, DC: Association of Maternal and Child Health Programs.

Centers for Disease Control and Prevention. (1988). Guidelines for effective school health education to prevent the spread of AIDS. *Morbidity and Mortality Weekly Report, 37*(S-2), 1–14.

Centers for Disease Control and Prevention. (1994). Guidelines for school programs to prevent tobacco use and addiction. *Morbidity and Mortality Weekly Report, 43*(RR-2), 1–14.

Centers for Disease Control and Prevention. (1996). Guidelines for school health programs to promote lifelong healthy eating. *Morbidity and Mortality Weekly Report, 45*(RR-9), 1–41.

Centers for Disease Control and Prevention. (1997a). Guidelines for school and community programs to promote lifelong physical activity among young people. *Morbidity and Mortality Weekly Report, 46*(RR-6), 1–36.

Centers for Disease Control and Prevention. (1997b). *Coordinated school health program infrastructure development: Process evaluation manual.* Atlanta: U.S. Department of Health and Human Services, Centers for Disease Control and Prevention.

Cohen, D. (1996, February). A Working Relationship. *Education Week, 15*(23), 29–32.

Colorado Department of Education. (1995). *Mobilizing our resources: Framework for comprehensive school health programs in Colorado.* Denver, CO: Author.

Dryfoos, J. G. (1994). *Full-service schools.* San Francisco: Jossey-Bass.

Grason, H., & Guyer, B. (1995). *Public MCH program functions framework: Essential public health services to promote maternal and child health in America.* Baltimore, MD: Child and Adolescent Health Policy Center, The Johns Hopkins School of Hygiene and Public Health.

Hayes, M., & Walker, D. K. (1997). The role of public health in assuring a system of health care for children. In R. E. K. Stein (Ed.), *Health care for children: What's right, what's wrong* (pp. 339–351). New York: United Hospital Fund.

Institute of Medicine. (1997). *Schools and health: Our nation's investment.* D. Allensworth, E. Lawson, L. Nicholson, & J. Wyche (Eds.). Washington, DC: National Academy Press.

Joint Committee on National Health Education Standards. (1995). *National health education standards.* Atlanta, GA: American Cancer Society.

Knoster, T., & Enterprise Group, Ltd. (1991). *System reform for children and their families.* Lansing: State of Michigan.

Kolbe, L. J., Kann, L., & Collins, J. L. (1993). Overview of the Youth Risk Behavior Surveillance System. *Public Health Reports, 108*(Suppl. 1), 2–10.

Kolbe, L. J., Kann, L., Collins, J. L., Small, M. L., Pateman, B. C., & Warren, C. W. (1995). The School Health Policies and Programs Study (SHPPS): Context, methods, general findings, and future efforts. *Journal of School Health, 65*(8), 334–343.

Lawson, H., & Hooper-Briar, K. (1994). *Expanding partnerships: Involving colleges and universities in interprofessional collaboration and service integration.* Oxford, OH: Danforth Foundation and Institute for Educational Renewal, Miami University.

Marx, E., & Northrop, D. (1995). *Educating for health: A guide for implementing a comprehensive approach to school health education.* Newton, MA: Education Development Center.

McCarthy, M., Langdon, C., & Olson, J. (1993). *State education governance structures.* Denver, CO: Education Commission of the States.

Melaville, A. I., & Blank, M. J. (1993). *Together we can: A guide for crafting a profamily system of education and human services.* Washington, DC: U.S. Department of Education and U.S. Department of Health and Human Services.

National Association of State Boards of Education. (1995). The role of state boards of education. *Policy Update, 3*(4), 1–4.

National Commission on the Role of the School and Community in Improving Adolescent Health. (1990). *Code blue: Uniting for healthier youth.* Alexandria, VA: National Association of State Boards of Education and American Medical Association.

National Conference of State Legislatures. (1997). *Adolescent health issues: State actions 1996.* Denver, CO: Author.

National Governors' Association. (1987). *Making America work: Bringing down the barriers.* Washington, DC: Author.

National Health & Education Consortium. (1995). *Putting children first: State level collaboration between education and health.* Washington, DC: Author.

The Policy Exchange, The Institute for Educational Leadership. (1994). *Linking schools with health and social services: Perspectives from Thomas Payzant on San Diego's new beginnings.* Washington, DC: Author.

Small, M. L., Majer, L. S., Allensworth, D. D., Farquhar, B. K., Kann, L., & Pateman, B. C. (1995). School health services. *Journal of School Health, 65,* 319–326.

Texas Department of Health. (1996). *Healthy children are prepared to learn.* Austin, TX: Author.

U.S. Department of Education. (1994). *Strong families, strong schools.* Washington, DC: Author.

Waters, M., & Byrd, S. (1995). *Florida's comprehensive school health program coalitions.* Tallahassee: Florida Department of Education.

The authors would like to acknowledge the valuable input and recommendations from the following focus group participants: Michael Everman, director of public affairs, Texas Association for HPERD, Austin, Texas; Jaynee Fontecchio, school health director, Infrastructure, State Department of Education, Santa Fe, New Mexico; Mary Jackson, program director, Health Promotion, Bureau of Women and Children, Texas Department of Health, Austin, Texas; Judy Jonas, project director, Texas Comprehensive School Health Initiative, Austin, Texas; William Kane, associate professor, Health Education, University of New Mexico, Albuquerque, New Mexico; Ellen Kelsey, American Heart Association, Austin, Texas; Kristine Meurer, program manager, State Department of Education, Santa Fe, New Mexico; Joyce Moore, health education specialist, Alabama Department of Education, Montgomery, Alabama; Patsy Nelson, school health director, Public Health Division, New Mexico Department of Health, Santa Fe, New Mexico; Donna Pike, director of CSHE Initiative, Rocky Mountain Center for Health Promotion and Education, Lakewood, Colorado; Emma Lou Rodriguez, New Mexico State Board of Education, Albuquerque, New Mexico; and David Smith, director, Prevention Initiatives Unit, Colorado Department of Education, Denver, Colorado.

Brenda Z. Greene, M.F.A.
Kristine I. McCoy, M.P.H.

12 The National Role in Coordinated School Health Programs

O rganizations at the national level can influence support for coordinated school health programs as well as their implementation at the
local level. In fact, many national organizations—both government
and nongovernment—have taken a leadership role in supporting school
health programs over the past several decades. Although their perspectives,
roles, and strategies are diverse, these agencies can link local school personnel and school health advocates to national efforts on behalf of coordinated
school health programs that are comprehensive and fully functioning.

National organizations fulfill their missions through a wide range of activities that include:

- issuing position statements
- encouraging cooperation and collaboration with other agencies
- disseminating information
- offering professional development
- developing program standards and assessments
- certifying of professionals and programs
- conducting research and evaluation
- advocating
- fund-raising
- providing technical assistance

Health Is Academic: A Guide to Coordinated School Health Problems. Edited by Eva Marx and Susan Frelick
Wooley, with Daphne Northrop. New York: Teachers College Press, 1998. ISBN 0-8077-3713-5 (pbk.), ISBN
0-8077-3714-3 (cloth). Prior to photocopying items for classroom use, please contact the Copyright Clearance
Center, Customer Service, 222 Rosewood Dr., Danvers, MA 01923, USA, tel. (508) 750-8400. © 1998 Education Development Center, Inc. All rights reserved.

Both nongovernment and government organizations that support coordinated school health programs use at least one of these strategies to provide leadership and assistance to those implementing at the state and community levels. This chapter describes the roles and capacities of national organizations in supporting coordinated school health programs, the context that influences their work, actions that they might take to contribute to local implementation, and ways that local stakeholders might affect national actions. It first discusses the activities of nongovernment organizations and then those of government agencies. Information on how national organizations support the individual components of coordinated school health programs appears in Chapters 3–10. Appendix 1 provides a sampling of groups that are concerned with the health and academic achievement of children and adolescents. Many more organizations that are not listed contribute to coordinated school health programs. The organizations used as examples in this chapter are only a few of those supportive of coordinated school health programs.

HOW NONGOVERNMENT ORGANIZATIONS SUPPORT COORDINATED SCHOOL HEALTH PROGRAMS

Missions and Membership

Young people's health and academic achievement are concerns for hundreds of national organizations and coalitions. They bring an array of perspectives and strengths to the advancement of coordinated school health programs. These professional and voluntary organizations include:

- *Organizations that focus on one or more components of a coordinated school health program.* Their membership comprises persons responsible for implementing a specific school health component, such as school nurses, health education teachers, physical education teachers, school social workers, school counselors, and school psychologists. These groups focus on only one or a few aspects of school health. Examples of such organizations are the National Association of School Nurses, the National Association of School Psychologists, or the American School Counselor Association.
- *Organizations that focus on schools or education.* Their members include state and local policy makers, superintendents, principals, curriculum specialists, university faculty, and teachers for subjects other than health. Health-related issues are complementary or secondary to their primary mission, and they might focus on only one portion of the continuum from kindergarten through 12th grade, such as elementary or middle schools. The National Association of Elementary School Principals, the American

Association of School Administrators, and the Association for Supervision and Curriculum Development are examples of this type of organization.

- *Organizations that address environmental and physical safety.* Persons who design, construct, or maintain school buildings or who have responsibility for ensuring a healthy, safe environment compose the membership of these groups. Such organizations represent fields such as risk assessment and management, architecture and building engineering, air quality, water quality, hazardous materials, and law enforcement. Their focus is usually broader than schools. Examples of these organizations are the National Environmental Health Association and the Public Risk Management Association.

- *Organizations that focus on improved health outcomes.* Members include persons involved in prevention or therapeutic health care, such as physicians, dentists, audiologists, nurses, dietitians, psychologists, substance abuse counselors, social workers, recreation therapists, and public health educators. Some organizations represent health care providers, such as hospitals and insurance companies, and others provide material resources such as businesses and foundations. These groups focus on all aspects of the health of children, adolescents, and adults, or more limited topics such as vision, hearing, oral health, nutrition, environmental health, and mental health. The health of children and adolescents is rarely their primary focus. The American Public Health Association, the National Association of Social Workers, the Robert Wood Johnson Foundation, and the American Dietetic Association are a few examples.

- *Organizations that encourage parents, families, and communities to nurture and protect youth.* Such organizations represent constituencies such as elected officials (other than school boards); specific racial and ethnic communities; clergy and religious institutions; advocates for children with disabilities, parents, families, and students; volunteers; and civic organizations. Health-related issues are usually secondary to the primary mission. Examples of these organizations are the National Conference of State Legislatures, the National Urban League, and the National Council of Churches.

Whatever its membership and the relationship between its mission and school health programs, an organization's main commitment is the needs of its members. A commitment can restrict a group's ability to take positions on issues and can, on occasion, pit one organization against others that represent related but competing interests.

Many national nongovernment organizations have state, regional, and local affiliates. For example, the National School Boards Association (NSBA) is a federation of state school boards associations and the school boards of states and territories with a central school governance entity. Members of the National PTA (parents, teachers, and others who advocate for the health, welfare, and education of children and youth) are affiliated with local parent-teacher associations linked to the national organization through state congresses.

Nongovernment organizations have both formal and ad hoc systems for providing leadership to their state or local affiliates and receiving input from their members. Groups disseminate information on research about effective programs, available resources (for example, funding to support program activities), and federal legislation that might support or disrupt local activities. At the same time, the affiliates inform their national leaders about local needs, challenges, and experiences related to implementing school health programs. For example, the National PTA communicates with its membership through mailings to local units, state offices, the national board, state boards, and state board leaders with specific portfolios (for example, chairs for health and welfare or HIV/AIDS education). To obtain feedback from its members, the National PTA conducts surveys, the executive committee of the board of directors attends state annual conventions, and the legislative program maintains a member-to-member network of important advocacy contacts in each state.

Position Statements

Many organizations demonstrate their support of school health by adopting position statements, policies, or resolutions that place on record the organization's commitment to school health programs or specific aspects of school health. The position statements of some organizations, such as the American School Health Association (ASHA), specify school health as the primary mission. The statements issued by some other organizations include a commitment to school health programs. For example, the National Middle School Association (NMSA) "is dedicated to improving the educational experiences of young adolescents by providing vision, knowledge, and resources to all who serve them in order to develop healthy, productive, and ethical citizens" (NMSA, 1995, p. ii). This resolution underscores the NMSA's imperative to address the academic needs of students in the context of their physical, social, and emotional needs.

An unpublished compilation in 1994 by the American School Health Association and the National School Boards Association of the resolutions and policy statements of ten national education and health organizations revealed that eight formally acknowledged their support for school health programs. Six had statements specifically addressing school health instruction, use and abuse of tobacco, steroids, and other drugs, and HIV/AIDS education. Although five or fewer of the organizations had policy statements addressing other components of coordinated school health programs, such as school health services, these diverse organizations clearly have common, mutually reinforcing goals that provide a basis for partnerships. Thus, advocates for coordinated school health programs can draw on groups' position statements to urge specific actions by schools and districts and to forge partnerships on behalf of the well-being of youth.

Cooperation and Collaboration

Because of the shared commitment to the healthy development of youth and the shared understanding that health is a key to school success, it is not surprising that national organizations have increased their cooperative and collaborative ventures in recent years. Such activities can be formal or ad hoc, and they can be implemented through structures such as large and small coalitions or consortia.

Formal Collaborations.   An increasing number of formal, ongoing coalitions or consortia focus on school health programs in general or on specific components of school health programs. Examples include the following:

- The National Health & Education Consortium (NHEC) was formed in 1990 by the congressional National Commission to Prevent Infant Mortality and the nonprofit Institute for Educational Leadership (IEL). The NHEC seeks to improve public policy, enhance coordination, and raise awareness of program models and practices to promote increased and improved relationships between the health and education sectors. It is a 58-member consortium of health and educational professional associations that represent about 12 million individuals.
- The National Assembly on School-Based Health Care (NASBHC) promotes the provision of quality primary physical and mental health care to children and youth through school-based health centers. It is a membership organization for professionals from various disciplines who are dedicated to the development of school-based health centers (see Chapters 7 and 8).

Ad Hoc Collaborations.   National organizations periodically meet to identify common goals and principles or to discuss specific issues. For example, the National Consensus Building Conference on School-Linked Integrated Service Systems convened in January 1994. The conference resulted in the publication of *Principles to Link By: Integrating Education, Health, and Human Services for Children, Youth, and Families,* which articulated the commitment of more than 50 national organizations "to create comprehensive support for every child and young person" (Ad Hoc Working Group on Integrated Services, 1994).

In 1992, the American Cancer Society (ACS) convened representatives of 40 national health, education, and social service groups to plan how to make comprehensive school health education an essential part of the nation's health and education agendas. This conference became a model for similar state-level collaborations ("Working Together for the Future," 1993).

Disseminating Information

Nongovernment national organizations use a variety of media to provide their constituents motivation to support or information on issues important to the organization and its members.

Publications. Persons involved in school health issues need up-to-date statistics, research findings, program ideas, health information, advocacy materials, policies, standards, and so on. National organizations serve this need by regularly producing newsletters, newspapers, magazines, journals, brochures, issue briefs, policy updates, fact sheets, and legislative updates.

Some examples of publications used to distribute information and organizational position statements are:

- Reports, such as American Psychological Association's (APA) *School Health: Psychology's Role,* which provides information about the importance of school health, the rationale for linking education and health, and specific ways in which psychologists can contribute to implementing the eight components of a coordinated school health program.
- Professional journals such as *Educational Leadership,* published by the Association for Supervision and Curriculum Development; *Journal of School Health,* published by the American School Health Association; *American Journal of Public Health,* published by the American Public Health Association; and *Adolescent Medicine,* published by the Society for Adolescent Medicine.
- Newsletters such as *School Health Program News,* published by Education Development Center, Inc. (EDC), *HExtra,* published by the American Association for Health Education (AAHE), and the National Middle School Association's *Midpoints.*
- Brochures such as *Healthy Children, Successful Students,* published by the National PTA. This brochure tells parents and local parent-teacher associations what steps they can take to support coordinated school health programs.

- Booklets such as *Be a Leader in Academic Achievement . . . ,* jointly published by the American Cancer Society, the American Association of School Administrators, the National School Boards Association, and the National School Health Education Coalition, that motivates its readers and guides their actions in supporting school health programs.
- Special mailings, such as *Readings on School Health Issues,* produced by the Council of Chief State School Officers. This three-ring binder was designed to help state education chiefs maintain a file of peer-reviewed journal articles related to HIV/AIDS policies and effective school-based programs to reduce sexual risk behaviors. The National Health & Education Consortium mails new reports to the executive directors, public information officers, and representatives of its member organizations, and the executive directors of members' state affiliates. In one year, the NHEC distributed three reports (on the relationship of violence to learning, elementary school-based health centers, and state-level collaboration between education and health) through special mailings.

Electronic Media.   As their in-house computer networking capacities grow, national organizations are expanding communication with their members. The National Education Association (NEA) has created an interactive forum, *NEA On-Line,* for members. The Comprehensive Health Education Network (CHEN), an on-line system run by the Council of Chief State School Officers, is available to organizations funded by the Division of Adolescent and School Health (DASH) of the Centers for Disease Control and Prevention (CDC), U.S. Department of Health and Human Services (DHHS). HandsNet connects its subscribers to a variety of information sources on health and other social policy issues. The Educational Resources Information Center (ERIC) maintains an on-line database on educational issues, including health education and physical education.

The Internet also provides a forum for two-way communication and research on information, data, and resources. Individuals can access information from the national organizations—both nongovernment and government—through a few keystrokes. Some groups have created home pages that facilitate direct access to their staffs and links to related information sources and services. For example, the CCSSO's home page is linked to its member state education agencies that also have home pages.

Professional Development

Most national nongovernment organizations offer education and training programs through conferences, legislative forums, and skill-building sessions. Some of these events are designed to increase their members' understanding of school health programs. For example, the Public Education Network (PEN), which provides technical assistance to a network of community organizations that identify resources to support local education, offered a conference session on how to develop plans for coordinated school health programs. In addition, the National Association of State Boards of Education (NASBE) periodically assembles a group of state board of education members and state education officials to explore school reforms and state policies that foster students' health and well-being.

Nongovernment organizations also educate their members about regulatory and fiscal changes that could affect students' health. In addition, as more managed-care groups provide school health services, training on accessing managed-care resources becomes essential. Advocates also need skills in persuading decision makers about the importance of supporting school health services and in using existing supportive structures to expand and strengthen school health programs. For example, at their annual conferences, the National Assembly on School-Based Health Care and the Association of Maternal and Child Health Programs include workshops on issues such as changes in Medicaid and the impact of the changing health care system on school services.

Interdisciplinary training is becoming recognized as an essential form of professional development. Education Development Center (EDC) recruited representatives of the National Association of School Psychologists (NASP), National Association of School Nurses (NASN), National Association of Social Workers (NASW), American School Counselor Association (ASCA), and American Psychological Association to design an interdisciplinary training model aimed at professionals who provide student services. This model illustrates how state-level teams of student services professionals can provide local school districts training and technical assistance on coordinated school health programs. The model incorporates ongoing reinforcement from the collaborating organizations (see Chapters 8 and 11).

Development of Program Standards and Assessments

As part of education reform, both school health education and physical education have developed program standards and ways to assess what students have learned and are able to do. In 1995, after two years of extensive study, outreach, and deliberation, a Joint Committee for National School Health Education Standards issued standards for health education. The committee included representatives of the American Cancer Society, the American Association for Health Education, the American Public Health Association, the American School Health Association, and the Society of State Directors for Health, Physical Education, and Recreation (SSDHPER). The standards received support for widespread distribution from the American Cancer Society.

The Standards and Assessment Task Force of the National Association for Sport and Physical Education (NASPE), an association of the American Alliance for Health, Physical Education, Recreation and Dance, published content standards based on work of NASPE's Outcomes Committee and input from hundreds of physical education professionals throughout the country (NASPE, 1995).

The Council of Chief State School Officers has led a State Collaborative on Assessment and Student Standards (SCASS) in health education as well as in mathematics and science. The health education project developed and tested assorted student assessment tools for health education, including selected-response and open-ended exercises and performance tasks ("Council's State Collaborative," 1995).

Research and Evaluation

Some nongovernment organizations conduct independent research to support program and constituent activities. In 1994, the American Cancer Society commissioned a Gallup Poll that found broad-based support for school health education among school administrators and parents. For the most part, however, the cost of effective research and evaluation prohibits nongovernment organizations from undertaking such endeavors independently. Instead, nongovernment organizations sometimes collaborate with the federal government on research studies. For example, in 1990 the National School Boards Association, the American Association of School Administrators, and CDC conducted a national study of HIV/AIDS and health education policies and programs (Holtzman et al., 1992).

Technical Assistance

Many national nongovernment organizations provide technical assistance on school health and related issues to their membership, other organizations, state and local education agencies, and school-level professionals. Assistance by telephone, printed materials, training programs, and specific staff contacts are available for many issues, including developing policy, organizing communities, educating peers, cultural competency, and developing a curriculum. For example, the National School Boards Association provides technical assistance on HIV/AIDS and school health policies, including sample policies, guidance on content and legal issues, and referral to other agencies with specific expertise.

HOW THE FEDERAL GOVERNMENT SUPPORTS COORDINATED
SCHOOL HEALTH PROGRAMS

The federal government has taken the initiative on many fronts to advance coordinated school health programs, including program funding and development of regulations and guidelines. Federal agencies also support school health programs in many of the same ways nongovernment organizations do.

Program Funding

The federal government supports state and community efforts to help schools prevent violence among youth, provide nutritious school lunches, develop health education guidelines, provide physical and mental health services in schools, and implement safety standards. Numerous federal agencies and departments provide funding through entitlement programs, block grants, competitive demonstration grants, and other means.

Examples of funding sources include Medicaid, the Maternal and Child Health Block Grant (Title V), and the Child/Adolescent Planning and System Development Program of DHHS; the Safe and Drug Free Schools Program of the U.S. Department of Education (DOE); and the School Breakfast and Lunch Programs from the U.S. Department of Agriculture (USDA). The Institute of Medicine (IOM) report *Schools and Health: Our Nation's Investment* (1997) describes these and other programs that support elements of a coordinated school health program. Some of this funding flows to school programs through state-administered programs, such as Medicaid and the school meals programs. By contrast, demonstration grants such as the High Risk Youth Demonstration Grant Program of the Center for Substance Abuse Prevention (CSAP), Substance Abuse and Mental Health Services Administration (SAMHSA), DHHS, go directly to schools and other community-based service providers. The DHHS publication *Healthy Schools: A Directory of Federal Programs and Activities Related to Health Promotion Through the Schools* (1992) catalogs federal programs for school health. The Division of Adolescent and School Health maintains an on-line database of federal funding sources for school health programs. Other public and private partners may add state and private level funding to this database.

Development of Regulations and Guidelines

Legislation creates most federal government programs. Federal agencies then establish the regulations under which the programs function. These regulations often stipulate who is eligible for government resources and, more important, provide standards of quality. Determining quality often involves give-and-take between the government and those whom the regulations will affect. The federal agency considers comments from the public on possible unnecessary fiscal or bureaucratic effects but strives to maintain the goals of the legislation. Also, political influence sometimes strengthens and sometimes weakens regulations. Occasionally public comments and political influence result in new legislation. For example, in 1995 the U.S. Department of Agriculture (USDA) created the School Meals Initiative for Healthy Children, which requires that school meals meet the Dietary Guidelines for Americans, supply certain proportions of recommended daily allowances of particular nutrients, include foods from different cultures, and appeal to the consumer. Because implementing these regulations proved difficult, new legislation was enacted to provide school districts increased flexibility to meet the Dietary Guidelines. To assist schools in meeting the new standards, USDA also developed tools to institute and monitor menu planning, established technical assistance for training food preparation personnel, created new recipes, and established the Team Nutrition program to build support within schools (see Chapter 9).

In addition to regulations, federal agencies have established guidelines for school health programs, particularly on coordination of health and social services. To encourage linkages among local agencies who serve children and families, federal agencies have begun issuing grant awards that require some coordination with other organizations. School health programs benefit because the requirement motivates schools, school-based providers, and other community service organizations to share information and create a cohesive system of services. These more flexible guidelines also can allow communities to consolidate funding that various agencies provide for activities such as substance abuse prevention for high-risk youth, parenting classes for pregnant teens, and referrals for children receiving health screenings at schools.

Cooperation and Collaboration

With the issuance of the *Joint Statement on School Health* in 1994 (Figure 12.1), the secretaries of education and health and human services committed their agencies to fostering cooperation and coordination between the education and health sectors. In this statement the two secretaries recognized the link between education and health and the convergence of the national health and education goals. The secretaries also announced the establishment of the Interagency Committee on School Health (ICSH) and the National Coordinating Committee on School Health (NCCSH), both chaired by officials of the Departments of Education, Health and Human Services, and Agriculture. The ICSH convenes representatives from nine federal agencies

FIGURE **12.1**

JOINT STATEMENT ON SCHOOL HEALTH
by
The Secretaries of Education and Health and Human Services

Health and education are joined in fundamental ways with each other and with the destinies of the Nation's children. Because of our national leadership responsibilities for education and health, we have initiated unprecedented cooperative efforts between our Departments. In support of comprehensive school health programs, we affirm the following:

■ *America's children face many compelling educational and health and developmental challenges that affect their lives and their futures.*

These challenges include poor levels of achievement; unacceptably high drop-out rates; low literacy; violence; drug abuse; preventable injuries; physical and mental illness; developmental disabilities; and sexual activity resulting in sexually transmitted diseases, including HIV, and unintended pregnancy. These facts demand a reassessment of the contributions of education and health programs in safeguarding our children's present lives and preparing them for productive, responsible, and fulfilling futures.

■ *To help children meet these challenges, education and health must be linked in partnership.*

Schools are the only public institutions that touch nearly every young person in this country. Schools have a unique opportunity to affect the lives of children and their families, but they cannot address all of our children's needs alone. Health, education, and human service programs must be integrated, and schools must have the support of public and private health care providers, communities, and families.

■ *School health programs support the education process, integrate services for disadvantaged and disabled children, and improve children's health prospects.*

Through school health programs, children and their families can develop the knowledge, attitudes, beliefs, and behaviors necessary to remain healthy and perform well in school. These learning environments enhance safety, nutrition, and disease prevention; encourage exercise and fitness; support healthy physical, mental, and emotional development; promote abstinence and prevent sexual behaviors that result in HIV infection, other sexually transmitted diseases, and unintended teenage pregnancy; discourage use of illegal drugs, alcohol, and tobacco; and help young people develop problem-solving and decision-making skills.

■ *Reforms in health care and in education offer opportunities to forge the partnerships needed for our children in the 1990s.*

The benefits of integrated health and education services can be achieved by working together to create a "seamless" network of services, both through the school setting and through linkages with other community resources.

■ *GOALS 2000 and HEALTHY PEOPLE 2000 provide complementary visions that, together, can support our joint efforts in pursuit of a healthier, better educated Nation for the next century.*

GOALS 2000 challenges us to ensure that all children arrive at school ready to learn; to increase the high school graduation rate; to achieve basic subject matter competencies; to achieve universal adult literacy; and to ensure that school environments are safe, disciplined, and drug free. HEALTHY PEOPLE 2000 challenges us to increase the span of healthy life for the American people, to reduce and finally to eliminate health disparities among population groups, and to ensure access to services for all Americans.

In support of GOALS 2000 and HEALTHY PEOPLE 2000, we have established the Interagency Committee on School Health co-chaired by the Assistant Secretary for Elementary and Secondary Education and the Assistant Secretary for Health, and we have convened the National Coordinating Committee on School Health to bring together representatives of major national education and health organizations to work with us.

We call upon professionals in the fields of education and health and concerned citizens across the Nation to join with us in a renewed effort and a reaffirmation of our mutual responsibility to our Nation's children.

Richard W. Riley
Secretary of Education

Donna E. Shalala
Secretary of Health and Human Services

and departments that seek to coordinate federal systems and programs that affect the health and education of children in the United States. The NCCSH, which is made up of over 40 national nongovernment organizations from the education, health, and social services sectors, provides a forum for leaders of NCCSH organizations and federal officials to discuss issues, trends, and initiatives that affect school health programs. Meetings allow interaction and foster collaboration between the many disciplines that support children's health and learning.

CDC has also been active in collaborating with nongovernment organizations. For example, CDC involved nongovernment organizations in developing guidelines for schools to prevent HIV infection (1988) and tobacco use and addiction (1994) and to promote healthy eating (1996) and physical activity (1997) among youth. In these efforts, CDC asked representatives of relevant national health and education organizations to help develop the content of these guidelines and help schools implement them.

Government agencies also collaborate with each other. For example, the Bureau of Primary Health Care (BPHC) and the Maternal and Child Health Bureau (MCHB), both in the Health Resources and Services Administration (HRSA) of DHHS, funded the Healthy Schools, Healthy Communities program, which supports model school health programs in more than 20 communities. The Division of Adolescent and School Health of CDC, BPHC, MCHB, the National Institutes of Health (NIH), and the Office of Population Affairs (all of DHHS) together with the U.S. Department of Education (ED) sponsored an Institute of Medicine analysis that examined school health programs (Institute of Medicine, 1997). ED and HRSA have developed a publication to inform community health centers and schools serving low-income populations of possible collaborations.

Information Dissemination

Government organizations use print materials, electronic media, and public campaigns to inform people of and involve them in implementing coordinated school health programs.

Print Materials.   Some federal publications highlight guidelines or research and evaluation findings; others such as *Together We Can: A Guide for Crafting a Profamily System of Education and Human Services* (Melaville & Blank, 1993) explore the joint roles of the health, social services, and educational systems in raising children. The federal government sometimes sends materials directly to school districts, state health and education departments, community health centers, and national organizations. National Coordinating Committee on School Health organizations also inform their members of the resources available.

Electronic Media. Federal agencies are increasingly using computer technology to make school health resources available to the public. For example, the National Coordinating Committee on School Health is establishing a school health home page to link its members, the public, and relevant federal and nonfederal agencies. As mentioned above, the Centers for Disease Control and Prevention with other partners in the Department of Health and Human Services has developed a database of federal funding sources for school health programs. The Maternal and Child Health Bureau supported the University of Colorado in its effort to develop long-distance interdisciplinary training via video conferences for school professionals in sparsely populated Western states. In addition, some federal clearinghouses make information on or resources for implementing various components of a coordinated school health program available through on-line systems, phone, and print (see Appendix 2).

National Campaigns. Occasionally federal health initiatives reach communities nationwide and become highly developed in schools. One such national campaign is the physical fitness initiative begun by President Eisenhower and strengthened during the terms of President Kennedy and President Johnson. With federal leadership, a surge of support for physical education occurred in the 1960s from individual teachers revamping their curricula to states allocating significant funds for the development of physical fitness materials, facilities, and personnel. The President's Council on Physical Fitness and Sports (PCPFS) established the Presidential Physical Fitness Award to recognize students with outstanding fitness. Although youth's physical fitness continues to be a priority of the PCPFS, the initiative has lost momentum and both physical education in schools and physical fitness among children have declined.

Another national initiative is the Team Nutrition program of the USDA (see Chapter 9). Through this program, the federal government and private partners strive to improve school meals. Similarly, the Food and Drug Administration has supported a campaign featuring the storybook character Curious George to teach children about nutrition labels on food. These efforts complement the publication of federally sponsored dietary guidelines and requirements for food labeling that have increased public awareness of the need for improved nutrition.

Professional Development. Federally sponsored conferences and training bring together school health professionals, often for cross- or multidisciplinary professional development. The largest such meeting focusing exclusively on school health is the annual National School Health Leadership Conference coordinated by CDC with co-sponsorship from ED, DHHS, and USDA. Other major conferences are the health-focused sessions sponsored by the Department of the Interior's Bureau of Indian Affairs at meetings of the National Indian Education Association and the National Indian School Boards Association and the grantee-tailored conferences sponsored by the Center for Substance Abuse Prevention. The Bureau of Primary Health Care and the Maternal and Child Health Bureau sponsor workshops for grantees that address specific aspects of a school health program, such as school-based health centers, supplemental health education, and building multidisciplinary teams.

Research and Evaluation

Numerous federal programs research specific school health issues. The National Institutes of Health has many ongoing research programs in schools, such as the Child and Adolescent Trial for Cardiovascular Health (CATCH) and Going Places; the latter looks at the effects of the transition to middle school on students' health behaviors and discipline. CDC has evaluated many school-based efforts to prevent HIV infection among youth. The Office of Technology Assessment (OTA), a congressional research office that was dissolved in 1996, conducted research that resulted in the recommendation that school health centers be established to meet the health needs of adolescents (U.S. Congress, Office of Technology Assessment [OTA], 1991). Another OTA study (1995) examined health risks to students in schools. In addition, the President's Council on Physical Fitness and Sports publishes digests of findings from physical activity and fitness research for persons who develop or administer school health programs.

Surveys are another major federal contribution to school health programs. The Youth Risk Behavior Surveillance System (YRBSS) (Kolbe, Kann, & Collins, 1993), the *Monitoring the Future* study (Johnston, O'Malley, & Bachman, 1996), and the School Health Policies and Programs Study (SHPPS) (Kann et al., 1995) are three federally sponsored surveys of behavior among youth. The YRBSS monitors youth's risky behaviors and the results are published in *Morbidity and Mortality Weekly Report*. The *Adolescent Health: State of the Nation* monograph series (CDC, 1993, 1995) combines YRBSS data with health outcome data to produce national and state profiles on subjects such as the leading causes of death among adolescents and the extent of sexual behaviors among teenagers. The *Monitoring the Future* study surveys drug use and related attitudes among American college students and students in the 8th, 10th, and 12th grades. This study includes annual surveys and a longitudinal survey of a subset of students into young adulthood. Data from the study include grade at first use, trends in use at lower grade levels, and intensity of drug use. The SHPPS examines the nationwide status of school health programs at the state, district, and school levels, including school-based health education; physical education; health services; food services; and health policies prohibiting violence, tobacco use, and alcohol and other drug use (Kann et al., 1995). This study is used to measure the nation's progress toward the *Healthy People 2000* objectives which schools can help to effect (USDHHS, 1991).

In addition to researching specific school health issues and conducting surveys on students' health and behaviors, the national government evaluates federally supported and other school health programs. The Bureau of Primary Health Care continuously evaluates the school-based health centers established by the Healthy Schools, Healthy Communities Program, and the BPHC publication *School-Based Clinics that Work* (U.S. Public Health Service, 1994) looks at six such programs considered successful by their communities. Similarly, the National Coordinating Committee on School Health has sponsored the publication of two compendia on evaluated school health programs, *School Health: Findings from Evaluated Programs* (U.S. Public Health Service, 1993; in press).

As they work to implement coordinated school health programs, schools can use this wealth of information at several stages of the process. It can be useful, first, to document that school health programs improve students' health, second, in planning effective programs, and, third, in obtaining community support.

Technical Assistance

The federal government provides technical assistance to its grantees, such as states funded by the Centers for Disease Control and Prevention to develop school health infrastructure (see Chapter 11), and communities funded by the Center for Mental Health Services, Substance Abuse and Mental Health Services Administration, U.S. Department of Health and Human Services, to develop systems of mental health care. Members of the public, including school staff, students, and their families, can receive ad hoc assistance by contacting federal agencies with expertise in their area of interest or through federally funded clearinghouses.

As states and communities assume more program responsibilities, federal agencies are likely to develop a stronger technical assistance role. This will avoid the need to develop such capacity in every state and give professionals across the country access to similar levels of support.

NATIONAL TRENDS THAT AFFECT THE IMPLEMENTATION OF COORDINATED SCHOOL HEALTH PROGRAMS

Political Context

Two public concerns that influence national-level decisions affecting education, health, and social programs and the implementation of coordinated school health programs are: (1) the belief that federal mandates (particularly unfunded mandates) and categorical funding interfere with policy and program decisions that are best made at the state or local level and (2) the drive to reduce the federal budget deficit. Decisions made within this political context might provide either opportunities or challenges for the implementation of coordinated school health programs. For example, restructuring categorical and entitlement programs into block grant programs might result in increased flexibility and thereby allow programs to be client-focused rather than program-focused. However, if each state rather than the federal government decides which programs to implement or which clients to serve with block grant funds, these programs might not address the broader priorities that affect the nation as a whole. In addition, federal funding for block grant programs might prove more volatile than funding for targeted programs. Regardless of who determines how funds are distributed, a cutback in federal funding concerns schools because "achieving flexibility and encouraging innovative efforts to solve problems requires adequate resources" (Hayes, 1995, p. 24).

Another political theme driving today's decisions about school health is the respective roles of schools and families with regard to the education, health, and welfare of children. For example, health-related matters are often considered more a family responsibility than a school responsibility. Thus, even if resources for coordinated school health programs are available, some schools might provide limited services to students because the schools defer to families to provide health-related services and education.

Education Reform

Since the early 1980s, education reform efforts have focused on producing an educated and productive workforce to ensure the nation's competitiveness in the world economy. At first, reform concentrated on raising academic standards, holding schools and teachers accountable for student achievement and emphasizing the basics of reading, writing, science, and mathematics and the increased application of technology. More recently, school reform efforts have focused on structural change, that is, more flexibility in implementing programs, shared decision making within each school, links between curriculum standards and assessment and accountability, family involvement, and options for which school students attend.

The interrelatedness of health and education is an issue that is gaining both advocates and momentum in discussions of education reform. Business leaders are among the most outspoken advocates for school reform. They recognize that one of the essential components of a successful education system is "health and other social services sufficient to reduce significant barriers to learning." However, schools should address students' health and well-being in partnerships with families and other persons in the community. Schools cannot and should not be expected to do the job alone (Business Roundtable, 1992).

The effort to link health and education in schools is compatible with the new emphasis on "improving the school climate, increasing parent and community involvement in the educational enterprise, and building collaborations among community agencies to solve the multifaceted family, social and financial issues that obstruct learning" (Chervin & Northrop, 1994, p. 12). The federal government's efforts to support education reform, such as the America 2000 and subsequent Goals 2000 programs, explicitly recognize the importance of health and physical education, appropriate health services, and healthy school environments in the pursuit of students' educational success (see Chapter 1). Yet, despite the recognition that health and education are intertwined, school health programs must still compete with other issues on the school reform agenda for resources, including teaching personnel, materials, and time in the school day.

Health Care Reform

In the early 1990s momentum gathered behind efforts to strengthen public health programs, reduce health care costs through prevention and treatment programs, and make care accessible to all American citizens. The rapidly changing health care environment with its trend toward market-driven systems that focus on cost-efficiency and quality has caused public health agencies to re-examine their role and shift their predominant activities from direct services provision to an emphasis on systems development (Hayes & Walker, 1997). Although sweeping health care reform has been rejected at the national level, the debate and incremental changes continue and efforts are playing out at the state level. Advocates of school health programs are working to ensure that these programs are part of health care reform initiatives at the state and local levels.

ACTION STEPS TO FACILITATE LOCAL IMPLEMENTATION
OF COORDINATED SCHOOL HEALTH PROGRAMS

Actions That National Organizations Can Take

Because of the diversity of national government and nongovernment organizations that influence the capacity of schools to produce educated, healthy, and productive citizens, no one-size-fits-all plan exists. However, all national organizations can provide leadership to raise support for coordinated school health programs. To provide such leadership, national organizations must identify, prepare, and support persons who recognize the value of school health programs and reassure others that a coordinated school health program will not usurp or minimize, but instead might enhance, their professional or parental roles. When constituents understand how coordinated school health programs can advance their personal mission and interests or those of their organization, they will be more likely to support these activities.

Information Sharing

- Tailor organizational messages about the benefits of coordinated school health programs to constituents' professional and personal goals for the well-being of children.
- Convene conferences and workshops with other organizations on common objectives at national, state, and local levels.
- Identify model programs and tell constituents and other organizations—especially state and local affiliates—about these successful school health programs.
- Increase the use of technology, such as the Internet, to connect local constituents to the information, resources, and technical assistance available from other organizations.
- Tell local constituents about funding sources that support local school health programs.

Professional Preparation

- Train persons to advocate for coordinated school health programs.
- Develop professional preparation programs that include multidisciplinary training for those working in school health programs.
- Establish credentialing requirements for persons who participate in coordinated school health programs.
- Develop incentives for professionals to pursue formal training with other disciplines, such as continuing education credits.

Research

- Fund and conduct research on "best practices" for what is needed and what works in coordinated school health programs.
- Provide data about current trends in health risks and behaviors.
- Provide technical assistance for evaluations.

Legislation

- Advocate for legislation that provides for or supports coordinated school health programs.
- Obtain examples of local problems and solutions that might influence or improve legislation and federal regulations.
- Suggest federal legislation and regulations that would enhance communities' abilities to implement coordinated school health programs.
- Push to minimize categorical funding that discourages comprehensive, coordinated approaches to students' health and educational needs.

Actions That Members of National Organizations Can Take

The staff of national organizations are not the organizations—the members are. The experiences, needs, and goals of those involved at the local level can help develop national strategies. Individuals at the local level can bring assistance and resources to their local communities and can affect national policies and priorities for research, information development and distribution, professional preparation, funding, and legislation.

Using National Resources

- Request programming (for example, speakers or technical assistance) to educate the organization's members on bringing about change at the local level.
- Obtain technical assistance, print materials, access to educational programming, and other resources from national organizations, and inform them about your specific needs and interests.
- Use the resources and technical assistance available from national organizations to mobilize broad-based support for coordinated school health programs in your schools.

Information Sharing

- Give feedback to the organization's leadership and staff about organizational goals, policies, programs, products, and communications.

- Advocate for policies and position statements that specifically support local implementation of coordinated school health programs.
- Respond to national surveys that gather data on local experiences, needs, and success stories.
- Provide copies of presentations, letters to the editor, successful local policies, and so on to the national organization as examples for organizational affiliates and members to use.
- Work with other disciplines and components of school health.

CONCLUSION

National organizations—both government and nongovernment—in partnership with their constituents can play a significant role in promoting and supporting local implementation of coordinated school health programs. The challenge is to maintain momentum as political, social, and economic climates change over time. Establishing a sustained and broad-based commitment to successful implementation of coordinated school health programs will require that staff and members of national organizations integrate actions on behalf of these programs within their organizational activities and goals. Those organizations that make coordinated school health programs a priority are responding to a fundamental national mandate to ensure the health and productivity of all children.

REFERENCES

Ad Hoc Working Group on Integrated Services. (1994). *Principles to link by: Integrating education, health, and human services for children, youth, and families.* Washington, DC: American Academy of Pediatrics.

American Cancer Society. (1994). *Values and opinions of comprehensive school health education in U.S. public schools: Adolescents, parents, and school districts.* Atlanta, GA: Author.

The Business Roundtable. (1992). *The essential components of a successful education system: Putting policy into practice.* Washington, DC: Author.

Centers for Disease Control and Prevention. (1988). Guidelines for effective school health education to prevent the spread of AIDS. *Morbidity and Mortality Weekly Report, 37*(S-2), 1–14.

Centers for Disease Control and Prevention. (1993). *Mortality trends, causes of death, and related risk behaviors among U.S. adolescents* (CDC Publication No. 099-4112). Atlanta, GA: Author.

Centers for Disease Control and Prevention. (1994). Guidelines for school health programs to prevent tobacco use and addiction. *Morbidity and Mortality Weekly Report, 43*(RR-2), 1–18.

Centers for Disease Control and Prevention. (1995). *Pregnancy, sexually transmitted diseases, and related risk behaviors among U.S. adolescents* (CDC Publication No. 099–4630). Atlanta, GA: Author.

Centers for Disease Control and Prevention. (1996). Guidelines for school health programs to promote lifelong healthy eating. *Morbidity and Mortality Weekly Report, 45*(RR-9), 1–40.

Centers for Disease Control and Prevention. (1997). Guidelines for school and community health programs to promote physical activity among youth. *Morbidity and Mortality Weekly Report, 45*(RR-98), pp. 1–36.

Chervin, D. D., & Northrop, D. (1994). *Education and health: Partners in school reform.* Atlanta, GA: BellSouth Foundation and Education Development Center, Inc.

Council's state collaborative on assessment and student standards for health education project. (1995, September 21). *CHEN News.*

Hayes, C. D. (1995). *Rethinking block grants: Toward improved intergovernmental financing for education and other children's services.* Washington, DC: The Finance Project.

Hayes, M., & Walker, D. K. (1997). The role of public health in assuring a system of health care for children. In R. E. K. Stein (Ed.), *Health care for children: What's right, what's wrong* (pp. 339–351). New York: United Hospital Fund.

Holtzman, D., Greene, B. Z., Ingraham, G. C., Daily, L. A., Demchuk, D. G., & Kolbe, L. J. (1992). HIV education in the United States: A national survey of local school district policies and practices. *Journal of School Health, 62*(9), 421–424.

Institute of Medicine. (1997). *Schools and health: Our nation's investment.* D. Allensworth, E. Lawson, L. Nicholson, & J. Wyche (Eds.). Washington, DC: National Academy Press.

Johnston, L. D., O'Malley, P. M., & Bachman, J. G. (1996). *National survey results on drug use from the Monitoring the Future Study, 1975–1985.* Rockville, MD: National Institute on Drug Abuse.

Joint Committee on National Health Education Standards. (1995). *Achieving health literacy: An investment in the future.* Atlanta, GA: American Cancer Society.

Kann, L., Collins, J. L., Pateman, B. C., Small, M. L., Russ, J. G., & Kolbe, L. J. (1995). The School Health Policies and Program Study (SHPPS): Rationale for a nationwide status report on school health programs. *Journal of School Health, 65*(8), 291–294.

Kolbe, L. J., Kann, L., & Collins, J. L. (1993). Overview of the Youth Risk Behavior Surveillance System. *Public Health Reports, 108*(Suppl. 1), 2–10.

Melaville, A. I., & Blank, M. J. (1993). *Together we can: A guide for crafting a profamily system of education and human services.* Washington, DC: U.S. Department of Education and U.S. Department of Health and Human Services.

National Association for Sport and Physical Education. (1995). *National physical education standards: A guide to content and assessment.* Reston, VA: Author.

National Institute on Drug Abuse, National Institute of Health. (1994). *National sur-*

vey results on drug use from the Monitoring the Future study, 1975–1993. Vol. 1 Secondary School Students. Washington, DC: U.S. Government Printing Office.

National Middle School Association. (1995). *This we believe: Developmentally responsive middle level schools. Position paper of the National Middle School Association.* Columbus, OH: Author.

U.S. Congress, Office of Technology Assessment. (1991). *Adolescent health: Vol. 1. Summary and policy options* (OTA-H-468). Washington, DC: U.S. Government Printing Office.

U.S. Congress, Office of Technology Assessment. (1995). *Risks to students in school* (OTA-ENV-633). Washington, DC: U.S. Government Printing Office.

U.S. Department of Education & U.S. Department of Health and Human Services. (1994). *Joint statement of school health by the Secretaries of Education and Health and Human Services.* Washington, DC: Office of Disease Prevention and Health Promotion.

U.S. Department of Health and Human Services, Public Health Service. (1991). *Healthy people 2000: National health promotion and disease prevention objectives, full report with commentary* (DHHS Publ. No. [PHS] 91-50212). Washington, DC: U.S. Government Printing Office.

U.S. Department of Health and Human Services. (1992). *Healthy schools: A directory of federal programs and activities related to health promotion through the schools.* Washington, DC: U.S. Government Printing Office.

U.S. Public Health Service. (1993). *School health: Findings from evaluated programs.* Washington, DC: U.S. Government Printing Office.

U.S. Public Health Service. (1994). *School-based clinics that work.* Washington, DC: U.S. Government Printing Office.

U.S. Public Health Service. (in press). *School health: Findings from evaluated programs* (2nd ed.). Washington, DC: U.S. Government Printing Office.

Working together for the future: Proceedings of the 1992 comprehensive school health education workshop sponsored by the American Cancer Society. (1993). *Journal of School Health, 63*(1), 7–70.

Eva Marx, M.H.S.M.

13 Summary: Fulfilling the Promise

*From an educator's perspective, it's important for schools to be concerned
with a child's health because healthy children are more effective learners. For
parents, it is very reassuring to know that their local school is concerned not
only with reading and writing, but is also looking out for their child's health
and well-being.*

—William Casey, District Superintendent, Brooklyn, New York
(Making the Grade, 1997, p. 11).

S chools typically measure the job they are doing by students' achievement on tests. But test scores do not tell the whole story about either students' academic achievement or their potential to become productive, responsible citizens. Helping students realize their full potential goes far beyond classroom instruction. For students to become productive, responsible citizens, schools also must help students develop health-promoting skills and behaviors and attend to the physical, mental, and social dimensions of their lives. Students' health and well-being must take on the same importance in a school as reading, writing, and mathematics because, as this book strives to make clear, health is academic, or characteristic of school. When students are not physically and mentally healthy, they do not achieve as well as they might in the classroom and consequently they are less likely to reach their potential later in life. Moreover, as this book also stresses repeatedly, a coordinated school health program that integrates eight well-developed, mutually reinforcing components—health education; physical education; nutrition services; counseling, psychological, and social services; school health services; health promotion for staff; family and community involvement; and a

Health Is Academic: A Guide to Coordinated School Health Problems. Edited by Eva Marx and Susan Frelick Wooley, with Daphne Northrop. New York: Teachers College Press, 1998. ISBN 0-8077-3713-5 (pbk.), ISBN 0-8077-3714-3 (cloth).

healthy school environment—holds promise for promoting students' health and advancing their learning.

Today's climate in education is in a state of flux. Public debate centers on how schools can do what they do even better—despite shrinking budgets and new challenges. But, as the authors of this volume assert, educational reforms will be effective only if students' health and well-being are identified as contributors to academic success and are at the heart of decision and policy making. Schools, in concert with students, their families, and communities, must consider how well schools are accomplishing their missions and how they can best help students realize their full potential.

A coordinated school health program, as described in the preceding chapters, can improve the future of millions of students. No data exist to demonstrate the efficacy of coordinated school health programs in improving student health and achievement. However, the potential for cumulative gain is apparent from a review of a few documented positive impacts of some individual components.

- *School health education* not only can positively change students' health behaviors and attitudes (Dusenbury & Falco, 1995; Gold, 1994; Kirby et al., 1994) but is also a cost effective public health measure (Rothman et al., 1993).
- *School-based health centers* can increase student attendance at school and reduce suspensions and dropout rates (Dryfoos, 1994).
- The quality of the *school environment* can either enhance or undermine the quality of a school health program (Center for Research on Elementary and Middle Schools, 1989; Comer, 1984, 1988; Slavin, Madden, Karweit, Dolan, & Wasik, 1992).
- Teachers participating in *school-site health promotion programs* have higher morale and fewer absences (Allegrante & Michela, 1990; Falck & Kilcoyne, 1984).
- *School nutrition services* can relieve short-term hunger and improve students' scores on standardized tests (Meyers, Sampson, Weitzman, Rogers, & Kayne, 1989; National Research Council, 1989; U.S. Department of Health and Human Services, 1988, 1991).
- *Family involvement* can increase students' adoption of health-enhancing behaviors (Perry et al., 1989).

All schools have implemented some aspect of a coordinated school health program, whether it be health instruction in the classroom, a school nurse who provides immunizations and emergency care, school food services that provide nutritious meals, a physical education program that helps students stay active, pupil services personnel who respond to students' mental health and social needs, policies that prohibit tobacco use on school grounds, smoking cessation programs for school staff, or annual health fairs that involve students' families and the community. But school health-related activities typically resemble the haphazard relationships depicted in Figure 13.1. It is the rare school that has implemented a *fully functioning* coordinated school health program in which each of the eight components is completely developed and integrated with the others in a seamless effort that meets the needs of students, their families, and school staff and is supported by the community.

MEETING THE CHALLENGE

Although coordinated school health programs function at the school building, campus, or cluster level, such programs can only exist with support from communities, school districts, colleges and universities, and state- and national-level organizations and agencies as well as in the school itself. Schools need the following support to meet the challenge of making coordinated school health programs a reality.

- *Commitment of leadership.* Leaders at the national, state, and local levels must be committed to a vision of schools as places that enable students, their families, and school staff to adopt health-promoting behaviors that can facilitate achievement and lifelong health. At the local level, the leadership and support of the school principal or chief administrator is key to implementation of a fully functioning coordinated school health program.
- *Collaboration.* A coordinated school health program represents a new way of working that requires interdisciplinary and interagency collaboration at every level. Such collaboration involves government and nongovernment agencies and organizations, education and health professionals, students, their families, community volunteers, and businesses. To be effective, collaborative structures need to define a common mission or vision, identify players, map available resources and sources of funding, conduct needs assessments, develop and implement an action plan, evaluate both processes and outcomes, and make adjustments based on evaluation findings.
- *Professional development.* Professional development must occur at both preservice and inservice levels. Colleges and universities can incorporate school health into the curriculum of all preservice programs designed to prepare professionals who will work in schools or with children. School administrators in particular need to understand the importance of and the process for implementing a coordinated school health program; health and education professionals need to understand how to implement their own

FIGURE 13.1. An Example of a Haphazard System

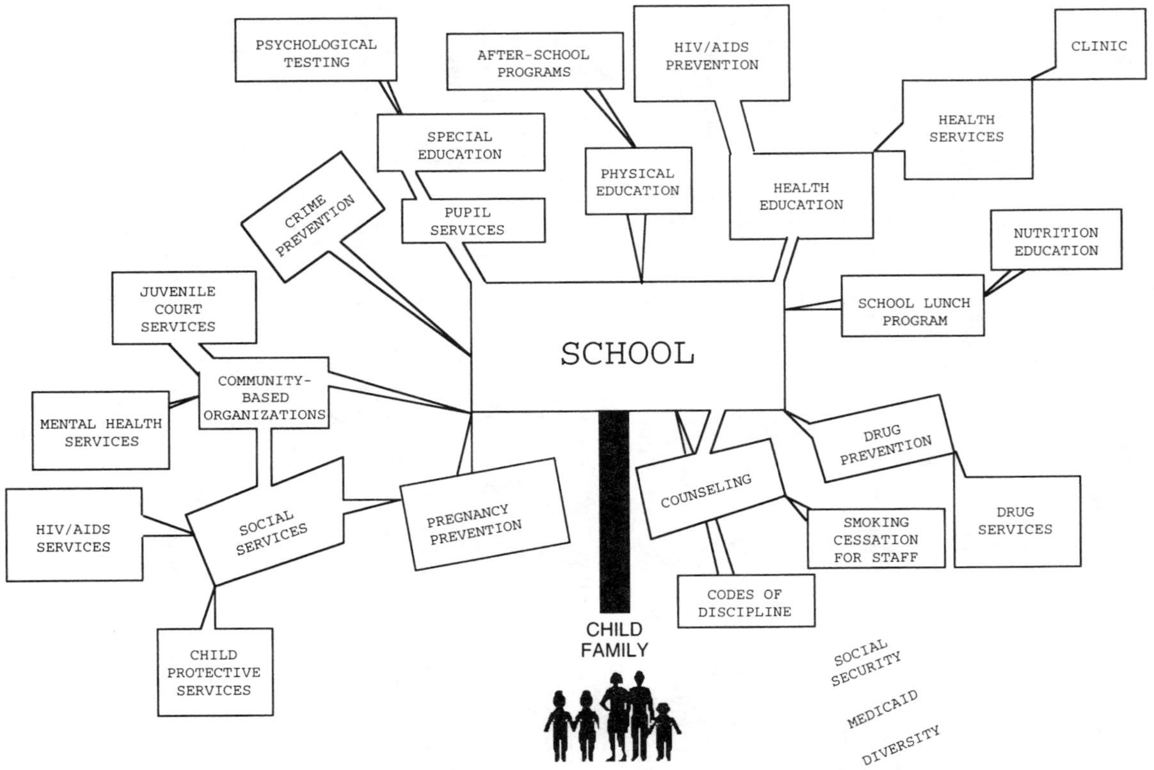

discipline in the context of a coordinated school health program as well as how to work with others. Health and education professionals and administrators must continue their professional development throughout their careers to ensure delivery of school health programming that helps students achieve optimal performance.

- *Personnel, time, and funding.* Fully functioning school health programs require adequate personnel, materials, and space. Safe, secure, and well-maintained buildings and grounds provide a supportive environment and reduce injuries. Hiring credentialed staff who are professionally prepared to address specific components within a coordinated school health program helps ensure implementation likely to improve students' performance. Providing adequate time in the school curriculum for health instruction and physical activity can maximize the benefits of these components. Release time for staff to coordinate activities and participate in ongoing professional development is essential. Creative coordination of existing assets can eliminate duplication and reduce the need for additional resources. Funding needs to be both flexible and stable to allow for long-term planning and development. The availability of these resources will not become a reality without support from decisionmakers at national, state, district, and school levels and their constituencies.

- *Enhanced communication.* Schools and communities have much to learn from one another. Examples of successful efforts to incorporate health into the fabric of schools and other youth-serving agencies abound and need to be shared with school administrators, health professionals in schools and communities, intra- and interagency task forces, school health committees, school health coordinating councils, and coalitions. Traditional channels such as newsletters, journals, and conferences are valid media for such communication but new technologies—including electronic media—offer immediacy, convenience, and broad accessibility.

- *Research.* In many areas decisionmakers need more data to help them interpret events and guide their decisions. Schools, local health and education agencies, state and national organizations, and colleges and universities need to continue to gather and share information about both successes and failures with respect to students' health and academic outcomes and the cost-effectiveness of fully implemented coordinated school health programs and their individual components.

BUILDING A SCHOOL HEALTH PROGRAM

As with all systemic change, developing and implementing coordinated school health programs takes time. The prospect of building and maintaining a coordinated school health program might seem daunting. Implementation requires the commitment and continuous involvement of school and community professionals, students and their family members, and community members. What a school can expect to accomplish in the first two years depends to some extent on what is already in place at the state and district levels as well as at the school level. Some components doubtlessly are better developed than others. These better developed components might become a catalyst for the other components to coalesce. Some schools have a strong health education component. Others might have well-developed student assistance programs or health services. Yet others have teams that have participated in a school staff health promotion conference. The following steps can lay the foundation for the institutionalization of a coordinated school health program.

- The school board and district administration support the view that health promotion is an essential part of the educational mission and understand the concept of a coordinated school health program.
- Faculty, other school staff, families, and students acknowledge that health promotion is an essential ingredient of the school's mission.
- Key members of the school community have attended at least one workshop that promotes understanding of coordinated school health programs.
- An interdisciplinary school health team or Healthy School Team (see Chapter 2) that includes administrators and representatives of all components of a coordinated school health program, students and their families, and community organizations meets regularly, either as part of a larger school management team or as an independent body. This team (1) promotes awareness of the need for health as an essential ingredient of the school's mission; (2) assesses the current status of the school's health program, resources in the school and community, and factors that impede students' success and well-being; (3) develops a plan with realistic, clearly defined goals and objectives that identifies the roles and responsibilities of each component and how the components can work together; (4) oversees implementation of the plan; (5) regularly evaluates progress in implementing the plan and outcomes of the implemented program; and (6) suggests ways to adapt strategies and activities based on evaluation findings.
- An individual with access to school decisionmakers coordinates school health program activities and has release time, space, and other necessary resources to coordinate this activity within the school, with other education and health agencies, and with the community.
- A system exists for communication among those responsible for the components of a coordinated school health program.
- Subcommittees of the school health team address the unique needs of each component of a coordinated school health program. The subcommittees meet regularly to clarify their roles, assess current status and unmet needs,

and identify ways of working with other components to promote the health and educational achievement of students.

- The school health team has inventoried and mapped existing school and community activities and resources that address the components of a coordinated school health program.
- The school health team has reviewed school and district policies to identify needed modifications to existing policies, develop proposals for new policies, and establish ways to enhance enforcement of policies to support a coordinated school health program.
- The school community demonstrates increased commitment to the health of students and school staff. For example, teachers explore ways to integrate health-related materials into their curricula, the cafeteria offers more healthy choices, physical education classes place greater emphasis on promoting skills for lifelong physical activity, policies support students' safety and well being, and employee benefits packages include health promotion activities.

These steps are but a beginning. Institutionalization will require time—as long as 10 to 15 years. As with any program, to become institutionalized the coordinated school health program will need consistent and stable support from the school and the community, including adequate resources and funding, qualified personnel, supportive organizational structures (such as community coalitions and agency partnerships), supportive policies, and committed leadership. An institutionalized program does not depend on a key individual and thus is less likely to be endangered by changes in administration or staff.

THE PROMISE FOR THE FUTURE

Schools can do more than perhaps any other single institution to improve the well-being and competence of children and youth. Only when schools view coordinated school health programs as essential as history, social studies, or language arts will they maximize academic achievement and positive health outcomes among the children and youth they serve. As a society, we cannot afford to have the promise remain unfulfilled.

REFERENCES

Allegrante, J. P., & Michela, J. L. (1990). Impact of a school-based workplace health promotion program on morale of inner-city teachers. *Journal of School Health, 60*, 25–28.

Center for Research on Elementary and Middle Schools. (1989). *Success for all*. Baltimore: The Johns Hopkins University.

Comer, J. P. (1984). *Improving American education: Roles for parents.* Hearing before the Select Committee on Children, Youth, and Families. Washington, DC: U.S. Government Printing Office.

Comer, J. P. (1988). Educating poor minority children. *Scientific American, 259*(5), 42–48.

Dryfoos, J. G. (1994). *Full service schools: A revolution in health and social services for children, youth, and families.* San Francisco: Jossey-Bass.

Dusenbury, L., & Falco, M. (1995). Eleven components of effective drug abuse prevention curricula. *Journal of School Health, 65*(10), 420–425.

Falck, V., & Kilcoyne, M. (1984). A health promotion program for school personnel. *Journal of School Health, 54*(6), 239–242.

Gold, R. S. (1994). The science base for comprehensive health education. In P. Cortese & K. Middleton (Eds.), *The comprehensive school health challenge, Volume 2* (pp. 545–574). Santa Cruz, CA: ETR Associates.

Kirby, D., Short, L., Collins, J., Rugg, D., Kolbe, L., Howard, M., Miller, B., Sonenstein, F., & Zabin, L. (1994). School-based programs to reduce sexual risk behaviors: A review of effectiveness. *Public Health Reports, 109*(3), 339–360.

Making the Grade, George Washington University. (1997). *The picture of health: State and community leaders on school-based health care.* Washington, DC: Author.

Meyers, A. F., Sampson, A. D., Weitzman, M., Rogers, B. L., & Kayne, H. (1989). School breakfast programs and school performance. *American Journal of Diseases and Children, 143,* 1234–1239.

National Research Council. (1989). *Diet and health: Implications for reducing chronic disease risk.* Washington, DC: National Academy Press.

Perry, C. L., Luepker, R. V., Murray, D. M., Hearn, M. D., Halper, A., Dudovipz, B., Maile, M. C., & Smythe, M. (1989). Parental involvement with children's health promotion: A one-year follow-up of the Minnesota Home Team. *Health Education Quarterly, 16*(2), 171–180.

Rothman, M. L., Ehreth, J. L., Palmer, C. S., Collins, J., Reblando, J. A., & Luce, B. P. (1993, October). *The potential benefits and costs of a comprehensive health education program.* Paper presented at the meeting of the American Public Health Association, San Francisco, CA.

Slavin, R. E., Madden, N. A., Karweit, N. L., Dolan, L. J., & Wasik, B. A. (1992). *Success for all: A relentless approach to prevention and early intervention in elementary schools.* Arlington, VA: Educational Research Service.

U.S. Department of Health and Human Services. (1988). *The surgeon general's report on nutrition and health.* Washington, DC: U.S. Government Printing Office.

U.S. Department of Health and Human Services, Public Health Service. (1991). *Healthy people 2000: National health promotion and disease prevention objectives* (DHHS Publication No. PHS 91-50213). Washington, DC: U.S. Government Printing Office.

National Organizations That Support Components of Coordinated School Health Programs

Advocates for Youth
1025 Vermont Ave., N. W., Ste. 210
Washington, DC 20005
Phone: (202) 347-5700
Fax: (202) 347-2263

**American Academy of Child &
Adolescent Psychiatry**
3015 Wisconsin Ave., N.W.
Washington, DC 20016-3007
Phone: (800) 333-7636
Fax: (202) 966-2891

**American Academy of Pediatric
Dentistry**
211 East Chicago Ave., Ste. 700
Chicago, IL 60611-2616
Phone: (312) 337-2169
Fax: (312) 337-6329

American Academy of Pediatrics
141 Northwest Point Blvd.
Elk Grove Village, IL 60007

Phone: (847) 228-5005
Fax: (847) 228-5097

**American Association for Active
Lifestyles & Fitness**
1900 Association Drive
Reston, VA 22091
Phone: (703) 476-3431
Fax: (703) 476-9527

**American Association for Health
Education**
1900 Association Drive
Reston, VA 22091
Phone: (703) 476-3437
Fax: (703) 476-6638

**American Association of School
Administrators**
1801 North Moore St.
Arlington, VA 22209
Phone: (703) 875-0755
Fax: (703) 807-1849

American Cancer Society
1599 Clifton Road, N.E.
Atlanta, GA 30329
Phone: (404) 329-7949
Fax: (404) 248-1780

American College of Sports Medicine
PO Box 1440
Indianapolis, IN 46206-1440
Phone: (317) 637-9200
Fax: (317) 634-7817

American Dietetic Association
216 West Jackson Blvd., Ste. 800
Chicago, IL 60606
Phone: (800) 877-1600
Fax: (312) 899-1758

American Federation of Teachers
555 New Jersey Ave., N.W.
Washington, DC 20001
Phone: (202) 879-4490
Fax: (202) 393-8648

American Medical Association
515 North State Street
Chicago, IL 60610
Phone: (312) 464-4065
Fax: (312) 464-5842

American Nurses Association
600 Maryland Ave., S.W.
Ste. 100 West
Washington, DC 20024
Phone: (202) 651-7068
Fax: (202) 651-7001

American Psychological Association
750 First Street, N.E.
Washington, DC 20002
Phone: (202) 336-6126
Fax: (202) 336-5962

American Public Health Association
1015 15th Street, N. W., 3rd Floor
Washington, DC 20005
Phone: (202) 789-5600
Fax: (202) 789-5661

American Public Welfare Association
810 First Street, N. E., Ste. 500
Washington, DC 20002
Phone: (202) 682-0100
Fax: (202) 289-6555

American Red Cross
8111 Gatehouse Road
Jefferson Park
Falls Church, VA 22042
Phone: (703) 206-7180
Fax: (703) 206-7673

American School Counselor Association
801 N. Fairfax St., Ste. 310
Alexandria, VA 22314
Phone: (703) 683-2722
Fax: (703) 683-1619

**American School Food Service
  Association**
1600 Duke Street
Alexandria, VA 22314-3436
Phone: (800) 877-8822
Fax: (703) 739-3915

American School Health Association
PO Box 708
Kent, OH 44240
Phone: (330) 678-1601
Fax: (330) 678-4526

**Association for Supervision &
  Curriculum Development**
1250 North Pitt Street
Alexandria, VA 22314
Phone: (703) 549-9110
Fax: (703) 299-8631

Association of State and Territorial Health Officials
1275 K St., N. W., Ste. 800
Washington, DC 20005
Phone: (202) 371-9090
Fax: (202) 371-9797

Association of State and Territorial Public Health Nutrition Directors
1275 K St., N. W., Ste. 800
Washington, DC 20005
Phone: (202) 789-1067
Fax: (202) 789-1068

Communities In Schools, Inc.
1199 North Fairfax St., Ste. 300
Alexandria, VA 22314
Phone: (703) 519-8999
Fax: (703) 519-7213

The Council for Exceptional Children
1920 Association Drive
Reston, VA 22091
Phone: (703) 620-3660
Fax: (703) 264-1637

Council of Chief State School Officers
One Massachusetts Ave., N.W.
Ste. 700
Washington, DC 20001
Phone: (202) 336-7035
Fax: (202) 408-8072

Council of the Great City Schools
1301 Pennsylvania Ave., N.W.
Ste. 702
Washington, DC 20004
Phone: (202) 393-2427
Fax: (202) 393-2400

Employee Assistance Professionals Association
2101 Wilson Blvd., Ste. 500
Arlington, VA 22201
Phone: (703) 522-6272
Fax: (703) 522-4585

Food Research and Action Center
1875 Connecticut Ave., N.W.
Ste. 540
Washington, DC 20009
Phone: (202) 986-2200
Fax: (202) 986-2525

Girls Incorporated
30 East 33rd Street
New York, NY 10016
Phone: (212) 689-3700
Fax: (212) 683-1253

National Alliance of Pupil Services Organizations
7700 Willowbrook Road
Fairfax Station, VA 22039
Phone: (703) 250-3414
Fax: (703) 250-6324

National Assembly on School-Based Health Care
1522 K St., N.W., Suite 600
Washington, DC 20005
Phone: (888) 286-8727
Fax: (202) 289-0776

National Association for Sport and Physical Education
1900 Association Drive
Reston, VA 20191-1599
Phone: (703) 476-3410
Fax: (703) 476-8316

National Association of Community Health Centers
1330 New Hampshire Ave., N.W.
Ste. 122
Washington, DC 20036
Phone: (202) 659-8008
Fax: (202) 659-8519

**National Association of Elementary
  School Principals**
1615 Duke Street
Alexandria, VA 22314
Phone: (703) 684-3345
Fax: (703) 518-6281

**National Association of Governor's
  Councils on Physical Fitness & Sports**
201 S. Capitol Ave., Ste. 560
Indianapolis, IN 46225
Phone: (317) 237-5630
Fax: (317) 237-5632

**National Association of Leadership for
  Student Assistance Programs**
Box 335
Bedminster, PA 18910
Phone: (215) 795-2119
Fax: (215) 795-0822

National Association of School Nurses
PO Box 1300
Scarborough, ME 04074-1300
Phone: (207) 883-2117
Fax: (207) 883-2683

**National Association of School
  Psychologists**
4340 East West Highway, Ste. 402
Bethesda, MD 20814
Phone: (301) 657-0270
Fax: (301) 657-0275

**National Association of Secondary
  School Principals**
1904 Association Drive
Reston, VA 20191
Phone: (703) 860-0200
Fax: (703) 476-5432

National Association of Social Workers
750 First Street, N.E.
Ste. 700
Washington, DC 20002-4241
Phone: (202) 408-8600
Fax: (202) 336-8310

**National Association of State Boards
  of Education**
1012 Cameron Street
Alexandria, VA 22314
Phone: (703) 684-4000
Fax: (703) 836-2313

**National Association of State NET
  Program Coordinators**
200 West Baltimore Street
Baltimore, MD 21201
Phone: (410) 767-0222
Fax: (410) 333-2635

**National Coalition for Parent
  Involvement in Education**
c/o IEL
1001 Connecticut Ave., N.W., Ste. 310
Washington, DC 20036
Phone: (202) 822-8405
Fax: (202) 872-4050

**National Coalition of Chapter 1 and
  Title 1 Parents**
National Parent Center
Edmond School Bldg.
9th and D Streets, N. E., Rm. 201
Washington, DC 20002
Phone: (202) 547-9286
Fax: (202) 547-2813

**National Conference of State
  Legislatures**
1560 Broadway, Ste. 700
Denver, CO 80202
Phone: (303) 830-2200
Fax: (303) 863-8003

National Council of Churches
475 Riverside Drive
New York, NY 10115
Phone: (212) 870-2297
Fax: (212) 870-2030

National Council of LaRaza
1111 19th St., N. W., Ste. 1000
Washington, DC 20036
Phone: (202) 785-1670
Fax: (202) 776-1792

National Education Association
1201 16th Street, N.W.
Washington, DC 20036
Phone: (202) 822-7570
Fax: (202) 822-7775

National Environmental Health
  Association
720 S. Colorado Blvd., Ste. 970
Denver, CO 80222
Phone: (303) 756-9090
Fax: (303) 691-9490

National Federation of State High
  School Associations
11724 NW Plaza Circle
Kansas City, MO 64195-0626
Phone: (816) 464-5400
Fax: (816) 464-5571

National Health & Education
  Consortium
1001 Connecticut Ave., Ste. 310
Washington, DC 20036
Phone: (202) 822-8405
Fax: (202) 872-4050

National Middle School Association
2600 Corporate Exchange Drive
Ste. 370
Columbus, OH 43231
Phone: (614) 895-4730
Fax: (614) 895-4750

National Network for Youth
1319 F Street, N. W., Ste. 401
Washington, DC 20004
Phone: (202) 783-7949
Fax: (202) 783-7955

National Peer Helpers Association
PO Box 2684
Greenville, NC 27834
Phone: (919) 522-3959
Fax: (919) 522-3959

The National PTA
330 North Wabash Ave., Ste. 2100
Chicago, IL 60611-3690
Phone: (312) 670-6782
Fax: (312) 670-6783

National Safety Council
1121 Spring Lake Drive
Itasca, IL 60143-3201
Phone: (630) 285-1121
Fax: (630) 285-1315

National School Boards Association
1680 Duke Street
Alexandria, VA 22314
Phone: (703) 838-6722
Fax: (703) 548-5516

National Urban League
120 Wall St., 8th Floor
New York, NY 10005
Phone: (212) 558-5300
Fax: (212) 344-5332

National Wellness Association
PO Box 827
Stevens Point, WI 54481-0827
Phone: (715) 342-2969
Fax: (715) 342-2979

President's Council for Physical Fitness
  and Sports
Hubert H. Humphrey Building
200 Independence Ave., S.W.
Room 738H
Washington, DC 20201
Phone: (202) 690-9000
Fax: (202) 690-5211

Public Education Network
601 13th Street, N.W., Ste. 290
Washington, DC 20005
Phone: (202) 628-7460
Fax: (202) 628-1893

Public Risk Management Association
1815 N. Fort Meyer Drive
Ste. 1020
Arlington, VA 22209
Phone: (703) 528-7701
Fax: (703) 528-7966

Society for Adolescent Medicine
1916 Copper Oaks Circle
Blue Springs, MO 64015
Phone: (816) 224-8010
Fax: (816) 224-8009

Society for Nutrition Education
2850 Metro Drive, Ste. 416
Minneapolis, MN 55425-1412
Phone: (612) 854-0035
Fax: (612) 854-7869

Society for Public Health Education, Inc.
1015 15th St., N.W.
Ste. 410
Washington, DC 20005
Phone: (202) 408-9804
Fax: (202) 408-9815

Society of State Directors of Health, Physical Education and Recreation
1900 Association Drive
Reston, VA 20191
Phone: (703) 476-3402
Fax: (703) 476-9527

State Directors of Child Nutrition
c/o ASFSA
1600 Duke Street
Alexandria, VA 22314-3436
Phone: (800) 877-8822
Fax: (703) 739-3915

Wellness Councils of America
7101 Newport Ave., Ste. 311
Omaha, NE 68152-2175
Phone: (402) 572-3590
Fax: (402) 572-3594

Federal School Health-Related Clearinghouses

CDC, Division of Adolescent and School Health
http://www.cdc.gov/nccdphp/dash
(Internet)

CDC National AIDS Clearinghouse
(800) 458-5231
(800) 342-AIDS (English hotline)
(800) 344-SIDA (Spanish hotline)
(800) 243-7012 (TTY/TDD)
(301) 783-6616 (Fax)
(301) 217-0023 (International line)
http://www.cdcnac.org (Internet)

CDC, National Center for Chronic Disease Prevention and Health Promotion
(404) 488-5080
http://www.cdc.gov (Internet)

Clearinghouse for Occupational Safety and Health Information
(800) 35-NIOSH
(513) 533-8326
(513) 533-8573 (Fax)
http://www.cdc.gov/niosh/
homepage.html (Internet)

Combined Health Information Database (CHID)
(800) 955-0906
http://www.ovid.com/dochome/fldguide/
chiddb.htm (Internet)
http://www.ovid.com/db/databses/chid.
htm (Internet)

CSAP's National Clearinghouse for Alcohol and Drug Information
(800) 729-6686
(301) 468-2600
(800) 487-4889 (TTY/TDD)
(301) 230-2867 (TTY/TDD)
(301) 468-6433 (Fax)
http://www.health.org (Internet)

ERIC Clearinghouse on Teaching and Teacher Education
(202) 293-2450
(202) 457-8095 (Fax)
http://www.aacte.org (Internet)

Family Life Information Exchange
(301) 585-6636
(301) 588-3408 (Fax)

Food and Drug Administration, Office of Consumer Affairs
(301) 443-3170
(301) 443-9767 (Fax)
http://www.fda.gov (Internet)

Food and Nutrition Information Center, U.S. Department of Agriculture
(301) 504-5719
(301) 504-6409 (Fax)
http://www.nal.usda.gov/fnic (Internet)

Indoor Air Quality Information Clearinghouse
(800) 438-4318
(202) 484-1307
(202) 484-1510 (Fax)
http://www.epa.gov/iaq (Internet)

National Center for Education in Maternal and Child Health
(703) 524-7802
(703) 524-9335 (Fax)
http://www.ncemch.org (Internet)

National Clearinghouse on Child Abuse and Neglect Information
(800) FYI-3366
(703) 385-7565
(703) 385-3206 (Fax)
http://www.calib.com/nccanch (Internet)

National Clearinghouse on Family Support and Children's Mental Health, Portland State University
(800) 628-1696
(503) 725-4040
(503) 725-4165 (TTD)
(503) 725-4180 (Fax)
http://www.rtc.pdx.edu (Internet)

National Health Information Center
(800) 336-4797
(301) 565-4167
(301) 984-4256 (Fax)
http://nhic-nt.health.org (Internet)

National Highway Traffic Safety Administration, U.S. Department of Transportation
(800) 424-9393 (Hotline)
(202) 366-0123 (Hotline)
(202) 366-5962 (Fax)
http://www.nhtsa.dot.gov (Internet)

National Information Center for Children and Youth with Disabilities
(800) 695-0285 (Voice/TT)
(202) 884-8200 (Voice/TT)
(202) 884-8441 (Fax)
http://www.nichcy.org (Internet)

National Injury Information Clearinghouse
(301) 504-0424
(301) 504-0124 (Fax)
http://www.cpsc.gov (Internet)

National Maternal and Child Health Clearinghouse
(703) 821-8955, ext. 254 or 265
(703) 821-2098 (Fax)
http://www.circsol.com/mch (Internet)

National Oral Health Information Clearinghouse
(301) 402-7364
http://www.nidr.nih.gov (Internet)

Office of Minority Health Resource Center
(800) 444-6472
(301) 565-6112 (Fax)
http://www.omhrc.gov (Internet)

Office on Smoking and Health, Centers for Disease Control and Prevention
(404) 488-5705
(800) CDC-1311
(404) 488-5939 (Fax)
http://www.cdc.gov/tobacco (Internet)

**President's Council on Physical Fitness
  and Sports**
(202) 272-3430
(202) 504-2064 (Fax)

**U.S. Consumer Product Safety
  Commission Hotline**
(800) 638 2772
(800) 638-8270 (TT)
(301) 504-0580
(301) 504-0399 (Fax)
http://www.cpsc.gov (Internet)

About the Authors

Howard Adelman, Ph.D., was a remedial classroom teacher before returning to graduate school in 1962. Since receiving a Ph.D. in psychology from the University of California, Los Angeles, in 1966, he has pursued interests in educational reform, with emphasis on improving interventions for students with learning, behavior, and emotional problems. In the late 1960s and early 1970s, he was a professor in the School of Education at the University of California at Riverside. In 1973, he returned to UCLA as a professor in the Department of Psychology and as director of the Fernald School and Laboratory. In 1986, with Dr. Linda Taylor, he established the School Mental Health Project at UCLA to focus on school-based programs; in 1995, the project established a center focused on mental health in schools (funded by the U.S. Department of Health and Human Services, Maternal and Child Health Branch).

Dr. Adelman is involved with national initiatives to enhance school and community efforts to address barriers to student learning and enhance the healthy development of children, families, and the professionals who serve them. He also collaborates with the Los Angeles Unified School District's *Early Assistance for Students and Families Project* and with the district and the Los Angeles Educational Partnership on the *Los Angeles Learning Centers* project (one of nine models supported by the New American Schools Development Corporation). This work, along with work at selected sites involved in the *Los Angeles Education Alliance for Restructuring Now* (LEARN), focuses on restructuring education support programs and services and their integration and linkage with community health and social services.

Dr. Adelman's latest works (co-authored with Dr. Linda Taylor) are *Learning Problems and Learning Disabilities: Moving Forward,* and *On Understanding Intervention in Psychology and Education.*

John P. Allegrante, Ph.D., is professor of health education at Teachers College, Columbia University, where he began his career in 1979. He was chairman of the Department of Health Education from 1980 to 1990 and director of the Division of Health Services, Sciences, and Education from

1989 to 1996. As director of the Center for Health Promotion, a multidisciplinary research and development group he helped establish in 1981, he has led the development of the college's program of research in health promotion and education.

Dr. Allegrante holds a joint appointment in Columbia's faculty of medicine as a professor of clinical public health in sociomedical sciences at the School of Public Health and is an adjunct professor in the Department of Medicine at the Cornell University Medical College.

He has published numerous articles and scientific papers in leading journals of health education, public health, and medicine and is co-author of *Investing in Employee Health: A Guide to Effective Health Promotion in the Workplace.* Dr. Allegrante has been a consultant to the National Institutes of Health since 1983, and an advisor to many other government agencies, private foundations, and universities. He is president-elect of the Society for Public Health Education (SOPHE).

Dr. Allegrante received a B. S. in 1974 from the State University of New York College at Cortland, and an M. S. and Ph.D. from the University of Illinois at Urbana-Champaign. He was W. K. Kellogg Foundation Fellow from 1985 to 1988 and spent a year in advanced study as a Pew Health Policy Fellow at the RAND/UCLA Center for Health Policy Study. He has been a Fellow of the New York Academy of Medicine since 1985.

Dorothy Caldwell, M.S., R.D., is special assistant for nutrition and nutrition education in the office of the Undersecretary for Food, Nutrition, and Consumer Services, U.S. Department of Agriculture. She was director of child nutrition for the Arkansas Department of Education from 1988 to 1997. She focuses on promotion of the team approach to child nutrition as part of school health. During her tenure, school breakfast programs expanded from fewer than 50% of the schools in the state to more than 95%. She has received grants to establish Health Action Teams in Arkansas schools and has been instrumental in the work of the Arkansas Comprehensive School Health Committee. She began working with child nutrition programs in 1968 as Director of Food and Nutrition for the Lee County, Arkansas, School District.

Ms. Caldwell has served as a member of the Institute of Medicine's Committee on Comprehensive School Health Programs, the National Coordinating Committee for School Health, the Advisory Board of the National Food Service Management Institute, the *Resetting the American Table* Speaker's Bureau, and several task forces for the United States Department of Agriculture.

She is past president of the American School Food Service Association and the School Food Service Foundation. The recipient of the American

Dietetic Association's *Medallion* Award, she is also a member of the expert panel for the association's Child Nutrition Campaign and vice chair of the School Nutrition Services Practice Group.

A registered and licensed dietitian, Ms. Caldwell holds a B. S. in home economics with a minor in dietetics from the University of Arkansas, and an M. S. in food systems administration from the University of Tennessee.

Pauline Carlyon, M.P.H., M.S., is retired from Johnson & Johnson Health Management, Inc. (JJHMI), in Santa Monica, California, where she provided consultation and administrative services for health education and promotion to Fortune 500 client companies. She also managed a network of health educators who provided on-site assistance to corporate clients' employees at field locations nationwide.

Before joining JJHMI, she was an independent health education specialist, directing workshops, institutes, and training programs in sexuality education and school/community health education for professional and community groups throughout the country. From 1975 to 1980, Ms. Carlyon directed the Comprehensive School/Community Health Education Project for the National Congress of Parents and Teachers. This project was among the first contracts awarded by the newly established Bureau of Health Education at the Centers for Disease Control, U.S. Department of Health and Human Services. Earlier, she spent six years as program director for family life education in the Bureau of Maternal and Child Health, Michigan Department of Public Health, and eight years on the health education faculty of the State University of New York College at Cortland.

Ms. Carlyon holds an M.P.H. from the University of California at Berkeley, an M. S. in family relations and child development from Cornell University, and a B. S. in health education from the State University of New York College at Cortland.

William Carlyon, Ph.D., is a writer, editor, and health education consultant. He is a former director of the American Medical Association's (AMA) Department of Health Education. While at the AMA, he served as secretary to its Committees on School and College Health and on Exercise and Physical Fitness. He was also responsible for planning the AMA's biennial conferences on physicians and schools.

Dr. Carlyon is an adjunct professor of health education at the University of New Mexico, Albuquerque. His writings have included professional and social criticism, poetry, reviews, and plays.

Paula Duncan, M.D., F.A.A.P., is the maternal and child health (MCH) director for the Vermont Department of Health. A pediatrician with subspecialty fellowship training in adolescent medicine and neonatology, Dr.

Duncan was on the full-time faculty in pediatrics at Stanford University for five years, and the University of Vermont School of Medicine for three years. She taught adolescent medicine and school health, and her research focused on the healthy development and parenting of young adolescents. As health services coordinator for the Burlington School District for five years, she was involved in the design and implementation of a K–12 comprehensive health education curriculum and a community-wide Success by Six program for preschoolers and their families. Dr. Duncan has also practiced primary care general pediatrics.

Dr. Duncan, who received her Vermont certification as a K–12 health educator, has served for the past ten years as a consultant to the Vermont Department of Education on health education curricular activities. She has continued on the clinical faculty at the University of Vermont School of Medicine, and in 1996, was appointed clinical associate professor of pediatrics at the university.

At the national level, Dr. Duncan was appointed chair of the American Academy of Pediatrics School Health Committee in July, 1995. She is also a member of the School-Aged and Adolescent Health Committee of the Association of Maternal and Child Health Programs. In 1996, Dr. Duncan was awarded a primary care policy fellowship by the U.S. Public Health Service.

Joyce V. Fetro, Ph.D., C.H.E.S., is an Associate Professor in the Department of Health Education and Recreation at Southern Illinois University. In the previous seven years, as supervisor and health education curriculum specialist for the San Francisco Unified School District, she was responsible for planning, implementing, and evaluating the district's comprehensive school health program. Other professional experience includes 13 years as a middle school teacher, two years as a university instructor, and three years conducting research and evaluation studies about the effectiveness of substance use, STD/HIV infection, and pregnancy prevention.

Dr. Fetro holds a Ph.D. in health education from Southern Illinois University. In addition to numerous articles in professional journals, chapters in books, and national presentations, she is the author of *Step by Step to Substance Use Prevention: The Planner's Guide to School-Based Programs,* and *Personal and Social Skills: Understanding and Integrating Competencies across Health Content.* She is coauthor of *Are You Sad Too: Helping Children Deal with Death and Loss,* and *Sexuality Education: The Consumer's Guide.*

In 1991, Dr. Fetro was named the American School Health Association's Outstanding School Health Educator of the Year. In 1996, she received the American Association of Health Education's Health Education Professional of the Year award. In 1997, she received an Award of Excellence from the Centers for Disease Control and Prevention for her imaginative and creative efforts toward positively influencing the advancement of HIV and comprehensive school health programs.

Brenda Z. Greene, M.F.A., has served as manager of HIV/AIDS education and school health programs at the National School Boards Association (NSBA) since the program's inception in 1987. She has responsibility for training programs, technical assistance, resource development, and cooperative activities with other organizations. Previously, as manager of editorial services, she was responsible for the association's school policy publications and services.

Ms. Greene is involved in a wide range of community activities related to education, health, and human services. She has served as a commissioner on the Northern Virginia Planning District Commission since 1982, and currently is chair of the Human and Community Services Committee, which fosters regional planning and program implementation on welfare reform, HIV/AIDS prevention and services, human services, and juvenile crime and justice. She also is a member of the Fairfax County Superintendent's Community Advisory Committee and School Health Advisory Committee. She was appointed by the mayor of the District of Columbia to the Metropolitan Washington Region HIV Health Services (Ryan White CARE Act) Planning Council when it was established in 1990, and currently serves as an alternate member representing Northern Virginia.

Ms. Greene is a member of the Community Advisory Board of the Whitman-Walker Clinic of Northern Virginia. An active member of the Fairfax County Interbranch Education Committee of the American Association of University Women, she served for several years as chair. In 1989, she chaired the Fairfax County ad hoc task force on AIDS/HIV.

Ms. Greene, who has been a professional stage designer and a professional sports writer, holds a B. A. and an M.F.A. from Brooklyn College of the City University of New York.

Alan Henderson, Dr.P.H., C.H.E.S., is a professor in the Health Science Department at California State University, Long Beach. He graduated from the University of California, Santa Barbara, with a bachelor's degree in economics in 1966 and earned an M.S.P.H. in 1973 and a Dr.P.H. in 1976, both in health education and health services administration at the School of Public Health, University of California at Los Angeles.

Dr. Henderson has been active in all phases of health education professional preparation. He has been a faculty member at Southern Illinois University and St. Louis University Medical Center. From 1978 to 1981, he directed the Role Delineation Project for Health Education as a staff member at the National Center for Health Education in San Francisco. This project, funded by the Public Health Service's Bureau of Health Professions, formed the basis for the development of the certification program of the National Commission for the Certification of Health Educators.

Dr. Henderson also has worked with schools and school districts in the west and midwest to improve health education programs. He authored *Healthy Schools, Healthy Futures: The Case for Improving School Environments,* and a chapter on healthy school environments in *The Comprehensive School Health Challenge.* He chairs the California Coalition for Comprehensive School Health Education, an initiative of the California Division of the American Cancer Society. He also has served as a consultant to health services agencies, corporations, and public health departments.

Dr. Henderson has served as a board member for the American Association for Health Education. He is president of the California Division of the American Cancer Society. Among his volunteer activities, he has led local and statewide efforts to create smoke-free public places and to support full funding for education and research from California's Proposition 99 tobacco tax. He represents the California Department of Education on the Scientific Advisory Committee for the University of California's Tobacco Research Program, funded by Proposition 99.

Judith B. Igoe, R.N., M.S., F.A.A.N., is an associate professor and the director of the Office of School Health at the University of Colorado Health Sciences Center. Earlier, she directed the school nurse practitioner program, which originated at the university in 1969. The Office of School Health continues to offer courses in this area, as well as additional teaching programs for school health services personnel. It also maintains a large resource collection on school health, conducts consumer education activities, and operates a data services program for school systems and other groups with an interest in program evaluation and policy analysis.

In 1984, Ms. Igoe received the William A. Howe Award from the American School Health Association. A member of numerous associations active in school health issues, she has served on the Institute of Medicine's School Health Study Committee, the American Academy of Nursing's Expert Panel on Adolescent Health, and the American Academy of Pediatrics' School Health Subcommittee on School Health Education. She holds a bachelor's degree in nursing from the University of Iowa, and a master's degree in public health nursing from the School of Public Health at the University of Minnesota.

David K. Lohrmann, Ph.D., C.H.E.S., is director of the Evaluation Consultation Center at the Academy for Educational Development (AED) in Washington, D.C. With funding from the Centers for Disease Control and Prevention, Division of Adolescent and School Health, this project provides evaluation technical assistance to education agencies and organizations across the country that deliver coordinated school health programs. Before joining AED in 1993, Dr. Lohrmann was a high school health education teacher and a member of the faculties at Syracuse University and the University of Georgia. From 1987 to 1993, he served concurrently as health education director and curriculum director for the Troy, Michigan, public schools and project director for a CSAP Community Partnership Grant. His work focused on the use of a health promotion planning model to develop and implement a broad-scale school and community alcohol, tobacco, and other drug abuse prevention program. He also was involved in the development of a policy on communicable diseases for students and staff, and the delivery of HIV/AIDS education within a K–12 comprehensive health education curriculum.

Dr. Lohrmann has served in leadership positions with numerous national and state professional organizations. Most recently, he was a member of the Joint Committee on National Health Education Standards, which developed content standards for students and opportunity-to-learn standards for states and school districts. The author or coauthor of more than 45 articles, reports, and books, Dr. Lohrmann holds a Ph.D. in health education from the University of Michigan.

Eva Marx, M.H.S.M., is associate director of the Center for School Health Programs at Education Development Center (EDC), in Newton, Massachusetts. She directs activities for the CDC-funded project that supported the development of this volume. As a precursor to this undertaking, she organized a partnership of pupil services organizations to pilot the dissemination of the coordinated school health program concept at the national and state level. She also coordinated the development and management of the Comprehensive School Health Education Network, which provided training and technical assistance for school health education and HIV prevention to all state and territorial education agencies in the United States.

Ms. Marx developed and co-edits a nationally distributed newsletter, *School Health Program News.* She is coauthor of *Educating for Health: A Guide for Implementing Comprehensive School Health Education,* which discusses how school districts can initiate and maintain school health activities, and *Choosing the Tools: A Review of Selected K–12 Health Education Curricula* to assist local curriculum decisionmakers. In her earlier work at EDC, Ms. Marx coordinated the integration of HIV materials into two nationally distributed health education curricula, *Growing Healthy* and *Teenage Health Teaching Modules* (THTM), and coauthored *Schools Face the Challenge of AIDS.* With support from the Bureau of Justice Assistance, U.S. Department of Justice, she also developed an implementation manual for Project DARE and directed the introduction of the program in Massachusetts.

Before joining EDC, Ms. Marx worked for the New England Resource Center for Children and Families at Judge Baker Children's Center, where she provided technical assistance to public and private child welfare agencies, developed program implementation manuals, and helped found the National Parent Aide Association. She graduated from Antioch College with a bachelor's degree in philosophy and holds a master's degree in human services management from the Florence Heller School of Social Welfare, Brandeis University.

Alice R. McCarthy, Ph.D., is an educator and writer. She holds a bachelor's degree from Cornell University in early childhood development and education, and a doctorate from Wayne State University, where her work concerned human growth over the life span and curriculum development. Since completing her degree work, Dr. McCarthy has focused on family education, research, and curriculum writing related to health and the family.

Dr. McCarthy is writing a curriculum for families, *Parents as Partners: Keeping Kids Healthy,* based on nationally distributed health curricula. She is also preparing a national curriculum in health for students in grades K–6, entitled *Health 'n Me!* Her book, *Healthy Teens: Success in High School and Beyond,* was published in September 1996, with the support of the school health programs of the State of Michigan's Departments of Community Health, Education, State Police, and the Family Independence Agency. Dr. McCarthy has also conducted several research projects on the health education needs of families.

Since 1992, Dr. McCarthy's company, Bridge Communications, Inc., has published three health newsletters for families: *Healthy Beginnings* for families with children in pre-kindergarten through grade 3, *Healthy Growing* for grades 4–5, and *Healthy Choices* for grades 6–8. She also developed a book for families on health and safety issues, *Healthy Preschoolers: At School—At Home.* Between 1987 and 1994, Dr. McCarthy prepared a column for the Parent Talk page of *The Detroit Free Press.* She currently writes a column entitled *All About Families.*

Dr. McCarthy is past chairperson of the board of regents of Lake Superior State University, Sault Ste. Marie, Michigan, and of the board of directors of the Merrill-Palmer Institute, Wayne State University. She has received many national and state awards and commendations.

Kristine I. McCoy, M.P.H., an independent consultant, was coordinator of school health programs for the Office of Disease Prevention and Health Promotion, a staff office of the U.S. Public Health Service in the Office of the Secretary of the Department of Health and Human Services. She was also a research associate in economic studies, working primarily on projects addressing the overall value of public health and cost-effectiveness analysis applied to health and medicine.

Ms. McCoy was the primary staff person for the Interagency Committee on School Health and the National Coordinating Committee on School Health, committees co-sponsored by the U.S. Departments of Health and Human Services, Education, and Agriculture. The first committee brings together staff from nine federal departments and agencies with an interest in school health to develop strategies for supporting community programs, building state infrastructures, and providing technical assistance. The second is comprised of more than 40 health, education, and human services organizations that support the use of the school setting to meet children's health and other needs. Within the U.S. Public Health Service, Ms. McCoy was responsible for developing policies that encourage communities to develop and sponsor health promotion programs, coordinating Public Health Service efforts in these areas, and promoting use of innovative evaluation and communication techniques.

Earlier she was involved in research in maternal and child health. She also has served as a patient counselor for a group of women's clinics and as an HIV educator for the San Mateo County, California Department of Health Services. She holds an A. B. in human biology from Stanford University, and an M.P.H. from the University of California, Los Angeles.

Floretta Dukes McKenzie, Ed.D., is president of The McKenzie Group, Inc., a comprehensive education consulting firm to both public and private organizations. Before starting the firm in 1988, Dr. McKenzie served seven years as superintendent of schools for the District of Columbia Public Schools. She was deputy assistant secretary in the Office of School Improvement, U.S. Department of Education, from 1979 to 1981. In this capacity, she administered 15 federal education discretionary programs and initiatives and directed the department's efforts to improve schools in areas ranging from basic skills instruction to women's educational equity. Dr. McKenzie represented the department at the 21st General Conference of UNESCO (Belgrade, Yugoslavia) and the Third Conference of Ministries of Education (Sofia, Bulgaria). Earlier, she was deputy superintendent of the Montgomery County, Maryland, Public Schools, and assistant deputy superintendent of the Maryland State Department of Education.

Dr. McKenzie is an active board member of Howard University, the University of Maryland Board of Visitors, the Lightspan Partnership, Inc., the Foundation for Teaching Economics; the Association of Governing Boards of Universities and Colleges, and Reading Is Fundamental. She received a B. A. from Teachers College, Washington, D.C., an M. A. from Howard University, and an Ed.D. from the George Washington University.

Marion Nestle, Ph.D., M.P.H., has been professor and chair of the Department of Nutrition and Food Studies at New York University since 1988. Her research focuses on factors that influence the development and acceptance of federal dietary guidance policies. She taught nutrition at Brandeis University, and from 1976 to 1986 was associate dean at the University of California, San Francisco, School of Medicine, where she directed a nutrition education training program for health professionals. From 1986 to 1988, she was staff director for nutrition policy in the Office of Disease Prevention and Health Promotion, Department of Health and Human Services, and served as managing editor of the 1988 *Surgeon General's Report on Nutrition and Health.*

Dr. Nestle is the author of *Nutrition in Clinical Practice,* a textbook for students and practitioners in medicine and other health professions. She was a member of the New York State Commission on Dietetics and Nutrition, and chair of the Advisory Committee for the 1996 Dietary Guidelines of the American Cancer Society. She recently completed terms as a member of the Food Advisory Committee of the Food and Drug Administration, and of the Dietary Guidelines Advisory Committee of the Departments of Health and Human Services and Agriculture. Dr. Nestle's professional credentials include a Ph.D. in molecular biology, and an M.P.H. in public health nutrition, both from the University of California, Berkeley.

Patricia Nichols, M.S., C.H.E.S., is the supervisor for comprehensive programs in health and early childhood at the Michigan Department of Education. In this capacity, Ms. Nichols supervises programs in school health, including comprehensive school health education, physical education, and HIV prevention education. As project manager for the department's coordinated school health program infrastructure project, she coordinates efforts to build state-level support for school health programs with her counterpart in the state's public health agency.

Ms. Nichols has worked in school health education and public health nursing since 1967. She has taught at both the school district and college levels, has experience in program and curriculum development at the local district level, and in working with children and families in the community health setting. Ms. Nichols has an M. S. in health education from Syracuse University.

Daphne Northrop, B.A., worked closely with the editors in the conceptualization, planning, and editing of *Health Is Academic.* She is a senior research associate at Education Development Center, Inc., (EDC), in Newton, Massachusetts, where she writes in the fields of health education, violence and injury prevention, and education reform. Ms. Northrop is coeditor of *School Health Program News,* a newsletter about school health issues, resources, and events for school health professionals. She is also coauthor of *Educating for Health: A Guide to Implementing Comprehensive School Health Education,* a manual for school districts, and *Education and Health: Partners in School Reform,* developed for the BellSouth Foundation as part of the New Partnerships Network.

Ms. Northrop served as editor of the *Teenage Health Teaching Modules* (THTM) curriculum and edited *Educating Professionals in Injury Prevention* (EPIC), a graduate-level curriculum. Ms. Northrop recently wrote and edited background papers on the health and education status of children around the world for the World Health Organization's Expert Committee on Comprehensive School Health Education and Promotion.

As associate project director for communication for the New England Network to Prevent Childhood Injuries, she developed and wrote educational materials to inform educators, legislators, the media, and key decision makers about the extent of the child injury problem. She wrote and edited selected chapters of *Injury Prevention: Meeting the Challenge.*

Before joining EDC, Ms. Northrop was director of publications and information at the Harvard School of Public Health. She also has been an editor and reporter for several newspapers. She holds a bachelor's degree from Macalester College.

Julius B. Richmond, M.D., is John D. MacArthur Professor of Health Policy Emeritus in the Department of Social Medicine at Harvard Medical School. In 1965, while Dr. Richmond was chair of the Pediatrics Department and dean of the School of Medicine at the State University of New York at Syracuse, he was called to Washington to direct the Head Start Program. He also served as director for Health Affairs, which initiated the Neighborhood Health Centers Program for the Office of Economic Opportunity. He returned to Syracuse in 1967. In 1971 he joined the faculty at Harvard Medical School as Professor of Child Psychiatry and Human Development and became director of the Judge Baker Guidance Center and chief of psychiatry at the Children's Hospital.

Dr. Richmond served as assistant secretary for health in the Department of Health and Human Services, and surgeon general of the U.S. Public Health Service from 1977 to 1981. Under his leadership, the agency published *Healthy People: The Surgeon General's Report on Health Promotion and Disease Prevention.*

Dr. Richmond's publications concern pediatrics, child health, child development, and public health policy. He has received the Aldrich Award of the American Academy of Pediatrics, the Martha May Eliot Award of the American Public Health Association, the Ronald McDonald Children's Charities prize, the Gustave Lienhard Award of the Institute of Medicine,

the Howland Award of the American Pediatric Society, the Sedgwick Medal
of the American Public Health Association, and the Ittleson Award of the
American Orthopsychiatric Association. He holds M.D. and M.S. degrees
from the University of Illinois at Chicago.

Werner Rogers, Ed.D., is executive director of Georgia Public Broadcasting and president of the Foundation for Public Broadcasting in Georgia. He
was Georgia's state school superintendent from 1986 to 1995. As state superintendent in Georgia, Dr. Rogers was a founding partner of The Family Connection, a public-private partnership to ensure children's academic success
through coordination and integration of services and pooling of resources.
Dr. Rogers served twice as president of the Council of Chief State School
Officers. During his tenure, he spearheaded efforts to encourage collaboration among the various service agencies for children and families. He serves
on the board of directors of the Agency for Instructional Technology, Georgia's Distance Learning Telemedicine Board, and the Georgia Center for Advanced Telecommunications Technology. He also is active in many civic associations and in regional and national broadcasting organizations.

Dr. Rogers holds a bachelor's degree from California State University
and a master's degree, an education specialist's degree, and a doctorate in
education administration from the University of Georgia.

Daryl E. Rowe, M.P.H., Dr.P.H., is the biological safety officer and an
adjunct professor of environmental health science at the University of Georgia. He teaches courses in environmental health science, including a course
on the institutional environment. Dr. Rowe's interest in school health began
early in his public health career and continues as part of his activities in
biological safety. He is the author of several articles and book chapters, and
speaks frequently on biological safety and environmental health issues.

Dr. Rowe received a B.S. in zoology from Ohio University; an M.P.H.
in environmental health administration from the University of California,
Berkeley; and a Dr.P.H. in environmental health from the University of
Michigan. He is a certified/registered professional in biological safety, envi-
ronmental health and safety management, and a diplomate of the American
Academy of Sanitarians.

Vernal D. Seefeldt, Ph.D., is a professor and director emeritus of the
Institute for the Study of Youth Sports at Michigan State University. He
taught high school science and elementary school physical education in the
Wisconsin public schools before assuming his position as a specialist in motor development at the university in 1966.

Dr. Seefeldt's professional efforts have been directed toward understanding the relationship among growth, maturation, and the physical fitness and

motor development of children and youth. His leadership role in the National Association for Sport and Physical Education is associated with programs such as the *National Justification of Physical Education Project,* the *Outcomes in Physical Education Project,* and *National Standards for Athletic Coaches,* and edited volumes entitled *Physical Activity and Well-Being,* and *The Value of Physical Activity.* As chair of the Michigan Governor's Council on Health, Physical Activity, and Sports, Dr. Seefeldt initiated a longitudinal effort to develop a model for performance-based physical education programs in the state. The focus of his 135 professional publications has been on the importance of motor skill acquisition and physical fitness in programs for all children and youth.

Dr. Seefeldt received a bachelor's in biological science and physical education at the University of Wisconsin–LaCrosse, and a doctorate in physical education and anatomy from the University of Wisconsin–Madison.

Donald Ben Sweeney, M.A., is chief of the school health unit at the Michigan Department of Community Health, and codirector of the Michigan Comprehensive School Health Infrastructure Project. He has worked extensively in the field of health education since 1972, with a recent focus on collaborative efforts.

He is one of the originators of the Michigan Model for Comprehensive School Health Education, a nationally recognized collaborative effort that works with seven state agencies and 115 voluntary and professional groups to deliver school health programs.

As a trainer, counselor, consultant, and program manager, Mr. Sweeney has a lifelong commitment to the betterment of children. He has presented throughout the United States on a variety of school health topics. He holds a bachelor's in psychology from the University of Michigan, and a master's in human sexuality and communications from Michigan State University.

Susan F. Wooley, Ph.D., C.H.E.S., the Executive Director of the American School Health Association, has consulted in health education for local, state, and national organizations, including the Society of State Directors of Health, Physical Education, and Recreation, the American Association for Health Education, and the U.S. Centers for Disease Control and Prevention (CDC). As a former health education specialist at the CDC Division of Adolescent and School Health (DASH), Dr. Wooley managed cooperative agreements with state and local education agencies and national organizations. In addition, she reviewed DASH-supported publications and coordinated a project for identifying curricula that favorably impact behaviors that put young people at risk.

Dr. Wooley spent four years on a curriculum development project for elementary schools, *Science for Life and Living: Integrating Science, Technol-*

ogy and Health, which took a behavioral approach to health education and incorporated cooperative learning and a hands-on approach to learning. Her first experience in curriculum development was as editor of *Snooper,* a health newsletter for children in grades K–4. As a faculty member at Delaware State College and consultant to the Delaware Department of Public Instruction, she helped develop a K–12 curriculum in health education for the state. Dr. Wooley also has experience with community health education and served as director of safety programs and of nursing and health programs for a local Red Cross chapter.

During her undergraduate work at Case Western Reserve University she received a National Science Foundation grant for biological research. She holds a master's degree in health education from the University of North Carolina at Greensboro, and a Ph.D. in health education from Temple University.

Index